THE
du Ponts
OF
Delaware

By William H. A. Carr

Illustrated with photographs and a map

DODD, MEAD & COMPANY
NEW YORK

To
Eileen Carr Strutz

Library of Congress Catalog Card Number: 64–13693

Printed in the United States of America
by The Cornwall Press, Inc., Cornwall, N. Y.

ACKNOWLEDGMENTS

A number of people and organizations have assisted in the gathering of material for this book.

Special thanks are due to Mr. Gilbert A. Camm, executive assistant of the New York Public Library, and the trustees and staff of the Library for their help, including the use of the Frederick Lewis Allen Room; to the staff of the Eleutherian Mills-Hagley Foundation; to the staff of the Library of Congress; to the John Price Jones Company; and to Dr. Norman Bursler; Mrs. Donald A. De Stefano; Mr. and Mrs. Charles Hanson; Miss Florence H. Luscomb; Professor Dumas Malone of the University of Virginia; Mr. Jackson Martindell, of the American Institute of Management; Mr. Raymond McDonough; and Mrs. Rhoda Truax Silberman.

The historical research of Mrs. Bessie Gardner du Pont has been an invaluable starting point for the original material here on the early development of the family.

The cooperation of members of the du Pont family was extended freely and without strings. For this I wish to thank the Honorable Alexis I. du Pont Bayard, Mr. Emile F. du Pont, Mr. Ernest du Pont Jr., Miss Ethel B. du Pont, Mr. Irénée du Pont Jr., and, above all, Mr. and Mrs. Samuel F. du Pont. Several members of the family who provided information wished to remain anonymous.

None of the persons mentioned above have seen the text of this book. The author alone is responsible for what is said in the following pages.

CONTENTS

I. DYNASTY ON THE BRANDYWINE   1

II. THE WATCHMAKER   7

III. A PATENT OF NOBILITY   14

IV. REVOLUTION   22

V. SHADOW OF THE GUILLOTINE   30

VI. FLIGHT TO AMERICA   41

VII. THE EIGHTH PLAN   50

VIII. MISSION FOR JEFFERSON   57

IX. BIRTH OF THE COMPANY   63

X. STRUGGLE FOR SURVIVAL   70

XI. BLEAK DAYS FOR VICTOR   76

XII. WAR SAVES THE COMPANY   83

XIII. BIGAMY 93

XIV. DEATH OF PAPA 100

XV. DISASTER AND COMPASSION 110

XVI. PASSING OF THE OLD ORDER 117

XVII. COMMUNAL LIFE 125

XVIII. SUNDAY SCHOOL 131

XIX. POWDER AND PANIC 138

XX. ACROSS THE CREEK 145

XXI. WHIGS, REPUBLICANS, DEMOCRATS 155

XXII. FATHER OF ANNAPOLIS 163

XXIII. CONGRESSIONAL MEDAL OF HONOR 173

XXIV. TIME OF ALARMS 178

XXV. A MIND DESTROYED 185

XXVI. THE POWDER TRUST 189

XXVII. THE LITLE WORLD ON THE
BRANDYWINE 196

XXVIII. REIGN OF EUGENE 204

XXIX. SENSATIONS FOR THE PRESS 212

XXX. I'LL BUY THE BUSINESS 222

XXXI. STRUGGLE FOR THE SENATE 231

XXXII. THE END OF THE POWDER TRUST 240

XXXIII. THE OTHER WOMAN 247

XXXIV. I'LL SEE THE FAMILY IN HELL! 255

XXXV. FIGHT FOR CONTROL OF THE
COMPANY 266

XXXVI. A PRESIDENTIAL BOOM 277

XXXVII. PROFITS OF WAR 284

XXXVIII. ALFRED MEETS HIS CHILDREN 290

XXXIX. SPREADING OUT 298

XL. THE LIBERTY LEAGUE 303

XLI. AUNT ZADIE ON THE PICKET LINES 313

XLII. THE DU PONT GIRL AND THE
PRESIDENT'S SON 319

XLIII. EYEWITNESS TO A NEW AGE 330

XLIV. TOO BIG TO BOTHER 336

XLV. THE FAMILY TODAY 343

BIBLIOGRAPHY 352

INDEX 357

ILLUSTRATIONS

Following page 112

Pierre Samuel du Pont de Nemours
Eleuthère Irénée du Pont de Nemours
Victor Marie du Pont de Nemours
Don Pedro, the merino ram
Bois des Fossés, the du Pont home at Nemours, France
The Investiture
Sketch of the powder mills and du Pont residence, about 1806
Rear Admiral Samuel Francis du Pont
Colonel Henry Algernon du Pont
Worker's home on Breck's Lane near the powder yard
Ruins of some of the powder mills as they appear today
Damage caused to workers' homes by the great explosion of 1890
Alicia Bradford Maddox du Pont
Alfred I. du Pont
Eleutherian Mills, the residence of Eleuthère Irénée
Miss Zara du Pont
T. Coleman du Pont
Pierre S. du Pont
Irénée and Lammot, Pierre's brothers
Ethel du Pont and Franklin D. Roosevelt, Jr. at their wedding
Alfred I. du Pont's palatial estate, Nemours
The big house at Winterthur
A view at Longwood Gardens

xi

THE LINE OF ELEUTHÈRE IRÉNÉE

(Drastically abridged to include only
people playing prominent roles in this book)

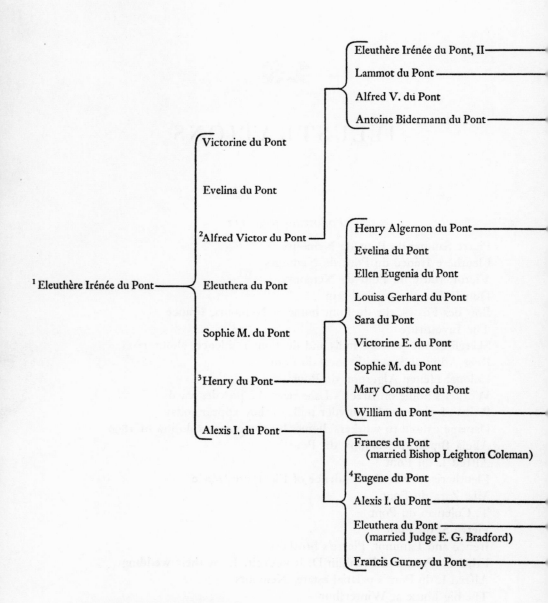

Eleuthère Irénée du Pont, II ————

Lammot du Pont ————

Alfred V. du Pont

Antoine Bidermann du Pont ————

Victorine du Pont

Evelina du Pont

²Alfred Victor du Pont ————

    Henry Algernon du Pont ————

    Evelina du Pont

    Ellen Eugenia du Pont

    Louisa Gerhard du Pont

¹Eleuthère Irénée du Pont ————

Eleuthera du Pont

    Sara du Pont

    Victorine E. du Pont

Sophie M. du Pont

    Sophie M. du Pont

    Mary Constance du Pont

³Henry du Pont ————

    William du Pont ————

Alexis I. du Pont ————

Frances du Pont
(married Bishop Leighton Coleman)

⁴Eugene du Pont

Alexis I. du Pont ————

Eleuthera du Pont ————
(married Judge E. G. Bradford)

Francis Gurney du Pont ————

Numbers identify successive heads of Company

Asterisks (*) identify the three cousins who
bought the Company in 1902

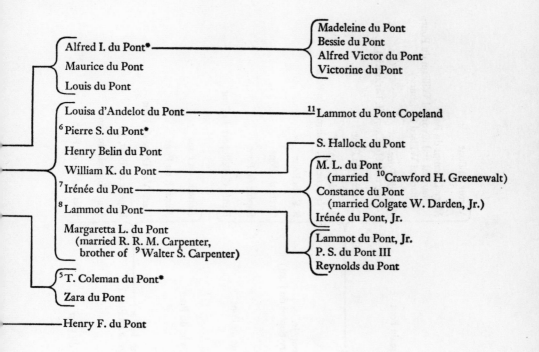

Alfred I. du Pont* —— Madeleine du Pont
Maurice du Pont   Bessie du Pont
Louis du Pont   Alfred Victor du Pont
                       Victorine du Pont

Louisa d'Andelot du Pont —— [11]Lammot du Pont Copeland
[6]Pierre S. du Pont*
Henry Belin du Pont   —— S. Hallock du Pont
William K. du Pont —— M. L. du Pont
[7]Irénée du Pont   (married [10]Crawford H. Greenewalt)
[8]Lammot du Pont ——   Constance du Pont
Margaretta L. du Pont   (married Colgate W. Darden, Jr.)
   (married R. R. M. Carpenter,   Irénée du Pont, Jr.
   brother of [9]Walter S. Carpenter)   Lammot du Pont, Jr.
                       P. S. du Pont III
[5]T. Coleman du Pont*   Reynolds du Pont
Zara du Pont

Henry F. du Pont

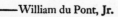

William du Pont, Jr.

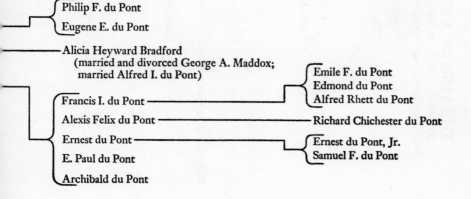

Philip F. du Pont
Eugene E. du Pont

Alicia Heyward Bradford
   (married and divorced George A. Maddox;
   married Alfred I. du Pont)
                       Emile F. du Pont
                       Edmond du Pont
Francis I. du Pont —— Alfred Rhett du Pont
Alexis Felix du Pont —— Richard Chichester du Pont
Ernest du Pont ——   Ernest du Pont, Jr.
E. Paul du Pont   Samuel F. du Pont
Archibald du Pont

THE LINE OF VICTOR
(Drastically abridged to include only
people playing prominent roles in this book)

Victor Marie du Pont

Amelia E. du Pont

Charles I. du Pont

Mary Van Dyke du Pont

Victor du Pont

Charles I. du Pont, Jr.
(married Mary Sophie du Pont)

Amelia Josephine du Pont

Admiral Samuel Francis du Pont
(married Sophie M. du Pont)

Nicholas Van Dyke du Pont

Amelia Elizabeth du Pont
(married Eugene du Pont)

Julia S. du Pont

Henry Ridgely du Pont

Victor du Pont

Mary Lammot du Pont
(married and divorced William du Pont;
married Willard Saulsbury)

Ethel du Pont
(married Hamilton M. Barksdale)

Charles I. du Pont

Alice du Pont
(married T. Coleman du Pont)

S. F. du Pont

Greta du Pont

Sophie du Pont

Rénée de Pelleport du Pont

Anne R. du Pont

Alexis I. du Pont

Mary Van Dyke du Pont

Eugene du Pont, Jr.

Amy Eugenia du Pont

Julia Sophie du Pont

COUSIN MARRIAGES
(Indicated by broken lines)

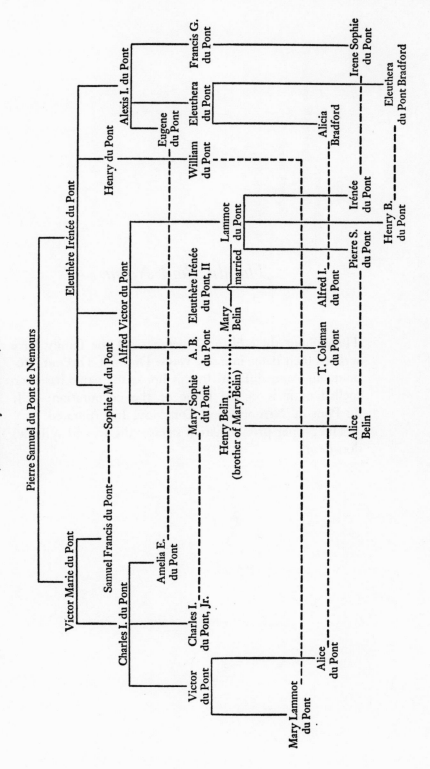

The du Pont Name

Throughout their history, members of the family have written their name in many ways: Du Pont, DuPont, Dupont, du Pont, duPont. In this book, the name has been spelled as it is in the name of the corporation: E.I. du Pont de Nemours and Company, Incorporated.

The proper pronunciation stresses the second syllable: doo-*Pont'*.

CHAPTER I

DYNASTY
ON THE BRANDYWINE

NORTH AND WEST of Wilmington, the countryside is folded into bold hills and deep valleys, crisscrossed by long, low walls of loose stones. The fields are green and yellow under the sun, and drowsy cattle, flicking their tails and shaking their heads to throw off the flies, shuffle slowly into the little streams that begin in the hilltop springs and trickle with a merry sound along their rocky beds, down and ever down until they plunge in small waterfalls over the steep bluff into the shady gorge of Brandywine Creek.

This is the heart of the du Pont country. Here seven generations of du Ponts have walked the earth, bred their tribe, fought their feuds, loved with "Brandywine propriety" and sometimes against the laws of God and man, consecrated the earth to their descendants with their very flesh and blood and bones, torn gaping holes in the valley with their explosives, labored long and weary hours in sweat and danger and the clinging dust of black powder, and wrought from their loins and dreams and determination the only true industrial dynasty in America.

The du Ponts are unique. There are families that have enjoyed wealth and power in the United States longer than they, but the

prosperite
richesse

du Ponts trace their origins to Frenchmen well-born when Christopher Columbus was returning from his discovery of the New World. A number of families have been as rich, but the du Ponts have conserved their wealth, adding to it generation after generation. Some families can truly boast that they have influenced history, but the du Ponts had a hand in bringing about the French Revolution, helping to force recognition of American independence from a reluctant British Crown, were instrumental in preventing a war between the United States and France, negotiated the Louisiana Purchase, and enjoyed the friendship and confidence of such men as Jefferson, Franklin, and Hamilton. There have been other families that have raised up magnificent palaces in America—James Gore King's Highwood, Jay Cooke's Ogontz, George Vanderbilt's Biltmore, William Randolph Hearst's San Simeon; but only the du Ponts built three baronial halls of such splendor as Longwood, Winterthur, and Nemours, and to them they added two dozen great estates of scarcely less imposing dimensions. The business empires put together by other families have fallen apart in a generation or two, but the du Ponts have constructed a complex, world-wide chemical combine on the keystone of one small black powder company.

Because of the du Ponts, northern Delaware is often called "America's chateau country." Alliteration is the curse they bear: "the barons of the Brandywine" is a favorite label for them, and many who talk about the du Pont country insist on calling it "the du Ponts' duchy of Delaware."

The land is covered with their names, so Gallic that the du Pont country sometimes seems like a slice of France itself: Montchanin, Granogue, Chevannes, St. Amour, Louviers, Bellevue, Guyencourt, Bois des Fossés.

Everything about the du Ponts must be stated in superlatives. They are the richest family in the world; their aggregate wealth is believed to be in the neighborhood of three billion dollars. There are sixteen hundred du Ponts today, and their numbers are increasing at the rate of about a hundred a year. Only about two hundred and fifty comprise the core group, and most of the family's riches are in their hands.

They have entered into more marriages of cousins than any other family in the United States, but they have married into more than one hundred and fifty other families, too. They have wed Jews and Germans, Irish and Scots, English and Swiss and Italians. In their genealogy are names like O'Banion and Kitchel and Huidekoper, Lickle and Farquhar and Kirwan, Van Deusen and Raichlen and Irving, Crowninshield and Greiner and Biasutti.

There are du Ponts who believe as firmly in their divine rights as King James ever did: these live in a travesty of formal elegance. Others are happiest when they are deep in the greasy gears of intricate machinery. And there are in-laws who look down their noses at the du Ponts because they are under the illusion that *Mayflower* descendants or F.F.V.'s are somehow more aristocratic. Many du Ponts are not rich at all, merely comfortably situated. Some live as economically as possible in rented quarters.

Although the public usually thinks of du Ponts as being ultra-conservative Republicans, their politics actually covers the whole spectrum all the way to the Socialist left. In between are moderate Republicans, conservative Democrats and liberals. Some du Ponts organized the American Liberty League; others have walked in picket lines during strikes. Du Ponts have been presidential electors, state legislators, governors, lieutenant governors, United States senators, judges, commissioners of one kind or another.

One du Pont won the Congressional Medal of Honor in the Civil War; another won high honors in the same war but later was forced to resign his command under a cloud. A leading du Pont put all the needy old people in his state on a pension paid out of his own pocket until the state was willing to accept its responsibilities. Another organized Delaware's school system and simultaneously served as the state's tax commissioner and liquor control commissioner. Several died heroically in catastrophic explosions in their powder works; one came to his end in a bordello. No family ever clung more closely together. Yet it was rent by a feud that produced slander suits and walls built by du Ponts to keep out other du Ponts, and an eye-gouging struggle for control of the company itself.

The family business—E.I. DU PONT DE NEMOURS AND COMPANY, IN-CORPORATED—has kept pace with the family in superlatives. It is the largest chemical company in the world, with assets of approximately $3,300,000,000—not counting the du Pont interest in General Motors now being shed under a court order. It is also, in the words of *Forbes' Magazine of Business and Finance*, "indisputably the most profitable among the U.S.'s billion-dollar industrial blue chips." Du Pont's *Products Book* takes one hundred and sixty-eight pages to list the twelve hundred products that are turned out by the ninety-three thousand employees—twenty-two hundred of them Ph.D.'s—in its one hundred and seventeen plants here and abroad, factories which have spread the du Pont names across the map. The *Post Office Directory* lists such places as Barksdale, Wisconsin; Du Pont, Washington; and Louviers, Colorado.

From the time an American gets up in the morning until he goes to bed at night, he pays tribute to du Pont. His tooth brush is made of du Pont nylon. The plastic cup with which he rinses his mouth is made of du Pont plastic. As he gets dressed, du Pont contributes its bit, too: his suit is Dacron and wool. His wife's girdle is made with the new Lycra, and so is her brassiere, and the sweater she wears with her skirt is made of Orlon. He smokes a cigarette while he's dressing, tearing the Cellophane wrapping off the pack. He peers out the window to see how the weather is and he notices in passing that the lawn looks good. It's been planted with du Pont grass seed and nourished with du Pont turf food, while the du Pont crab-grass killer got rid of that nuisance. The house has been freshly painted—inside with Lucite, outside with Dulux.

And so it goes all day. His golf balls are covered with Neoprene HC. He buys shotgun shells made by du Pont—Remington is a subsidiary—for the weekend skeet-shooting. The gasoline in his car contains an anti-knock additive made by du Pont; the brake fluid is du Pont's, and so is the wax as well as the paint it covers, plus many other features of the auto. His dentist uses du Pont X-ray film. And so on—and on—and on.

Although the first du Pont product was made in Delaware just outside Wilmington, only three of the company's plants are situated in the state now: two pigment factories, at Edge Moor and Newport, and a nylon mill at Seaford. But the company's home offices are there and so are its research facilities, and the du Pont impact on Wilmington is so great that one is almost tempted to think of it as a company town.

"It is certainly not a large city," Charles Wertenbaker, a native son, once wrote anonymously in *Fortune*. "But into it is poured nearly all the wealth of a score of du Pont businesses, each one an industry in itself. Wilmington is the home city of the du Ponts, from which they have steadfastly refused to depart; it is their background and their responsibility. Delaware is their back yard."

It is significant that Wilmington is the only American city below the rank of metropolis honored by the *Social Register* with an edition partly to itself—because of the du Ponts, of course.

And the du Ponts' riches have raised the per capita wealth of Delaware to first place in the entire nation.

Drive into the state from New Jersey, and you will cross over the soaring Delaware Memorial Bridge, whose construction was guided by Francis V. du Pont. Once in Delaware, you can drive north to Wilmington by two routes: one, close by the river, will take you past Eden Park with its merino rams in masonry, a memento of the time when a du Pont partner, Pierre Bauduy, owned the place; the other route is the Coleman du Pont Highway.

When you reach the center of town, you will find it dominated physically by the two tall buildings that house the du Pont company. Should you have an accident en route, you will be taken to a hospital whose board includes at least one du Pont. Across the street from the company is the public library, built on land contributed by a du Pont. You'll check into the Du Pont Hotel, owned by the people you'd expect. If you pick up a local newspaper, you're buying a du Pont product: the du Ponts own the only daily newspapers in the state. You may notice a few items in the news—school problems, for example, involving the Alfred I. du Pont state board district and the Alexis I. du Pont special school district.

Drive out of the city toward the northwest, on the Kennett Pike —bought, paved, and given to the state by a du Pont—past the Du Pont Road, and soon you'll be passing the du Pont estates, most of them standing so far back from the road that the houses cannot be seen. You can go to the Hagley Museum, however, in the midst of one hundred and sixty-five acres of Brandywine land and see the ruins of the old powder mills. The property, a scene of beauty and tranquillity these days, is maintained by the Eleutherian Mills-Hagley Foundation. If you stay on the highway past the Du Pont Country Club, you'll find that the du Pont estates have spilled over into Pennsylvania, too; Delaware, our second smallest state, isn't big enough to hold all the du Ponts and the *lebensraum* they need today. They've pushed across the line into Maryland, too.

Drive back along the Kennett Pike toward Wilmington, but turn off it to the east on Buck Road just below Greenville. Follow it past the Montchanin Road to the top of the bluff that leads down to the Brandywine. Here, at the top on your left, is a stone gateway. Pass through and you will find yourself at the du Pont family grave-yard, an unpretentious, quiet corner in what was once the Sand Hole Woods. There are only two tall monuments here, one for Samuel Francis du Pont, a Civil War naval hero, the other—a tall column broken in two to symbolize sudden death—in honor of Lammot du Pont who lost his life in an explosion because he was too courageous. The other graves are marked by simple headstones.

One of the tombstones marks the last resting place of Pierre Samuel du Pont de Nemours, the founder of the American family. Near him rests his younger son, Eleuthère Irénée du Pont de Nemours, who established the company that still bears his name.

"The fortunes of the family and the corporation," said Charles Copeland who married Louisa d'Andelot du Pont and fathered the current president of the company, "are identical and rise and fall together."

Here, in the sanctuary above the Brandywine, is the beginning—as it must be the end—of the du Ponts.

CHAPTER II

horloger

THE WATCHMAKER

Ilgem

Pierre samuel du pont—the designation "de Nemours" was added relatively late in his life—once traced his family back to Roman times. In a letter to his longtime friend, Thomas Jefferson, du Pont wrote, "The du Ponts, beginning with Pontius Comminius, who bore letters from Camillus to the Capitoline and crossed the Tiber without a boat (and he didn't even know how to swim!), have always been men of resolution and courage. I do not want them to be mere wealth of no value."

He wrote it tongue in cheek, of course, but he was undoubtedly prompted by his wistful longing for a noble past, the inevitable search for roots of a self-made man. For Pierre Samuel was a man who had raised himself from the *bourgeoisie* into the nobility under a monarchy notoriously absolute, corrupt, and rigid in its class structure.

He was a study in contrasts. A brilliant economist better known in America in his own time than Adam Smith, he was unable to understand the financial operations of his son's business: he could see without difficulty through the complexities of a nation's economy, but he could not cope with the problems of managing his own income. Famed for his prudence, he could also be so bold that he spent his life getting into trouble with a succession of French regimes and even with the American government, and he almost

7

lost his head to the guillotine. A true democrat who valued each man on the basis of his individual character, he was also an inveterate name-dropper and snob, with an unconscious but obvious awe of the great statesmen among whom he moved as an equal. An honest man but a prig, simultaneously imaginative and foolish, farsighted and wildly impractical, witty and pompous.

Du Pont is a name almost as common in France as Smith in the English-speaking countries. Pierre Samuel's family stood out from the other families of that name in eighteenth century France for one reason: they were Huguenots, Protestants in a predominantly Catholic country. Since at least 1500, they had lived in Rouen, and they were happy to have achieved the status of small merchants and traders. It was a shaky position, for they were subject to periodic persecution for their faith. This was reflected in the hostility Pierre Samuel displayed toward the Church of Rome to the end of his days—when it was prudent to show his feelings. The family had suffered in the massacre of the Huguenots on St. Bartholomew's Day in 1572, and in 1591 they and their co-religionists had been expelled from Rouen, their properties confiscated by the Crown. When, in 1598, the Edict of Nantes permitted them to return, they resumed their trades. That branch of the family from which Pierre Samuel was descended was engaged in watchmaking.

His father, Samuel, had been christened a Catholic after his birth on April 19, 1708, but there is reason to believe that the Roman ceremony was only a device to protect the family from further anti-Protestant decrees; there was probably a secret Huguenot baptism, too. Samuel was the first of his family to leave Rouen and seek his fortune in Paris, where he set up shop in the Rue de Harlay, the street of the fine watchmakers.

Across the street from du Pont's place was the shop of Pierre de Montchanin and his brother Alexandre. They were of an ancient family of the lower nobility deprived of its estates because of its loyalty to the Huguenot faith. Their father had been overseer of a large estate in Burgundy owned by a Catholic cousin, the Chevalier de Jaucourt, but the sons had come to Paris and become watchmakers.

One day a new face appeared in the window above the Montchanin shop—the pretty face of the brothers' fifteen-year-old sister

Anne Alexandrine. She had been separated from her brothers since the age of three, when de Jaucourt, with her parents' permission, had carried her off to Paris to be a playmate for his own infant daughter. Anne had been reared as another daughter of the family and had known all the advantages of growing up as a young noblewoman. But one day the Chevalière called Anne to her for a discussion of the girl's future. Without dowry or title she could not hope for a noble marriage, her patroness pointed out as gently as she could. And yet the girl had been groomed for life in a noble household. The solution proposed by the Chevalière was employment in the de Jaucourt household, with her salary to be saved toward her *dot*. She would be in charge of the servants, Madame la Chevalière explained.

To Anne, the idea was repugnant. She felt she would be merely a domestic in a household where she had known the happiness of a daughter of the family. In tears she fled to her brothers.

They patted her awkwardly on the shoulder, gave her a kerchief to wipe away her tears, peered anxiously into her anguished face and tried their helpless, masculine best to cheer her up. To take her mind off her troubles, they put her to work painting watch faces, fine work calling for careful attention.

One day, as she looked up from her work, she saw a tall, strong-faced young man practicing fencing in a window across the street, lunging and parrying as though he were one of Louis XV's own guardsmen. A handsome sight—small wonder the youthful Anne should find herself attracted to the virile fellow. But a few minutes later, the young man re-appeared in the window, this time struggling, not with an *épee*, but with a flute that appeared to be losing the battle, judging from the painful sounds issuing from it. Anne found she could not stop from giggling at the cacophony.

The strapping fellow, pausing in his musical efforts, looked across the street and saw the merriest girlish face he had ever seen. He determined to meet his lovely young neighbor.

In the course of time, Anne de Montchanin and Samuel du Pont did meet. In the beginning, he must have considered the slim young girl with her patrician ways unattainable for a *petit bourgeois* like himself. But he was a tall, handsome man who epitomized masculinity, and Anne was a lonely and impressionable young lady. Two

years after they met, they were married. That was in 1737, when
he was twenty-nine and she was twelve years his junior. First there
was a civil ceremony in Paris and then they slipped away for a
secret Protestant religious service in Tournai, returning to Paris to
set up housekeeping.

Their first child, a boy, died as an infant. That their second child,
Pierre Samuel, survived is remarkable. In those days it was customary for reasonably prosperous Parisians to board out their babies
with peasant families, on the theory that country air and country
food would build healthy children. The du Ponts did this with their
son after his birth on December 14, 1739. But Pierre Samuel's first
foster mother gave him so little food that he nearly starved. When
his mother found this out, she took him away and put him with
another peasant family. The "country air" he enjoyed with them
was in the village tavern where the man of the house, something of
a sot, used to take the child. When the baby cried, he was given
brandy to keep him quiet. By the time he was three, Pierre Samuel
was pale, thin, and anemic; he walked with a limp; his joints were
swollen and painful. He was clearly suffering from rickets.

Appalled at his condition, Anne carried her baby back to Paris.
In time, he was able to walk without a limp, but his joints remained
abnormal. He never attained his natural growth. He would never
have been a handsome man, and a fall, at the age of five, that broke
his nose, did not improve his appearance. The damaged nose remained a prominent part of his features all his life. In his old age, he
looked like Benjamin Franklin with a prize-fighter's battered face.

To his adoring mother, however, Pierre Samuel was a thing of
wonder and a solace for the disappointment she found in her marriage. Samuel du Pont had not proved himself to be the exciting
personality she had expected, but—rather—a dull, unimaginative
burgher. So Anne poured into her relationship with little Pierre
Samuel all the love and the intellectual vitality she found lacking in
her role as a wife. She was determined that her son be given every
opportunity to rise above his father's station in life.

A good education was to be the beginning. Her husband thought
this a foolish extravagance for a watchmaker's son, but in the end
he acceded gracelessly, grumbling about the cost and the waste of

time. "Remember," he warned the boy's teacher, "my son is not to write verses. I won't have a poet in the family."

But Pierre Samuel's teacher, recognizing at once an exceptional talent, cultivated it lovingly. The lad read every book he could find. When he was twelve, his teacher proudly arranged a public demonstration of his pupil; several hundred spectators heard the boy "translate at sight passages from the best Latin authors, answer questions on French and Latin grammar, on logic, rhetoric, fables, poetry, literary style, and civil law." Even his father was pleased with him that day and his mother was nothing less than ecstatic.

Still trying to save her son from life as a watchmaker, Anne told her husband that Pierre Samuel had a vocation to be a Protestant minister. Even a man as stubborn as Samuel du Pont could not argue against a divine calling, so he agreed, reluctantly, that the boy could have more schooling. Protestant theology was added to his intellectual diet, and so were mathematics, physics, metaphysics, the philosophies of the ancients.

Smallpox put an end to all that. The boy fell critically ill. And then the night came when the physician turned to the du Ponts and told them that he could detect no pulse, no heartbeat. Anne collapsed in grief and her husband, drawn close to her in the loss of their only child, helped her out of the room. A woman friend sat with the body in keeping with a custom of the day.

A few hours later, the woman screamed hysterically. The "dead" boy had moved and spoken! Pierre Samuel recovered, but the sight in his right eye was permanently impaired.

During his convalescence, his father decided to teach him the art of swordsmanship to counteract the bookish leanings of the boy and to strengthen his body by physical exercise. Every day the two spent a good deal of time fencing with the foils, but Pierre Samuel was still the son of Anne de Montchanin: he immediately began studying books on military science and dreamed of a career in the army. In disgust, his father put his foot down. As soon as the boy was strong again, Samuel put him to work in the shop learning the watchmaker's craft.

When Pierre Samuel was sixteen, his mother, just thirty-six years old but worn out by two successive still births, died. Her last words were a plea to her husband and her son to act toward each other with love and understanding.

It was a vain hope. Without Anne as a buffer, Samuel and his son couldn't get along together at all. Bitterly the widower viewed his son as the object on whom his wife had lavished love that should rightly have been given to him, her husband. And Pierre Samuel, in his heart, despised this alien man who had not been able to make his mother happy, who could never share the vision of an exciting world of beauty and knowledge that Anne and her son had known.

The conflict between them came to a head when Pierre Samuel grew interested in a neighborhood girl and his father gave him a flogging because of this. The boy left home in a rage—he never returned.

Pierre Samuel went to work for another watchmaker and shared quarters with a fellow apprentice. A few months later the other youth fell ill; after a sickness of several weeks, he died. By that time young du Pont and his roommate's physician, a man named du Bourg, were fast friends. With his characteristic enthusiasm for new knowledge, Pierre Samuel read medical texts, studied anatomical drawings, besieged Dr. du Bourg with questions, slipped into lectures. Dr. du Bourg made it possible for him to visit clinics and observe surgical operations. In those days medicine was a simple discipline; and before long, du Pont had mastered the current store of knowledge. Thereafter he always spoke of himself with pride as a physician and, during a time of danger in the Revolution, he worked actively as a medical man.

For five years du Pont continued as a watchmaker, but in his free time he wrote plays for a group of amateur actors and performed in them, met artists and students, and enjoyed the pleasures of mind and flesh that Paris offered to an active, spirited young man. In those days the gusts of change were beginning to sweep through the ancient streets of Paris, whipped along by Montesquieu and Rousseau and Voltaire.

The philosophical ferment of the time was intoxicating to du Pont, but he was a young man and other, more primal, forces were stirring within him, too. On his time off from his work, he fell into the custom of visiting a couple by the name of Doré, friends who had moved from Paris to the village of Nemours about fifty miles south of the capital. The sentimental Madame Doré had asked him to call her *Maman*. She loved to listen to his poems.

So, too, did Madame Doré's young cousin, Nichole Charlotte Marie Louise Le de Rencourt, usually called by the simpler name of Marie Le Dée. She was a lively girl, three years younger than du Pont. The daughter of a minor government official, she was a gay, light-hearted lass with a quick and eager mind. Du Pont treated her rather like a younger sister until the day he found her sobbing pitifully. He begged her to tell him what was wrong. Sniffling between tearful outbursts, she told him that Madame Doré was arranging a marriage for her with a certain Monsieur des Naudières, a widower of fifty-five. "Looks even older!" she exclaimed.

Off to confront Madame Doré went the young gallant. He protested that she was forcing an old satyr on such a sweet, pure, beautiful young girl. Madame pointed out, reasonably, that Marie was nineteen and not getting any younger; it was time she was married. And the prospective groom, despite his age, was a good catch, a man of property.

"But I, too, will have property!" du Pont burst out. "I shall earn a fortune with my pen. Give me two years to prove it and I will marry Marie!"

Looking back over the perspective of centuries, the whole episode seems like a put-up job that ended just the way Madame Doré and Marie Le Dée had expected—and hoped—it would end. It is recorded that du Pont was astonished at himself for having proposed marriage and that he was equally surprised when Madame Doré accepted his plea. His delighted fiancee hurled herself into his arms and dried her tears, with possibly a surreptitious wink at her helpful cousin. And Pierre Samuel felt very manly and protective as his friends poured their best wine in celebration of the event.

Family legend says that he went back to Paris and fashioned the most exquisite watch he had ever made, finely wrought of gold with intricate, delicate tracery. And on New Year's Day, 1763, he took the watch to his dour father and showed him what he had engraved on the back:

Du Pont filius composit, fecit, dedicavit patri suo—"The son of du Pont designed this, made it, and dedicates it to his father."

It was the last watch Pierre Samuel ever made.

CHAPTER III

A PATENT OF NOBILITY

IN THE FOLLOWING MONTHS, the young ex-watchmaker, who started out with just six hundred francs in his pocket, contrived to win acceptance by possibly the most distinguished coterie of intellectuals in the world of his time—the Encyclopedists.

Apparently it was through his distant relative, the Chevalier de Jaucourt, that the door was opened to du Pont. But Pierre Samuel himself won the respect and admiration of Diderot, d'Alembert and the other Encyclopedists through his cogently reasoned essays on political economy and the marvelous agility and brilliance of his mind in the duels of wits that took place in the fashionable salons to which he was soon a welcome guest. There he met the aristocracy—intellectual, political, and hereditary—of France.

For du Pont, the most important friendship he made at that time was with François Quesnay who was then trying to work out a new theory of political economy. It was du Pont who gave the theory the name it has retained through history, "physiocracy," and when Quesnay's followers became numerous, du Pont became a kind of party secretary for the group. In 1763 he published his first work, an essay entitled *Reflections on the Wealth of the State*—this was more than a decade before Adam Smith's *Inquiry into the Nature and Causes of the Wealth of Nations*. Ironically, in this and other works, du Pont, who was to found a great industrial dynasty, spent his life attacking those who favored the development of manufactures. Like Jefferson, he glorified agriculture and distrusted industrialization.

Quesnay, who was advisor to the king's mistress, Madame de Pompadour, invited du Pont to join him at Versailles, and it was at the suggestion of his preceptor that Pierre Samuel wrote a study on the importation and exportation of grain which was published in April, 1764. It doesn't sound like a very exciting piece of work, but political economy was all the rage then, and du Pont's treatise, well received at court, marked the beginning of his reputation. He received several assignments from the government for economic surveys, entered into a correspondence with Voltaire, then living in Switzerland out of reach of the king's police agents, and, in the summer of 1765, accepted an appointment as editor of a newly established government periodical, *Journal de l'Agriculture, du Commerce et des Finances*.

Now he was ready to return to Nemours and claim his bride.

The long betrothal had not been easy on either du Pont or Marie Le Dée. At first her father had regarded him with suspicion as a suitor of scant prospects. A respectable man ran a farm or a shop, stayed in one place, knew his position in society, and ignored all those incomprehensible but no doubt evil ideas that were so fashionable in the capital. But this du Pont—no. He was full of confusing talk about all sorts of things—politics, economics, and what not; he hadn't had a regular income until his appointment as editor of this new journal; he mixed into all manner of things at court and elsewhere that were no business of simple folk. He was, worst of all, a damnable Huguenot!

To get around Papa de Rencourt, du Pont made a formal denial that he was a Huguenot—which was probably true, for by this time, he had already discarded his belief in institutionalized religion. He also made a written pledge that any children of the marriage would be brought up as Catholics. And, turning all of his considerable charm on his prospective father-in-law, he pointed out that now, as an editor, he had a regular income.

With some misgivings, de Rencourt consented to the wedding. The banns were proclaimed. On January 28, 1766, Pierre Samuel du Pont and Marie Le Dée were married in the Church of St. Sulpice in Paris.

And then, in the fall, du Pont lost his job. He was expelled from his post for opposing a government move against the Breton parliament in a dispute over an unpopular tax.

With a young wife to support, du Pont had no income.

Another powerful physiocrat, Turgot, who was in charge of the province of Limoges, came to his aid, employing du Pont as a statistician. It was the beginning of a long and intimate association.

The du Ponts were thus able to continue living in Paris, in a comfortable apartment in the Rue et Faubourg St. Jacques. Their first child, Victor Marie, was born there on October 1, 1767. The child's godfather was the Marquis de Mirabeau.

In the spring of 1768 du Pont became the editor of another review, *Les Éphémérides du Citoyen.* This periodical was a private enterprise lacking government support. It also lacked funds. While du Pont built an international reputation by his campaigns for freedom of the press and of conscience, public education, a single tax on land, the abolition of slavery in the colonies, and other issues, his thrifty wife did her best to stretch the dwindling income from the review. To add to their problems, Pierre Samuel came down with the gout, a complaint that plagued him intermittently for the rest of his life, and the baby fell ill with smallpox at a time when Marie was again pregnant. Victor recovered, but the second child died a few days after birth.

But the success of du Pont's first major work, *Physiocracy, or the Natural Constitution of that Form of Government Most Advantageous to the Human Race*, sustained the spirits of Pierre Samuel and Marie. The book was acclaimed all over the western world.

"There is such a freedom from local and national prejudices and partialities, so much benevolence to mankind in general, so much goodness mixed with the wisdom in the principles of your new philosophy that I am perfectly charmed with them, and wish I could have stayed in France for some time to have studied in your school," Benjamin Franklin wrote to him after reading the book.

Du Pont, the quondam watchmaker, was now moving in the most exalted circles in France—indeed, in all Europe—a scant decade after leaving the Rue de Harlay. Was the country girl he had married able to measure up to the other women in this glamorous atmosphere?

Apparently she was. Franklin, on a visit to France, spent a good deal of time in du Pont's company. Later he wrote to Pierre Samuel from London to say, "Would to God I could take with me [to America] Messrs. du Pont, du Bourg, and some other French friends with their good ladies! I might then, by mixing them with my friends in Philadelphia, form a little happy society that would prevent my ever wishing again to visit Europe."

The letter arrived at the du Pont apartments late in 1770, just about the time Marie learned that she was going to have another baby. Her delighted husband wrote to Turgot, asking him to be the child's godfather. Turgot accepted with pleasure. "If it is a boy," he wrote, "will you not call him Eleuthère Irénée, in honor of liberty and peace? If a girl, the names Eleuthèrie and Irène would be equally as good."

Eleuthère Irénée was born June 24, 1771, the second living son and the last child to be born to Pierre Samuel du Pont and his wife Marie.

Less than a year and a half later, the political censors decided that du Pont had gone too far too often: the *Éphémérides du Citoyen* was suppressed, and another period of financial distress began for Pierre Samuel. Somehow he scratched together a living by writing monthly letters of economic intelligence to King Gustavus III of Sweden, the Margrave of Baden at Karlsruhe in Germany and other European rulers. When he was offered a post as tutor to the Prince Royal of Poland and director of that country's Council of Public Education, he couldn't refuse—especially when the perquisites included a suite in the royal palace, carriages and various honors. The salary and living allowances were very generous, and at the end of ten years he would receive a bonus of 100,000 francs. One-third of the bonus was to be paid on his acceptance of the post.

With 33,000 francs, the advance on his bonus, in his pockets, du Pont decided he could now become a landowner. He and Marie happily scouted the countryside about Nemours looking for just the right place. They finally chose a small estate near Chevannes about five miles away, put down their money for it and named it Bois des Fossés—meaning, literally, "Forest of the Trenches," there being a number of deep ditches on the land said to have been built as trenches by the Romans.

Off to Warsaw went Pierre Samuel, Marie and their two babies, on a long, uncomfortable journey by jouncing, jolting carriage over the deeply rutted roads.

Scarcely had the du Ponts arrived, settled down and become acquainted with the Polish court, when word came from France that Louis XV had died of smallpox, passing on the crown to his twenty-year-old grandson, now Louis XVI, the fat, clumsy, shy, pious, dull-witted husband of the exquisite, charming, frivolous, extravagant, cruel Marie Antoinette. Among the new king's ministers was Turgot, now in charge of finance.

Du Pont's friend summoned him at once from the Polish court. As a courtesy to a fellow monarch, the Polish ruler released Pierre Samuel from his service, and by January, 1775, he was installed at Versailles. But his tenure there was brief. In a regime plunging headlong toward bankruptcy, Turgot tried to curb the spending of "Madame Déficit," as the queen was called, only to be dismissed from office. And du Pont went with him. The year was 1776.

Banished to Bois des Fossés, Pierre Samuel resumed his economic intelligence reports to various European rulers, while his efficient wife, as practical as he was not, set about making the farm self-sufficient. From time to time, du Pont would go to Paris for long conversations in the salons with his friends: Turgot, Vergennes who was now foreign minister, Mirabeau, Necker who had taken Turgot's place in the government, the Abbé de Périgord—better known as Talleyrand. He could also show off his decoration, the Order of Vasa, awarded him by Sweden's Gustavus in acknowledgment of the value of his reports. And he could hear the latest news from America where some of his friends, Lafayette among them, were fighting beside the colonists against the English.

After four years of private life, du Pont was called back into government service by Vergennes and given two missions, both of the utmost importance: to open negotiations with the English in an effort to induce them to recognize the independence of the American colonies; and to draw up a treaty which, by covering all aspects of commerce between France and Britain, would bring to an end the war between the two European rivals.

Years before, du Pont had met James Hutton, "a very able man who was one of the instructors of the sons of the king of England," as Pierre Samuel later said. Even during the war, they had somehow managed to carry on a friendly correspondence. Now du Pont suggested that his friend ask the English government to authorize him to act as its representative in secret negotiations with the French. Between them, Hutton and du Pont drew up a rough draft of an agreement, finally signed in 1783 as the Treaty of Paris, by which Britain acknowledged the independence of her erstwhile colonies. Four years later, the Franco-British commercial treaty was signed.

Thomas Jefferson, one of the American representatives in Paris, wrote to John Jay regarding du Pont: "I have found him a man of great judgment and application, possessing good general principles on subjects of commerce and of a friendly disposition towards us."

Louis XVI, too, recognized the value of du Pont's diplomatic achievements by bestowing on him a *lettre de noblesse*, a patent of nobility which raised him to a rank roughly equivalent to the British knighthood. A coat of arms was one of the honors accompanying the distinction. Du Pont at once adopted the motto, *Rectitudine Sto*—"Be Upright"—that was emblazoned under a crest depicting a column probably representing Learning on a plain field, the whole surmounted by a vizored casque. Today, the coat of arms can be found in many du Pont homes on everything from dinner service to match books.

To cap Pierre Samuel's pleasure, his financial problems were over —temporarily. That year the thrifty Marie was able to write a joyful announcement from Bois des Fossés to her husband in Paris: "We are out of debt—let it be for always!"

During the next summer, 1784, while her husband remained in Paris busying himself with official matters, Marie worked briskly about Bois des Fossés, supervising the peasants who tilled the fields, tending to the livestock herself, and caring for her two growing boys, Victor, now sixteen, and Irénée, thirteen. They were as active and ready to get into difficulties as any teen-agers. After Irénée fell out of a tree from which he had been trying to steal a bird's nest, his father wrote to him on the subject of climbing for nests—"a very *lofty* subject," said Pierre Samuel who dearly loved a pun— gently reproving his son for "despoiling a little home."

Toward the end of August, Marie began to feel unwell. It was nothing very definite at first, just a general malaise and fatigue, and she assured her husband that she would be all right soon, that she was merely tired and suffering from a headache. But it took a good deal more than a trifling indisposition to put Marie Le Dée du Pont to bed. She was seriously ill. It is probable that she had fallen victim to typhoid fever.

On September 3, she died, barely forty-one years old. Her stunned husband came posthaste from Paris, and she was buried in the churchyard at Chevannes. No cross was placed on the grave. This led later members of the family to assume she had died a Protestant.

A few days after the funeral, Pierre Samuel summoned his sons for a curious ceremony which the father's melodramatic imagination had just devised. It has since been referred to in the family as "The Investiture."

The elder du Pont sat in a high-backed chair, a cushion on the floor in front of him. A bust of his dead wife was at his left and, on a bench at his right, was a hat and a sword that he intended to bestow on Irénée: whether he had earlier gone through this pompous rigmarole with his first-born, Victor, history does not say. Pierre Samuel's own sword was at his side.

He ordered the boys to pledge eternal honor and respect to France and to their parents. Then he struck Irénée on the left shoulder, saying, "This blow that I give you, my son, is to teach you that you must bear any blow when it is honorable and right to accept it."

Then he said the words which the more conscientious members of the family have repeated to their children to this day: "No privilege exists which is not inseparably bound to a duty."

The right to wear a sword, he reminded his younger son, carried with it the obligation to fight for the public good. Pierre Samuel gave the sword on the bench to Irénée and then commanded both boys to draw their swords, salute each other and embrace.

"Promise one another," he said, "that you will always stand together, united, that you will comfort one another in every sorrow and distress, that you will help one another in all your endeavors, that you will stand by one another no matter what the difficulty or the danger."

When they had pledged themselves, he concluded the ceremony with these words:

"I bless you, my children, and may heaven also bless you. Bless your labors and your children. May your families be carried on by wives who are good, sensible, courageous, economical, generous, simple, and modest like the mother you have lost. May each generation of your descendants struggle unceasingly to pass on to its children a better heritage than it received."

CHAPTER IV

REVOLUTION

I N OCTOBER, 1787, Pierre Samuel du Pont, now a councilor of state and director of commerce and one of the most important and influential men in France, obtained an appointment for his son Victor as unpaid secretary to the French legation in New York, then the capital of the United States. Victor was made for the diplomatic life: he was handsome, intelligent, witty, gay, personable beyond belief, attractive to women, companionable to men, but he was utterly incapable of hard work.

Earlier in the year du Pont *père* had drawn on his friendship with Antoine Lavoisier, the father of French chemistry, to place his younger son Irénée in the National Powder Works, a government monopoly managed by Lavoisier. Irénée had a certain superficial resemblance to his brother. Like Victor, he was tall and well-formed; his nose was prominent and his chin was deeply cleft—two characteristics that have continued to appear on most du Ponts down through the years to the present. But the two brothers were as dissimilar in personality as two men could be. Irénée was earnest, sober, uncommunicative, shy, easily hurt, and a tireless, persistent worker.

In Philadelphia, Victor saw a good deal of Benjamin Franklin, who confided to friends, "I like young du Pont very much. He seems to me to be a young man of intelligence and ability; I think he will give much satisfaction to his father."—a prediction that proves Franklin could be something less than infallible in his judgments.

While his older brother was in America, most of Irénée's time was spent at the Essonnes gunpowder mills, where he was quickly becoming used to the frequent accidental explosions that were an inevitable part of the life there. The choice of such a dangerous calling had been Irénée's own. His father, disgusted by the inelegant life his son had picked, resigned himself to it with a shrug, saying, "A man may become distinguished even at making watches."

Pierre Samuel, however, had other things on his mind beside his sons' careers. The years of corruption and scandal and extravagance among the ruling class and the years of poverty and hunger and hopelessness among the poor were now bearing their bitter fruit. Riots broke out in Paris with increasing frequency. A city crowded with beggars and vagabonds from all over France was ripe for disorders. From time to time, soldiers were stoned, houses were burned, stores were looted. Mobs led by the worst cutthroats were a constant danger as a weak king vacillated, and law and order collapsed. "There is now no safety in Paris except that which is enforced by the courage, the coolness, and the swords of the citizens themselves," Irénée wrote his brother in America.

When the frightened but petulant king finally permitted the election of a Constituent Assembly in April, 1789, Pierre Samuel du Pont was elected deputy from the district of Nemours to the Third Estate—the "commons." There were a number of other du Ponts in the Assembly, so Pierre Samuel, to distinguish himself from the others, began styling himself "de Nemours."

In the turbulent weeks that followed, du Pont de Nemours was a key figure, putting his head together with other Assembly leaders who were being driven toward positions ever more revolutionary because of the intransigence of the Crown, the aristocracy, and the Church. Liberals like du Pont cheered that summer when the king yielded reluctantly and instructed the privileged orders to meet with the Third Estate in a true National Assembly; this then appointed a committee to draw up a constitution. But after the king dismissed the reform ministers and put the reactionary court party in power, the people rose up in open rebellion. When the Bastille was taken on the 14th of July, du Pont cheered again. He was even more delighted the next day when the king came in person to the Assembly to announce that the troops would be withdrawn from Paris and Versailles, where they had been moved in an attempt to cow the populace.

The work of the Revolution moved ahead inexorably. Many of the changes that were wrought were measures that du Pont had been urging for years, but some of the other proposals seemed to him of doubtful value. In that atmosphere of wild, revolutionary enthusiasm, it appeared that few besides du Pont were willing to subject matters to the unflattering light of logic.

But on August 27, du Pont signed with satisfaction the Declaration of the Rights of Man. Then, in September, in a speech wildly cheered in the Assembly, he proposed the confiscation of the estates of the Church, thus at last avenging his Huguenot ancestors.

However, not all his opinions were greeted with popular approval. In October, when he spoke in opposition to the further issuance of paper money, a mob tried to dunk him in the Seine and would have succeeded but for the timely arrival of a detachment of the National Guard. This militia, organized by order of the Assembly to defend the Revolution, had a new recruit now—Eleuthère Irénée du Pont de Nemours, whose company elected him lieutenant in command.

By this time, Victor had returned from America, and he was in the hall on that hot August day in 1790 when his father was elected president of the National Assembly.

Like many of the moderates, du Pont belonged to the Club of '89, one of the many political organizations which had sprung into being with the coming of the Revolution. But the tide was already running with the extremists who were banded together in the Jacobin Club.

When the Constitution of 1791 was adopted, it contained a provision barring members of the National Assembly from the new Legislative Assembly for three years, so du Pont could no longer take part in parliamentary developments. But he had not retired to private life; instead, he had reached the highest level to which a courtier might aspire. In the words of the *Cambridge Modern His-*

tory, "the private advisors of the Court at this time were Barnave, Malouet, du Pont of Nemours, and Mallet du Pan."

Louis XVI had neither the wit nor the wisdom to accept the advice of his counselors, however, and matters continued to slide from bad to worse. By now the king, after trying to escape from France with Marie Antoinette, was a virtual prisoner with her in the Tuileries.

Personal as well as national problems were worrying du Pont by this time. His government salaries and allowances, amounting to 30,000 francs a year at the beginning of the Revolution, had been gradually whittled down by the Jacobins. His income was running low, and Marie was no longer alive to manage these things for him. At fifty-two, du Pont, who for years had known nothing other than the life of a politician, suddenly had to earn a living.

Thinking of his friend Franklin, he decided to open a printing house. On the Ile Saint-Louis across from Notre Dame Cathedral, he bought the town house of the Bretonvilliers family to shelter his presses. And on the Rue de Richelieu, he opened a shop to sell his pamphlets and books.

But then he came to the end of his money.

In his usual way he had embarked on an ambitious project without adequate funds. Now, however, his friend Lavoisier came to the rescue. For a four percent mortgage on Bois des Fossés to be repaid in twelve years, Lavoisier lent du Pont 710,000 livres.

Lavoisier had quit his post at the National Powder Works to become one of the commissioners of the national treasury. With his idol gone, Irénée du Pont, no longer interested in remaining at Essonnes, joined his father in the operation of the Paris publishing house.

Probably Irénée's major reason for wanting to go to Paris was to be closer to a girl there. Born at Metz on July 22, 1775, Sophie Madeleine Dalmas was a tradesman's daughter. She was sixteen and Irénée was twenty.

As one might have expected, Pierre Samuel bitterly opposed the match. With much difficulty he had raised himself from the ranks of the *petite bourgeoisie*, and here was Irénée marrying beneath himself, marrying a *petite bourgeoise* girl. With all the heat his passionate nature could summon, Pierre Samuel denounced the very idea. He said he would never accept the marriage, that Irénée would break his heart, that such a marriage would put an unbridgeable chasm between his son and himself.

A rival for Sophie's hand made Irénée's suit even more difficult. A man named Perdonet had boasted, quite in the manner of a stage villain, that he would have the maiden by fair means or foul—or so the family legend goes. Tradition says that Irénée fought two duels with Perdonet—once with swords, a second time with pistols; and on the second occasion he managed to inflict a wound that kept Perdonet *hors de combat* for several months.

During those months, Irénée waged a ceaseless campaign to win over his father. In a long, moving letter to him, Irénée mentioned Pierre Samuel's acid predictions about the effect such a marriage would have on the rest of the family and on the elder du Pont's friends.

"As to the first," Irénée wrote, "I care very little for their opinions—I did not choose them for my relatives; as for your friends, who are the relatives you have chosen, they should have more consideration." There were many other letters in the same vein, for father and son, although living in the same house, were no longer talking; their only communication was through letters.

By this time, Victor had returned to America to be French consul general at Philadelphia. He, too, made plain his opposition to the match with as little success as his father.

Finally Papa du Pont gave up and consented to the marriage. Perhaps it was Victor's opposition that turned the trick, for Pierre Samuel had come to have little regard for Victor's sagacity. A year later the elder du Pont would write in his journal, "My son Victor, born with great ability, active, gentle, honest, gifted with a just mind and unusual versatility, came near being ruined and would have been quite so if fortune had not ruined us first. He squandered 40,000 francs very foolishly, because I was noble, a chevalier, lord of a manor, councilor of state, working with the ministers. He believed it beneath him to consider order and economy, to refrain from wasting money, to make his own reputation instead of profiting by mine. I think that now the loss of my fortune and my position, the danger of asserting relationship with me, and the growth of his own intelligence have entirely corrected him."

So at last it was with his father's blessing that Irénée married Sophie in Paris on November 26, 1791.

The newlyweds had very little time together, for the momentous events begun almost three years earlier were now rushing toward their climax. France's European neighbors, apprehensive and angry over her Revolution and its challenge to the existing order in all countries, began to make threatening gestures, a state of affairs not unwelcome to French politicians, many of whom, unable to gain power in the political chaos that existed, hoped that a war would provide the opportunity to win control. These pressures led France to declare war on Austria on April 20.

In the midst of all this, the lives of ordinary men and women still went on, as they have in all times and places, and Sophie found that she was pregnant. She would bear Irénée a child in August.

It was an upsetting, nerve-wracking, terrifying time to be carrying a baby. Hunger griped the guts of the city. One dull-witted radical achieved a measure of immortality as a footnote to history with his unintentional epigram in a letter to a friend: "All goes well here; food is not to be had." Famished, penniless, hopeless, men turned to banditry. Mobs roamed the streets at will, with none daring to challenge them. Wild rumors flew through every district of Paris, each accepted as fact until the next rumor sprang up. Without the credit of the nation behind it, money became almost worthless in a skyrocketing inflation.

Even the liberals were now losing hope of persuading the Revolution to retain the king under any circumstances; many of them began to join the Royalists in flight. But not Pierre Samuel du Pont. He published broadsides flaying the mobs, denouncing the excesses of the people and the parliament. He did more: he organized himself, his son Irénée and thirteen other men into a little company ready to do battle for law and order. Little by little the troop grew, until at length there were "sixty men of the greatest courage" in his band.

The call to action came on August 10. A messenger arrived breathlessly at the du Pont printing house to tell of a mob on its way to the Tuileries—the king and queen were in danger. Frantic with worry over Sophie who might give birth at any moment,

Irénée nevertheless whipped off his printer's apron, buckled on his sword and pistol and dashed with his father out into the street.

At the Tuileries, the du Pont troop arrayed itself beside the Swiss Guards as the mob—shouting, cheering, singing, shaking fists and upraised weapons—rushed toward the palace, appearing first on the Place de Carrousel. The timid king made up his mind to appeal to the Assembly for protection, so he and the queen slipped away without the knowledge of the rabble.

As Louis XVI left the palace, he passed du Pont. "Ah, Monsieur du Pont," he said, "one always finds you where one has need of you."

With the royal couple gone, most of the National Guard and the *gendarmerie* fraternized with the armed throng across the square. But the du Pont troop stood firm. Pierre Samuel's foolish pride compelled him to go on fighting for an absent monarch who wasn't worth an honest man's blood. Retreating with the Swiss into the palace proper, they prepared to stand off the besiegers. There were several volleys and then, for nearly an hour, scattered shots that kept the mob at a distance. At length the Swiss and their handful of steadfast French allies made a sally that cleared the square of their opponents without bloodshed.

At that moment an order came from the king: they were to stop fighting. It was an order to commit suicide. The Swiss Guard obeyed and they were slaughtered, most of them shot down as they crossed the broad gardens of the Tuileries, the rest massacred in a church where they had been confined, unarmed.

The French, who had fought for the royal couple beside the Swiss, were butchered to a man when the mob could lay hold of them. To prevent that, the du Pont band fought fiercely until it had been reduced in numbers from sixty to a mere eight including Pierre Samuel and Irénée. That scant handful made its escape by sheer bravado, thanks to Papa du Pont's audacious imagination. Aware of how dirty he and his friends were—smeared with soot and powder and with rivulets of sweat running down through the grime on their faces—it occurred to him that the disheveled little troop actually looked as disreputable as the *sans-culottes* they had been fighting.

Slipping out of sight of their assailants for a few moments, they organized themselves into the likeness of a revolutionary detachment. Then Pierre Samuel, looking for all the world like a villainous Jacobin, marched his seven men, all wearing the *bonnet rouge*, the red liberty cap, out of the palace and across the square as though they were on their way to report to the Hôtel de Ville. The ruse succeeded. Out of sight of the mob, the little group of survivors scattered hastily.

Obviously, the elder du Pont was in danger: several men in the mob had recognized him during the melee and had called him by name. He was, after all, a well-known public figure. Irénée was not, so he might be safe. It was unlikely that anyone would know that he had fought at the Tuileries, especially since he was a lieutenant in the National Guard and was known for his real devotion to the Revolution. It was agreed, therefore, that Irénée should remain at the publishing house to manage it, while his father went into hiding.

The dome of an observatory served as Pierre Samuel's refuge. There was no bed, and the astronomer in charge, Le Français de Lalande, could bring him only bread and water. While he remained under cover, the Austrians, advancing into France, got as far as Verdun. Panic maddened the Parisian rabble and, on September 2, the mob started to smash its way into the jails in order to massacre the helpless Royalists held prisoner there. For five days the outrages went on, until the blood lust of the people was sated, and in the excitement and confusion, when the guards at the city gates had deserted their posts briefly to join in the tumult, Pierre Samuel made good his escape from Paris.

Reaching a house owned by a cousin at Cormeilles, he disguised himself by an eye shade that partly obscured his face. He claimed to be an elderly physician and, falling back on his early training, he treated all who came to him.

In the meantime he had become a grandfather.

CHAPTER V

SHADOW

OF THE GUILLOTINE

Victorine Elizabeth du Pont was born to Sophie and Irénée on August 31, 1792, while her grandfather was hidden in the observatory. A month later Irénée took mother and child to Bois des Fossés where they would be safer than in strife-torn Paris.

Back to Paris went Irénée, for there was work to be done. In its search for the elder du Pont, the mob had sacked the printery, and Irénée had to get things in order again and resume business. Even in a revolution, men must sweat for their bread.

The parted lovers wrote to each other every day. Most of these letters have been preserved; they show a couple well matched. Reserved, taciturn, even cold as he might appear to others, Irénée was as warm, affectionate, romantic, passionate as Sophie herself. Their correspondence proves they retained a profound love for each other until the end of their days.

Sophie's first letter to Irénée was dated at Bois des Fossés, September 26, 1792. She wrote:

> My dear Irénée,
> I am very anxious to know whether you have arrived in good health. Mine is fairly good but I still have some pain; I hope, how-

ever, that it will not amount to anything. The little one is very well; she loves and embraces you, my dear. If you could know how I love you, you would know what I suffer in your absence. I would have left here before now had it not been for our child. I am very unhappy away from you and need all my resolution to stay so long. I cannot tell you what I feel when I think that you love me and are perhaps as sad as I am. Yes, you must be, for even when we are parted, we are only one—our hearts are united forever.

I beg you, my dear love, to write to me as often as you can. You know it is my only comfort. Above all, tell me how you are. Be careful not to overtire yourself or fall ill. I should die of sorrow if anything happened to you and I were not there to care for you. You know that I am your little mother and that I love you first as your sweetheart and then as your wife. Yes, my dear, I am your wife and your love and shall be so always. I tremble with joy when I think that—though others may say that people love less after they are married—I know that judging by myself they love more.

My dearest, I wish the two weeks were gone that must pass before you come to see me, but you must finish your work, and when you can come you will let me know you are coming, so that I may go to meet you. Oh! my Irénée, how sweet will be the moment that reunites us! I believe that if you did not let me know in advance I would die of joy and gladness. . . .

Irénée's reply was dated Paris, October 2, 1792, "the second year of the happiness of my life"—New Year's Day now fell on September 22 in the republican calendar that the Revolution had introduced:

I have received your dear letter, my sweet love. It is impossible for me to tell you with what pleasure I have read and reread it. . . . Oh! if I could have done on Saturday as I wished and as I wrote you in my last letter, I could have left on Sunday as soon as I received yours and you would have been wakened in the night by your lover's kisses. But the duty which my heart must hear first kept me. I was unable to accomplish on Saturday what I wrote you of—yesterday was decided on. It should have been a happy day and it was, my Sophie, as happy as is possible without you. You will not be jealous, my dear love; your heart and mine are one, and I am sure you shared with me the pleasure of that day.

I am delighted, my dearest, to know that our dear child is well, but I implore you, in the name of our love, to take the greatest care of yourself lest you become ill. You know that I am unhappy enough at being so far from my Sophie, without having additional distress and anxiety. You know, my dear angel, we are and always will be one. Our souls, our bodies are forever united. I am sure that if you were ill, I would soon be so. Remember that, dearest, and take care of yourself for the sake of your lover and his dear child.

I send you, best and dearest, the tenderest and warmest kisses. Embrace our angel for her father, for her mother's lover. . . .

In the next few years, Sophie and Irénée spent most of their time apart, she at Bois des Fossés, he in Paris, and their correspondence continued on a letter-a-day basis except when he was able to get away from Paris to be with her. Her letters are full of family gossip, news about the farm, and homely requests: "Please, my dear, have a little tin bath tub made for her [the baby], thirty inches long and wide in proportion. . . . The edges must be rounded so they will not cut."

Irénée's letters are full of vivid pictures of revolutionary Paris: "Gudin [a cousin] has arrived—fat and well and covered with some glory and much dirt. . . . Trouble is brewing. This morning at 10 o'clock we learned that the barriers were closed. This step, which is doubtless only a precaution, has given some alarm; they are beating to arms everywhere. It is said that the object of all this is to search for arms by making a house-to-house check. . . ."

Ten presses were installed in the new du Pont printing plant located in a former monastery, and pamphlets and periodicals began to pour forth from *l'imprimerie du Pont*. Anxiously Pierre Samuel tried to keep an eye on the business from a distance; the danger was still too great for him to venture out from Bois des Fossés where he was now living very happily with the daughter-in-law he had once opposed so vehemently. He praised her as "beautiful and good" and predicted that she would "give to our family wisdom, moderation, happiness."

Bois des Fossés was an island of tranquillity in a world gone mad. The monarchy had been abolished; Louis XVI had lost his head to the Revolution; and Great Britain, Spain, and Holland had joined the Holy Roman Empire and Prussia in the war against France. In June, 1793, the Reign of Terror began—just about the time Victor du Pont arrived home from America.

He looked like a perfect candidate for the guillotine, this tall and very handsome young dandy dressed "in the English fashion," his bearing carelessly superior. France was a very dangerous place that summer for anyone of gentle birth, and no one could look at this fastidious, debonair gentleman and believe that he really accepted the doctrines of *égalité* and *fraternité*.

But to Gabrielle Josephine de la Fite de Pelleport, Victor was the only man she had ever seen who quickened the beating of her heart and filled her soul with excitement. Years later, recalling her first sight of him, she said, "I had never before seen, either at court or in town, a figure and a face which so immediately attracted one's attention and so easily held it."

Gaby was the daughter of the Marquis de Pelleport who had died in 1783, a few months after his wife. That summer when she met Victor, Gaby was living with her half-sister, Reine Marguerite de la Fite de Pelleport, a nun until the Revolution ordered the abolition of the religious orders. The two young women had taken shelter with other secularized nuns in an abandoned convent at Ferrières. Among their acquaintances in the area was the Vicomtesse de Segur, an incorrigible matchmaker even in those grim days, who delighted in telling them about a young gallant just back from America to whom she wished to introduce them.

On a day when Victor was to dine with her, the Vicomtesse arranged for the Pelleport sisters to join her too. "We went," Gaby recalled later. "He did not arrive. Madame de Segur kept glancing at the clock. When at last she gave him up, she stamped her feet with anger and told us with the most amusing volubility that he was unbearable, that he never answered letters, that his indifference was inconceivable. My sister and I were choking with laughter. Fortunately she was too angry to see it."

The next day the sisters went with the Vicomtesse to the fête of La Magdaleine at Montargis, and there Madame de Segur spotted Victor and called him to her. And that was the beginning of his courtship of Gabrielle de Pelleport.

At the time of his return to France, all the young men were being conscripted for military service. An old family friend, an official of the Commune, suggested that Victor join the *gendarmerie*. "I will see that you are stationed at Ferrières where you will be near home," the friend promised. "This step will prove your patriotism and that of your father which is seriously doubted." Irénée sent money for Victor's uniform and equipment as a gendarme and the scheme worked. Victor was not drafted.

Before long, however, his work became intolerable. The increasing number of arrest orders for Royalists with whom he secretly sympathized was demoralizing. Besides, he was in love with Gaby. And she would not marry him while he was a gendarme who might even be ordered to arrest Gaby herself any day.

It would have been too dangerous for Victor to have resigned from the *gendarmerie;* that would have exposed him to the suspicion of being Royalist in sympathy. As a device to get out of the force safely, he feigned illness. Spinach juice smeared on his face gave him a convincingly sick appearance. Pretending that he wasn't able to swallow food, he ate only by stealth. He made so credible a picture of a jaundiced, wasting young gendarme that a friend in the Commune was able to obtain his medical discharge.

Even after Victor was out of the *gendarmerie*, Gaby refused to marry him. She said she wouldn't consider herself properly wed unless the ceremony were performed by a priest, but most of the curés had been arrested by the anti-religious regime. However, Victor could be resourceful. He went to the curé of Branles and pleaded with him to perform the ceremony. At first the priest refused because of the danger to himself if the authorities learned that he had performed a religious wedding, but Victor finally persuaded him that it could be done with such secrecy that no one could ever learn of it. A closed room at Bois des Fossés was chosen for the ceremony, but Victor, to maintain absolute secrecy, didn't even tell Gabrielle about his plans lest she tell someone else.

"I had not supposed that Victor would be able to arrange this," Gaby wrote in later years, "especially as the curé had refused at first, and I was overcome with embarrassment and perplexity when he called me and led me to a room where I found his father, his cousin, and the old priest. I asked to be allowed to call my sister who was watching a game of backgammon downstairs, but they refused. I had not one moment for consideration; he held my hand and would listen to nothing; and I took the most important step of my life under circumstances so precipitate, so incomprehensible to myself, that I could scarcely believe it or explain to my sister a few minutes later why she had not been permitted to assist at this most unceremonious ceremony. But she was kindness itself and quite understood that I had had no choice; she embraced me tenderly and never referred to it again."

For three weeks there was no outward change in Gaby's life so as to avoid letting the authorities in on her secret. She continued to live at Ferrières and Victor at Bois des Fossés. Then, once their documents were in order, they were married in a civil ceremony at Chevannes on April 4, 1794, and went back to Bois des Fossés to live with Pierre Samuel and Sophie, to whom Victor had long been reconciled.

Irénée was still in Paris, operating the renovated du Pont printing house now in the former Convent des Nouvelles Catholiques, Rue Helvétius Number 57, and carrying out his duties in the National Guard. He had not lost his faith in the essential righteousness of the Revolution, but he was sickened by the Terror, which now claimed the life of even his beloved Lavoisier. Nevertheless, he could be cool and detached, could appreciate that the Revolution, despite its horrors, had brought a new and better life to most Frenchmen. After the celebration of Bastille Day that year, Irénée pondered on the change in the character of festivals. Before the Revolution, the people were "often more bored than amused by what they had come to see," but now "it was different—a real merry-making, not merely a spectacle. They were citizens, brothers, who rejoiced— joy and gaiety showed everywhere; it was one immense family who celebrated together the happy events that are delighting everyone, interesting everyone."

Ironically, two days earlier—although Irénée didn't know it—an order had been issued for the arrest of his father who was described in the warrant: Aged fifty years [it should have said fifty-four], living at Chevannes, department of Loiret, height five feet, eight inches, hair and eyebrows gray, forehead high and bald, eyes blue, nose flat, mouth large, chin cleft, face oval and full.

At Bois des Fossés the family was disturbed by the sound of horses' hooves and jangling bridles outside. There was a banging on the door and a party of soldiers burst into the house. Sophie, distraught, insisted on going with her father-in-law, but the soldiers wouldn't permit her to ride in the same coach. It was a stormy night, but Sophie, imploring Victor and Gabrielle to look after Victorine, set off resolutely on a mule with a peasant boy as her only escort. She rode several miles on the beast until she reached an inn where she could wait for a public diligence to Paris.

It was a sad reunion for Irénée and Sophie. Irénée at once sought out his politician friends and those who had been associated with his father in the past, trying to win the release of Pierre Samuel, or, failing that, at least to prevent his falling victim to the guillotine. Every day Sophie, dressed in peasant clothes, filled a basket with books and food and made her way to La Force prison. She could leave a basket there for her father-in-law, but she was not allowed to visit him.

Inside the prison, Pierre Samuel in his most debonair fashion was making himself at home. He found a number of old friends there who greeted him warmly but regretfully. "It was impossible to know the man and not to love him," the Comte de Beugnot wrote in his memoirs many years later. "No man ever bore misfortune—I will not say with greater courage, for courage implies an effort—but with such perfect calmness; when it forsook him, it was only to give way to wit or gaiety."

With the insouciance of a D'Artagnan, du Pont told his friends, "I am here like a conscript in a regiment. It is for you to educate me."

Instead, he himself promptly set up classes in political economy and proceeded to deliver learned lectures to his captive audience. His "students," who attended because they had nothing else to do, found themselves actually listening and arguing—and forgetting for a few precious minutes the tumbrils that every day carried some of them to the guillotine.

None of the du Ponts knew that sentence of death had already been passed on Pierre Samuel. He was to go to his execution July 30.

Three days before that date, he was walking in the courtyard of

La Force, arguing as usual—this time about slavery—when he suddenly held up his hand in a gesture for silence.

The tocsins were sounding everywhere in the city as they always did when revolutionary events were coming to a climax. The prisoners of La Force assumed that once again the mob was about to break into the prisons and slaughter the Royalists. Most of the prisoners gathered in the central hall to listen apprehensively to the wild ringing of the bells. They were close to panic when du Pont demanded their attention and began a harangue.

The Comte de Beugnot has recalled the substance of du Pont's remarks: "When the alarm bell rings, it is possible that they are going to repeat the massacres of September in all the prisons, but as for him, he intends to sell his life dearly. He exhorts us to do the same and tells us his plan for defense. There are twelve of us who can arm ourselves more or less well with the fire irons which fortunately had not been removed, the two daggers that we possessed among us, our knives, and the legs of the chairs. We must adopt the ancient order of battle—that is to say, the strongest one shall be in the front rank, two more in the next, three in the third, and four in the last. . . . However alarming was the situation, it was impossible not to laugh at the seriousness with which this beloved du Pont arranged his line of battle."

Humorous or not, every man of them expected to fight for his life before the night was out. During the hours of dark, the tension continued. There were unusual noises and the jailors kept telling the prisoners the latest rumors: Robespierre, chief figure in the Reign of Terror, was a prisoner . . . he wasn't a prisoner, but his brother was. . . . Robespierre's men had rescued him. . . .

Not until later, after the dawn of that fear-filled day, did they learn the truth. His fellow revolutionaries had turned on Robespierre and had shot him; the next day the man who had sent so many to the guillotine lost his own head to the blade.

In a fortnight the Terror was over and by the end of August, du Pont was out of prison and back at Bois des Fossés. Irénée remained in Paris, managing the printing house and carrying out his official duties, one of which was the collection of money for the poor, a task he really enjoyed for, as he wrote to Sophie, "of all the duties of a citizen, that of helping the unfortunate is of course the most agreeable." A less agreeable responsibility was leading his company of the National Guard into the fighting against the extremist followers of the dead Robespierre when they tried to seize power.

At Bois des Fossés, things were far from tranquil. Love was causing problems. Gabrielle's half-sister, Reine, had fallen in love with Victor, although she was careful to conceal her passion from him and Gaby. Nevertheless, the shrewd Sophie sensed the truth which she confided only to her husband. "She is most unhappy," Sophie wrote after coming across Reine in tears upstairs. "I am very sorry for her, for I can see how she suffers." But in the fall, Reine found an excuse to end the situation and went to stay with another of her sisters who lived at Villefranche. Less than a year and a half later, she died of gangrene after a long, painful illness.

About the time she left Bois des Fossés, Victor and Gabrielle made their departure, too. The foreign minister, a pre-Revolutionary friend of Gaby's family, sent Victor to America again. This time he and Gabrielle lived at Charleston, S.C., where he was consul.

But even while Reine was being tormented by her love for her half-sister's husband, love was also causing pain to the patriarch, Pierre Samuel. He had always harbored a secret passion for Madame Lavoisier, and now, with her husband dead, he felt that he could with propriety avow his love. Her reaction was a painful blow to his ego: she said she had always thought of him as a father. And then she made it plain that she expected him to pay off Lavoisier's mortgage on Bois des Fossés at once because she was without funds. Of course, du Pont was equally penniless, and the poor widow grew increasingly icy in her attitude toward him.

During this period of distress, Papa du Pont said, "Sometimes I think I will end it all by writing to Citizeness Poivre, getting her to come here, and marrying her. But that is a very radical step to take. . . . My head is tired and my heart is sad and the sadness is increasing."

Madame Françoise Poivre, the widow of a French colonial official who had died in 1786, was an old friend of the du Ponts. Victor had once sought to marry her daughter, Julie Ile de France, but she had chosen Lafayette's aide, Bureaux de Pusy, instead. Madame Poivre was a sentimental, soft-hearted, ineffectual woman who worshipped Pierre Samuel as a philosopher on a plane with the gods.

And now, after his painful rebuff by Madame Lavoisier, the elder du Pont found his old admirer's outright adoration balm to his soul; in fact, he was so carried away that he married the widow in the Town Hall at Chevannes on September 26, 1795.

The following month saw him win election to the upper house of the new parliament, the Council of Ancients. He also established a newspaper, *l'Historien*, which soon found itself consistently opposing the policies of the government now run by a five-man Directory. His narrow escape had not taught Pierre Samuel political discretion.

Meanwhile, the ranks of the du Ponts were growing. A girl born to Sophie died after two days, but on May 31, 1796, she produced another girl, christened Evelina Gabrielle. And in America, her sister-in-law, Gaby, gave birth to Amelie Elisabeth on January 3, 1796, and Charles Irénée on March 29, 1797.

Throughout 1796 and 1797, the struggle between Jacobins and constitutionalists continued. It came to a head on September 4, 1797, when the three left-wing members of the Directory staged a *coup d'état*, suppressed all the opposition journals, including *l'Historien*, and encouraged the mobs to pillage the du Pont printing house.

The next day Pierre Samuel was arrested again and thrown into La Force. This time Irénée was arrested, too.

To their surprise, the du Ponts were only in prison for one day. But on their liberation, they found that Pierre Samuel's political allies were being deported to French Guiana, part of it just set aside as a penal colony soon to be known as "Devil's Island." The elder du Pont was on the list for deportation, too, but he was saved by an old friend. Madame de Staël had connections in every political group and at her suggestion, Joseph Chénier, a left-wing extremist, appealed for clemency on behalf of du Pont because, so said Chénier, he was in his eighties. This was untrue, of course, as Chénier and most of his listeners knew full well—du Pont was not yet sixty. But the deputies went through a solemn pretense of believing Chénier and with straight faces they asked the Directory to nullify du Pont's banishment.

Nevertheless, the du Ponts realized that a France which had imprisoned them twice for their political opinions, had threatened their lives, had twice ravaged their publishing house, offered no hope for a tranquil future.

They decided to emigrate to America.

They didn't know that a warrant for Pierre Samuel's arrest would soon be issued by the American government.

CHAPTER VI

FLIGHT TO AMERICA

As a FRENCH DIPLOMAT in America, Victor du Pont was in an increasingly uncomfortable position. Relations between his country and the United States had deteriorated to an extent unbelievable at the close of the War of Independence. Revolutionaries in deed but not in temperament, many of the American leaders had been appalled by the excesses of the French Revolution, especially by the execution of the king and queen and the bloody harvest of the Reign of Terror.

By 1798, matters had come to such a pass that the United States had repudiated its treaties with France, the French had retaliated with raids on American shipping by their privateers, and men-of-war of the two countries had engaged in armed combat. An undeclared naval war broke out.

At this inauspicious time Pierre Samuel du Pont de Nemours made up his mind to go to America.

Like most Frenchmen, including the Directory then ruling France, he was unaware of how sharply American public opinion had turned against his country. The French thought that only President Adams and his Federalists were hostile. Du Pont himself mistakenly believed that most Americans still loved France. So he was sure that he could live in greater safety and respect in the United States than in a France gone berserk.

His position in his homeland was even more precarious than he realized. Although he did not know it, the police were secretly investigating him two months after his release from La Force. The authorities at Orléans had received a tip from an informer that all the Royalists for some distance around Nemours were making clandestine visits to the elder du Pont—although Pierre Samuel, like Irénée, was now a confirmed republican. The investigation was conducted by a lieutenant of gendarmes at Montargis and not by the commissioner of du Pont's own canton. The latter was distrusted because he was known to be a friend of Pierre Samuel. But after a careful inquiry, the lieutenant reported that Papa du Pont wasn't plotting with the monarchists; he had been busy with wine-making and had received no visitors at all, despite the fact that he "is much loved at Chevannes."

It was during their brief incarceration in La Force that the du Ponts resolved to emigrate. As soon as the heavy doors swung open for them, they set to work on their plans. The first step was to obtain information, so they questioned anyone who might know about conditions in the New World. Among those consulted was a French emigré back home on a visit; he urged them to settle on the Potomac. But the American inventor, Robert Fulton, then in Paris experimenting with submarine mines, recommended a site in Kentucky not far from the Ohio River.

Before the year was out, a prospectus for a company to finance the venture was issued. Its unrestrained and unrealistic optimism bore the unmistakable imprint of Pierre Samuel. Among the attractions it listed were these:

1—No danger; no risk of loss of capital.

2—The certainty of possessing for each share a considerable property in a country where liberty, safety, independence really exist in a temperate climate, where the land is fertile and bountiful, in Virginia and the western counties.

3—The certainty of drawing interest—first at four percent, then at six, then at eight.

4—Finally, after twelve years, the certainty of a capital that has been quadrupled, probably increased tenfold, possibly even twice tenfold.

In Pierre Samuel's vision, the company would establish a colony —he named it, somewhat prematurely, "Pontiana"—on the Ohio, beginning with a nucleus of seventy-five hundred acres in Kentucky owned by Jacques Bidermann, a Swiss banker in Paris. Cleared of forests, the fertile soil would yield abundant crops, model villages would rise, small manufactories—sawmills, gristmills, distilleries, potteries, and so on—would be developed to make the colony self-sufficient, and the necessities of social life—schools, hospitals, churches, inns—would spring into existence. It was all so easy and idyllic as Papa du Pont saw it.

There would be an office in New York, but headquarters would be in Alexandria, Virginia, just across the Potomac from the future site of the federal government chosen by President Washington in 1790 and scheduled to become the seat of national power in 1800.

The cost of the entire venture was estimated at 4,000,000 francs, with shares pegged at 10,000 francs each. Many of the most illustrious names in France agreed to subscribe, but their total pledges amounted to only 3,200,000 francs—800,000 short of the need. And when the time came to make good on the pledges, most of the subscribers reneged. Only 450,000 francs were actually paid in.

The stock company, Du Pont de Nemours Père, Fils & Cie., was off to a bad start.

One copy of the prospectus was sent to Victor, who was appalled by its naiveté. He knew, however, that he would not be able to escape involvement in his father's scheme, for the prospectus bragged at some length about Victor's long experience in America, his knowledge of the land, the people and the language, and his influential connections.

At that point, early in 1798, Victor himself was ordered to move from Charleston to Philadelphia where he was to be consul general. In May he arrived there. This was poor timing because, on April 3, the XYZ Affair, an attempt by high French officials to extort money from the United States government, had been made public. As a result, the nation became passionately hostile to the French.

When Victor presented his credentials, President Adams refused to accept them. Adams's action was not intended as a slight to Victor personally, even though the President distrusted Papa du Pont as being—of all things!—"too Jacobin," but as a rebuff to France.

Without diplomatic standing, Victor had no reason to remain in America, so, on June 7, after a private talk with Thomas Jefferson, then Vice-President, he sailed for France—three weeks before the Alien and Sedition Laws became effective.

In Paris, Victor wrote a long report for Talleyrand, the foreign minister. Savagely attacking the anti-American policy France had been following, Victor warned that an all-out war that would throw the United States into the arms of France's hated enemy, England, was imminent unless the Directory changed its attitude. The French had committed so many crimes against the United States, Victor said bluntly, that the catalogue of them would fill many volumes. He charged that French privateers, with the sanction of their government, had been guilty of "acts of violence, of brigandage, of piracy." He urged a complete turnabout in policy: an end to the spoliations, the resumption of normal diplomatic relations with the appointment of new consuls not identified with the past policy, and the reopening of negotiations to bring about a *rapprochement* in Franco-American relations. Such a policy, Victor pointed out, would also help the anti-Federalists—the Democratic-Republican Party headed by Jefferson—to win the approaching elections. And the anti-Federalists tended to be Francophiles.

The day after he received Victor's report, Talleyrand transmitted it to the Directory with a covering letter endorsing Victor's observations and his recommendations. On July 31, the Directory adopted the policy that du Pont had suggested. Richard Codman of Boston, an American speculator in Paris, wrote to Federalist congressmen that du Pont had opened Talleyrand's eyes to the dangers of the old French policy. The anti-Federalist press in America played up the Directory's action. This had a favorable effect on neutral opinion in the United States.

"By respecting du Pont's advice," wrote Samuel Eliot Morison, the American historian, "the Directory made it impossible for the Hamiltonian wing of the Federalist Party to force a war with France, strengthened the Democratic opposition, and gained time for the peaceful acquisition of Louisiana from Spain."

It is ironical that a son of Pierre Samuel argued America's case with Talleyrand; for, at the very moment that Victor was urging a reasonable, equitable, conciliatory policy toward America, the

United States government was taking secret action against Papa du Pont.

It all began when Rufus King, United States minister to England, wrote to Secretary of State Pickering, saying that du Pont and a delegation of French philosophers from the National Institute—he was wrong about that, of course—had obtained passports from the Directory to go to the United States. King understood that they planned to settle on Spanish land in the upper reaches of the Mississippi just outside the borders of the United States—wrong again. He didn't think, King concluded, that the United States government would be happy at the prospect.

He was right. President Adams was unwilling to let du Pont or any other "French philosopher" come to the United States "in the present situation of our country." Adams added irascibly, "We have had too many French philosophers already and I really begin to think, or rather to suspect, that learned academies, not under the immediate inspection and control of government, have disorganized the world, and are incompatible with social order."

In October, Pickering got a report that a French plot was afoot to seize the western part of the United States for France. He submitted blank arrest orders for the President's signature. Three of the warrants bore names, one of them being Pierre Samuel du Pont de Nemours—"if he is to be found."

By the time Pierre Samuel actually arrived in the United States, the Alien Act had expired and the American nation had recovered from its flirtation with authoritarianism. Apparently he never knew how close he had come to jumping out of the frying pan into the fire. Which is just as well, for he was still full of an ecstatic enthusiasm for America. In August, 1798, while Adams and Pickering were privately discussing what steps to take against him, the oblivious du Pont wrote to Jefferson from Paris: "I wish to die in a country in which liberty exists not only in the laws, always more or less well, more or less badly carried out, but even more in the fixed habits of the nation."

But he wasn't doing very much to achieve that desire. All Pierre Samuel really did was rush around talking about the grand scheme to anybody who'd listen, while Irénée and Sophie worked feverishly to make the emigration possible. Sophie, somewhat handicapped by the birth of her third living child, Alfred Victor, on April 11, 1798, had to decide which of her treasured possessions to take to America and which must be left for lack of space. Meanwhile, Irénée was selling the printing house and trying to find a buyer for Bois des Fossés.

Bureaux de Pusy, son-in-law of Pierre Samuel's second wife, had fought beside Lafayette both in the American Revolution and in the war against Austria. Recently he had been imprisoned with Lafayette at Olmütz. When Pusy was set free, it was specified that he must go to America without entering France even to set his personal affairs in order. His wife was pregnant, so it was decided that she should remain behind until after her confinement, but her mother, her husband and her daughter left for America from Hamburg as the advance guard of the du Pont group.

The spring of 1799 turned into summer and summer into fall before Victor managed to find a ship to carry the du Ponts to America. It was the *American Eagle*, owned and commanded by a Captain Brooks. Seized by a French privateer two years earlier, it had been rotting away at La Rochelle ever since, until the authorities of the port finally condemned it. But Victor appealed to Talleyrand, who ordered the vessel returned to Captain Brooks and given clearance to leave the port. The captain could not afford to have his ship repaired properly or outfitted adequately, but somehow he managed to get the vessel ready for sailing.

There were thirteen in the du Pont party on October 2, 1799, when the *American Eagle* finally weighed anchor—seven adults and six children: Pierre Samuel; Madame de Pusy and her baby, Maurice; Victor, his wife and two children; Irénée, his wife and three children; and Sophie's brother, Charles Joseph Dalmas, then twenty-four years old.

Columbus took little more than two months to cross the Atlantic; the *American Eagle*'s passage consumed ninety-one days, almost three weeks longer. Barnacles that had accumulated for more than two years encrusted the ship's bottom, slowing her progress. The vessel leaked, the weary sails ripped, worn and weathered shrouds and sheets parted when any strain was put on them. Half the time a distress signal flew from the masthead. A terrible northwestern wind blew them far off course. The captain lost his bearings and the ship wandered confusedly across the sea in a general westerly course. If two English ships at different times had not given them food and bearings, they might have perished.

A family tradition insists that the du Ponts were saved from starvation by an enormous paté Sophie had brought along with her. More credible is another family legend that the famished passengers were finally reduced to eating a soup made by boiling rats trapped aboard the old tub. The passengers—the du Ponts were a minority— quarreled among themselves and so did the crew. Fights broke out. The sailors, becoming mutinous, broke into the passengers' trunks to steal what they could. The du Pont men had to guard their belongings with their swords.

Papa was the only person aboard ship who was not disheartened. He played with the children, encouraged the passengers to sing songs in order to keep up their spirits, involved everyone in long debates on philosophy, history, economics, and painted glowing pictures of the bright future that awaited them all in America.

The du Ponts bid the old century good-by at sea. The next day— New Year's Day, 1800—the ship limped into the ice-packed harbor of Newport, Rhode Island, frozen in the grip of one of the coldest winters in its history.

Chilled to the bone, half famished, ears and noses reddened by a frigid wind, the du Pont party disembarked and trudged up the street from the dock, looking for shelter and food. Stopping at the first house, they banged on the door, but there was no response. They peered through the frost-glazed windows and saw a cheery fire on the hearth and a table set with food. The occupants apparently had just left to visit neighbors or perhaps—considering the large Catholic population of Newport—to go to church for the celebration of the Feast of the Circumcision.

For the newcomers, the temptation was too much. Finding the door unlocked, they went in and made themselves at home. After getting warm before the fire as they waited in vain for the return of the people who lived there, the du Ponts finally could stand the sight of food no longer. They fell to and enjoyed what seemed the best meal they'd ever had in their lives. The occupants still had not returned when, the meal concluded, the du Ponts departed. Various versions of the story disagree on whether they left money in payment for the food.

The du Ponts' arrival in America was reported by the *Philadelphia Gazette* and the *Newport Journal*. The latter newspaper spoke warmly of "Mr. Victor du Pont, whose devotion to American interests in France deserves the gratitude of all Americans."

George Washington, too, welcomed the family, saying that "our people . . . are sensible to [Pierre Samuel du Pont's] contributions to his own land and more especially to this country in arranging the late peace." And Jefferson called the elder du Pont "the ablest man in France."

From Newport, the immigrants traveled by stage to New York City. There they were met by Bureaux de Pusy and Pierre Samuel's wife. By sloop they crossed the Upper Harbor of New York to Bergen Point where Pusy had bought a house, Good Stay, about where Jersey City and Bayonne meet today. It was nine miles by ferry and road from New York in those times, but because Good Stay was far out in the country, it was less expensive than a house on Manhattan Island. However, even with the wings that Pusy had added, it was crowded quarters for the sixteen men, women and children.

The company occupied buildings in New York, first at 61 Pearl Street and later at 91 Liberty Street. From these offices the company issued a broadside, grandiloquent like all of Papa du Pont's announcements, proclaiming the firm's entrance into the export-import business, the handling of remittances, and the administration and investment of funds. The backgrounds of Pierre Samuel, Victor, and Bureaux de Pusy were set forth in glorified detail, but all that was said of Irénée was one drab sentence: "Eleuthère Irénée du Pont has had much experience of business methods in France, in agriculture, manufactures, and the useful arts."

To his friends back in Europe, the elder du Pont wrote enthusiastically that his new homeland was "the best one in the world."

His attitude endeared him even to those Americans who might otherwise have regarded Pierre Samuel with disfavor. When du Pont retained Alexander Hamilton as lawyer for the new company, the Federalists were completely won over.

Nevertheless, Papa du Pont's natural inclination was toward the anti-Federalists, who, of course, included his best American friend, Jefferson. The Vice-President gave him valuable advice during his first months in America, cautioning him against land purchases while prices were wildly inflated.

Because aliens could not own land in many states, it was decided that Victor must become a citizen quickly. This could be done where the only qualification for citizenship was ownership of real estate. So Victor was dispatched to Alexandria, Virginia. There he bought a small house, leased it, and then became naturalized.

About this time, at Jefferson's request, Pierre Samuel sat down to make suggestions for the curriculum that should be followed at a state university in Virginia. He ended up with a long, verbose treatise, *On National Education in the United States of America*. Out of this welter of words, Jefferson eventually did cull some ideas that he used when founding the University of Virginia.

The dissertation on education, of course, did nothing to help the company financially. The du Ponts were using capital for living expenses and little or no money was coming in to replace it. Unable to follow their original plan of colonization, they turned to other business schemes. They prepared to engage in an extensive trade with Guadeloupe in the West Indies, but a revolution there ended that prospect. They then proposed a fleet of packets operating on a regular schedule between France and the United States, but that plan required the consent of both governments: the Americans liked the idea, the French didn't. After that, they dreamed up a rather shady deal for smuggling gold to the Spaniards then at war with England; they planned to conceal the precious metal inside pigs of lead which would be used as ballast in American flagships. However, the Peace of Amiens, concluding the Spanish-English war and the need for such smuggling, was signed just as Bureaux de Pusy arrived in Madrid to complete arrangements.

The outlook for the du Ponts was getting darker all the time.

And then Irénée took his gun and went hunting—and found his place in America.

CHAPTER VII

THE EIGHTH PLAN

Iʀᴇ́ɴᴇ́ᴇ's ʜᴜɴᴛɪɴɢ ᴄᴏᴍᴘᴀɴɪᴏɴ on an autumn day in 1800 was Colonel Louis de Tousard, who had come to America to fight for the colonies and lost his arm doing so. Along with many other Frenchmen, he lived on the Lancaster Road outside Wilmington, in one of the many French colonies that existed along the seaboard in those days, communities settled by refugees both from revolutionary France and from Haiti, whose black slaves had recently risen successfully against their French masters.

In the course of their hunting over the Delaware countryside, the two men ran out of ammunition and stopped at a country store to fill their powder horns. The poor quality and high price of the gunpowder appalled Irénée who recalled the finer product made by Lavoisier at Essonnes. But Tousard assured him that the price and the quality were typical of American gunpowder. The only good powder to be bought in the United States was imported from England, a matter of some concern to American leaders who distrusted Britain's attitude toward her former colonies.

With a new and hopeful idea in mind, Irénée asked Tousard to take him to an American powder mill. They went to the factory of William Lane and Stephen Decatur at Frankford, Pennsylvania. Irénée's opinion of their operations wasn't very favorable. Although the saltpeter they used was better than that available in France, they refined it so badly that it had little strength. Their mills were inefficient, producing little powder at great effort with too many workmen. Much of the powder was reduced to dust and lost in the manufacturing process.

Excited by the possibilities presented to his alert mind, Irénée hastened back to Good Stay. There he told his father of a plan to build a gunpowder factory in America where the need was great and competition weak. A powder mill could count on a high price and a sure market for its product, especially in a pioneering country that was growing in population and area. For not only did the armed forces need dependable powder, but so did the frontiersmen who were pushing the wilderness westward beyond the Alleghenies. In addition, the plantations of the South and of the West Indies required powder to blast out stumps and rocks and to perform a million and one other tasks.

The elder du Pont was lukewarm to the project. This was not a venture on an epic scale like the Pontiana colonization scheme or the packet ship plan or any of the other ideas so noble in scope. This was prosaic, dull stuff—working with one's hands in a wretched factory like any common laborer. Besides, he had always regretted that his younger son had chosen an ungraceful career in the powder mill at Essonnes. Now that deplorable prospect was in view again. Nevertheless, the family's funds were draining away and very little was coming in to replace them. Perhaps, sighed Papa du Pont, this might be a profitable notion after all.

At Pierre Samuel's suggestion, Irénée reduced his plans to writing. In his prospectus, he reckoned that one stamping mill and one wheel mill in operation two hundred working days a year would produce 100,000 pounds of powder annually. Gunpowder had three major ingredients: saltpeter, sulphur, and charcoal. The latter two were inexpensive, but saltpeter was relatively costly. The labor costs would include the director—Irénée himself, a foreman, four journeymen powdermen, and twelve other workmen. The capital requirements for such an enterprise would total $36,000. The annual profit was estimated at $10,000.

By this time, a list of seven projects for the du Pont firm had already been drawn up by Papa du Pont. Now, reluctantly, he added the powder mill to the list. He also decided that both of his sons should sail for France. While in their native country, Victor was to raise more money for the company and Irénée would order equipment for the powder mill.

In a letter to his original backer, Jacques Bidermann, the Swiss banker in Paris, Pierre Samuel rhapsodized about the first seven projects. Then he added, "My second son will explain to you the eighth plan that we have in view, and what we believe we can accomplish here by the manufacture of gunpowder—for which his skill in this art, the ignorance of it in America, the needs of government, those of the country, and even of the West Indies, gives us not hope but a positive certainty of great profits."

The more Papa du Pont thought about the powder mill project, the more ardent he became. He fired off a letter to Jefferson, telling him about Irénée's plans and—inevitably—he ended up bragging that du Pont gunpowder would "send bullets a fifth farther than English or Dutch bullets travel." The letter concluded with a plea for consideration in the granting of government munitions contracts.

On January 5, 1801, the brothers du Pont sailed for France. A month later they landed at Le Havre.

A major task faced Irénée. In addition to ordering the necessary machinery and studying the latest developments in French powdermaking, he also had to raise money. For his father, dubious of the safety of investment in a factory that might be blown to smithereens at any time, had only agreed to put up two-thirds of the required capital. So the firm of Du Pont de Nemours Père, Fils et Cie. was advancing $24,000, leaving $12,000 still to be raised for the project. The earnest Irénée got what he needed. It came from Bidermann, Duquesnoy, who had been in La Force with his father, and Louis Necker, uncle of Madame Germaine de Staël and brother of Louis XVI's onetime finance minister.

The French government took a lively interest in Irénée's proposed powder works. Although it was on the point of signing the Treaty of Amiens and thus making peace with England, the French government considered this merely a pause allowing both sides to catch their breath. The peace lasted, in fact, only twenty months. And so the French were delighted at the prospect of a French-owned factory that would cut deeply into England's virtual monopoly of the American powder market. The government, therefore, behaved with unusual generosity toward Irénée. He was enabled to buy machinery at cost; new processes, developed since his time at Essonnes, were made available to him; experienced powdermen were invited to listen to his recruitment talks, and some agreed to migrate to the United States.

While Irénée was in France, busily engaged in preparing for his project, events in American politics were entering an era more favorable to the du Ponts. Jefferson moved up from Vice-President to President. This suggested a pun to Papa du Pont who dearly loved a play on words: "You have never had but one Vice," he wrote the Sage of Monticello. "I compliment your country and both hemispheres that you have at last lost it."

In Paris on April 21, Irénée's company was incorporated for the "manufacture of military and sporting powder in the United States of America." It was capitalized at $36,000, representing eighteen shares valued at $2,000 each. Bidermann, Duquesnoy and Necker each held one share, the parent du Pont firm, Du Pont Père, Fils et Cie., had pledged itself to take eleven shares, and four were to be made available for possible American investors. Irénée and the parent firm would have the sole right to determine when dividends should be paid. The dividends were to be split into thirty parts: eighteen for the shareholders, nine for the director—Irénée, and three reserved for a slush fund to be used in obtaining government contracts.

While Irénée was hard at work coping with such mundane matters, his carefree brother was enjoying one last taste of Parisian society as it existed under First Consul Napoleon Bonaparte, who had come to power in November, 1799, by a *coup d'état*. His regime aped the opulence and grandeur of the old order and when Talleyrand made known his friendship with Victor, the doors of the most fashionable salons were opened to him. He dined at Madame de Staël's, went to tea at the home of his father's old love, Madame Lavoisier, and renewed his friendship with a Lafayette now grown fat. At a huge *soirée* in Bonaparte's honor, Victor had an opportunity to see at close range the Corsican and his mistress, Italian soprano Josephina Graziani.

In July, when Irénée sailed back to America, Victor decided, for some reason that is unclear, to remain in Europe for a while. Certainly it was not because he preferred Europe to America, for Victor, since his first visit to the United States, had become truly American in outlook. That summer of 1801, while traveling in Spain, Victor sent home to his wife in America a poem of his own composition which was more notable for its pro-American ardor than for its lyrical qualities The poem, *"Mes Adieux a l'Europe"* ("My Farewell to Europe"), began by listing many of the things in the Old World that Victor was happy to leave behind. The second stanza said:

> In order to find
> Peace, virtue, wisdom, humanity,
> The spirit of independence and sweet equality,
> Innocence of manners and happiness of hearth,
> A good people, good laws, liberty—
> To know living, industry, ease, activity—
> O! my dear friends, one must
> Cross the Atlantic!
>
> * * *
>
> On my return
> To America,
> I am able to say, with truth:
> The more I see other countries,
> The more I love America!

After thirteen months in Europe, Victor returned to the United States. Ten months earlier, in July, 1801, Irénée had come back to Good Stay, bringing with him Paris clothes for Sophie and dolls and toys and coloring boxes for the children. Seeds and plants he carried from Europe for cultivation in du Pont gardens here, and there were seven merino sheep from Spain, a breed renowned for its long and silken fleece.

Having rested up from his voyage, Irénée started looking for a site on which to build his powder mill. Even before the proper location was found, Pierre Samuel wrote to President Jefferson, asking for a government contract once the du Pont powder mill was in actual operation. And because he believed that only government work could make the mill profitable, the elder du Pont urged his son to build the factory near Washington.

Like a dutiful son, Irénée scouted the territory around Federal

City—as the national capital was then called. He had already looked at several places in the Hudson River valley and had made an unsuccessful attempt to buy the Lane-Decatur mill at Frankford. After scouring parts of Maryland and Virginia lying near the capital, Irénée wrote wearily to his father, "The country, the people, the location are all worthless." Then he added, almost as an afterthought, "I shall stop off in Wilmington for a day to see the Brandywine."

The Brandywine Creek tumbled down one hundred and twenty feet in its first four miles, picking up speed as it rushed over a rocky course from Pennsylvania, winding past Chadds Ford and through the Quaker and Swedish farmlands of northern Delaware, until it mingled its waters with the Christina River at Wilmington and then poured forth into the great expanse of the Delaware River. In and about Wilmington there were many French immigrants to whom du Pont was introduced by Tousard. Among them was Jean-Pierre Bauduy de Bellevue, a refugee from Haiti. Bauduy—he styled himself Peter Bauduy in the United States—was a man of artistic temperament. A wealthy planter in pre-revolutionary Haiti, he was also an accomplished painter. His American neighbors, recognizing his talent, had even asked him to design the Wilmington town hall.

Bauduy, whose brother Alexandre was already a friend of Victor, became enthusiastic at once about Irénée du Pont's powder project. He offered to subscribe for some of the shares held open for American participation. In the end, these shares were divided between Bauduy and Archibald McCall, a Philadelphia merchant.

With Bauduy as his guide, Irénée was able to take a close look at the properties along the Brandywine. The stream was essential, for his machinery must be turned by water power. Two pieces of property appeared to meet his needs: one, close to Wilmington, was owned by a man named Harvey; the other, farther out in the country, belonged to a Quaker squire, a dour and tight-fisted man named Jacob Broom. In 1795, Broom had built a cotton mill on his property, but it had been destroyed by fire within a short time and he had never restored the mill.

The Broom property appeared almost ideal to du Pont, but the owner set too high a price for his land. Using Bauduy as his agent, Irénée continued his negotiations with Broom from New Jersey, hoping to win agreement on a lower price. In the meantime, he kept looking at other possible sites.

In the end, he bought the ninety-five acres belonging to Broom for $6,740. Because the law in Delaware, as in several other states, prohibited ownership of property by aliens, Alexander Hamilton, as the du Ponts' attorney, consulted James A. Bayard, then a member of the House of Representatives from Delaware and later a senator. Hamilton wondered if there was any chance of persuading the state legislature to pass a special act permitting Irénée to own real estate. But among many influential men there was still, Hamilton found, an "unreasonable animosity against the French" and the du Ponts were unable to obtain the necessary dispensation. Therefore, the property was finally transferred, not to Irénée but to William Hamon, a naturalized Frenchman and a friend of Bauduy.

When June came, du Pont's young brother-in-law, Charles Dalmas, left Good Stay on the schooner *Betsy of Patterson* with dogs, sheep, and as many of the du Pont possessions as the family could cram into boxes and barrels. He was put ashore at New Castle, Delaware, and carted everything by wagon the eleven miles to the farm Irénée had bought. On July 15, Irénée and Sophie, herding their offspring into a wagon already piled high with furniture, trunks, and other impedimenta, bade farewell to the house on Bergen Point. After four days of teeth-jarring riding over dusty roads on which countless other wagons had cut deep tracks, they arrived in Wilmington, a journey of one hundred and thirty miles.

Three months earlier, Papa du Pont in a letter to Jefferson had touched on the dichotomy, more apparent than real, between Irénée's principles and his plans. With a play on the meaning of his son's given names, Eleuthère—"peace" and Irénée—"liberty," Pierre Samuel wrote, "This peaceful friend of liberty, although he manufactures gunpowder, hopes that it will not be used for war but for those deeds which prevent war, those functions to which our military and our youth must devote themselves—that is, to the business of the country, to hunting, to the opening of mountains and canals, to all public works."

CHAPTER VIII

MISSION FOR JEFFERSON

W HILE IRÉNÉE AND HIS FAMILY had been preparing to move to the Brandywine in that spring of 1802, Pierre Samuel and his wife had been packing, too. They were going back to France.

Papa du Pont had decided the trip was necessary because Victor had failed in his European mission to obtain additional capital for the parent company. The elder du Pont thought that he himself, with his great personal prestige, might better persuade investors to put their money in Du Pont Père, Fils et Cie. Moreover, some of the original shareholders were growing restless, and Pierre Samuel hoped to allay their fears and at the same time whip up support for the company's new ventures.

There was also another reason for the trip that Papa du Pont did not even discuss with his sons. He was homesick. Although he knew many of the most prominent men in America, he was not happy in the United States. The language remained strange to him, although he sometimes spiced his conversation by using an English word or phrase. Besides, he was sensitive to the prejudice against the French that was still so prevalent throughout the cities of America.

It was widely believed, and with good reason, that Napoleon intended to reconquer Haiti and then use it as a rallying point where a fleet and an army could be assembled for an eventual landing in

Louisiana and an invasion of the United States from the southwest.
As a result, Franco-American relations were worse than they had
been at any time since Victor du Pont had induced the Directory
to end the depredations against American shipping four years earlier. These were the circumstances that drew Pierre Samuel du Pont
de Nemours into a new series of diplomatic negotiations.

His involvement began before he left the United States. When
he wrote from Good Stay to President Jefferson, telling of his
plans, the President quickly replied with a letter asking his old
friend to come to Washington for a discussion of matters so delicate that they "could not be committed to paper." Despite the air
of urgency in the letter, du Pont was unable to take the time to go
to Washington before sailing, so Jefferson was compelled, in the
end, to put the matter in writing.

Jefferson's grim words shocked du Pont, for the President bluntly
warned that French occupation of the Louisiana Territory, acquired
from Spain by Napoleon under the Treaty of San Ildefonso, meant
war.

"The day that France takes New Orleans," Jefferson wrote in a
letter dated April 25, 1802, which he asked du Pont to deliver to
Robert R. Livingston, United States minister to France, "we must
marry ourselves to the British fleet and nation."

The shaken du Pont than read the letter addressed to himself. In
it Jefferson wrote that France—in New Orleans—and the United
States could not live peacefully side by side, even if the French
were to guarantee American access to the sea by way of the Mississippi. If Bonaparte sent troops to Louisiana, Jefferson would consider it an act of war, although the President was anxious to avoid
a conflict. If the French actually took possession of Louisiana, he
would arrange with the British a joint action against the French.
With the aid of England, the United States would then launch an
attack on New Orleans. The entire Louisiana Territory would be
occupied to prevent any new European power from gaining a foot-
hold on the North American continent. Jefferson assumed that
Britain and the United States would wipe out the French fleet and
gain complete domination of the seas. Then South and Central, as
well as North, America would in effect be "appropriated by them."

Du Pont instantly realized that such a frank threat, laid before

Napoleon, would certainly provoke that hot-tempered militarist into an immediate war with the United States, for Jefferson was saying in plain language that France must give up Louisiana or the United States would take it. National honor would force Bonaparte to embark upon a war in defense of the French territory of Louisiana.

Replying to Jefferson, du Pont pointed to a weakness in the President's plans: if the Administration committed itself to such a chauvinistic course, it would strengthen the hand of the American jingoists—especially the Federalists, including those who had been calling for a military conquest of Mexico.

Moreover, Pierre Samuel pointed out, an alliance with the British would not strengthen, only weaken, American seapower, for the English would never permit the rise of the United States to the first rank of maritime nations.

In du Pont's letter to the President, a compromise was suggested: let France pledge free access to the sea to "the territories of the Cumberland, the Wabash, and both banks of the Ohio." As everyone knew, France and England were about to go to war with each other again, so why not propose to Napoleon a swap—a free hand in conquering Canada in return for Louisiana?

If no other solution could be found, du Pont concluded, why not turn to commerce instead of war by purchasing Louisiana from the French government?

Thus the Louisiana Purchase originated in the mind of Pierre Samuel du Pont de Nemours.

Jefferson wrote back that the United States, having very little money, could not possibly afford to buy Louisiana. But his letter, negative though it was, indicated that he was interested in the idea.

A purchase would be much cheaper than war, du Pont pointed out in his next letter. Recalling the undeclared naval war with France which his son had helped to terminate, du Pont said, "Calculate what that very slight armament cost you, which you made three years ago. Consider what the most fortunate war with France and Spain would cost you. And contract for a part—a half, let us say. The two countries will have made a good bargain. You will have Louisiana and possibly the Floridas for the least possible expense, and this conquest will be neither animated by hatred nor sullied by blood."

His arguments were persuasive. Jefferson agreed that Napoleon should be sounded out on the possibility of selling Louisiana.

Just before sailing from New York, du Pont informed Jefferson that his son had decided to establish his gunpowder works on the Brandywine near Wilmington. He promised that the American government would be able to get the finest powder from the du Pont mill, adding, with a rueful recollection of Jefferson's bellicose attitude, "But, my excellent friend, do not use it against us [the French]. Sell it rather in our colonies."

By then Pierre Samuel had already won his case, although he didn't know it. For the President now wrote a confidential letter to Livingston, asking him to find out how the French might consider a sale.

Once in France, du Pont had his work cut out for him. Unfortunately Chancellor Livingston, the American envoy, was a tactless diplomat. Livingston prided himself on his candor and it was all du Pont could do to keep Talleyrand from exploding with wrath at his offensive statements.

Meanwhile, in America matters were drifting from bad to worse. The Spanish authorities at New Orleans barred the port to the Americans bringing goods from upriver. The frontiersmen of the Ohio River valley were ready for war and the fever was spreading along the seaboard. In November James Madison aligned himself with the war party, and a month later President Jefferson, in a message to Congress, said that if the French were to take possession of Louisiana, it would make "a change in the aspect of our foreign relations" which would require Congressional action—in other words, appropriations for war.

And then, just when war appeared inevitable, Jefferson asked the Senate to approve the appointment of James Monroe as a special envoy to France with full powers to join with Livingston in negotiating "a treaty or convention with the First Consul of France [Napoleon], for the purpose of enlarging and more effectually securing our rights and interests in the river Mississippi and in the territories eastward thereof."

The reason for Monroe's appointment was a letter from du Pont that had raised Jefferson's hopes for peace. Scoffing at the pessimistic reports that Livingston had been sending to Washington, du Pont offered a tentative outline for a treaty under which Louisiana would be sold for $6,000,000. Du Pont hoped that Monroe would be able to conduct the negotiations with more skill than Livingston. Jefferson followed up the appointment by sending a letter to du Pont expressing satisfaction at his efforts. The President said he couldn't agree entirely with the terms of the treaty but he welcomed the proposal because it held out the hope of an eventual accommodation.

Apparently Jefferson did not wholly trust du Pont—at least in so far as du Pont's loyalty to France might conflict with his affection for the United States. Even while he was protesting that $6,000,000 was more than the United States could pay, Jefferson was secretly authorizing Monroe and Livingston to pay up to twice that much for Louisiana. But candor is never an attribute of statesmen, no matter how high-principled; Jefferson was no exception. While he was deceiving du Pont about the price he was prepared to pay, he also emphasized in his communications with the Frenchman the trust that the United States, as well as France, placed in him. Because he enjoyed the confidence of both countries, Jefferson said, du Pont was in a peculiarly advantageous position to help both countries without any conflict of conscience. And it was possible for du Pont to operate with greater freedom than the diplomats of either nation because he was not restricted by the protocols of government service.

In Paris, negotiations continued apace. Du Pont conferred frequently with Talleyrand and Consul Lebrun on the one side, and with Monroe on the other. The latter's instructions from Washington had been explicitly based on du Pont's recommendations. Apprehensive of a blunder by Livingston that could upset the delicate dealings, Monroe and du Pont kept the minister in the dark about the arrangements that were slowly taking shape. Jefferson leaned heavily on the reports he received from du Pont and Monroe and ignored Livingston's pompous bleatings; which was just as well, for Livingston was certain that du Pont was a hindrance rather than a help to the American cause.

Ultimately a peaceful solution to the Franco-American crisis was found—not merely through du Pont's efforts, to be sure, but also as a result of other events such as the failure of Bonaparte's attempt to reconquer Haiti and the necessity for the French to conserve their strength for the coming war with the British. In the end, even Napoleon had to face the fact that his dreams of North American conquest must be abandoned.

When Bonaparte reached that point, a treaty was quickly concluded. In that document signed May 8, 1803, but antedated to April 30, France sold the entire Louisiana Territory to the United States for $15,000,000. It was more money than Jefferson had intended to pay, but he got far more land than he had bargained for. He had been seeking title to Florida and the Gulf Coast east of the Mississippi, but the treaty gave him New Orleans and an immense tract stretching from the Mississippi to the Rockies, from the Gulf of Mexico to Canada—828,000 square miles, a wilderness empire that doubled the size of the United States.

And when, in October, the United States Senate finally approved the treaty, Jefferson wrote to his old friend again, thanking him for his help in a transaction which would result in "blessings to unborn millions of men."

CHAPTER IX

BIRTH OF THE COMPANY

IT WAS HOT AND HUMID, that July of 1802, when Irénée, Sophie, and their menage arrived on the Brandywine. On the property there was no house worthy of the name, just a tiny, two-room cottage of stone built into the hillside, a crude structure with low ceilings and few windows, a pathetic contrast with the spaciousness of Good Stay or the ordered beauty of Bois des Fossés. Rattlesnakes and copperheads abounded in the rocky valley of the stream.

The arrival of the du Ponts created a good deal of interest in the area. Delaware was then, and remained until 1830, one hundred percent rural. Its total population in the 1800 census was a little more than sixty-four thousand. And when the du Ponts arrived, Wilmington itself probably had fewer than four thousand souls. So the appearance of this large household was bound to cause excitement.

The purchase of the Broom farm by the du Ponts bewildered the people of the area. The barren tract of rocks wasn't of much value as farmland; and what else could it be used for?

The indomitable Sophie set to work unpacking pots and pans, bedding and clothes, staples and toys, and the little cottage was soon in order, a neat little corner of France transplanted to America. Irénée's hunting dogs sought shade under the trees nearby, and the bleating of the merino sheep added to the din caused by the cries of

63

the children, the shouts of the workmen, and the hammering and blasting that marked the construction of the powder mill.

To build the mill, Irénée had recruited men from Chester and Philadelphia as well as Wilmington—masons, carpenters, teamsters— all of whom camped in the valley as they labored on the factory. At first the work went badly, for the boss spoke very poor English with a strong French accent, and the workmen thought he issued his odd orders regarding the specifications for the mill buildings because he didn't understand their tongue well enough to make his wishes clearly known. When at length they understood that he really wanted the buildings built so strangely, they decided he must be a little crazy.

Actually Irénée was employing the sound precepts that he had learned from Lavoisier. Powder-making is a hazardous undertaking; a man who enters upon such a labor without anticipating disastrous accidents is a fool. Irénée, no fool, planned for misfortune. Instead of one big building, he put up several small ones. He allowed for a generous space between each, so that a fire or an explosion in one would be less likely to spread in a chain reaction to the others. Three sides of each building were constructed of stone walls three times as thick as those of an ordinary structure. The fourth side, facing the creek, was not as high as the wall opposite and it was not as strong. The roof, which slanted down toward the stream, was only a flimsy cover of wood. The reason for this design was simple: when an explosion occurred, the force of the blast was directly upward and toward the creek, thus minimizing the damage and the number of casualties.

That Irénée was able to carry on the work to its completion is a tribute to his doggedness, for the construction consumed much more time than anyone had expected. Sickness struck most of the household, including Irénée himself, and he suffered terribly from the emotional depression that recurred again and again throughout his life, blighting what could have been very happy periods.

"We have accomplished an astonishing amount of work since August," he wrote to his father in France in the late winter, "but I am dismayed when I think of what is still before us. Within three months we have built a large house and barn of stone and the greater part of the refinery; we have repaired the water-course and

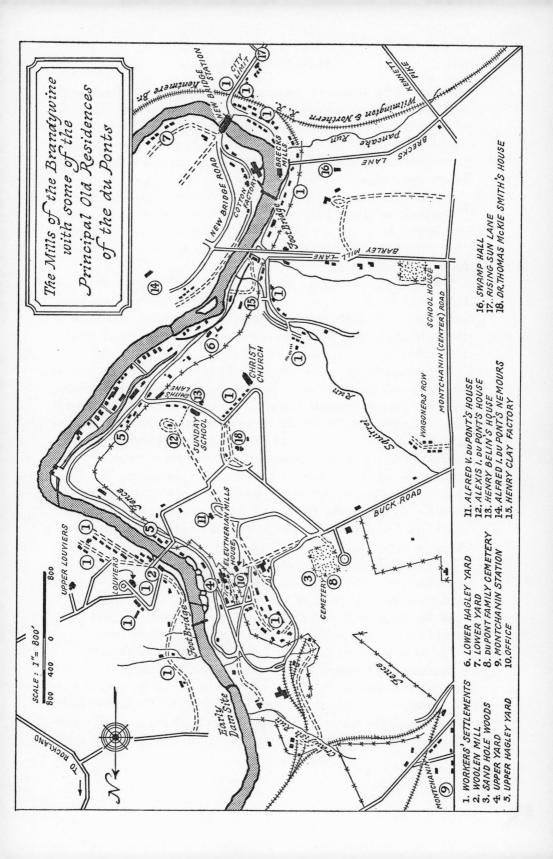

The Mills of the Brandywine
with some of the
Principal Old Residences
of the du Ponts

SCALE : 1" = 800'

800   400   0   800

N

TO ROCKLAND

UPPER LOUVIERS

LOUVIERS

Foot Bridge

Early Dam Site

FENCE

FENCE

MONTCHANIN

Crawfish Run

CEMETERY

BUCK ROAD

Squirrel Run

ELEUTHERIAN MILLS

CHRIST CHURCH

SUNDAY SCHOOL

SMITHS LANE

New Bridge Road

COTTON FACTORY

Foot Bridge

BARLEY MILL LANE

Kennett Br.

CITY LIMIT

NEW BRIDGE STATION

N. R. R.

BRECKS MILLS

Brecks Run

Pancake Run

PANCAKE LANE

Wilmington & Northern

KENNETT PIKE

SCHOOL HOUSE

MONTCHANIN (CENTER) ROAD

WAGONERS ROW

1. WORKERS' SETTLEMENTS
2. WOOLEN MILL
3. SAND HOLE WOODS
4. UPPER YARD
5. UPPER HAGLEY YARD

6. LOWER HAGLEY YARD
7. LOWER YARD
8. DUPONT FAMILY CEMETERY
9. MONTCHANIN STATION
10. OFFICE

11. ALFRED V. DuPONT'S HOUSE
12. ALEXIS I. du PONT'S HOUSE
13. HENRY BELIN'S HOUSE
14. ALFRED I. DU PONT'S NEMOURS
15. HENRY CLAY FACTORY

16. SWAMP HALL
17. RISING SUN LANE
18. DR.THOMAS McKIE SMITH'S HOUSE

the sawmill in which we prepared the wood for our framework and a part of that used for the machines. This month we have still to build three mills and one or two other buildings; to dig a new race for one of the mills; to make the drying place, the magazine, the workmen's quarters. It is evident that we cannot make powder before the autumn."

In the same letter he mentioned the sickness in the household. "The position of our little house at the very bottom of the valley and in the damp air of the creek is not a healthful one," he said, "but I think that when spring comes and we live on the hill, I shall be quite strong again."

Spring came, but Irénée could not shake off his moodiness. A letter from the Brandywine in April said, "The activity of my work helps me and is good for me, in that it gives me less time to yield to the melancholy that never leaves me and that, I am afraid, affects my health."

Depression often causes fatigue and lethargy, but Irénée was as energetic and active as ever. He collected seeds and young plants, shipping them to botanist friends in Europe. In this he had an ulterior purpose, for apparently he was not as confident of success with his powder mill as he tried to make his father and his financial backers believe, so it had occurred to him that there might be profit in keeping up his interest in botany and agriculture. "By these shipments and some successful work with plants and trees," he reasoned, "I may make for myself a position in France, and some day in the future obtain a place in the Administration of Forestry." A return to his homeland, an official appointment, an assured income —how wistfully the French emigré, struggling with an outlandish language and a back-breaking responsibility in a barely civilized land, must have dreamed of them!

In his despondency, Irénée found it impossible to believe he would ever be accepted in America, ever feel at home here.

"In spite of the equality, the rights of liberty, and the excellent government of this country," he wrote, "we foreigners are always in a position inferior to that of other citizens; we are not, as you say, among our equals; that is a truth that I have learned from daily contact with Americans. This suggestion of inferiority—this prejudice of which one often feels the influence—offsets in my mind many of the advantages of America and makes me believe that if we could be free from debt we would all be happier in France."

The avarice of Jacob Broom did nothing to improve Irénée's opinion of Americans. The wily Broom, watching the powder mill take shape, realized that du Pont needed a swift current in Brandywine Creek for the water power to turn his machinery. Broom owned another small piece of property upstream from the land he had sold du Pont. On his remaining land Broom now built a dam across the creek, thus braking the force of the current. Then he told du Pont that he would sell him the dam *and* the land on which it had been erected. The price was exorbitant.

Furious at Broom, Irénée stormed back and forth along the bank of the stream for a couple of days. And then he hit upon a solution. A dam, he suddenly realized, stretches from one side of a body of water to another. Broom only owned the land on one side of the Brandywine. Irénée sought out the owner of the property on the other side at the opposite end of the dam, and paid him one hundred dollars for the water rights alone. Once he owned the water rights, he was able to destroy half of the dam and the Brandywine flowed as swiftly as before.

The cost of constructing the mill increased, however, beyond expectation. Bauduy, who was taking a very active part in the business, paid for two more shares in the company, bringing his total investment to $8,000. As the need for more capital grew, Bauduy arranged for bank loans totaling $18,000, secured by his personal notes. It is scarcely surprising that Bauduy began to feel that the mill was as much his as Irénée's.

By the summer of 1803 du Pont was able to process the first saltpeter, but it was not until the spring of the next year that the first finished black powder was poured into barrels at the mill. As soon as he was able to refine saltpeter, however, Irénée wrote to Thomas Jefferson, asking his help in obtaining government contracts. In reply he received a letter from the Secretary of War, giving the du Pont mill an order for the refining of the saltpeter then in the government's possession as well as the making-over of damaged powder. The letter also promised that the du Pont firm could look forward to government orders for new powder as it was required.

Irénée's abhorrence of war now had to live with his need to sell gunpowder. As early as July, 1803, he wrote to Pierre Samuel, "The condition of war that exists in Europe is very promising for my enterprise. I will do all I can to profit by it."

When the time came to choose a name for the factory, Irénée wanted to call it the Lavoisier Works, but his father talked him into lending his own name to the enterprise, and so it became the Eleutherian Mills.

Early in 1804, Irénée shipped his first barrel of gunpowder. It went to Victor, in New York.

"You may be sure that I will do my best to sell the powder and I will certainly succeed," the older brother wrote.

Victor suggested that a notice be put in the newspapers:

> E.I. DU PONT DE NEMOURS GUNPOWDER
> MANUFACTORY
> Wilmington, Delaware
> This new and extensive establishment is now
> in activity and any quantity of powder, equal
> if not superior to any manufactured in Eu-
> rope will be delivered at the shortest notice.
> Samples to be seen at
> V. DU PONT DE NEMOURS ET CIE.
> New York

Bauduy was more impetuous. Without consulting Irénée, he ordered cards printed advertising the powder mill. This was a little thing, but it blew up into a major crisis. Irénée's rage at Bauduy was out of all proportion to the offense. Undoubtedly the printing of the cards was simply an excuse for Irénée to quarrel with his partner; their real differences lay in the contrasting temperaments of the two men. The tall, blond du Pont once conceded that his own manner was marked by "coldness and sensitiveness." His pride was like scraped skin, flinching at the slightest touch. His silence and his moodiness made strangers believe, wrongly, that he was unfeeling and hostile. Bauduy, on the other hand, was open, bluff, and cheerful. As rash and unthinking as du Pont was prudent and rational, Bauduy was forever blundering into difficult situations. Even in philosophy the two men were far apart: Bauduy, the onetime slave owner from Haiti, had no sympathy for the libertarian ideals of Eleuthère Irénée du Pont.

It had been Bauduy's understanding that he was to boss the external affairs of the company—deal with suppliers, customers, agents, and the government. And so he took over the business correspondence without discussing the matter first with his partner, and proceeded to sign his name to all the letters that were sent out. He had thought that Irénée was to confine himself to the production end of the firm.

Irénée, furious, charged that Bauduy was trying to cut him down to the level of head powderman. Bauduy promptly shot back that Irénée wanted to demote him to a mere chief clerk.

The climax came when Irénée found that Bauduy was signing the name of the firm, "Du Pont, Bauduy & Company."

On this point, Irénée would not budge. The name, he insisted, would be—*must* be—E.I. du Pont de Nemours & Company.

"If, as I hope," he said, "it earns a reputation greater than that of others, and if it makes a name—that name should be mine."

He won his point.

The bickering came to a temporary end when Victor stepped into the row as mediator. Diplomatically soothing the ruffled feelings of both men, he worked out compromises regarding the partners' responsibilities and privileges. The solutions were acceptable to each side.

An uneasy truce emerged from these negotiations. From that time forward, Irénée and Bauduy harbored a hidden dislike for each other.

CHAPTER X

STRUGGLE FOR SURVIVAL

Despite initial difficulties, the du Pont mill started producing powder at an opportune moment. War had broken out in Europe, and American-made products did not, for the time being, have to compete with imports from abroad.

In the mills by the Brandywine the dangerous work of making powder was carried on steadily. In the stamping mill, saltpeter, sulphur and charcoal—the ingredients of black powder—were moistened and pounded and thoroughly mixed. Next the powder was taken to the press house, where it was forced into compact cakes from which the moisture was squeezed. The third stage was in the graining—or corning—mill where the cakes were broken up and the powder passed through sieves to produce the various sizes of gunpowder. The last step took place in the glazing mill; here the grains of powder were moved about in barrels of graphite to make each grain rounder, drier, and coated against dampness.

In 1804, the du Pont mill turned out 44,907 pounds of powder, and Irénée applied for the first patent issued to the company. It covered a new graining machine that did the work of six men with less waste and danger.

Within a year the firm was able to organize a network of sales agents throughout the country to help it market the powder. The business was showing "more favorable results than we ever hoped for," Irénée reported. In the beginning he had planned on selling his powder at $36 a hundredweight, but by the first winter of production, he had raised his price to $40, helped by the national shortage of gunpowder and the quick popularity of his product. Despite the higher price, "it sells as rapidly as we can make it," he wrote his father.

Pierre Samuel did his bit to help drum up trade. After all, he *had* helped the United States accomplish the Louisiana Purchase, and the old courtier was a man who knew how to use his influence to best advantage. From Paris to the White House went a reminder to Jefferson: "You promised me your support and protection for my fine gunpowder factory, which has no equals in the two worlds. Have you given it your saltpeter to refine and your gunpowder to rework? I beg your Excellency not to forget that it is a useful establishment which the zeal of my children created and which is conducted by my second son, the best pupil of the greatest chemist in Europe, and that it belongs to your friend."

This approach wasn't subtle, but it was effective. Soon after receiving the letter, Jefferson sent a confidential message to Irénée, whose spirits rose as he read that the Army and the Navy would be buying du Pont powders "whenever their wants may call for them."

The first government use of du Pont powder came almost immediately. For years, the Barbary States of North Africa had been raiding shipping in the Mediterranean, but the corsairs' depredations now became intolerable. Congress authorized action against the pirates. The United States Navy consumed 22,000 pounds of du Pont powder as its ships hurled cannon balls against the citadels of Tripoli and Derna in the short, successful war, and scores of Americans who had been enslaved were freed and carried back to their homeland. When some of these emaciated men, burned black by the tropical sun, returned to Wilmington, the du Pont workmen were proud at having contributed in a small way to their liberation.

Before the war—even before the letter from Papa du Pont—Jefferson had suggested to the Secretary of War that it would be in the national interest to let contracts to the du Ponts since this would encourage progress in "one of the most essential manufactures." But after the war with Tripoli, General Henry Dearborn, the crusty Secretary of War, ordered comparative tests of available gunpowder, including the du Pont product. English powder also was tested. The du Pont powder, Irénée reported gleefully to the family, "proved so superior that old Mr. Dearborn, in spite of his unwillingness, sent us about 120,000 pounds to remake, and a part of his saltpeter to refine, and he announced publicly on the Fourth of July before the officers, who were delighted with our powder, that in future we will do all the government work."

With such sales, money should have been coming into the du Pont coffers at a satisfactory rate, and it was. But expenses continued to exceed income and the firm was still operating in the red. In the next few years, however, the company began to show a steady profit as sales rose from $10,000 in 1804, to $33,000 in 1805. The following year, after the Tripolitan War sales ended, the firm's income dropped slightly, totaling $32,000. Happily, in 1807, sales jumped to $43,000.

"But in spite of this success I am still somewhat embarrassed," Irénée wrote to his father, "and as yet have been unable to pay any part of the $11,000 that I borrowed from the bank, because the first expenses and the completion of the establishment cost more than I had calculated, and because in that calculation I forgot the credit of six months and more that we must necessarily allow on all sales; thus there is from $25,000 to $30,000 due us now."

Unexpected difficulties kept cropping up. In the winter of 1805, Irénée heard a rumor that his powder was being sold to the Haitians, an accusation that could have ruined du Pont's reputation with many influential Americans horrified by the bloody excesses of the revolution there. To put an end to the report, Irénée offered to open his books to any responsible person. In addition, he announced that he would pay $10,000 to anyone who could prove that du Pont powder had knowingly been sold to the Haitians. Then, after learning that the canard had been started by the French commercial attaché, Irénée met privately with him and the French ambassador. He persuaded both men that the allegation was untrue, and he made them understand that any further insinuations against the du Pont name would boomerang.

In the midst of his efforts to strengthen the young firm, Irénée was presented by Sophie with his fourth child, a girl named Eleuthera, born December 7, 1806.

Three years earlier, the family had moved out of the little two-room stone cottage which still stands beside the Brandywine today. Pierre Bauduy had insisted on designing a new house for Irénée, but du Pont's personal tastes were embodied in the building he called the Eleutherian Mills. It was two stories high, topped by an attic and over that a low cockloft—a structure five bays in width, two full rooms in depth, with a generous central hall. The walls were of gray stone blasted out of the site on which it stood but covered with stucco. A warm, inviting home, it sat on the brow of the hill, with groves of trees on both sides. From the balconies that originally graced the east side of the house, a large part of the powder yards could be seen.

The mills at that time gave employment to about one hundred and forty men. They worked a twelve-hour day in summer and nine hours in winter. By today's standards, those are deplorably long days, but in the early nineteenth century they were unusually short. The textile worker in those days often was a child; yet he worked a fourteen-hour day. The typical adult factory-hand worked from fourteen to sixteen hours in summer and up to twelve hours in winter. Du Pont workers labored shorter hours for more money than did employees of most other contemporary companies.

Most of the original workmen were French, and the little community above and below the Hagley Falls was essentially a French hamlet—French in its speech, its customs, its outlook. As French indeed as its masters in the houses on the hill.

Those first few years the head workman was Charles François Parent, recruited for Irénée by his old colleagues at Essonnes. Parent proved to be a painful disappointment. Having made up his mind that he had arrived in a semi-barbaric country, he assumed an absurdly fastidious manner and kept complaining about the hardship of living "in the middle of the woods." Less than a year after his arrival, he was discovered plotting to break his contract and build a powder mill in competition with the du Ponts. Irénée forestalled this scheme in forthright—if somewhat high-handed—fashion: he had Parent thrown in jail. After three months in those uncomfortable lodgings, Parent agreed to a compromise solution. Iréneé, by now as eager to be rid of Parent as he was to get away, gave him $1,000 worth of machinery and tools on the promise that Parent would build his mill in New Orleans, far from the du Pont sales area.

Fortunately, such difficulties with employees were rare; the du Ponts usually got on very well with their workmen. These powdermen were brave men—only courageous people would undertake jobs that might cost them their lives at any moment. To minimize the hazard, the men wore no metal in their clothes and there were wooden pegs, instead of nails, in their boots. The shafts of the machinery were made of hardwood, too. The machinery had been so contrived that the starting and the stopping—the most dangerous parts of the process—could be controlled from outside the building. Yet all these safeguards were not able to prevent occasional "accidents"—the du Pont euphemism for explosions.

The first explosion occurred on August 18, 1807. Irénée gave a vivid description of it in a letter to his father.

Tired of building and forced by the demands [of Bauduy] to start manufacturing as soon as possible, I was obliged to use a structure that was already built—sixty feet from the graining mill—to make a heated dry-house. Attached to this building was another one that was formerly used in the cotton manufacture [by Broom] and that I use for a charcoal house, having no other. I knew that the charcoal had lighted spontaneously several times at the Essonnes mills and at other mills in France; I knew the danger of having powder and charcoal under the same roof; but my partner did not think as I did. We were tired of building and we had to start.

On the 18th of August, we had taken the charcoal out of the furnace with the fire absolutely extinguished. When we stopped work in the evening, Dalmas and I went to look at the charcoal to be sure that there was no danger; we saw none. After supper Dalmas said, "We should go back and look at the charcoal—it is too dangerous. Will you go or shall I?" Then he added, "You are tired; I will go."

In less than fifteen minutes after he left, the drying house exploded with a tremendous roar.

I was in my writing room. The window came in on my head before I heard the report.

I ran down, convinced that the other building so nearby would go, too, and perfectly sure that Dalmas was lost. Judge of my joy when he was the first to answer my call. By good luck he had stopped for a moment on the way down to talk to Jandelle, and, going on, he was less than twenty paces from the dry house when the blast occurred—the stones and boards went over his head.

The two houses were knocked down on the ground and several others were shaken.

The ruins burned so fiercely that the men had to toil through the night to put out the flames. It was hot, tense work; a single spark, carried by the breeze, could have caused another of the buildings to explode, perhaps killing the fire-fighters. Bucket brigades stretched from the creek and the millrace to the blaze; through the long night, heat and exertion made the sweat stand out on the foreheads of the men as they passed the pails of water from hand to hand, the flickering light of the flames reddening their faces.

In all the houses nearby, their women were cleaning up the shambles caused by the explosion. The blast—750 pounds of black powder had blown up in the drying house—had rattled dishes and broken windows in every neighboring home.

Irénée saw the gaping windows in the morning as he wearily climbed the hill after the fire had been extinguished. Passing a sooty hand across his smoke-blackened forehead, he reflected that there was at least one lucky thing about the accident besides his brother-in-law's escape: it was summer and there'd be plenty of time to replace the windows before cold weather set in.

CHAPTER XI

BLEAK DAYS FOR VICTOR

T HE NAME DU PONT is invariably associated with moneymaking, but only one of the first three du Pont men—Pierre Samuel and his sons, Victor and Eleuthère Irénée—who came to the United States succeeded in avoiding bankruptcy.

Victor was the most ill-starred of the three. Some men seem fated to undergo endless disappointments and failures. Such a man was Victor Marie du Pont, who somehow managed to laugh at his many misfortunes.

Unsuccessful in securing additional financial support for Du Pont Père, Fils et Cie. while in Europe, Victor had, however, been able to arrange a business deal. He obtained letters from Talleyrand and other high officials recommending that Louis André Pichon, the French consul general in the United States, co-operate with him in financing the purchase of supplies for the French expedition to reconquer Haiti. The du Pont commissions on such huge purchases would amount to a fortune, so Victor was pleased with himself when he set sail for America.

But he landed to find everything awry. His father had already tried to persuade Pichon to give the firm the Haitian expedition's business, but Pierre Samuel, used as he was to dealing with men on the highest levels of government, had forgotten how to conduct himself with lesser officials. "He treated me like a little boy!" Pichon told Victor indignantly.

Displaying his usual tact, Victor somehow placated Pichon. The French consul general finally said that he would like to see Victor get the business, but not that father of his. So Victor came up with a proposal for Papa du Pont: Victor would withdraw from the parent firm and set up a new, nominally independent company to be called V. du Pont de Nemours et Cie. of New York. The parent firm would transfer to it, as capital, the house at Bergen Point with twenty acres of land; the shop at Alexandria, Virginia, which Victor had bought for his naturalization; and Bidermann's six thousand acres of land in Kentucky.

Pierre Samuel, who wanted to go back to France anyhow, leaped at the idea, for it meant that he could move the parent firm's headquarters to Paris. Many friends in high places had been urging him to come home. They were certain that Napoleon would find a place of honor for such a great statesman and philosopher. And Madame du Pont had been urging him incessantly to leave America and return to France, especially since her daughter, Madame de Pusy, had been repatriated with her husband now prefect of Moulins.

For perhaps a year Victor's business appeared to go well. He did a good deal of trade with the French West Indies, re-exporting shipments to France. Then fortune turned against him. Two ships laden with valuable cargoes were lost. Many of his debtors failed to pay their accounts. By March, 1803, he was writing to Irénée that he could not send the $6,000 owed to his younger brother for the powder venture. He would try to "send it little by little, the later the better," but he didn't hold out much hope of ever raising the full amount which represented the balance of the parent company's interest in Irénée's project.

The agreement with Pichon, by which Victor pledged himself to share with the consul general his commissions on the Haitian provisions, was the keystone of the elder brother's hopes for his own financial success. Victor kept paying out money for supplies for French ships.

On one of those ships was Jerome Bonaparte, nineteen-year-old brother of Napoleon. In 1803, Jerome deserted his warship and proceeded to enjoy himself in America. He capped his escapades in December of that year by marrying an eighteen-year-old Baltimore belle, Elizabeth Patterson. To celebrate his nuptials properly, Jerome needed large amounts of money. These Victor advanced to him as loans after receiving assurances that Jerome would put in a good word for him with Napoleon.

By that time, Victor was beginning to realize that he might need a friend at court, for Napoleon had decided that Pichon was a crook trying to make a good thing out of the Haitian campaign. Undoubtedly Napoleon, smarting from the failure of his plans to conquer Haiti, really was looking for a scapegoat and Pichon was "it." At any rate, the Emperor growled that he would honor no more drafts from Pichon, and precious few drafts from anyone if the expenses involved the Haitian expedition.

In Paris, Pierre Samuel tried desperately to persuade the government to pay its obligations to Victor. Napoleon, frankly suspicious, would not listen to the old man's long and involved explanations of the bills. "An opinion is growing that is very bad for us," the elder du Pont wrote to Victor. "Everyone who holds Santo Domingo [Haitian] drafts is suspected of trickery and his honor is more or less questioned. And if my own reputation lifts me a little above that class, I have been made to feel it. It had kept me out of the Senate and out of the Legion of Honor."

Everything now rested on Jerome's influence with Napoleon. When the French leader had first learned of Jerome's marriage, he had merely commented disparagingly about his own family. But now the First Consul had had himself crowned Emperor and, in the manner of parvenus, took a loftier view of Family. The more he thought about Jerome's middle-class wife, the more outraged he grew. When Jerome and his Betsy reached Europe, Bonaparte's troops surrounded the ship; the young bride was refused permission to accompany her husband when he landed. She never saw him again. Napoleon had the marriage annulled and saw to it that his brother was wed to Catherine of Württemberg and crowned king of Westphalia.

Anyone who had helped Jerome in his ill-starred romance with Betsy Patterson became the object of Napoleon's wrath. Now he ordered that the name of Victor du Pont de Nemours was not to be mentioned again in his august presence.

It was clear that Bonaparte would never pay Victor the $140,000 owed to him in French government drafts and in loans to Jerome. Victor's position was impossible; he was bankrupt in August, 1805.

In his hopelessness, Victor was ready to clutch at any straw. One was held out to him by Philip Church, scion of a rich New York family and nephew of the great Alexander Hamilton, also, it will be recalled, attorney for the du Ponts. Philip's father, John Barker Church, who had known Papa du Pont for a quarter of a century, had purchased a 100,000-acre tract of land on the Genesee River in western New York State. Philip was going to develop it—a plan which, he suggested, offered an opportunity to Victor du Pont.

As early as January 28, 1805, when he saw financial disaster approaching, Victor wrote to Irénée that he was "considering a plan for settling on the Genesee on Mr. Church's estate and in the town of Angelica where I could establish a store." A month after his firm failed, Victor reached a hurried decision: he would make the long journey by sloop up the Hudson and west along the Mohawk, completing the last part of the trip on horseback by wilderness trails. His family was left behind, for Victor was only reconnoitering this time, and besides, Gabrielle was pregnant.

When he learned that Victor had gone, Irénée hurried to Bergen Point, for he and Sophie understood how dejected and worried Gabrielle and Victor must be. Irénée, insisting that Victor and his family spend the winter in Delaware, prevailed. He personally escorted Gabrielle, her three children, and their nurse to the Brandywine. When Victor returned from his scouting excursion, he joined them there.

So it was in her Uncle Irénée's home that Victor's fourth child, Julia Sophie Angelique, was born on June 3, 1806. The third given name, of course, was bestowed on her in expectation of a happy and successful settlement at Angelica.

Fortunately—or perhaps unfortunately—Gabrielle still had a little money in her own name which she had inherited. Using it, Victor bought a 500-acre parcel of land near Angelica in what is now Allegany County. But he made two mistakes: he paid too much for the land—$3,000—and he paid cash, which left him short of working capital.

With his natural optimism, Victor was sure he'd be successful on the Genesee. Others were less sanguine. Gabrielle, who would never learn to like life in the United States, was utterly opposed to the idea. It seemed impractical to her. And the thought of living in the backwoods, without the amenities of urban life, was appalling to this long-suffering daughter of the French nobility. Her views were echoed by Irénée who foresaw nothing but calamity. But Victor, desperate now to prove that his judgment was sound and his business ability keen, insisted that everything would work out well. So Irénée—"our good brother," as Gabrielle always called him, "most unhappy at our departure"—saw his brother and the family off, "but sent with us a wagon loaded with powder worth $1,000."

Arriving too late on the Genesee to beat the onset of winter, Victor was unable to clear the land and build a home, so he used the last of Gabrielle's money to buy a small house in Angelica. That first winter was uncommonly severe even in comparison with most cold winters in that part of the country. In the spring Victor built a store on a lot adjoining the house.

But settlers were not moving into the area as quickly as Victor had hoped. Ultimately the success of the land promotion depended on Philip Church. If he persuaded farmers to buy land in his broad tract, others would come along and buy Victor's five hundred acres—at an inflated price, of course. Or so Victor thought.

Victor's land remained unsold. The store was unprofitable. Even personal relationships deteriorated. As Gabrielle wrote later in her memoirs, "Captain Church at Angelica became the Bauduy of the Brandywine; everything began to go wrong."

Victor and his family, Irénée wrote to his father in February, 1808, "are quite ruined if they persist in staying on a farm of 500 acres covered with enormous forest trees, for which he has not paid, which he has no means of cultivating, and by which he cannot possibly support his family, much less give his children any kind of education."

One day Amelia, then twelve years old, was playing a piano in the cabin when she suddenly screamed at the sight of an Indian at a window. With her virtually unshakable poise, Gabrielle told her daughter to go on playing. Then the mother opened the door and confronted a group of Indians. She welcomed them into the dwelling as gravely as though they were French nobles of the highest rank. In they crowded, until there were fifty of them jammed into the little house, listening enthralled to the unaccustomed sounds from the piano. Gabrielle fed them all and then they left as quietly as they had come.

When they were gone, Gabrielle collapsed into a chair, shaking uncontrollably from reaction to the strain. Victor returned to the cabin to be told that this was the end: they must go back to civilization.

It was an ultimatum with which he could not argue, for by then a depression had laid a blight on almost all business in the country, and his prospects were bleaker than before. Irénée's powder sales were still good, however, because the economic slump had been caused by the Embargo Act proclaimed by the United States, and this did not affect the domestic powder trade.

At this point, Irénée was so determined that Victor should leave the Genesee and move to the Brandywine that he himself made the long trip to Angelica to argue the matter in person. With him he took his accountant, Raphael Duplanty, a Breton emigré who had lost his father and two brothers to the guillotine in the French Revolution. Duplanty knew Victor well, and it was Irénée's plan to set up Victor and Duplanty in business together; he thought that Duplanty could contribute the business acumen that Victor unquestionably lacked.

During the spring of 1809, Victor abandoned Angelica. To pay some of his debts, he sold a slave, "my black wench named Charlotte," and her four-week-old son to August d'Autremont, one of his friends, for two hundred dollars. The house, the store, and the five hundred acres were assigned to Irénée and other creditors.

Still another humiliation awaited Victor. He stopped briefly at Good Stay that June on his way to Wilmington and was promptly arrested. A deputy United States marshal took him into custody in New York, and, then, after Irénée had sent the money to bail him out, he was again detained in New Jersey. The New York arrest resulted from Victor's default on a $278 Custom House bond. An impatient creditor caused the New Jersey difficulty.

By the end of summer, however, Victor and his family were able to move into a handsome new stone house above the Brandywine. Situated on the east bank, designed by Irénée himself, it was a graceful Regency mansion whose plans had been approved by Thomas Jefferson. The two-story colonnade on the west portico reminded Gabrielle of the plantations of South Carolina. She and Victor called their new home Louviers.

On the Brandywine, they were welcomed not as the vanquished are, with pity, but—like the Prodigal Son, with love. There was nothing patronizing in the attitude of Irénée or Sophie, only genuine joy at having part of the family reunited once more.

CHAPTER XII

WAR SAVES THE COMPANY

I T IS ONE OF THE IRONIES of history that the du Ponts, whose name is indelibly associated with synthetic fibers, helped to found the woolen industry in the United States.

One of Pierre Samuel's friends in France before and during the Revolution had been Étienne Delessert, a banker and breeder of merino sheep. The upheavals in his homeland had forced Delessert to flee to the United States, where he bought a farm at Rosendale in the Catskills near Kingston, New York. At one time Irénée had considered setting up his powder mill near Delessert's estate.

In 1801, when Irénée was in France, he arranged for four of Delessert's merino stud rams to be shipped to America as Delessert had requested him to do. In return for this favor, Delessert agreed that the rams might go first to Good Stay, to service the du Ponts' ewes. Only one of the rams, however, a stalwart beast named Don Pedro, survived the voyage. After covering nine ewes at Bergen Point, Don Pedro was shipped to Delessert's farm.

Four years passed. Then, as political stability of a sort returned to France, Delessert prepared to go back to his homeland. The Delessert farm was sold, but not before Irénée had bought Don Pedro for sixty dollars. The long, silken fleece of Don Pedro's offspring proved to Irénée that his money would be well spent.

On the Brandywine, Irénée already had a flock of respectable proportions, the result of Don Pedro's breeding with the du Pont ewes at Bergen Point. The mighty ram now proceeded to multiply the numbers of the flock in a way satisfactory to the du Ponts, himself and, presumably, the ewes.

This suggested the possibility that Victor and Duplanty might launch a woolen factory. And so a contract was signed on June 19, 1810, by which the signatories agreed to "form a company for the purpose of establishing on the Brandywine a cloth manufactory under the name of the Merino Wool Factory." In addition to Irénée, who provided a part of the capital, and Victor and Duplanty, who were to handle the actual management of the woolen mill, there was a fourth partner—Bauduy. Despite the now-concealed hostility between him and Irénée, Bauduy had always been fond of Victor and he still was. Bauduy supplied most of the money for the enterprise; he planned to put his son, Ferdinand, to work in the mill.

It was agreed that the firm should be called Du Pont, Bauduy and Company, the name that Bauduy had earlier wanted to give the powder works.

The prospects appeared excellent. An act of 1809, intended to encourage the raising of sheep, made them non-taxable. Sheep-raising became very popular. Merinos—and their fleece—were especially prized; it was not uncommon for a farmer to pay $300 to $500 for a ram. By 1814, the hills above the Brandywine were said to be "clothed with rich verdure and covered with sheep." There were 4,300 sheep in the Wilmington area, including 700 merinos. Although his own interest in the sheep was subordinate to his major occupation, Irénée was elected vice president of the Merino Society of the Middle States of North America. The stud, Don Pedro, was as famous as an animal can be, and in a technical journal of the time, Dr. James Mease wrote a respectful biography of the beast, saying that "Don Pedro is believed to be the first full-blooded ram introduced into North America."

With Victor's business affairs now apparently on an even keel, Irénée presently found himself unexpectedly involved with romantic problems. The difficulty involved his first-born, Victorine. "She is well-informed, gentle, and attractive," Irénée wrote to his father on November 22, 1809. "The devil of it is that others are beginning to find her so. She and I could have got on without them for two or three years more. I admit that I was really vexed at the first proposal that was made to me for her," Irénée went on with humorous self-mockery. "I had no idea that anyone thought me old enough to have a marriageable daughter."

Duplanty was one of Victorine's suitors, although no one, including the girl herself, realized this at first. After all, she was only seventeen and he was more than twice her age. In the tight little colony on the Brandywine, everyone saw a great deal of everybody else, so it was natural that Victorine often found herself in Duplanty's company. Then, in October, Duplanty began to imagine that his beloved reciprocated his feelings. She was more vivacious and friendly than usual—or so he thought. He was certain now that she realized the seriousness of his admiration and had decided to accept his attentions.

The girl's mother, more sensitive about such matters than Irénée, summoned Victorine one day for a heart-to-heart talk. She pointed out that Tini—as her daughter was called in the family—had created a situation of great emotional intensity. Did she realize that Duplanty loved her and did she feel the same way about him?

At first, Tini could not believe that her mother had interpreted Duplanty's feelings correctly. When she was finally convinced, she said that henceforth she would refrain from any words or acts that might encourage the man.

Suddenly, then, Duplanty found Tini completely changed in manner. She was as cold as she had once been warm and friendly. Hurt and puzzled, he asked Bauduy to persuade one of his daughters, a friend of Tini's, to find out how she felt.

Bauduy did as Duplanty asked, but he also told Irénée of the contretemps that had developed. And then Bauduy himself got a shock: he found that his own son, Ferdinand, was also in love with Victorine!

"My son has told me that ever since he left college, he has seen and thought of no one but Victorine," Bauduy told Irénée.

The father of Tini swore a great oath, slammed his right fist into the palm of his left hand and stomped off for a long, solitary walk to ponder the situation. The devil! Two men in love with his little girl and neither of them worthy of her—not that he had ever met anyone who deserved her as a wife.

Irénée went home and talked over the matter with Sophie, who knew that her daughter was fond of young Bauduy. In the morning he sat down and wrote to his father about his predicament. Despite his anxiety, he had not lost his sense of humor as the letter showed.

"If the question were for myself," he wrote, referring to Duplanty, "I would marry him with pleasure." But Duplanty was too old for Tini. And Ferd, at nineteen, was too young for the responsibilities of marriage. "I was, to be sure, only twenty when I married," Irénée conceded, perhaps recalling his father's opposition to that match, "but I was much older than he is." A statement which was undoubtedly true.

At the bottom of Irénée's objection to Ferd, of course, was his suppressed hatred for the boy's father. "Ferdinand is a nice boy," Irénée said grudgingly. "He has no vice that I know of. The match would be perfectly suitable. But his father has behaved to me in a way that it is hard to forget, though I have nothing to find fault with now."

In the end, Duplanty was firmly, but gently, rejected. As for young Bauduy, who had been planning a two-year visit to France, Irénée ruled that he could pay court to Tini after he returned if he and she both still wanted to get married. But Irénée flatly refused the boy's suggestion of a formal betrothal before he left.

Privately Irénée growled, "It is the factory he wants to marry," remembering how the elder Bauduy had sought to gain the upper hand in the powder company.

That firm was growing more substantial all the time, although Irénée had never overcome the anti-French bias of the government procurement officers. For example, in 1807, the Navy bought 1,200 kegs of English-made powder at $10 a keg, although it had proved inferior in the Navy's own tests to du Pont's powder which cost only $8.50 a keg.

Two years later the government asked a Dr. Hunter, a Philadelphia apothecary, for his opinion of du Pont's powder. Criticizing it as an inferior product, he said he could do much better himself. Having offered to refine saltpeter for the government for one cent a pound compared with the one- and a half-cent price of du Pont, Hunter was given a one-hundred-ton order. According to friends who reported back to the du Ponts, the saltpeter refined by Hunter was impure, coarse, and very wet. This didn't really matter, though, for he had already been given a second contract before he fulfilled the first. At the same time, du Pont received an order for only twenty-five tons.

Then the government admitted that it was dissatisfied with Hunter's saltpeter. Precisely what was wrong with it? the officials asked. How was it different from du Pont's? The unsuspecting Irénée replied by explaining in writing just how he refined saltpeter. The government promptly turned over his letter to Hunter so that he could improve his own methods. Hunter was also permitted to raise his price to the same level as du Pont's.

"Things are done here much as they are in France," Irénée concluded with resignation.

But fortunately, du Pont's sales to other consumers kept mounting. In 1810, John Jacob Astor, head of the American Fur Company and the Pacific Fur Company, ordered 5,250 pounds of du Pont gunpowder, making it plain to du Pont's agent that "he wishes the price to be as low as possible." The agent added, "Mr. Astor tells me that he may be in want of about 500 kegs every year."

In the beginning, the du Pont product had been labeled Brandywine Powder, but its success led competitors to set up a mill in Connecticut in 1808. The rivals named their millsite "Brandywine" and put the same name on their powder. The du Ponts had no legal recourse. So the product of Eleutherian Mills henceforth was called Du Pont Powder. Even its famous Eagle brand was sold as Du Pont's Eagle Powder.

Powder below du Pont's standard was sold as the product of A. F. & Company, the name being derived from Andrew Fountain who sold the cheaper powder at his country store near the mills.

There was always difficulty from shady competitors. At one time a group of Richmond, Virginia, business men determined to open a powder mill. To find out how du Pont powder was made, they employed a mechanic, Charles Munns, to go to Wilmington on a scouting expedition. Today it would be called industrial espionage. Munns bribed a du Pont powderman, Joseph Baughman, to steal some models and small pieces of machinery, but Irénée caught up with Munns, gave him a thrashing, and had him thrown in jail in

New Castle, Delaware. After a while Munns escaped to Virginia. Later he sued Irénée for malicious prosecution, but nothing ever came of his suit. However, the year 1812 was still only a few days old when part of the powder mill blew up. An investigation by Irénée proved that the explosion was "the result of malice for the purpose of injuring us." Security measures about the mill were tightened.

A month later, Dr. Thomas Ewell, a near relative of Secretary of the Navy Paul Hamilton, signed a contract with that department to handle most of its powder business. Ewell built a powder mill at Bladensburg, Maryland, seven miles from Washington, although he knew nothing of the making of explosives. Failing to hire any du Pont workmen away from the Brandywine, he offered Irénée "a connection" with his firm. When Irénée declined the partnership, Ewell began making threats against him, vague but increasingly vehement. He merely succeeded in goading Irénée into publishing a pamphlet entitled "Villainy Detected," which set forth the whole story of Ewell's corrupt dealings with the government. The affair swelled up into a great political *cause célèbre*. Despite his governmental shenanigans, Ewell was unable to make a go of the powder works. Years later—in 1817—when the Bladensburg mill was put on the auction block, Irénée was invited to bid for it; he refused.

However, late in 1811 as the danger of war with England heightened, the government was forced to turn to the du Pont firm, by then the largest powder works in the country, with an order for 50,000 pounds of gunpowder. War broke out the following year and 200,000 pounds were ordered for combat. By 1813, the government had increased its orders to 500,000 pounds.

On paper the orders looked good. But the government was very slow to pay its bills, as most states are—a painful truth that Victor had learned a decade before. And du Pont's other customers paid slowly, too. Storekeepers expected—and got—six months in which to settle their bills. Every dollar of income that could be spared had to be plowed back into the business, so Irénée's profits were not in cash but in raw materials, machinery, powder awaiting shipment, customers' notes, and accounts receivable. None of the original backers understood this, including Irénée's father who never could fathom economics except on a cosmic scale.

Just before the war broke out, this misunderstanding became critical to the welfare of the firm. In 1811, the Parisian firm of Du Pont Père, Fils et Cie. failed in a general panic that swept France. The only assets on the company's books were its twelve shares in the powder works, although those shares had never been paid for in full, Pierre Samuel having advanced to Irénée only $16,470.90 instead of the $24,000 the shares should have cost the parent firm. And even the full price would have been deceptive, for the original capital had proved inadequate, and Irénée, with considerable help from Bauduy, had raised a good deal of additional money, until the real capitalization now stood at $65,200. Thus the actual money paid in by the parent firm now amounted to only about one-fourth of the total capital.

Even worse, Pierre Samuel, in 1807, had borrowed 100,000 francs, equivalent to $20,000, from Talleyrand. Irénée had not asked his father for this money. What's more, he didn't receive all of it—actually only $12,000, the remaining $8,000 being retained by his father in Paris. But on the books of Pierre Samuel's concern the entire loan was charged against the powder company.

An additional complication was caused by Papa du Pont's inability to refrain from boasting. In its first six years, the powder company's profits had amounted to a little more than $43,000. In 1810, the profits were more than $30,000, and in the following year, they rose to about $45,000. But, as we have already seen, the profits were all tied up in the business, so the firm was plagued with a persistent shortage of cash. Pierre Samuel bragged about the profits but neglected to mention that there were scarcely any liquid assets.

Not surprisingly, the French creditors, after Pierre Samuel's bankruptcy, demanded that Irénée at once make good his father's obligations. As a minimum, they demanded payment of all the profits on the firm's books. When Irénée tried to forestall them by writing innumerable long, pleading letters to explain—without criticizing his father—how they had been misled, the backers made it clear that they did not believe him. And why should they when even his own confused father got the impression that Irénée was trying to evade his legal responsibilities to his stockholders? Even the threat of liquidation was raised by the Paris financiers.

It was a problem that continued to bedevil Irénée until the day

he died. And yet there is no indication that he ever bore his father
any resentment.

Through it all, Irénée clung to one thought: this was *his* company. He had built it, poured his hopes and heart and knowledge
into it. This was the heritage he would leave his children, a legacy
to which he would go on adding every day of his life.

What had to be done was done, regardless of pressure from the
creditors. In 1813, when war orders from the government were
overwhelming the company, Irénée overrode the protests of Bauduy and bought the Hagley Farm from Thomas Lea for $47,000.
Hagley was adjacent to Eleutherian Mills on the downstream side
and it would provide room for the mill to expand. Bauduy and many
others were fearful of expansion should the demand for powder fall
off too sharply after the war, but Irénée, with greater faith in the
economy, mortgaged his powder works to pay for the new property.

Although the War of 1812 was opposed by many Americans, it
had Irénée's full support. "Should the present war in its final result
produce no other good but to secure the establishment of home
manufacturers, so that we could manufacture our own produce for
our own use," he wrote, "it would repay the nation ten-fold for
every expense or loss the war may create. . . . Manufacturing . . .
is a true creation of wealth. It is taking cotton which costs twenty
cents a pound and making it *worth* several dollars. It is taking wool
at $1 and selling it again at $6 or $7 when it has received its metamorphose from our industry. Let us reap then the full advantage
that this war my produce. Let us secure forever the establishment
of American manufacture. . . . Almost every kind of goods can be
manufactured in this country as cheaply as in Europe."

During the first year of the war, the fighting was on the Canadian
frontier or at sea. But in the following year, Irénée received an
urgent message showing the amateurish nature of American defenses:

Wilmington, March 19, 1813.

Dear sir,
   I this morning received a letter from Governor Hazlet stating
that considerable depredations in burning of vessels, etc., are committed by the British vessels of war about Lewes Town in Sussex

and requests of me to forward him six kegs of your best rifle powder or such as is used for musketry, perhaps one or two of the
kegs had best be of cannon powder. I wish you to have it sent in
to Paul McGin's this evening or early in the morning, as we wish
to forward it tomorrow with some lead I am procuring.

Yours sincerely,
John Warner

P.S. Please send me a bill of the powder.

Three weeks later General John Stockton notified Irénée that
the British ship *Belvedere* was firing broadsides at Lewes and the
American shore defenses needed ten more kegs of cannon powder.

In May, Irénée got a tip that the British intended to move
against the du Pont powder works which were vital to the United
States war effort. Irénée appealed to the government for protection; troops were sent from Philadelphia to Delaware to ward off
any attack. None was attempted.

In the meantime, Irénée had been donating musket and cannon
powder to the local militia. He organized his own employees into a
company prepared to join in the defense of the mill if that should
become necessary. The Brandywine Rangers, as they were called,
later included men who worked for other manufacturers along the
creek.

In the election of 1814, the Brandywine Rangers became a political issue. The anti-war group charged that Victor du Pont had
paraded the Rangers for political purposes and marched them to
the polls in an attempt to overawe and cow opposition voters.
Tempers grew short and there were shouts against "du Pont's men"
whenever the Rangers appeared. Once Victor was ambushed by a
mob of twenty or thirty ruffians armed with stones and clubs. Before serious injury could be done, a party of "du Pont's men" appeared and drove off his attackers.

There must have been widespread feeling that the allegations
against Victor and the Brandywine Rangers were well founded,
for later in the year, the Delaware Legislature outlawed all such
military organizations set up by manufacturers.

The war actually never came very close to Wilmington. Even in
August, 1814, when the British burned Washington in reprisal for
the burning of York—now Toronto—in Canada the previous year,

enemy troops ventured only so far as the Sassafras River where they set fire to Georgetown, Maryland.

Although du Pont propagandists have sometimes suggested that the War of 1812 was a vexing period to the company because of the heavy demands laid on the firm by the government, it must be remembered that the powder mill was handsomely paid for these orders. Sales in 1812 totaled $148,597 and the following year they were $107,291. There were two shifts at the works as the powder-making went on day and night and wagons and ships rushed the ammunition to the fighting men.

At a time when the company was still in a shaky condition and in urgent need of financial support, its profits from the war made a great difference—possibly the margin between success and failure.

CHAPTER XIII

BIGAMY

THE FIRST MARRIAGE on the Brandywine was not Victorine's, but that of her cousin Amelia.

Amelia was Victor's eldest child, a shy, homely girl with a dumpy figure and a beautiful heart. She was an accomplished musician and an introspective, thoughtful person.

Nobody had ever paid much attention to her—certainly not romantically—before the spring of 1811, when William H. Clifford was hired to run the woolen mill. Clifford was an Englishman who had met a friend of the du Ponts on board ship to America. He appeared to be well educated and he claimed twenty-two years of experience in the woolen cloth line, having worked with his father from childhood in the family spinning mill in Gloucester. In those days, weavers and other experienced men were in great demand, so the du Ponts were delighted to snare such a jewel on his arrival. Clifford was to receive a salary of four dollars a week, plus his board and lodging "and washing" in the home of Irénée's bookkeeper. At the end of each year he was promised a bonus of four hundred dollars.

A short time later, Don Pedro, the merino ram, died. Letters of condolences arrived from livestock breeders all over the country, even from Thomas Jefferson himself. Don Pedro appeared in the trademark of Du Pont, Bauduy and Company, which showed two

Indians, one of them riding a merino ram, the whole surmounted by a bald eagle with outspread wings.

To prove that du Pont cloth would be the equal of Europe's best, Victor instructed Clifford to make cloth of a quality suitable for fashionable clothing. Samples of the material were sent to many prominent people. "Its quality is certainly superior to anything we have ever seen done in America," Jefferson wrote to Irénée. "With such manufactures as these, we need never regret the want of the English market."

Because of the small size and the democracy of the Brandywine settlement, the manager of the woolen mill saw a good deal of the owner's family. Soon he was paying particular attention to Amelia; this must have delighted Victor and Gabrielle. It was a whirlwind courtship, and on September 12, 1812, the plain little du Pont girl, not yet seventeen, was married to the twenty-seven-year-old Clifford. To all appearances, fate for once had been kind to Victor and his family.

The first sign of trouble came in three or four months when the partners began to suspect that the groom was not the competent, far-seeing manager he had claimed to be. "Evidently we have been deceived by Clifford, who has led us into very serious extravagances in order that we might begin on a large scale before our business was organized, even before he himself knew whether he could manage it," Irénée told Bauduy. In Irénée's opinion, the woolen company should have started on a small scale and devoted all its efforts to turning out inexpensive fabrics.

Irénée was also troubled by Clifford's character. After he became a member of the family, he seemed a different person from the modest, ingratiating man they had known. "Instead of an establishment among friends that might have succeeded by mutual effort," Irénée fumed, "we have a factory governed by the dictation and the caprices of Clifford, who, in his excessive and misplaced vanity, rejects every good idea that is not his own."

Unfortunately, Amelia was already pregnant. Her uncle's affection for her made him cautious in handling the Clifford problem. On June 8, 1813, Amelia gave birth to a girl named Gabrielle Josephine.

A few months later, an English weaver came to the Brandywine, looking for work. Seeing Clifford, he told one of the workmen that the manager of the woolen mill seemed familiar. The workman explained that Clifford was the boss's son-in-law. "That can't be," said the stranger, "I knew that man in England, and he had a wife and family there! And his name wasn't Clifford."

The stranger was whisked off to a private meeting with the du Ponts. As soon as he had told them what he knew, Clifford was summoned. He did not deny the accusations against him. Victor ordered him to leave the Brandywine at once.

The marriage was quietly annulled and Victor went to court to have the baby legitimatized. Amelia spent the rest of her life with her parents, a lonely, saddened woman, haunted by the memory of a few brief weeks of love.

During that same summer of 1813, Ferdinand Bauduy returned from France and Irénée no longer could think of any good excuse to forbid the boy's marriage to Victorine. Tini herself was dreamy-eyed with love now, completely won over by her suitor's constancy during the long absence. So the couple were betrothed.

Pierre Samuel, in Paris, wrote to express his disappointment. He said he had always hoped Tini would marry her uncle, Charles Dalmas, a union that would have been legal in France.

Actually, both the du Ponts and the Bauduys viewed the approaching wedding with mixed emotions. This was, of course, a mating of Montague with Capulet. Both sides hoped for an end to the feud that had been smoldering for years. Yet Irénée feared that his future son-in-law might help the elder Bauduy seize control of the powder company, and Bauduy undoubtedly wondered whether his son might not be cheated out of his heritage by Irénée du Pont.

The smiles of their elders were therefore somewhat forced on that day—November 9, 1813—when Victorine du Pont and Ferdinand Bauduy exchanged vows. But the young couple were obviously very happy. Their happiness lasted just eleven weeks.

In mid-January, Ferd came down with pneumonia. On January 21, 1814, he died in his father-in-law's home. Two days later the grief-stricken Bauduy, who had been away from Wilmington at the time of his son's death, wrote to Irénée, "May this sorrow unite us; be my friend, for I have lost the best friend I had." But that was not to be. The death of Ferdinand, in fact, put an end to the restraint both older men had exercised.

The following June, without telling Irénée, Bauduy wrote to the European backers protesting against his partner's alleged mismanagement of the powder company. "We now have $140,000 invested in buildings, water power, and land on the Brandywine—a piece of madness that I was unable to prevent," he reported.

And now Bauduy had an ally: the widow of Bureaux de Pusy. After her husband's death, she had come to America with her two children, ready to claim the thousands of dollars in profits that her stepfather, Pierre Samuel du Pont de Nemours, had led her to believe were there for the asking. Like Irénée's father, she never did comprehend the correct state of affairs or the real equity she held in the firm. Over a matter of months she changed from warmly affectionate to merely friendly to distantly cordial to outspokenly hostile. Part of the change was Irénée's fault. He obviously underestimated the importance of her concern. When she asked for financial statements, he kept putting her off because he was too busy. But she grew angry and so was in a receptive mood when Bauduy told her that Irénée was stalling because he was cheating her.

The shareholders now informed Papa du Pont that his sons would not honor the agreement he had made with his creditors. The harassed old man, his nerves frayed by years of financial struggles, lost his temper and wrote a savage letter to Irénée and Victor. In it he threatened to disown them, to denounce them publicly as thieves and unnatural sons. In fact, he even talked of coming to America personally to sue them in the courts unless they lived up to their obligations or what he considered to be their responsibilities. Soon after posting the letter, however, he felt pangs of remorse, realizing that his sons could not have behaved as he had been told; their enemies must be spreading tales intended to destroy them.

Another who was upset by the letters from America was Jacques Bidermann, whose firm had failed in a general panic. His du Pont investment was important to him; he wanted to be sure it was properly managed. To learn the true state of affairs, he sent his son, Jacques Antoine Bidermann, to the United States to look into the matter. Only twenty-four at the time, young Bidermann already had a shrewd head for business. He studied the books and understood at once what Irénée had been trying for years to explain to his father. He found that the stockholders' equity had more than quad-rupled, thanks to Irénée's sensible policy of putting the profits back into the business. As for Bauduy's claims that he himself had been bilked, Bidermann found that Bauduy had in fact reaped more than $100,000 in dividends and commissions over a period of twelve years on an original investment of $8,000, although Bauduy had also helped to negotiate loans for the firm. Irénée himself, on the other hand, had taken only $16,500 from the business—far less than he was entitled to.

There is real poignancy in a letter written by Irénée in June, 1814, replying to suggestions from his relatives and friends that he return to France: "I do not see what I could do in France," he said wearily. "I have spent my life here building up a very difficult in-dustry and the disappointments I have had to bear have given me an habitual dullness and melancholy that would be very out of place in society. Besides, how could I go? My position here is a very trying one: I have used all the credit I could get to start Vic-tor's establishment and to buy sheep, and neither of these enter-prises has been nearly as successful as the powder. I owe more than sixty thousand dollars, chiefly in notes at the banks, so that my debts amount to far more than my profits from the powder. I am forced to stay here; the signatures that must be renewed every sixty days on bank loans put me in exactly the situation of a prisoner on parole who must show himself to the police every month."

It is not surprising, then, that Irénée suffered from depression, bearing as he did a back-breaking, heart-breaking burden of debt, much of it unfairly imposed on him by his father's carelessness about financial details. He was forced to worry about the welfare, not only of his own family but also that of his father and of his older brother.

Something that Papa du Pont once wrote to Irénée was perhaps more pertinent than he intended. "I am perfectly convinced," he said, "that every personal advantage we experience is a motive and an obligation for us to do our duty to our fellow men. Those who are courageous are made to defend others, and those who have wisdom, to enlighten them."

Irénée's burdens were lightened by young Bidermann, who

helped Irénée oust Bauduy from the firm. Bauduy filed suit for an accounting of the money due him, a legal action not terminated until 1824, when Irénée finally won a complete victory.

The other thorn in Irénée's side, Madame de Pusy, continued to raise a rumpus after Bauduy left the firm. Whenever her stepfather saw her—for she was now back in France—she made him miserable by telling him of the lawsuits she was filing against his son. "One should avoid founding business associations and should never form them with family," he wrote to Irénée ruefully. With unusual understatement he added, "It weakens affection and sometimes destroys fortunes." Was Pierre Samuel's gout worse than before, or was his pain merely a reflection of the mental anguish he now felt?

Then, of a sudden, everything looked brighter to the elder du Pont. French politics had gone through one of those somersaults for which it was even then famous. In the spring of 1814, overwhelmed by military defeats and with the armies of his enemies occupying Paris itself, Napoleon had abdicated unconditionally. His foes had exiled him to a toy kingdom, the island of Elba, with an army of four hundred men instead of the countless legions he had led for so long. A provisional government came to power in France, headed by Talleyrand. He asked du Pont to accept the post of secretary. Thus, it was Pierre Samuel who actually certified the abdication of Napoleon at Fontainebleu on April 11.

After a fortnight, du Pont was appointed a councilor of state. He was also named a chevalier of the Legion of Honor. Affairs of state kept him busy now, and that was good for the old man. But family matters still gave him concern. Toward the end of the year, his wife fell from a carriage and was seriously injured and confined to her bed.

The following March all Europe was astounded to learn that Napoleon had escaped from Elba and landed near Cannes. The leaders of the government during his exile knew they were marked for Napoleon's revenge. Most of them fled to safety. On March 20, 1815, when Napoleon reached Paris, du Pont was still there. But he was already making plans to disappear.

He could not take his bedridden wife with him. Sadly he bade her farewell, knowing in his heart that they would never see each other again. And then he fled posthaste to the west of France, using a false American passport. By April 22, he was halfway across the Atlantic aboard the *Fingal*. Now seventy-five, he wrote to a friend in France to explain that he had left his homeland "to go to America so as not to be passed from hand to hand like a courtier or a courtesan." Even in his bitterness, Pierre Samuel could not resist a play on words.

He found his sons' families larger than they had been. Victor's last two children, Samuel Francis and Julia Sophie, had been born after his earlier visit to the United States. There were three grandchildren in the other house—Irénée's children—whom he had never seen: Eleuthera, nicknamed "Tata," born December 7, 1806; Sophie Madeleine, September 18, 1810; and Henry, August 8, 1812.

With his resilient temperament, du Pont felt his spirits restored now that he was once more in the bosom of his family. His customary exuberance returned. "I have seen the factory," he wrote to his wife. "It is gigantic, inconceivable that only one man was able to design and execute such things, especially this hydraulic machinery and these mechanical devices. . . . Irénée is a great man, with talent, courage, perseverance ten times greater than I had ever dared hope, although I have always held him in high esteem."

Thus, after so many years of thankless toil and trouble, Irénée had finally won the recognition that was most important to him.

CHAPTER XIV

DEATH OF PAPA

THERE WERE FOUR GENERATIONS of the du Ponts on the Brandywine in the summer of 1815, ranging from Pierre Samuel to
his great-grandaughter Gabrielle, Amelia's daughter.

In addition to the powder works, the du Ponts also controlled a
tannery, the woolen mill, and a cotton factory. At the time that
Bauduy was forced out of the powder company, he also withdrew
voluntarily from the woolen firm because it had never been profitable. Victor's eldest son, Charles Irénée du Pont, only seventeen,
had been managing that enterprise for a year, ever since the abrupt
departure of the bigamist Clifford. Even before that, Duplanty had
ended his participation in the woolen factory. Victor's main role
in Du Pont, Bauduy and Company had been to keep the peace between Duplanty and Bauduy; they were always at each other's
throats.

Irénée, regretting the disappointment that Duplanty had suffered
as Victorine's rejected suitor, provided the capital needed by his
friend to enter into a partnership with Archibald McCall. This
Philadelphia merchant had sold out his interest in the powder mill
some years earlier but was still involved in business dealings with
Irénée. Now Duplanty, McCall and Company spun cotton in a
mill later to be known as the Henry Clay Factory.

At this time the powder works were in two parts on the west
bank of the creek: the Upper Yard, containing the original build-

ings, faced Victor's Louviers Woolen Mill across the stream; and a short distance downstream was the new Hagley Yard. Later, when the powder company again expanded downstream on the west side, the newest group of buildings was called the Lower Hagley Yard to distinguish it from the older, or Upper Hagley, works. Just below Lower Hagley was the cotton plant.

It was in the Upper Yard that a mill blew up on June 8, 1815, about a month after Papa du Pont arrived from France—his first experience of a powder yard accident. The earth shook with a tremendous roar as nine men lost their lives in an explosion that also destroyed $20,000 worth of machinery and materials.

From Pittsburgh where he had gone on a sales trip, Bidermann wrote anxiously to find out what had happened and to urge that the widows and orphans of the blast victims be pensioned by the firm, although the company was still very short of money. Irénée immediately replied, "It is with very great pleasure that I saw by your last letter . . . that your first thought was like ours—to provide for the widows of the unfortunate who have died while working for us." He had already done what his young associate suggested. It marked the beginning of a company policy uniquely humane and compassionate, especially in an age before workmen's compensation laws and when few people carried life insurance, an era in which most employers acknowledged no responsibility at all for their employees except to pay them for their labors.

Now that the War of 1812 was over, English and other European goods were being dumped on the American market. This was, in part, the result of a deliberate policy aimed at wrecking the American economy. It was at this time that a member of the British House of Commons declared, "It is well worth while to incur a loss upon the first exportation in order—by the glut—to stifle in the cradle those rising manufactures in the United States which the war has forced into existence, contrary to the natural course of things."

In 1816, a United States tariff act increased duties on some foreign goods, including woolens and cottons, to the satisfaction of Irénée. He had used all his growing prestige on behalf of the measure. Despite the protective tariff, however, American textile manufacturers, including the du Ponts, continued to be hurt by the influx of British merchandise. And of the family enterprises, only the powder company kept making money.

Even that source of revenue wasn't enough to offset the financial drain from other ventures. The damage caused by the 1815 blast had already depleted the firm's cash reserves when, in Juy 1816, a fire broke out in the Upper Yard. The conflagration was contained but not until the main graining mill blew up. Fortunately there was no human toll; the material damage, however, was extensive. Irénée had to borrow $30,000 from William Warner of Philadelphia in order to get back into full production.

Collections were infuriatingly slow. Sometimes it took as long as a year to collect. Almost fifteen months after the Peace of Ghent, the United States government still owed E.I. du Pont de Nemours and Company more than $7,600. In the country as a whole money was so tight that businessmen found it difficult to obtain the credit that is the life-blood of commerce and industry. The nation was struggling with a paper economy.

"Houses without number have been built of paper," Pierre Samuel wrote to one of the creditors in Paris, explaining why his son was strapped financially despite a handsome record of profits, "water power for factories and the factories themselves—of paper; canals and roads—of paper; beautiful and useful steamboats—of paper." Irénée had profits in hand—on paper—paper that amounted to IOU's from his customers.

Moreover, he was now faced with a new challenge from an old quarter. Advertisements appeared in newspapers throughout the country; this one was typical:

Notice

PETER BAUDUY'S BEST GUNPOWDER

Having for thirteen years been concerned in the manufactory of gunpowder of E.I. du Pont (de Nemours) and Co. and having last year withdrawn from the said concern, I have established a manufactory of the same article under my particular care, and beg leave to inform the public that a constant assortment of gunpowder will be found with my agent Mr. John Roberts, merchant, of Alexandria, which will be warranted to be of the first quality, and will be sold on the most reasonable terms.

Peter Bauduy

Brandywine, August 25

That dateline—Brandywine—was misleading, an obvious attempt to cash in on du Pont's reputation. Actually, Bauduy and his son-in-law, J. P. Garesché, had built their powder mill at Bauduy's estate, Eden Park, which was, and is, to this day, south of the Christina River. Instead of waterpower, Bauduy used the energy of horses. In design his mill was patterned on the du Pont works. "But even though he has taken many of our workmen," said Pierre Samuel, "though he uses almost the same machinery and methods of mixing, no powder compares with ours—all because of Irénée's skill and his marvelous industry."

A distinct asset now to Irénée's firm was young Bidermann, who proved a tireless, intelligent, buoyant, even gay worker. He liked the United States and quickly became as American as Victor. In a matter of months his signature was transformed from "Jacques Antoine Bidermann" to "James Anthony Bidermann." Forever on the go, he hurried from city to city, despite the uncomfortable, inconvenient transportation of the time, arranging for local merchants to act as du Pont agents and negotiating contracts with large-scale customers.

Young Antoine Bidermann had more than a financial stake in the du Pont enterprise. He had fallen in love with Irénée's daughter Evelina. On September 14, 1816, they were married.

Earlier that year, on St. Valentine's Day, Irénée's wife had given birth to their last child, a boy named Alexis Irénée du Pont. He was the seventh living child born to Sophie, then nearly forty-one years old.

The baby's grandfather, Pierre Samuel, was suffering a good deal of pain from his gout which also caused chronic insomnia, but he was happy. He received a mighty boost to his ego when the revolutionary leaders of South America sent a representative to him asking for suggestions regarding a constitution for the "Equinoctial" states, the countries now known as Colombia, Ecuador, and Venezuela. At that time, this territory was in the final stages of its struggle for independence from Spain.

From France came letters in the hand of his invalid wife. Since her injury had confined her to bed, she had languished with such voluble resignation that she almost seemed to be glorying in her ordeal. Her satisfaction could be sensed in every self-pitying missive sent to her distant spouse. "Ah! dear love," she exclaimed in one note, "why did we not die together years ago, before my fall compelled our separation?"

Pierre Samuel himself had no such death wish. Without responsibilities now—his distant wife was independently wealthy—he was free to relax and expand in the atmosphere of adoring offspring and admiring friends. The great Portuguese botanist, José Francisco Correa da Serra, was appointed Portugal's minister to the United States. Upon his arrival in America, one of the first men he sought out was "du Pont de Nemours," as the senior of the family was called by statesmen. Thomas Jefferson invited both men to visit him at Monticello. Unfortunately, a misunderstanding occurred: the visitors thought Jefferson was expecting them in December, 1815, but when they arrived at his home they found he was off inspecting a distant estate. They waited three days for him, entertained by his daughter Martha, and then gave up and went home. The incident greatly embarrassed Jefferson.

The former President and du Pont were still corresponding regularly, although with less frequency than a dozen years before. Some of the letters were practical, like the message in which du Pont asked the Sage of Monticello to use his influence to gain an appointment as a naval officer for Victor's son, Samuel Francis du Pont. By return mail Jefferson replied that he had written to President James Madison at once and was sure that du Pont's request would be granted.

Du Pont's grandson, then barely twelve years old and a student at a boys' school at Mount Airy near Philadelphia, was appointed a Navy midshipman and also received the option of attending the Military Academy at West Point, thus having the choice of a career in either the Navy or the Army. The boy chose a naval life. In 1817, when he was fourteen, Midshipman du Pont began his sea service with the Mediterranean Squadron.

Often the du Pont-Jefferson letters dealt with philosophical and political matters. Both men were somewhat disillusioned about the speed of social progress and the enthusiasm with which the people would accept basic change. "As yet we can sow only acorns on land rather badly prepared," the Frenchman wrote. "Oaks will grow, under which—some centuries after us—men and animals will walk and propagate in safety, abundance, and delight."

Philosophically, each at an early age had committed himself to the dominance of agriculture, but the ironies of life had conspired against them. Du Pont's son was now a major industrialist; and about this time, Jefferson admitted "that manufactures are now as necessary to our independence as to our comfort."

Du Pont himself always believed that he and Jefferson shared the same point of view in politics, but he was wrong. Jefferson thought that conditions in America were unique; a republic of the kind he had helped to construct here could not, in his opinion, be adapted to suit the French temperament and traditions. He felt the French should emulate the British system of constitutional monarchy.

In their attitudes toward their fellow men, the two old philosophers were in the sharpest, if friendly, conflict. This disagreement was shown in Jefferson's letter to du Pont regarding Pierre Samuel's proposed constitution for the "Equinoctial republics"—New Granada, Cartagena, and Caracas, as they were then called. In keeping with physiocratic principles, du Pont had divided the populace into two classes: the landowners and the landless. The landholders alone would have the vote, but only they would be subject to taxation. The landless—those who worked for their livelihood for other men—would not be given the ballot, but they would be exempt from taxes; they would also be protected in their political, economic, and religious liberties.

In setting forth this recommendation, du Pont, who really had no interest in American politics despite his residence here, did not realize that he was espousing the views of Jefferson's—and his own son's—bitter political enemies, the Federalists and their successors. At that very moment these men were desperately but vainly attempting to prevent the passage of legislation in the states providing for universal male suffrage.

Jefferson's letter commenting on du Pont's draft constitution has become a classic statement of his political philosophy. "We of the United States, you know, are constitutionally and conscientiously democrats," he wrote to du Pont. Later, in the same letter, he neatly capsuled the difference between his stand and du Pont's: "We both consider the people as our children, and love them with parental affection. But you love them as infants whom you are afraid to trust without nurses; and I as adults whom I freely leave to self-government."

While his father was engaged in endless speculation and discourse on political theory, Victor had plunged into practical politics. In June, 1815, he successfully ran for a seat in the Delaware House of Representatives. His victory and the part played by the du Ponts in supplying powder to the armed forces in the war largely ended the prejudice against this foreign family. Some vestiges of the old bias, however, could be detected for a good many more years. In 1817, Victor was elected to the state Senate where he served until 1824. Apparently he never tried to put into practice the restrictive ideas of Pierre Samuel.

For his part, the practical Irénée had little time for abstractions. He was pleased when, as a result of his efforts, the duty on powder was raised two cents a pound. But he found himself fighting for the very life of his company in the summer of 1816, when a brief but savage depression made it more difficult than usual to obtain payments from his customers and orders from prospects. And there was always Bauduy, as ubiquitous as he was malicious.

On May 24, 1817, Irénée, who was in Washington trying to get a Navy contract for which Bauduy also was bidding, mixed business, hatred for Bauduy, and love for Sophie in a strange letter to his wife: "The time I have passed here is as hard as any that I remember in my life—without friends, without acquaintances, scarcely knowing anyone to speak to—but forced to assert myself, absolutely against my nature, in order to counter-balance the audacity and great impudence of that infernal Mr. B., whom I meet everywhere. What I have had to swallow, to endure, and to fight surpasses my ability to describe; and I had no kind of consolation. When I am unhappy and can get to you I soon forget it; if I were more poetic I would compare your effect on me to that which Anteus felt when he touched the earth and therefrom gained new strength to fight Hercules; where you and I are concerned, the comparison is not bad, but that fool of a Bauduy is a poor sort of Hercules. He has, however, done me one good turn, for I would long ago have told the Navy board to go to the devil had it not been that I could not bear to give in to him and lose the chance to beat him."

Irénée won the contract. He was now on his way to a national reputation as an industrial leader. His views were being sought on many matters of general importance. In an unobtrusive way he was a man of influence in political affairs, too. His allies had been winning elections. On June 3, 1817, Irénée wrote from Philadelphia to tell Sophie that James Monroe, inaugurated as President a few weeks earlier, was soon coming with him to visit the du Pont powder works. "Have your caps washed and dress yourselves up to receive him," Irénée teased.

His father, however, was not well. During the preceding Christmas holidays, Pierre Samuel had decided to surprise Victor and his family by rowing across the Brandywine and showing up for dinner unexpectedly. But the boat overturned as he stepped into it and the old man was plunged into the icy water. He was fished out and rushed home, drenched to the skin but in high spirits. As he was put to bed, hot bricks wrapped in cloth at his feet, comforters piled high, he chuckled and said, "Ah, my children, your old father never before went through the ordeal by water but he came out victorious!"

Nevertheless, in the following months he had suffered from recurrent periods of illness. The final blow to his health was an indirect result of an accident in the powder yard.

It occurred the night of July 16, 1817, while Irénée was away from the Brandywine on a business trip. A charcoal maker emptied a cylinder an hour after it was burned and left the charcoal in hogsheads. Not properly cooled, the charcoal rekindled. Soon the entire charcoal drying house was in flames and the dread fire gong was sounding in the valley, summoning every available man to the dangerous task of fighting the blaze before it ignited the powder. Even old Papa du Pont responded to the call. The pumps went dry in a matter of minutes, but a bucket line was organized to pass up water from the creek. The walls of the burning building collapsed, the chimney falling away from the structure and almost hitting Charles Dalmas. At one point Bidermann noticed that the highly inflammable tar barrels were in danger. But the kegs were too heavy to be carried away, so they were overturned instead. Soon the men were in tar up to their knees as the sticky material poured down the slope and covered the road. Fortunately, there was little wind, and the slight breeze that came up now and then was blowing away from the other buildings.

Sick as he was, the seventy-seven-year-old Pierre Samuel had insisted on pulling on his clothes and tottering out to help fight the blaze. He took his place in the bucket brigade, exchanging cheerful remarks with the powdermen beside him as they all worked together through the long, wild, uncertain night. By morning, the hands of old du Pont were raw from the unusual labor; his clothes were soaked and his face blackened by soot. His voice was hoarse from the effort of shouting over the noise. He was in pain and exhausted.

When he was finally able to tumble into his bed, it was immediately obvious that he was very sick. Before long his family could not deceive themselves; they knew that life was ebbing from his aged body. Refusing to give up this last fight of his eventful life, he clung to consciousness until August 5, when he sank into a coma.

Two days later, on August 7, 1817, Pierre Samuel du Pont de Nemours died at three o'clock in the morning, his family around his bed.

The newspapers carried the report of his death, and Irénée sent personal messages to his stepmother, to Lafayette, to Jefferson, and other friends of his father.

To Lafayette, the notice was "terrible news." He wrote to Irénée, "I need not tell you how I am suffering."

Jefferson sent a letter of sympathy in which he said, "Of no man who has lived could more good have been said with more truth. . . . His object never varied, that of the general good. For this no man ever labored more zealously or honestly; of which he has left abundant monuments."

A graveyard, which would from that day forward be the family burial ground of the du Pont family, was cleared in Sand Hole Woods, on what is now Buck Road, just west of Eleutherian Mills. There, among the oaks, beeches and hickories, the founder of the American family was laid to rest. At the head of his grave a slab of white sandstone was set up. On it were inscribed these words:

Sacred to the memory of
PIERRE SAMUEL DU PONT DE NEMOURS
Knight of the order of Vasa, of
the Legion of Honor and of the
order du Lis; Counsellor of State,
member of the first Constituent Assembly, President of the Council
of Ancients and member of the Institute of France. Born in Paris,
December, A.D. 1739. Died at the
Eleutherian Mills August 17, A.D.
1817.

CHAPTER XV

DISASTER AND COMPASSION

THE DU PONTS had scarcely recovered from the loss of their patriarch when disaster struck their mills.

It was March 19, 1818, and Irénée was in Philadelphia on business. On the Brandywine, the Marquis Emmanuel de Grouchy had been visiting Victor du Pont's home, Louviers, and his woolen mill. At ten o'clock in the morning he and his son were about to be taken across the creek to see the powder works. In Wilmington, people were enjoying a sunny spring day—still chilly but warming under a clear sky.

Suddenly the earth shook in Wilmington and even as far away as Lancaster, Pennsylvania, forty-three miles to the northwest. A moment later there was a second tremor. Houses moved perceptibly, setting their doorbells to ringing, the tingling incongruously cheery in a panic-stricken city. Windows rattled; many shattered from the earth movements or the shock waves that followed seconds later. Dishes rolled off shelves and smashed on the floors. Babies began wailing and older folk were just as frightened and confused. Men and women ran into the streets of Wilmington. "The steamboat!" somebody cried, remembering the strange new vessel on the Delaware. "Milnor's steamboat—it's full of passengers. It must have blown up!" Others screamed "Earthquake! Earthquake!"

Down from the Kennett Pike dashed a farmer on a foam-spattered horse. "Leave your houses!" he cried, waving his hat. "It's the powder works and the grand magazine is about to explode!"

Most of those who heard him fled in terror to the other side of the Christina River, but scores of people, showing the morbid curiosity that often attends catastrophes, began streaming out the pike toward the du Pont mills, on foot, on horseback, in carriages and wagons. They were lucky: they had not had time to reach the danger area when a third shock moved the ground and smote the faces of the onrushing hordes with a fierce gust of wind. Up from the gorge, in a column that folded and unfolded, rose dense black smoke, corkscrewing above the willow trees into the serene sky.

A glazing mill in the Upper Yard had been the first to go. The reason was never discovered, but one man, at first believed lost in the disaster, later was reported to have been seen running away from the mill, so either carelessness or malice may have been the cause. When the glazing mill exploded, orange-red flames and black smoke belching from door and roof, blazing fragments of its wooden roof were hurled far and wide. Some brands fell on the drying house which blew up almost at once. In this first stage of the accident, two other mills "blew"—the powderman's word—for a total of four, but the detonations were so close that only two shocks could be felt. The third shock came when thirty tons of powder stored in the magazine, a large room carved into the solid rock of the hillside, erupted. All that was left was a big hole in the hill.

The human toll was awful. Thirty-six perished instantly or within a few minutes; four more died of injuries during the next few days. Not all of the dead were workmen: many powdermen's houses had been crushed in as much as half a mile from the scene of the blast, and heavy stones flying through the air endangered their wives and children. When Irénée galloped home from Philadelphia after learning of the disaster, he found that his wife Sophie had suffered an injury to her side from which she never fully recovered. Another minor casualty was her brother, Charles Dalmas. After the first explosions, he had run to a pump to get water for a powderman's wife who had fainted with horror at the sight of the broken and torn bodies in the millyard. When the magazine blew up, falling rock and timber broke his arm.

Everyone pitched in at once to help put out the fires ignited by burning brands. Kegs of powder were rolled into the creek to cut down the possibility of more explosions. Rubble was explored for survivors. The injured were carried out of the danger zone for treatment; all the du Pont homes were converted into hospitals, with improvised beds on the floors of every room and hall. Selected groups of powdermen searched grimly for the bodies of their friends. Only eight could be identified. Human fragments were found at great distances from the Upper Yard, even in the tree tops on the lawn of tranquil Louviers.

Like everyone else, Marshal Grouchy and his son were pressed into service; they were asked to care for the maimed victims being sheltered at Louviers. Grouchy had planned to spend the night there, but the sight of the survivors' ghastly, mutilated bodies, the cries of pain, the gore, the knowledge that the hillside outside was still covered by pitiful bits of what had once been men—all of this was too much for him to bear. Perhaps he was reminded too vividly of Waterloo, a defeat that Napoleon had blamed on him personally. At any rate, in the middle of the night Grouchy disappeared with his son. A search party found them, pale and wild-eyed, trudging along the road in what they hoped was the direction of Philadelphia. Brought back to the Brandywine, they were bedded down for the night in a house at some distance from the scene of carnage.

In this, as in later emergencies, the women of the du Pont family worked with their men, swallowing the nausea that rose at the gruesome sights to which they were exposed. They cleaned and dressed wounds, fed the injured, comforted widows, rounded up orphans and told them lighthearted stories to take their minds off the fate that had, without warning, turned the sun-dappled gorge into a valley of death.

Again and in spite of its shaky financial position, E.I. du Pont de Nemours and Company did its best to provide for the families of the dead workers. Widows received a pension, a place to live, and firewood. Children who lost both parents were made wards of the du Ponts. They provided these orphans with shelter, clothing, food, and schooling.

Born in compassion, this policy turned out to be good business as well. Only two employees were so demoralized by the catastro-

Pierre Samuel du Pont de Nemours,
founder of the family

Eleuthère Irénée du Pont de Nemours,
founder of the company

Victor Marie du Pont de Nemours

Don Pedro, the merino ram whose offspring produced the wool for Victor's factory

Bois des Fossés, the du Pont home at Nemours, France, from which they left for America

Eleutherian Mills-Hagley Foundation

The Investiture, as it has been called by the du Ponts: Pierre Samuel, about to bestow his first sword on Eleuthère Irénée, admonishes him while Victor Marie looks on. From a painting by Stanley Arthurs.

A sketch of the powder mills and du Pont residence on the hill, drawn about 1806 by Charles Dalmas, brother-in-law of Eleuthère Irénée

Rear Admiral Samuel Francis du Pont,
Civil War naval hero

Colonel Henry Algernon du Pont,
winner of the Congressional Medal of
Honor

Worker's home on Breck's Lane near the powder yard

Eleutherian Mills-Hagley Foundation

Ruins of some of the powder mills as they appear today

Eleutherian Mills-Hagley Foundation

Damage caused to workers' homes by the great explosion of 1890

Alicia Bradford Maddox du Pont, center of the biggest scandal

Alfred I. du Pont, who saved the company and later lost control of it because of his romance with Alicia

Eleutherian Mills, the residence of Eleuthère Irénée, as it appears today. The center part is the original house; the wings were added about the middle of the nineteenth century. The old office building is at the left.

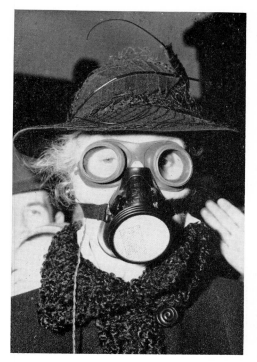

Miss Zara du Pont as she appeared in gas mask on a Boston picket line in the 1930s, protesting police use of tear gas against strikers

Wide World Photos

T. Coleman du Pont, Miss Zara's brother and president of the company in the 1900s, later United States Senator

Pierre S. du Pont, who, with Alfred I. and T. Coleman, took over the company in 1902; Pierre directed its development for nearly half a century.

Karsh, Ottawa, Courtesy of E. I. du Pont de Nemours and Company, Incorporated

Irénée (left) and Lammot, Pierre's brothers, each of whom headed the company at one time, as they appeared before the Senate munitions investigators in 1934

Wide World Photos

Ethel du Pont and Franklin D. Roosevelt, Jr. at the time of their wedding in 1937

Alfred I. du Pont's palatial estate, Nemours, as it appeared at the time of his death. The main house is at the top of the picture; the structure just below the center is a Temple of Love, modeled after one at Versailles.

The big house at Winterthur, now the Henry F. du Pont Winterthur Museum, as it is today, with all the wings that have been added since 1839. The enormous collection of American antiques finally forced Mr. and Mrs. du Pont to move out; they now live in a smaller house on the estate.

Henry Francis du Pont Winterthur Museum

Longwood Gardens Photograph

A view at Longwood Gardens: the central part of the vast conservatories, as seen across the fountain gardens

phe that they quit. All the rest, with full knowledge of the hazards, remained to work again with the gritty black powder.

One of the most painful duties of the du Pont women was to take inventory of the personal effects left by the victims. These were poor people, even in a time when living standards were low. Most of their possessions were simple necessities: coarse clothing, bed coverings, cooking utensils, and so on. Almost everyone had a few cherished treasures. Michael Tonner and his wife, both killed in the 1818 explosion, had a big looking glass, a set of brass candlesticks, one tablecloth, and six silver teaspoons. A bachelor who died that day owned a prized silver watch.

Besides the terrible toll in lives, the disaster had a tremendous impact on the powder company. The Upper Yard had been utterly destroyed; it was a whole year before repairs could be completed and operations resumed there. Irénée's house had been damaged, so he and his family moved into Louviers with Victor's family until the building could be made livable again. For several weeks Irénée's family slept on pallets at Louviers.

All the costly rebuilding of the Upper Yard and the damaged living quarters had to be done at a time when credit was at low ebb because of the countrywide depression. And yet du Pont made powder sales on extended credit. In 1818, a panic had occurred, setting in motion a depression that would not lift for four years. All over the country business houses failed, and some of them were agents of du Pont. This meant that a certain number of large accounts would never be able to pay. From 1817 to 1819, Irénée lost $140,000 from bankruptcies, explosions and other direct causes, and another $50,000 was gone from his books because of the deterioration of real-estate assets. Adding to his difficulties were some of the old problems of his father's making. Talleyrand, for example, politely but firmly demanded the 100,000 francs he had lent to Pierre Samuel many years before. Madame de Pusy's nephew, the arrogant, hot-headed Denizot, came to join forces with Bauduy and take Irénée into court. His intention was to dissolve the firm and he almost succeeded, for, after he published notices accusing du Pont of having misused company funds, the firm's credit suffered and Irénée had trouble obtaining working capital.

Fortunately, in sixteen years of toil he had acquired a reputation for integrity and responsibility—meaning, in bankers' terms, that he paid his bills. So bankers were willing to lend him money now.

Going back over the records, it seems incredible that Irénée could keep track of all the notes he had signed. He was constantly riding off to Philadelphia to meet a note that had fallen due. "It is cruel to ride sixty miles every five or six days to meet one's notes, and so to waste one's time and one's life," he complained. "God grant that some day I may get to the end of it."

He never did. But, paradoxically, after the disaster of 1818 the financial pressure did let up somewhat. Apparently accepting the fact of du Pont's straitened circumstances, Talleyrand agreed to give Irénée ten years to pay off his father's old debt. And the French creditors who had received powder-company shares when Du Pont Père, Fils et Cie. went bankrupt agreed to accept long-term notes.

The Upper Yard was rebuilt, and the mills at Hagley just a few hundred yards downstream never stopped rolling. A sizable community of industry had sprung up now along the Brandywine. Besides the powder works, there were three other firms owned in whole or in part by du Pont: Victor's woolen mill; the Duplanty-McCall cotton factory; and a tannery managed by Alexandre Cardon de Sandran who had accompanied Pierre Samuel to America. A little farther downstream, fourteen other textile mills were owned by Quakers.

Honors were coming to the du Ponts. Before the end of the War of 1812, Victor had begun to dabble in politics. From 1815 on, he was a Whig legislator for several years in the Delaware House of Representatives and later in the state Senate. Always convivial, he was in his element at Dover, the state capital, playing cards, telling jokes, and consuming huge quantities of food and drink with political allies and opponents alike. Everyone liked Victor. With age his body, never slim, was going to fat, but he was probably happier than he'd ever been in his life.

To run the woolen mill during his lengthening absences, Victor summoned his eldest son, Charles I. du Pont, home from Mount Airy College in Germantown, Pennsylvania, when he was only sixteen years old. This was a painful wrench for the boy, a rather scholarly, reflective youth, but he obediently swallowed his protests and did his best. In fact, he soon proved himself superior to his father as a business man. With the condition of the company healthier all the time, Victor faced this cold truth: his son was better for the firm than he; so, as time passed, Victor was seen at the office of the company less and less.

Irénée, too, was becoming more involved in public life. When Caesar A. Rodney ran for the United States Senate, Irénée closed his mills for the day so that all the men could vote for his friend. Then, in December, 1822, Senator Rodney notified Irénée that he had been named a director of the second Bank of the United States, a privately owned, federally chartered institution. As repository for the government's funds, this bank was supposed to stabilize the currency much as the Federal Reserve System does today. Irénée remained a member of the bank's board for the rest of its life except for a brief period when Victor took his place there.

Among their neighbors, the du Ponts were already reckoned people of substance. Their weddings, more frequent as the first American-born generation came of age, were the most eagerly awaited social occasions of Wilmington. On May 12, 1824, Victor's daughter Julia married Irvine Shubrick, a twenty-six-year-old Navy officer who eventually rose to be a commodore. In October, there were two du Pont weddings: Irénée's eldest son, Alfred V. du Pont, married Margaretta Lammot; and earlier in that month, Victor's son Charles exchanged vows with Dorcas Montgomery Van Dyke, daughter of United States Senator Nicholas Van Dyke.

Although Irénée and Victor had relatives named La Motte in France, it was through Alfred's marriage that the Anglicized version of the name, Lammot, came into the family. It later became a very common du Pont first name. Like the du Ponts, Margaretta was of Huguenot stock; her ancestors had sought religious liberty in America in the seventeenth century.

The wedding of Charles and Dorcas was the biggest event of its kind that Delaware had ever seen, for the aged Lafayette was touring America at the time and consented to give the bride away. The du Pont girls bubbled over with excitement. A great ball in honor of Lafayette was held in Philadelphia a few days before the wedding which took place in New Castle, Delaware. Each of the girls wore her best finery for the ball, and each needed a different gown for the wedding, of course.

During his visit, Lafayette, as a friend to both parties, tried unsuccessfully to resolve the dispute between Madame de Pusy, still in France, and Irénée.

All of Delaware turned out the next summer when Lafayette went to Chadds Ford on the Brandywine just over the Pennsylvania line, to visit the site of the Revolutionary War battle in which he had been wounded. Afterwards he traveled downstream to Irénée's home to spend the night. Eleuthera presented her album to him for his signature.

The old warrior wrote: "After having seen the banks of the Brandywine a scene of bloody fighting nearly half a century ago, I am happy to find it now the seat of industry, beauty, and mutual friendship. Lafayette"

Before he left, Lafayette climbed the hill to Sand Hole Woods. Leaning on a cane, he gazed sadly on the grave of his old friend. The crowds of Americans, gathered for a glimpse of their country's greatest French friend, kept a respectful distance. For the moment, even the powder mills were still.

CHAPTER XVI

PASSING OF THE OLD ORDER

Despite his success in politics, the increasing prestige of the family and the profit his woolen mill was showing under his son's management, Victor du Pont, with the assistance of his gambling cronies, kept sinking ever more deeply into debt. Always imprudent in handling money, he demonstrated that neither years nor misfortunes had impressed on him the virtue of thrift. His appointment to the board of directors of the Bank of the United States can only be regarded as a triumph of politics over judgment.

For a time he was troubled by ill health. Following surgery, he recovered fully. A year later a slimmer, clear-eyed Victor showed the effects of a strict diet and an enforced rest.

Soon after New Year's Day in 1827, he and a friend, Wilson Hunt, jointly bought a ticket in the New York Consolidated Lottery. In those days, lotteries were legal and widespread; they made possible many public improvements. This time Victor said he felt lucky.

On January 30, he went to Philadelphia on business. On the street there he encountered an old friend who remarked on his cheerful and robust appearance. "I never felt so well," Victor said expansively.

A half hour after this meeting, he collapsed in the street. He was carried a block or two to the United States Hotel where he had been staying. There he died an hour later; he was in his sixtieth year. A doctor certified the cause of death as "rupture of a cavity in the artery of the heart." A few days after his death, his family was notified that Victor's lottery ticket, still in his pocket when he died, had won. The ticket was worth eight hundred and fifty dollars.

The two brothers, so different in temperament, so close in affection, had been warm friends as well. Irénée found the loss almost unbearably painful. Although he recognized Victor's shortcomings, he had always understood that those weaknesses, in large measure, had stemmed from his brother's good nature. Victor had been one of those people who gain in love what they lose in esteem. To Irénée, he always remained the big brother who could do scarcely any wrong. Once, when Victor lamented that he had become a financial burden on him, Irénée replied feelingly, "We are as twins —when one dies, the other dies."

Not death, but a deepening of the melancholy from which he had always suffered was Irénée's lot these days. One thing that could usually draw him out of his depression was an inquiry about the company he had labored so hard and so long to establish. When Hezekiah Niles, a Wilmington man who had gone to Baltimore and founded there one of the country's most influential newspapers, *Niles' Weekly Register*, asked Irénée for information about the powder mill, du Pont's reply was full of pride. Employees numbered one hundred and forty, not counting "waggoners, shallop men, and so forth"—shallop men carried powder kegs in small boats from the shore to cargo ships. Production was at the rate of 800,000 pounds a year. The du Pont company, Irénée asserted, had put the American powder industry on a sound footing by its fight against imported powder and had helped substantially to reduce the price of gunpowder. For some reason, Irénée failed to mention the other products that his mills made at that time: refined saltpeter, charcoal, pyroligneous acid—a red dye called iron liquor, and creosote.

An increasing share of the business burden was falling on the shoulders of Evelina's husband, Antoine Bidermann, and Irénée's eldest son, Alfred. Bidermann, always close to Irénée, became his only real confidant after Victor's death. Alfred, who had grown up in the mill yards, went to work for the firm at nineteen after studying chemistry at Dickinson College in Carlisle, Pennsylvania. A slow but thorough thinker, making up in persistence what he lacked in brilliance, Alfred had his father's bent for chemistry. "Alfred has just contrived a new instrument as simple as it is ingenious and has proved an interesting fact—that there is no relation between the strength and quickness of gunpowder," Irénée wrote proudly.

His young chemist son reminded Irénée of himself many years ago—before the emigration to America, before the Reign of Terror, before the Revolution—of a young Irénée du Pont de Nemours, listening with awe and excitement to the words of his great teacher, Lavoisier, in a far-off place called Essonnes. Many other things reminded Irénée and Sophie of France. They often found themselves, alone at night before a fire in Eleutherian Mills, no longer a raw new house but a mansion mellow with twenty years of living, talking about their homeland—about Paris and its endless fascination, about their relatives with whom they had maintained a faithful correspondence, and most of all, about Bois des Fossés where they had lived as a young couple in the first flush of married love. Soon they would go back to France for a long visit, they vowed, even though Irénée disapproved vehemently of the Bourbon regime.

But the trip to France was not to be. Early in July Sophie fell ill. It seems likely that she was suffering from cancer. Her legs swelled and she suffered pain in every part of her body. Irénée was torn with anguish and fear.

"I am not able to attend to business affairs as I should," he wrote to a friend. "My only thought is for my wife, who is painfully and dangerously ill and has been so for several weeks. I am unable to work or sleep."

Two days later, on August 5, 1828, Irénée wrote, "Mrs. du Pont is so ill today that I hardly know what I am writing." He spent every minute by Sophie's bedside, comforting her, smiling at her and trying not to let his anxiety show through, feeding her, giving her medicine. She faded as the weeks wore on; rallied briefly; then declined again.

On November 27, 1828, she died at the age of fifty-three.

Irénée never really recovered from the blow. In the years that followed, he tried to bury himself in his work, but now he was fighting a losing battle against depression. Often he could be seen, sitting at his desk or standing with one foot on a rock by the Brandywine, just staring into space.

Public affairs could still command his attention, but the old spirit was gone. Earlier he had served on the survey committee that laid out the Chesapeake and Delaware Canal which shortened the water between Philadelphia and Baltimore by three hundred and nineteen miles. In 1831, when a Society for Promoting Manufactures was organized, Irénée was named to a four-man steering committee.

In purely political matters, too, he remained active, so much so that the *New York Courier and Enquirer* attacked him savagely in 1830. A friend, discussing the newspaper's denunciation, said, "You are held up as a powerful personage and as having influenced the late election in Delaware . . . and even as having, through the multitude of your dependents and workmen . . . decided it."

The following year Irénée was one of a committee of five appointed to inform Henry Clay that he had been nominated by the Whigs at their convention in Baltimore. During the subsequent election the Whigs swept most of Delaware's offices, but Clay was defeated by the incumbent President, Andrew Jackson.

By this time, party labels had undergone a transformation. The Federalist Party had died. The anti-Federalists, then known as the Republican Party, had split, the right wing forming the National Republican Party and the left calling itself first the Democratic Republican Party and later simply the Democratic Party. The du Ponts remained Whigs until the new Republican Party was organized in the middle of the nineteenth century. Since then most of the du Ponts have been Republican.

The first breach between North and South occurred in the early 1830's. It involved the du Ponts intimately. South Carolina, enraged by two successive high tariffs passed by Congress, enacted an Ordinance of Nullification which claimed that states' rights were superior to federal law and that any federal statute repugnant to a state could be rejected and declared void within that state. This was an ominous controversy, because the South Carolina legislature authorized appropriations for arms and the raising of a military force to be used, if need be, against the federal government.

At this point South Carolina's state government, through du

Pont's New York agent, placed an order for 125,000 pounds of cannon and rifle powder, worth $24,000. The Southerners offered to pay cash.

Irénée lost no time in rejecting the order. He wrote, "The destination of this powder being obvious, we think it right to decline furnishing any part of the above order. When our friends in the South will want sporting powder for peaceful purposes, we will be happy to serve them."

A month later, du Pont, as a leading Whig and an important manufacturer who had been campaigning for higher tariffs, was called to Washington to help work out a peaceful solution to a problem that was coming dangerously close to war. In the end, a compromise was reached: Congress passed a more moderate, lower tariff and agreed not to move with force against South Carolina, if the Southerners in turn agreed to drop the nullification argument.

In March, du Pont's Charleston agents, Pitray, Viel and Company, received a letter from Irénée, written, as du Pont letters customarily were, in the third person. Irénée said, "Our E.I. du Pont has been in Washington assisting at the treaty of peace between your friends, the Nullifiers, and ours, the monopolist manufacturers of the North. Now that the affair has ended so amiably, I almost regret that we refused to supply the powder. We would be very glad to have that $24,000 in our cash box rather than in that of your army."

A dependable supply of saltpeter, essential in the making of black powder, was always a problem. The best saltpeter came from India, a British possession. Thus du Pont's purchases were always in danger of being held up any time that Anglo-American relations happened to be bad. Before the War of 1812, du Pont considered making a trip himself to the caves recently discovered in Kentucky and what is now West Virginia, to examine the quality of the saltpeter found there.

Twenty years later, when his nephew, Lieutenant Irvine Shubrick, set forth on a voyage to South America, Irénée asked him to look into the saltpeter deposits of Peru and Chile. Shubrick's detailed report was a model of conciseness. Written at Valparaiso on November 18, 1832, the letter covered mining, refining, prices, transportation, composition, and uses: "It is said here that its basis is nitrate of soda and unfit in the composition of gunpowder, and that in France it is principally used for acids, glassware, soap . . ." Shubrick wrote.

Nevertheless, Irénée experimented with a quantity of the South American chemical. He came to the conclusion that sodium nitrate, the South American compound, could not be used in the making of black powder which required potassium nitrate. In his customary careful fashion, Irénée wrote a detailed account of his experiments and filed it away. Later in the century, a grandson would use that paper as the basis for his own successful experiments with South American saltpeter.

Irénée celebrated his sixtieth birthday comforted by the knowledge that the company was finally emerging from its financial bog. The debt to Talleyrand had long been paid off. Over the years, most of the shareholders in France had been bought out. Only a few remained, and there were scarcely any serious debts on the books of the firm. It was as prosperous as Irénée had always dreamed it might be. But the three people for whom he had labored to erect this profitable enterprise were no longer alive to enjoy it. To his children, some of them now parents themselves, he found himself talking a great deal about his illustrious father, his charming brother, and, most of all, his beloved wife.

Not that Irénée was always gloomy. Far from it. On June 27, 1833, for example, he looked proud and happy. That day he threw his home open to the family and their friends and neighbors for the wedding of his daughter, Sophie Madeleine du Pont, to Victor's son, Lieutenant Samuel Francis du Pont, United States Navy. And yet the marriage of this daughter, named for his dead wife, must have brought back bittersweet memories; some of his gaiety may have been forced. This was the first of the cousin marriages for which the du Ponts later became famous.

In the following year, Irénée's only unmarried daughter found the protection of a husband. Eleuthera du Pont married Thomas McKie Smith, a physician who had settled on the Brandywine. The ceremony took place on September 18, 1834. And with it Irénée may have felt that the last of his responsibilities had been fulfilled.

Late in the following month he had to go to Philadelphia on business. He appeared in good health when he left Wilmington October 29, but about four o'clock the next afternoon, as he was returning to the United States Hotel, he stumbled in the street. A block farther on, he fell to the ground. Passersby rushed to his side. At his request, they picked him up gently and carried him to his hotel room a block away.

There he died eleven hours later, at three o'clock on Friday morning, October 31, 1834, almost exactly as Victor had died nearly eight years before. He was sixty-three. One account says that Irénée, too, died of a heart attack; another blames his death on cholera which was sweeping Philadelphia at the time.

During the night, travelers arriving in Wilmington from Philadelphia brought the news that du Pont was seriously ill, for he was sufficiently prominent—and both cities were still so small—that such a misfortune became quickly known. In the morning, anxious crowds gathered on the town wharf to await the first sloop from Philadelphia, for the vessels that sailed up and down the Delaware were the fastest means of communication. When the news came that Irénée was dead, the townspeople left the wharf and walked slowly into town, talking solemnly as they went. For du Pont had made himself sincerely admired and liked in the area. "Prosperous in his own business," the *Delaware State Journal* said, "he made use of that prosperity to promote the happiness, to advance the welfare, and to increase the comfort and prosperity of all around him. Frugal and simple in all that related to himself, he seemed to regard the ample means which Providence and his own industry had placed in his hands as a trust fund for the benefit of others." The editorial concluded, "We have lost a friend whom we loved and venerated, this community a benefactor, our state its most useful and valuable citizen."

That afternoon Irénée's body was brought back from Philadelphia on the steamboat *Wilmington*. A large number of people were waiting at the wharf. Silently, on foot and in carriages, they accompanied the hearse on its slow journey to Eleutherian Mills five miles away.

The following afternoon, Irénée was laid to rest in the tree-shaded family burying ground in Sand Hole Woods. His brother, as the first-born, had been interred on the right of their father. So Irénée's resting place was on Pierre Samuel's left.

And thus the du Ponts are always buried to this day—those of the older branch on the right, those of the younger on the left.

CHAPTER XVII

COMMUNAL LIFE

T HE DEATH OF THE FOUNDER left a vacuum of leadership threatening the very existence of the company. The business had to be set on a firm footing now so that it could survive without Irénée. Moreover, the few remaining French shareholders, still an annoyance, must be paid off. Three sons had survived Irénée, but none of them could be trusted at this time to handle the difficult problems posed by their father's death.

Alfred, the eldest, was able to keep the mills running, but he could not handle delicate financial matters of the kind that had plagued his father so long. Now thirty-six, Alfred had spent the past sixteen years making powder, but it was the chemistry of explosives that interested him. At heart he was not a business man. In some ways he resembled his grandfather more than his father or his uncle. As a boy, he had been happiest helping old Pierre Samuel labor over his long, contemplative essays on public affairs, science, and philosophy. Although he had begun to work in earnest in the yards when he was twenty, his health, never robust, had often kept him away from the mills for months at a time.

His brothers were equally unqualified to take over the firm. Henry was only twenty-two and lacked experience in the business. His first love had been the army; he had been graduated from West Point on July 1, 1833, and commissioned a brevet second lieutenant.

A year later, at his father's request, he had reluctantly resigned his commission after seeing duty at Fort Monroe, Virginia, and in the Creek Nation. Alfred's lack of managerial ability caused Irénée to summon Henry home. But with only five months' experience at the time of his father's death, Henry obviously could not yet assume responsibility for the firm.

The third son, Alexis, was just eighteen. Although already a hard-working powderman, he was far too young to be trusted with the welfare of the firm. A powder mill owner had to deal with governments that might disown their debts or even be overthrown; with business men whose companies might be wiped out in the financial crises which were beginning to sweep the country every few years; and with transportation companies not eager to convey such dangerous cargo to customers.

In this crisis of leadership, a du Pont in-law stepped forward to carry on the company, setting a precedent that would be followed in later years. Antoine Bidermann, Evelina's husband and brother-in-law to Alfred, Henry and Alexis, took over the management of the firm. The logical choice for the job, he had worked with Irénée for twenty years. The two men had been more than in-laws; they had been warm friends, sharing their homesick memories of France, their love of America, and their utter absorption in the making of gunpowder.

After two years as head of the firm, Bidermann took a trip back to France with his wife and child. The company had prospered so well in that time that he was able to meet with the European creditors or their heirs and pay off the firm's obligations. Now, too, Pierre Samuel's debts were satisfied.

At long last, E.I. du Pont de Nemours and Company was American-owned, family-owned.

This task accomplished, Bidermann sailed back to America and reorganized the company as a partnership on April 1, 1837. There were seven partners, but Bidermann, at his own insistence, was not one of them. The seven were the children of Irénée: three sons and four daughters.

After the partnership was formed, Bidermann was never again active in the company, although he continued to live in the du Pont settlement on the Brandywine. His wife, to be sure, was of the generation that had now come to the fore, but Bidermann himself represented the past, and awareness of that must have colored his attitude.

When Victor's widow, Gabrielle, died on November 11, 1837, Bidermann's last link to the past was gone.

The new partners elected Alfred head of the firm, but only because he was the oldest of the brothers. Conscious of his own shortcomings, Alfred insisted that Henry and Alexis join him in a triumvirate of operating partners, thus setting a pattern that lasted three-quarters of a century. For as long as the company remained a partnership, there were several partners, with three of them serving as a kind of executive committee and one member of that triumvirate becoming the real head of the firm.

Victor's children, it will be noted, were excluded from the partnership, although some of them, over the years, worked for the company. His elder son, Charles, had the woolen mill; the younger, Samuel Francis was well embarked on a career in the Navy. The Victor branch of the family did, however, have an indirect voice in the management of the powder company through Sophie. As a daughter of Irénée, she held a partner's share.

Sophie's marriage to her first cousin had delighted the entire family, serving as it did to tie the two branches more tightly together, and it had the sanction of the dynasty's founder, although Pierre Samuel had been long dead when they were wed. Dreaming of his Utopian "Pontiana," he had written, "The marriages that I should prefer for our colony would be between the cousins. In that way we should be sure of honesty of soul and purity of blood."

But cousin marriages were as much the result of the family's isolation as of philosophical determination. The tiny community on the Brandywine, still decidedly French in atmosphere, had relatively little intercourse with the busy social life of the Quakers, the Swedes, and the Irish of Wilmington, even though the du Ponts took an active part in Delaware politics and, as the years went by, members of the family gradually married into many of the state's most distinguished families.

In part, their aloofness from Wilmington reflected their concern for the security of their powder-making. The du Ponts had introduced new methods in their mills, and they did their best to prevent competitors from learning about those refinements. This secretive attitude made the du Ponts appear to be hostile—or, at best, suspicious—of outsiders.

The reaction of many of their neighbors and of the uneducated people of Wilmington was, therefore, rather unfriendly. Du Ponts born and raised in the United States were sometimes labeled "foreigners."

The social isolation of the du Ponts is apparent in the letters and other records of Irénée. Although he had a broad business and political acquaintance, he rarely mentions entertaining friends or neighbors in his home. The same is true of his children. For at least three generations, the du Ponts remained an exclusive, closed group, although this was truer of Irénée's offspring than of Victor's. They found within the family whatever social intercourse they desired. Consanguineous marriages were an inevitable result of this way of life.

The cousin marriages also resulted in endless repetition of the same first names, a condition that still exists. In the first two generations after Eleuthère Irénée, for example, the given name Irénée occurs five times.

To distinguish among the many members of the family, servants, mill hands, and tradesmen used simply the first name, prefaced by the appropriate title of respect: "Mr. Alfred," "Miss Amelia," and so on. In writing or speaking to outsiders about company business, the family always followed the same formula: "Our Mr. Alfred V. du Pont says...." Even the writer of a business letter often referred to himself, although not invariably, in the third person, prefaced by "our."

The du Ponts, encysted in their own little world on the Brandy-wine, became a unique family; disciplined to an unusual degree, because powder-making was too hazardous to permit breaches of discipline; secretive, because they felt a need to hide their manufacturing processes from curious eyes; hard-working, because this was an essential part of Irénée's nature, a necessity to the family's survival in a strange land and, most of all, an integral feature of the Protestant ethic which formed the background of all the family's traditions; loyal to the family, because they felt walled off from the Americans about them; simple in their tastes and habits, partly because of their Huguenot beginnings but even more because of the company's peculiar character.

Theirs was a communal life. Indeed, this little family colony might be considered the only successful communal property society in America—a thought that might be greeted with something less than enthusiasm by the more conservative du Ponts. In those days, none of them owned the house he lived in or the carriage he rode in or the horse that drew it. Everything belonged to the company— even the broad farmlands that the du Ponts gradually acquired north and west of Wilmington, mostly west of the Brandywine but including some properties all the way east to the Delaware River above Wilmington. No one was even paid a salary; each member of the family drew cash to meet his needs.

There is in existence a note from Alfred to his brother Henry, written after Alfred's retirement from active participation in the company:

> My brother,
> I must go to Phil. before the 31. I have been putting it off nearly 3 weeks. My object is to pay off every small debt I owe. To do this, I wish you to send me a check on Phil. Bank for $100 and I shall draw $400 out of Union Bk.
>
> Your brother,
> Alfred V.
>
> I should wish to have the carriage at 11 o'clock, for Meta must go with me. . . .

This was a feudal society, despite its devotion to the principles of the Enlightenment. The center of the society was the family, and the family acknowledged its fealty to the patriarch. The members of this little society recognized their interdependence, and each knew he could rely on the others. In such an inward community, jealousies and petty rivalries were bound to arise, but all of them knew that in time of need the others would stand ready to give aid. They were comfortable with each other but ill at ease, for the most part, with outsiders. Social poise was not a characteristic of the average du Pont until very recent times. They had their own customs, some of them carried over from Europe. For example, on New Year's Day, which the family in the French manner enjoyed more than Christmas, all the du Pont men went from house to house, visiting all the du Pont women and bestowing on each of them a gift, usually a box of candy. The custom still prevails. Henry Seidel Canby, who grew up on the Brandywine knowing the du Ponts, recalled that even their speech was different: "There was among the youngsters a lingo of family reference hard for the visiting youth from town to understand."

To the outsiders who came into contact with them, the du Ponts were, understandably, objects of considerable curiosity. Many people, largely because they didn't understand this life along the Brandywine, considered the family rather an odd bunch. Amateur eugenicists among the neighbors, according to Canby, "used to say that the numerous eccentrics and rather frequent suicides among the du Ponts were the results of inbreeding, like the very characteristic du Pont face" with its Roman nose and cleft chin. But practical geneticists—livestock breeders, say, like the du Ponts themselves, who have always prized well-bred animals—know there's nothing harmful about careful inbreeding. In technical terminology, the du Ponts might be said to have reproduced themselves by line-breeding, a very mild form of inbreeding in which outbreeding is implicit. Line-breeding, properly carried on, usually produces the best stock if the initial stock is good.

Cousin marriages continued through the nineteenth century, although even members of the family sometimes worried about them. At one time, Henry du Pont, then head of the company and patriarch of the tribe, forbade any more consanguineous marriages, warning that he would discharge from the company any du Pont guilty of loving a relative. As he might have foreseen, the ukase was ineffective: even one of his own children married a cousin, and, worse still, that marriage ended in the family's first divorce.

CHAPTER XVIII

SUNDAY SCHOOL

IN THE BEGINNING, the du Ponts' attitude toward religion tended to scandalize their pious neighbors, mostly Quakers and Swedish Lutherans, plus a few scattered Episcopalians. The great majority of the du Ponts had little regard for organized religion. Their rejection of the Church was vehement.

In 1819 or 1820, Alfred V. du Pont said, "I wrote to a very reverend and good clergyman that he should be ducked in the creek the first time he could be found on our property."

During the early, hopeful days of the French Revolution, Pierre Samuel du Pont de Nemours had been the first to cry out in the National Assembly for confiscation of the estates of the Roman Catholic Church, an act that must have pleased the shades of his persecuted Huguenot ancestors. Pierre Samuel himself had no affiliation with institutional religion, Protestant or Catholic.

It is true that he and his son, Victor, were both Masons: Victor helped to found a New York lodge, *La Sincerité,* in 1801, and in 1813 he joined Washington Lodge Number One at Wilmington, later transferring to the Franklin Lodge there. But by then the Masons had dropped their requirement of a formal religious affiliation; a Mason simply had to believe in a moral law governing the universe.

And that is about as far as the du Ponts' religious beliefs went.

They have sometimes been described as agnostics, but it is more accurate to describe them as free-thinkers or deists, like Jefferson and Franklin and many other of the foremost men of the late eighteenth century. This was a time of revolutionary ideas in religion and philosophy as well as in politics and economics. Deists believed in a somewhat vague Divine Order in the universe, but they rejected revealed religion and its institutional forms.

This attitude was strongest in Irénée and his sons. Alfred apparently never enjoyed the pleasure of giving the unknown reverend an irreverent baptism despite his threat, but he and Henry made it plain, in the words of a family chronicle, that they "looked askance" at religious instruction. From boyhood, however, Alexis showed signs of weakening. When he was at the Dwight School at New Haven, he asked permission to be baptized. His father was so horrified at the idea that he made the then arduous journey all the way to Connecticut just to prevent it.

Irénée's letters are full of sarcastic references to Jesuits and other men of the cloth. In a note to a friend in 1827, he said that the schools of France used to be unexcelled, "but who can tell what may have become of those schools under the withering hand of the Bourbons, who—as much as they have been able to do it—have given up to priests the education of the youth of France."

At times, to be sure, Irénée grew curious about religion. In 1821, on a business visit to Providence, Rhode Island, he slipped into a church just to observe the service. Unfortunately, he entered during the sermon and his squeaking shoes drew the attention of the entire congregation. Cursing himself silently, the red-faced intruder, with a forced smile, declined the whispered invitations to join the faithful in their pews. His intrusion disrupted the service so much that the clergyman paused in his sermon for a moment until du Pont, in desperation, finally edged into a pew. "I left as soon as I decently could," he said afterward.

Despite his personal antipathy to religion, Irénée himself was indirectly responsible for the establishment of what has long been called "the du Pont church"—Christ Church Christiana Hundred, an Episcopalian congregation. It came about in this way:

After the death of her husband of a few weeks, Victorine du Pont Bauduy had been so overwhelmed with grief that nothing could arouse her to an interest in life. As her depression went on for weeks and then for months, her parents grew increasingly concerned.

Irénée was mulling over this problem, one Sunday in 1815, as he took his way to the home of John Siddall on a social visit. Siddall was an Englishman who operated a cotton mill near his home on the east bank of the Brandywine, downstream from the du Ponts. To his surprise, Irénée found a number of children in the dining room of the Siddall home. They were being taught reading, writing, and "ciphering." This was a Sunday school, for in those days before free public education became general, Sunday schools were simply classes held on the Sabbath; religious instruction was only a part of the curriculum.

Of course, any son of Pierre Samuel would have been an advocate of education, but Irénée had more than enthusiasm for education as a motive when he offered Siddall a room in the cotton factory of Duplanty, McCall and Company for the use of the school.

Irénée hoped that the Sunday school might be a means to give the widowed Victorine a new interest and lift her out of her grief.

On his return home, he told Sophie and the rest of the family about the school with such excitement and conviction that all four of his daughters agreed to go with him on a visit the following Sunday. The sight of the classes—the realization that it lay within her power to free hundreds of youngsters and adults, too, from the curse of illiteracy—had the desired effect upon Victorine. A week later she was teaching her own class in the school. In 1817, under the name of the Brandywine Manufacturers' Sunday School, Irénée —religious skeptic though he still remained—incorporated the organization. He contributed the land and most of the money for a school building.

Victorine's interest did not wane. Before long she was superintendent of the school, and she remained active in its affairs to the end of her life.

She never remarried. The young woman, who had always been surrounded by admirers and would-be suitors, who had won the hearts of both Raphael Duplanty and Ferdinand Bauduy, had become a self-conscious, unsure woman. One day, when acting as hostess for her father, she was so unnerved by the presence of a young man that she "deposited the contents of the teapot into the sugar bowl."

Victorine's sisters helped her in the Sunday school work, and the school led to their joining the Episcopalian Church soon after they began teaching there. Also Eleuthera's husband, Dr. Thomas Mc-Kie Smith, was a warden at Trinity Church in Wilmington, and Charles Breck, rector of Trinity and of St. John's Church in Wilmington, was connected with the du Ponts, his brother William having married Gabrielle Josephine du Pont, the child of Amelia's unfortunate marriage with the bigamist Clifford.

In time, church authorities decided that a minister should be sent to the Brandywine to establish a new parish. The Reverend Samuel Crawford Brincklé, a simple, godly man, was assigned to the task. In his diary under the date of February 26, 1849, he wrote of having asked Dr. Smith if "the Messrs. du Pont would assist" in founding the church. "He replied that they would do nothing, and that if they did not oppose us it would be as much as we could expect," Mr. Brincklé noted bleakly.

Mr. Brincklé had, however, one steadfast ally in his gentle crusade—Victorine. That lonely, inhibited woman conceived at their first meeting an affection for the minister that burned warmly for the rest of their lives. There was nothing improper about it: the parson was happily married to a very understanding woman and "Madame Bauduy," as everyone called her, was too restrained and respectful to permit herself to think of any closer relationship. It is a situation not uncommon with clergymen. In her heart, Victorine loved him; that is clear. She always called him "Dear Mr. B." One year on her birthday, he gave her roses with a card that read, *"Souvenir d'un ami."* She replied, "Nothing could be handsomer than the delicate pink of the flowers, nor more precious than its name."

One of the du Pont men—Victor's son, Samuel Francis, now a Navy captain—became a pillar of the church and a useful ally when he was not away at sea, for he could influence his male cousins, being also their brother-in-law.

One of those cousins, Alfred V. du Pont, was in the odd position of having religious services held in his own home despite his personal skepticism. His wife, Margaretta, was the daughter of Daniel

Lammot, Jr., one of the original organizers in the United States of the Church of the New Jerusalem, a Swedenborgian communion with strongly spiritualist overtones. For a time, meetings of the New Church, as the group was often called, were held in the home of Alfred and Margaretta, who, during her lifetime, was the largest single contributor to the church.

Three years after Mr. Brincklé arrived on the Brandywine, an accident took a leading member of his faith. Eleuthera gave some medicine to her husband, Dr. Smith, because he felt sick. The medicine turned out to be a fatal dose of aconite, an alkaloid also known as monkshood or wolf's bane. The poison was in the house because doctors often used it as a sedative and a pain-reliever. As soon as he took the drug, Dr. Smith realized what had happened. He told the people about him to give him emetics, but efforts to save the doctor were futile. On January 20, 1852, he died.

His death had a powerful effect on his brother-in-law, Alexis I. du Pont, who had witnessed his agony. Inclined toward religion since childhood, Alexis several times had narrowly escaped death in explosions that had killed other men in the powder mills. Now, saying, "The man who follows my business should be ready at any moment to meet his God," Alexis was baptized and confirmed at the same time and became a vestryman of the newly established Christ Church Christiana Hundred.

When the church building was being erected—or so the story goes—a stonemason named Robert Merchant produced a full bottle of whisky to inspire himself and his mates. Just then Alexis came into sight. Merchant hastily hid the bottle inside the thick stone wall they were building. Although the men didn't know it, Alexis had seen the bottle. Without indicating he realized that anything was amiss, Alexis sat down and proceeded to chat with the men, watching them at work as they slowly and unhappily built up the stone wall and sealed it with mortar, interring the whisky for as long as Christ Church should last.

Like many converts, Alexis became somewhat intolerant in religious matters. In time he became displeased with Christ Church because it was low church, and in arguing with his cousins over the theological issue, he tended more toward Trinity Church which was high. He could be quite fierce in his religious battles.

Eventually religion became a public issue along the Brandywine. The powder mill workers, originally French, had been almost wholly supplanted by Irish powdermen. The first Irish workmen had been hired by Irénée in 1803. By 1839, only a handful of du Pont employees were not Irish. They were well suited for the explosives industry, the du Ponts believed. As a newspaper of the time put it, "They [the Irish] are the only persons who will do just what they are bid, in every respect. This is absolutely necessary in this business, both for security and for excellence of workmanship." But throughout the country, the Irish, the first mass immigrants, were generally despised, being stereotyped as dirty, dishonest, treacherous, pushy, and so on. They were "ignorant and uncivilized," said Eleuthera du Pont Smith, referring to the du Pont house servants who were the sisters and daughters of Irish powdermen.

They were also Catholics. This alone probably would have caused prejudice against them because of the strong feelings that most people then had about religion, but public sentiment against them was intensified by the Catholic position on education.

In 1829, Delaware had become the first state to provide for general, free, state-aided public schools. In 1840, Archbishop Hughes demanded that tax funds be allocated to parochial schools too. Many Catholic clergymen began attacking the public schools. Captain Samuel Francis du Pont, in letters to friends, spoke bitterly of the "arrogance of their priests in interfering with the district schools."

The controversy came to a head in 1852, when the parish priest, the Reverend John S. Walsh, preaching in the Church of St. Joseph's-on-the-Brandywine which had been erected with financial help from the du Pont family, showed his congregation a book used in the public schools and then ripped out of it the pages dealing with the lives of Martin Luther and Samuel Adams. It was the opening gun in a school election campaign in which religious partisanship was the determining factor. Most of the du Ponts threw their influence on the side of the Protestant candidates who won by a very narrow margin. Later that year, Mr. Brincklé wrote in his diary, "Alexis du Pont called. Was very pleasant. Spoke of the Roman Catholics here, and their complete subjection to the priests, and opposition to the public schools. Said it had taught him one thing, which was, when vacancies occurred among the work-people, to give preference to Protestants."

Fortunately, that policy was never put into effect. The du Ponts often have been more progressive and enlightened in their actions than in their statements even to the present day, but their impulsiveness has inspired many a rash public pronouncement.

Actually the clan would never have taken an anti-Catholic stand, for part of the family was, and is, Catholic. As early as 1828, a missionary priest was celebrating the Mass in the home of Madame Victor du Pont. Victor's daughter, Amelia, was a devout Catholic and a benefactor of that church.

Victor's son, Charles I. du Pont, as a state senator, introduced a bill, subsequently passed, which freed Catholic organizations from certain disabilities under which they had suffered previously. And the following year he declared his opposition to the Know-Nothings because of their proposed "proscription of all foreigners and particularly the poor oppressed Irish Catholics." Charles recalled how his father and grandfather fled from misgovernment in France and found a welcome in America. He even became a trustee of St. Joseph's although he was not a Catholic. At the same time, he was serving as a vestryman of Christ Church, but he was not an Episcopalian, either.

CHAPTER XIX

POWDER AND PANIC

WHILE THE LITTLE COMMUNITY on the Brandywine lived through its own small crises, great changes were taking place in the wide world beyond, changes that affected the fortunes of the du Ponts and their company.

In the year of Irénée's death, 1834, a great panic had caused hundreds of business failures in Philadelphia, New York and Washington. There was a brief recovery and then, three years later, a speculative boom in land, canals, turnpikes and railroads ended in another crash so bad that banks suspended specie—coin—payments for a time. And so it continued; every few years—boom, then bust. In 1841, at the low point of a four-year depression, a business man wrote to Alfred, "All the states are insolvent, if by insolvent we mean unable to pay their bills." The following year found the federal government itself unable to meet its bills, including those for du Pont gunpowder, and the firm was notified that "there is a meeting of the holders of bills against the government called to take place in Washington on June 23." Economic conditions improved as the 1840's passed, but there was a recession in 1854, and a brief, sharp panic in 1857.

Under those chaotic conditions, it required careful husbanding of a company's resources to insure its survival. E.I. du Pont de Nemours and Company had that kind of management; the firm's profits in good years were stored away to help tide the company over the bad.

And the good years were very good, for the country was growing, expanding, and du Pont powder was essential to its progress.

Mid-century, the United States filled out from sea to sea. The Oregon Territory was opened up. Texas was annexed. The Mormon state of Deseret was founded. The discovery of gold set off a world-wide wave of excitement that peopled California. The Treaty of Guadalupe Hidalgo added enormous tracts of land to the southwestern part of the United States, and so did the Gadsden Purchase.

The need for gunpowder was everywhere. Before heading into the mountains, gold and silver miners packed du Pont blasting powder in kegs strapped across the backs of their burros. With powder from the Brandywine, Missouri farmers blew tree stumps and heavy rocks out of the ground. Using du Pont's Eagle Powder in their pistols and rifles, bearded men killed bear in the Rockies, lawmen brought order to the wild towns of the frontier West, and blue-uniformed troopers imposed the white man's rule on the Indians. The great ditches for the canals linking the Ohio and the Mississippi with the Great Lakes were blown through rock. The right-of-way for the railroads then spreading across the entire United States as fast as the West became tamed, was cleared with the aid of the products of Wilmington. It is no exaggeration to say that the West was won with du Pont powder.

Moreover, war—although it might be the universal curse of mankind—brought prosperity to the du Ponts. As the War of 1812 had produced a rush of orders at a critical moment in the firm's early years, so other wars and the threat of wars increased the demand for du Pont war materiel made in the heart of Quakerland. In 1836, there was fighting in Texas against the Mexican government. Because of friction between the United States and the Canadian governments, especially along the Niagara Frontier and the Maine-Quebec border, 1838 to 1840 were tense years.

But the Mexican War gave the Brandywine a greater prosperity than it had ever known before. During that conflict the government bought from the du Ponts more than a million pounds of gunpowder. Additional mill buildings were built well below the Hagley Yard; the new group was called the Lower Works. Even after the end of the war, the company was producing more than 10,000 pounds of powder a day. The mills were being operated around the clock; the men worked by the light of kerosene lamps for fourteen hours daily, a hair-raising experience when dealing with highly explosive material.

Shortly after the war broke out, the firm received from Havana an order for 200,000 pounds of powder, a very large quantity for ostensibly peaceful use. Suspecting from its size that the order was intended for the Mexican government, Alfred, as the head of the firm, went to Washington and told the President, James K. Polk, about it. The Secretaries of War and of the Navy were called to the White House to discuss the matter; they agreed that du Pont's suspicions were undoubtedly correct. Returning to Delaware, Alfred penned a refusal to Morrison, De Carrick and Company of Havana. "However unjust our proceedings may be, and however shameful our invasion of Mexican territory," he wrote, "we cannot make powder to be used against our own country."

To those who think of the du Ponts as munitions makers, the letter must seem curious, bristling as it does with frank disapproval of the "Manifest Destiny" aggression against Mexico. The du Ponts had not forgotten the idealism of the founder of the family.

However, they never saw any contradiction between disapproving of a military adventure and producing the gunpowder that makes such an outbreak possible. As the undertaker profits from death but is not blamed for it, and as the clergyman makes his livelihood from the sins of others but is himself innocent of iniquity, so, they felt, the munitions maker ought not to be forced to bear the burden of guilt for war. Indeed, they were proud of their patriotism: they never sold to enemies of the United States nor to any foreign government without the permission of Washington. On the other hand, their resources were always at the call of their own country. They saw themselves as minutemen, ready to provide the United States with the necessities of war whenever the country found itself in a fight.

After the Havana order, another attempt was made by Mexican agents to get du Pont gunpowder for the enemy. This time a Frenchman and a Spaniard placed the order with New York and

Philadelphia agents. Again, the amount requested was 200,000 pounds; again, it was turned down.

At least one du Pont saw combat in the Mexican War. He was Samuel Francis du Pont, son of Victor and husband of Irénée's daughter Sophie. A commander at the time of the Mexican War, he was named skipper of the sloop-of-war *Cyane*, a vessel of five hundred and thirty-nine tons carrying eighteen guns. In a matter of months, du Pont succeeded in destroying thirty enemy ships, sweeping the waters off California and Mexico's Pacific Coast clean of hostile craft. Moreover, loving a good fight, he was even willing to leave his ship and take to land if there was a good prospect of tackling the enemy there.

Du Pont learned that a party of Americans, including women and children, was confined to a mission house three miles inland from San Jose on the Gulf of California. There for twenty-one days they had been fighting off Mexican assaults. Without hesitation, the commander took every available man from his ship—one hundred and two in all—and marched them overland to the mission under fire. The sailors were welcomed as saviors, and with reason. They found the beleaguered Americans sick with fever and dysentery, with many men wounded and two lost as captives to the Mexicans. The enemy outnumbered the trapped men six to one. Food was becoming scarce and the well from which the Americans drew their water had come under fire.

In his official report to Washington afterwards, du Pont described the group's leader, Lieutenant Charles Heywood, as "indomitable." The same adjective might have been applied to Commander du Pont who considered his little amphibious operation a lark. With hardly any casualties to his own band, despite heavy enemy fire, du Pont not only carried the rescued Americans back to his ship but even managed to kill a score or more of the Mexican government troops. Subsequently he organized a number of other expeditions into the interior of the country to clear it of hostile forces.

The du Pont reports went to the commander-in-chief of our naval forces in the Pacific, who happened to be Commodore William B. Shubrick, uncle of Irvine Shubrick, du Pont's brother-in-law. During the Mexican War, Commander du Pont's nephew,

Irvine's son Thomas, was killed in action during the battle of Vera Cruz and his body was brought back to Wilmington for burial. Handsome, charming and gifted, young Tom and his twenty-one-year-old cousin, Mary Van Dyke du Pont, daughter of Charles I. du Pont, had been secretly in love—a fact which the family discovered only when Mary collapsed upon hearing of Tom's death. Mary never married; in fact, she never recovered fully from the shock of her loss.

Six years after the Mexican War, another great conflict brought more orders into the du Pont offices. This time the United States was not involved, so the firm was able to sell to both sides with a clear conscience. This was the Crimean War in which the British, the French and the Turks were allied against the Russians. English and French powdermakers were unable to meet the demand for ammunition; orders crossed the Atlantic to the du Ponts. But the Russians needed powder, too, and the du Ponts were delighted to sell to them as well. During the year-long siege of Sevastopol, the Russians became critically short of gunpowder. The Czar's forces ordered a shipload but the British got wind of the transaction. The admiralty dispatched several frigates to lie off Chesapeake Bay in international waters, ready to intercept the Russia-bound cargo. Alfred's son Lammot, then twenty-five years old, volunteered to take the munitions ship through the blockade, although one lucky cannon-ball hit would blow her up. Nevertheless, Lammot assumed charge of the ship, and, with his personal knowledge of Chesapeake waters, managed to evade the British men-of-war. The powder reached its destination safely.

Throughout these years the du Pont product remained essentially the same, although it was being gradually improved. When a Swiss inventor, Frederick Schoenbein, announced a new kind of explosive in 1846, the news aroused considerable interest in this country. Du Pont received frequent inquiries about the new development. Alfred told his customers that the discovery was "brilliant," but years would pass before guncotton could come into common use because of the high cost of manufacturing it. Alfred was right. Almost half a century elapsed before the use of guncotton became widespread.

Not only the cost of guncotton, but also its explosive weakness, its absorption of moisture, its corrosive action on gun barrels and its fumes were serious faults, as Alfred analyzed it. He suggested an experiment: "Take a small lock [of guncotton] between your thumb and finger, holding it with no more pressure than you would hold a pen in writing; fire one end and you will find that the fire will be cut off at the point of compression, the piece held between the fingers remaining unburnt; now, what dependence can be placed on a substance so easily affected by pressure?"

The company's stock in trade remained black powder. One of the major problems was transporting it to the customers. Because of gunpowder's explosive nature, du Pont usually shipped it by water whenever possible. But canals and even rivers were often frozen in winter. And if the powder was carried by sailing ship, a jittery captain might jettison it when a storm threatened. In the early days, ships were loaded in the Delaware River off Marcus Hook, a settlement just over the Pennsylvania line. Barrels of powder were carried from wagons to small boats, then out to the ships. The wagons didn't leave the Brandywine until the vessels signaled that they were ready to take the cargo aboard. If the weather became bad before the wagons reached Marcus Hook, the ships might be forced to weigh anchor and leave without the cargo. To avoid this sort of thing, the company built a pier and a magazine on the river three miles above Wilmington, just above the present city line at Edgemoor.

As railroads began to spin their webs out across the country, du Pont occasionally employed them in the transportation of gunpowder. But those first trains, spewing hot cinders and sparks into the air, added to the natural hazards of moving explosives. Many railroads even refused to carry powder. Occasionally they would add to the danger by announcing that "friction matches will not be carried except in the cars that carry gunpowder." Which was something like saying that alcoholics would only be accepted as passengers in cars with whisky as cargo. Rail transportation was more expensive than alternate means, too: the Camden and Amboy Railroad in 1835 charged a dollar twenty-five a hundredweight to carry gunpowder from Camden to New York, compared with about fifty cents by schooner from Wilmington to New York. Francis Gurney Smith, du Pont's Philadelphia agent, detailed that railroad's arrangements in a letter to the Brandywine: "It would be necessary and unavoidable that they should use a locomotive engine which should be placed behind the train of cars, so as to *propel* instead of *drawing* them. Precaution . . . would be taken by covering the cars, which are tight-roofed and sided, with cloths dampened so as to prevent accidents from sparks."

The most dangerous, but dependable, method of transportation was mule train. Six mules were used to pull a Conestoga wagon. It was slow transportation: six weeks were required to convey a wagonload of powder from the Brandywine to Pittsburgh. As the wagons creaked and bounced over the rutted, rocky roads, the teamster cheerfully cursing in the classic manner of muleskinners, other travelers scrambled to get out of the way. Everyone—even the powdermen whose own jobs were, God knows, too dangerous for most people's taste—respected the mule drivers as a rare and brave breed. They were not even required to harness their mules or to take care of them in the big stables near the office.

The job justified its reputation for danger. More than one teamster joined his animals in a sudden trip to Kingdom Come. In May 1854, three du Pont wagons, loaded with four hundred and fifty kegs of powder, were rolling through the heart of quiet, orderly Wilmington, jouncing on the cobblestones, when they suddenly blew up, digging a huge hole in the street, knocking down nearby walls and houses and killing two bystanders as well as the three drivers and their eighteen mules. Wilmington, busy with its own affairs, had hitherto not been very conscious of the danger of having powder mills so near; but now the community was bitter at the du Ponts for sending their wagons through tranquil city streets. Newspapers in all parts of the country carried the report of the mishap, and everywhere frightened burghers passed laws barring powder wagons from their thoroughfares.

It was the du Ponts' first experience with adverse publicity. It would not be the last.

CHAPTER XX

ACROSS THE CREEK

B Y MID-CENTURY, explosions were an old story to the du Ponts. There was an accident on an average of once every fourteen months, and the average blast killed three persons. Recognizing that the hazardous nature of powder-mill work might discourage some good men, the du Ponts made the material rewards of work in their yards unusually attractive. The powdermen were well paid and they were treated well on—and off—the job. If a man was maimed in an accident or otherwise disabled, easier work was found for him. Writing to Dougal White, whose brother had died a natural death while in the du Pont employ, Alfred said, "During the last year, his health declining, he became of comparatively little use; still he was not discharged, for we always, in case of illness or accidents, remember the past services of our people."

This paternalism is hard to accept a century later, but to the workmen of that time, struggling in the dark ages of the Industrial Revolution when the work day was long, pay was low, pensions were rare, and workmen's compensation and unemployment insurance laws were a half century or more in the future, the du Pont policies were humanitarian and enlightened.

The widows of workmen received small pensions as well as tenancy of a company house. These were not like the ramshackle houses in most company-owned mill towns; these were substantial stone houses built to withstand the tremendous shock waves of the explosions—houses, some of which remain standing today, still providing sound and sturdy shelter. In her house many a widow took bachelor powdermen as boarders; the company sent prospective lodgers to any widow who wanted to take them in, and more than one of them found a second husband this way. For the widows there were also milk from du Pont cows and vegetables from du Pont gardens and fields and firewood from du Pont woods. Their daughters might find work as maids in du Pont family homes and their sons could expect work in the powder mills when they grew big enough.

There were many causes for the blasts. Once an investigation disclosed that the metal rims on the wheels of a cart had struck a spark when the cart was backed against the stone wall of a glazing mill. To avoid such a spark, the horses that pulled cars on a little narrow-gauge railway running through the yards were unshod. The powdermen had no metal in their clothing, and the tools they used—even their shovels—were entirely wooden. Nevertheless, metal sometimes crept into the operations. An old nail or a scrap of broken iron might slip through in the mixing process, throwing a spark at a critical moment. If a mill building was not carefully cleaned of powder before carpenters and masons began to repair the structure, sudden death might be the result. Occasionally there were strong grounds for suspecting that a mill had been blown deliberately: once by a psychotic powderman who had a grudge against two men employed in the building that was wrecked; two or three times by disgruntled workmen who had been fired. Once the partners came to the conclusion that an explosion had been part of a successful plan of suicide by one of the victims.

It took very little to cause an accident—a spark, and suddenly there was a deafening boom echoing and re-echoing in the gorge until no one could tell where it came from. The mill spewed forth flame and smoke, and everything inside the building was hurled across the creek—machinery, men, stones, and wooden wall and roof—all mixed together in a ghastly mass. At the same time the shock of the blast sped out like a tidal wave of wind and sound, shattering windows and rattling crockery, often for considerable distances. "The impact was terrific," Henry Seidel Canby recalled.

"I have felt it like a blow on the face, in Wilmington, three miles away."

The casualties were not always limited to the men inside the danger zone. Despite its sturdy construction, a powderman's house sometimes was unable to withstand the tremendous shock, and more than once a dead wife and baby were found beneath the fallen stone.

There were alarm bells to tell of fire in the powder yards. But when an explosion occurred without warning, no one had to notify the next-of-kin that an accident had occurred. The sound could be heard, the shock could be felt for miles, and the willows would bend with the rush of wind. Billowing clouds of smoke rose out of the valley of the Brandywine, and soon the bitter, stinging, irritating smell of burnt powder would be everywhere.

And the women of Henry Clay and of Rising Sun and of the other settlements along the creek would feel their throats close for a moment in the terrible lightheadedness of fear. They would stand stockstill for one awful instant, chilled with panic, and then run white-faced from their snug stone homes down the hill to the gates of the du Pont powder works, there to wait, weeping or biting their lips, for an agonizingly long time until a member of the du Pont family came out to read off in a husky voice the names of the brave men whose luck had run out.

The funeral was always paid for by the company. In the latter part of the nineteenth century, the undertaker was Michael Dougherty who sometimes worked as a powderman himself and also ran a barber shop in Long Row on the Creek Road. A member of the du Pont family always attended the funeral and made a visit to the widow to assure her of the firm's continuing interest in her welfare and in the care of her children. The du Ponts considered this part of their heritage an extremely painful but solemn and unavoidable responsibility.

The powdermen never spoke of being blown to bits. Their euphemism for that fate was to "go across the creek." One rolling mill boss always chased away any stray dog that came near. "When I go across the creek, I don't want no hound's bones mixed up with mine," he used to say, spitting a stream of tobacco juice into the mill race: for obvious reasons, the men were not permitted to smoke, so most of them chewed plug. The men were wont to say that day-dreaming was dangerous; when a man got to musing, it was time to look for him "on the other side of the creek."

Under the circumstances, a body of legend and myth inevitably grew up about the works. Superstitious powdermen would talk of one night crew that saw an unbelievable sight in the middle of the night—two young girls, garbed in white, dancing from boulder to boulder in the middle of the Brandywine. After their watch was over, the crew told their wives and other workmen about the apparitions. On the following night, nine men went "across the creek" when a mill blew up.

And there was the story that Mrs. Pierre Boissou used to tell about Mickey Mullin. Mrs. Boissou, the widow of a powderman, took in boarders and Mickey was one of them. One day Mickey received a letter from Ireland; it was from his mother, pleading with him to come back to the "Ould Sod" so that she could see him once more before she died. Mickey decided to think it over for a few days. Then he came off the night shift one morning, walked into the house with his lunch pail and told Mrs. Boissou, "You know, last night I heard me mother crying."

"Where?" his landlady asked.

"Out on the rocks," Mickey replied.

"It was only an owl," Mrs. Boissou said reassuringly.

"Just the same," the shaken powderman insisted, "I'm going back to Ireland soon."

That night Mickey perished when his rolling mill exploded.

When a man's time was up, he'd go, the powdermen always said. Once a man quit the company because he'd decided the work was too dangerous. A week later as he was walking up the east bank of the creek on his way to see a man about a job, a powder mill blew up across the stream. An enormous piece of stone from the mill's wall was hurled through the air. It struck the man's head, killing him instantly.

It took a strong stomach and steel nerves to clean up the works after an explosion. This was a small community in which a man knew all his fellows, from the senior partner to the lowliest yard hand. The dead were not strangers: they were men with whom one had spoken a short time ago, whose families one knew. Next time it may be my turn to go, each man told himself as he faced the grisly task of helping to collect the remains. Parts of the bodies might be recovered as far away as the lawns of the du Pont homes on the top of the hill; sometimes scarcely anything was found, just hideous stains on the stone walls. All the mills had been rebuilt many times after explosions, and the whitewash on the rough walls covered the blood of many courageous men.

Living with danger, these powdermen could not take chances. They had no use for a co-worker who was stupid, foolish or reckless, for such a mate threatened the lives of all. A man known to possess undesirable characteristics didn't hold on to his job in the powder yard very long. But sometimes he was there a little too long. In 1852 Mills #7 and #8 exploded, killing two men. Investigation disclosed that a third man working in that part of the yards, Christopher Cowan, had caused the accident by carelessness. Cowan was fired, but he could not leave behind the memory of the victims' mangled bodies after the blast. Haunted by his sense of guilt, Cowan hanged himself a year later.

In 1847, an explosion in one mill set off a chain of blasts in other nearby buildings in the Upper Yard, a not uncommon characteristic of accidents. The disaster took place early in the morning; sheer luck spared Alexis I. du Pont. He had left his home later than usual, having paused to prepare an egg for the breakfast of one of his children. He reached the yard just as the detonations began. Later he found that one of the buildings destroyed by the explosions was the mill in which he had planned to begin his work that day. Others were not as fortunate: eighteen men had lost their lives.

A vivid account of that accident—and of the reactions of the du Ponts to such occurrences—appears in a letter from Charles I. du Pont's wife, Ann, to a cousin. Writing from her home, Louviers, she says the blasts began at six o'clock. Her husband had just risen, but she was still in bed.

"It was a bright morning," Ann wrote, "one of those days when nature seems to be full of smiles, and I was debating whether I would lose in sleep these sweet hours or get up. In an instant, without the slightest warning, there came a shock that seemed so terrific in its nature that I could only compare it to the meeting of heaven and earth. It appeared not to be local but a crash of the world—our window sashes, chairs, ceiling, all in the twinkling of an eye laid prostrate. The concussion, the breaking of glass and furniture, the horrid reports of the powder, the flash and the sudden pressure of the atmosphere, with the bursting of the doors— all formed a combination of horrors. . . .

"After the first instant of the explosion I looked up and found my husband pale and bleeding. It was, however, only a scratch from a piece of broken glass. He was pale from fear of his family on the other side [of the creek]. He knew not who was spared, yet a kind Providence saved them all, though their houses are dreadfully shattered. *We* have but one habitable room and that is made so by carpets and blankets nailed to the windows, and I have written this letter at 11 o'clock in the day by candlelight.

"While we have thankful hearts for the safety of those dear to us, we must mourn for the grief of the families who have lost husbands and fathers in this calamity. The shrieks of the wives and the children so soon made widows and orphans rose in sad succession to the preceding horror. Human heads, arms, and feet were found on that peaceful-looking bank of the Brandywine where you and I have walked. . . ."

Alfred had seen many sickening accidents before this, but he was aging now and tired from overwork, and peculiarly susceptible to this nervous strain, this tension that never let up. He had always been a kind, thoughtful, imaginative person; he had been able to function in the powder works only by closing his mind to its hazards. But this gruesome catastrophe could not be forgotten: he never recovered from the assault on his emotions.

For another two or three years Alfred attempted to carry on, but the effort was now beyond his strength. The memory of human obliteration, like a Rorschach in red, could not be exorcized. Alfred's nerves were shot. His emotional distress took physical form. The man who had been frail as a boy now became a semi-invalid to escape from the nightmare of the powder works.

Even the words of the Litany from *The Book of Common Prayer* made Alfred shudder when he heard them, the words that the du Ponts always regarded as their family prayer: ". . . From sudden death, good Lord, deliver us."

The withdrawal of Alfred from active participation in the firm in 1850 made a shifting of jobs necessary. Henry became the new head. The other members of the triumvirate now were Alexis I. du Pont and Eleuthère Irénée du Pont II, the son of Alfred, then a mere twenty-one years. If he had been older, he might have taken over the reins, but under the circumstances that was out of the question. Henry, who had been restless but submissive under Alfred's rule only by a great effort in self-control, had long been eager to run the whole show himself.

Alfred spent the next six years in declining health. On the day of his funeral, October 6, 1856, the mourners had hardly returned from the family graveyard when one of the most terrifying sounds that can be heard in a munitions factory broke forth—the clanging of the fire alarm. A great fire had broken out in the Hagley Yard and the powder was threatened. The blaze had begun by spontaneous combustion in the composition house and then spread to the sawmill. Flames were reaching high in the air, scattering sparks on the brisk fall breeze. At any moment an explosion might be set off.

The men of the du Pont family, as always, pitched into the fight against catastrophe alongside their workmen. Each was conscious that the next moment might be his last. Alexis directed the efforts of the men to contain, arrest, and extinguish the blaze, and he himself was in the thick of the battle. He kept men at work pouring water on the roof of the press room, a frame building, so sparks could not take effect. Alfred's second son, Lammot, joined James Stewart, one of the workmen, on the roof of the old graining house, wetting the roof and walls. Suddenly the roof gave way under Lammot and he plunged through it, down into a mixing box. In the dark, powder-filled building, he stumbled about, until finally he found his way outside, where the crackling of flames, the splashing of water, the shouts of the men created pandemonium. At last the fire was out; the composition house and the sawmill were ruined, but they were a small price to pay for saving the works from an explosion. As he turned away from the smouldering ruins, the weary Alexis realized that his hands hurt; he looked at them and became aware, for the first time, that he had burned them beating out some of the flames with his bare hands.

That night Sophie du Pont wrote in her diary that every male member of the du Pont family had been in the fight against the fire. "Explosions," she pointed out, "might very conceivably have wiped out the entire clan."

The tribe would survive, but some of its men would perish, along with their workmen, in explosions during the years ahead. Indeed, only ten months after that fire, an accident claimed the life of a du Pont for the first time.

This grim event took place on Saturday, August 22, 1857. On Monday the masons were to begin repairs on a graining mill in the Hagley Yard. Late Saturday afternoon Alexis, on an inspection of the works, looked into the mill and saw that the mixing box, a huge, heavy iron pot, had not been removed. The box was encrusted with powder. If the masons happened to knock against it accidentally with a stone, a hammer, or a trowel, an explosion might result. Alexis summoned seven workmen to help him lift the box and carry it out of the building. Afterwards, powdermen said that the box was so heavy that twenty men should have been assigned to the task. But there were only eight, including Alexis, grunting and puffing with the exertion of moving the awkward receptacle off its bed and through the door of the mill. There wasn't much room to maneuver. One end was already through the door when the side of the box struck the stone wall of the doorway. There was a spark, and the powder in the box flared up. The men dropped the box and frantically tried to beat out the sudden flash of flames with their bare hands. A tongue of fire sizzled across the powder-covered floor to a tub of waste material. The tub blew up, killing three of the men instantly. A fourth man was hurled thirty feet by the blast. He rose to his feet in a daze and staggered away helplessly. He got as far as his home and dropped dead at the feet of his wife.

Alexis du Pont had himself been blown thirty feet. With his clothes ablaze, he leaped into the mill race to put out the flames and save himself. Then, as he stood in the mill race, he saw that a burning brand from the wrecked mill had been hurled onto the roof of the press room nearby. There was a full charge of powder in the press. If that blew up, the whole works might be destroyed.

Dripping water, Alexis climbed out of the mill race and ran to the press room to get rid of the burning fragment. He had just reached the building when it exploded.

Alexis suffered a compound fracture of the thigh, an injury to his back, and two broken ribs, both of which punctured his lungs. He was also burned so severely that most of his body was "blackened." Nevertheless, he retained his composure. To check the bleeding from his mangled leg, he instructed his seventeen-year-old son, Eugene, who had come running at the sound of the first blast, to take off one of his suspenders and fashion a tourniquet of it. The surviving workmen—all the men who had been helping Alexis were dead or terribly injured—laid their boss on a window shutter and carried him home.

The fact that Alexis' injuries were so obviously mortal caused sorrow to everyone who had known him. A tough, friendly, unpretentious man with natural leadership ability, he had always been able to get more work out of the men with a joking word than others could do with a stern order. He had an impish sense of humor. One day a powderman's wife complained to Alexis that her son had swallowed gunpowder.

"This is a bad place, where a boy can gulp down gunpowder," she said. "What am I going to do, Mr. Alexis?"

"Ma'am," he replied, "I suggest that you give him two rifle balls to swallow and make sure you don't point him at any other human being for a week."

In his dying, as in his living, Alexis won the admiration of his men. For twenty-four hours during which he remained fully conscious and in great pain, Alexis lay on his death bed. He asked that the men with whom he had grown up and with whom he had worked be brought to his bedside so that he could say good-by to them. One by one the powdermen, in their rough work clothes and heavy boots, grimy, weary and full of grief at this latest accident, filed into the bedroom, to press silently the hand of Mr. Alexis and then walk out, swallowing hard.

On Sunday night, Mr. Brincklé wrote in his diary, "At six o'clock a summons to attend the deathbed of Alexis and to administer the communion. Reached there twenty minutes past six. Found him perfectly composed."

Less than two hours later Alexis died. He was forty-one years old. He was the first du Pont to be buried from Christ Church.

Standing by the grave in Sand Hole Woods, the other du Pont men remembered something that Alexis had told them as he lay dying. He had said that, after the first explosion when he was putting out the flames in his clothes in the mill race and saw the fire threatening the press room, he suddenly remembered a line from the Catechism: ". . . to do my duty in that state of life unto which it shall please God to call me."

CHAPTER XXI

WHIGS, REPUBLICANS, DEMOCRATS

L UCRETIA MOTT was both an abolitionist and a suffragette, and thus doubly damned in the eyes of most slave holders. In 1841, when she appeared to speak against slavery from the steps of the courthouse at Dover, capital of the slave state of Delaware, it was not surprising that a mob threatened violence. Any untoward incident, however, was prevented by a man who stepped forward to stand by the side of Mrs. Mott and demand a hearing for her. It was a truly courtly gesture, for the man was Henry M. Ridgely, one of the most influential politicians in the legislature, a slave owner himself and a Southern sympathizer. As a gentleman, Ridgely regarded it as his duty not only to defend the Quaker woman's right to speak, but even to offer her the hospitality of his home for the night.

A rather large group of relatives and friends took dinner at the Ridgely house that night, to argue politely but warmly with Mrs. Mott. Among them were Ridgely's daughter Ann and her two most ardent suitors, one of them State Senator Charles I. du Pont. So far Ann had been unable to decide between the two men.

In the course of the evening, Mrs. Mott sat down where she

thought her chair ought to be. But she had misjudged the spot, and, missing the chair completely, she took an embarrassing pratfall to the floor.

While his rival laughed at the discomfiture of the abolitionist, du Pont helped her to her feet with such kindness and courtesy that her chagrin was somewhat lessened. At that moment, Ann Ridgely made up her mind to marry Charles du Pont.

They had met a short time before when he went to Dover to take his seat in the senate for the first time. A few days after his arrival, he was invited to dine at the Ridgely home, and there he saw Ann, who was, at twenty-six, eighteen years younger than he. Yet, since her teens, she had beeen mistress of her father's house as a result of her mother's invalidism and the death of an elder sister. She was widely admired for her beauty, wit, charm, poise and breadth of knowledge.

Charles I. du Pont had been a widower for three years. His first marriage had been remarkably happy. Five children had been born to the union, although only three, Mary V., Victor, and Charles I. du Pont, Jr., had survived infancy. At the time their father met Ann Ridgely, they ranged from fifteen down to eleven years of age.

It was a whirlwind courtship that set the leading families of Delaware to gossiping excitedly. In January or February of 1841 they were introduced to each other. In the succeeding weeks du Pont was a constant visitor at the Ridgely home. In April their engagement was announced, and the marriage was performed in the first week of May.

Ann's family approved of the match. They called Charles "the kindest man alive" and they approved of his family, too: Ann's brother Nicholas, a minister, praised the "kindness and affection, as well as the taste and intelligence" of the du Ponts. One of Ann's friends said it was unusual "in our go-ahead country" to find "a society of congenial minds large enough for enjoyment without going beyond . . . near relatives."

The marriage turned out well. Tender, considerate, and understanding, Charles was the kind of man with whom Ann could share a love that encompassed emotional and intellectual companionship, bringing light and warmth into both their lives. After many years of marriage, Charles was able to write to her, "It is really unfashionable to love one another as we do."

Ann had married a remarkable man, although he has since been almost forgotten in the annals of the du Ponts. He had the courage to fight for the right of Roman Catholics to organize their churches as they wished, a stand that cost him the governorship in 1860. When hatred of the Irish immigrants was well nigh universal and some of his political allies joined the Know-Nothing movement, Charles publicly challenged the general prejudice, asserting that he "knew of no population more moral, more temperate and industrious, and more liberal in their donations to public schools."

He also knew the value of money, once lightly telling his wife that a new contract he hoped to obtain might permit them to employ French instead of Irish maids, go to Newport to "recreate a little," and "die rich yet." Nevertheless, he expressed his approval of a son who didn't care to take part in what Charles called "the race of accumulation which seems to pervade all minds in this country."

Charles, like most of the du Ponts, was a Whig. When that party crumbled, cousins found themselves in disagreement on the course to be followed. In the election of 1860, Charles supported the candidate of the southern Democrats, John C. Breckinridge, although he opposed the slave states' proposal to secede from the Union. Henry du Pont, the head of the powder company, supported the Constitutional Union candidate, John Bell, who favored compromise with the South but insisted on maintaining the United States intact. Captain Samuel Francis du Pont was a supporter of the newborn Republican Party and its standard-bearer, Abraham Lincoln. Others in the du Pont circle were more extreme: Henry Belin, the powder company bookkeeper and virtually a member of the family—his daughter did marry into it a short time later—was an ardent secessionist.

In the election, Delaware as a whole gave only a quarter of the vote to Lincoln, but in Brandywine and Christiana Hundred—a "hundred" is a political area based on an ancient tax assessment district—Lincoln won 617 votes against a total of 664 for the three other candidates: Bell, Breckinridge, and Stephen Douglas, the candidate of the northern Democrats. On election night, Henry sat

tensely by the telegraph in his office at the powder mill, getting
the returns as they came in. Other members of the family crowded
the small building or strolled over to Henry's residence, Eleutherian Mills, a few feet away. At three in the morning, when it
was clear that the Republican, Lincoln, had been elected, Henry
went to bed.

The next day he wrote a letter to his son, Henry A. du Pont,
then in his last year as a cadet at West Point where the elder Henry
had gone himself years before. "Your father, like all good men and
good patriots," the head of the powder company said, "does not
believe in the possibility of disunion, and thinks that the dark hints
we see in the newspapers are mere sensation articles." His daughter, seventeen-year-old Ellen, also sent a letter to the Military
Academy. In it she told her brother, "I think it is miserable that
Lincoln's elected—whenever I think of our having such a President,
from such a party, it makes me feel like tasting green persimmons
does to the children. . . . I wish the Republicans and abolitionists
were in the Atlantic, when we would be at rest." Within a year
her own father was a Republican. In 1864 he supported Lincoln,
and by 1868 he was a Republican presidential elector, an honor he
continued to enjoy for twenty years thereafter.

Before the week was out, the South Carolina legislature met and
passed the first secession resolution; the crisis of the republic was
at hand. "If South Carolina is allowed to withdraw," Captain du
Pont, now commandant of the Philadelphia Navy Yard, told a
friend, "then our nationality has been a fiction, a compact without
solid foundation. On the other hand, coercion creates a Southern
Confederacy and sooner or later a Civil War. One thing is certain,
there never was so little cause for secession."

The attack on Fort Sumter on April 12, 1861, unified most of
the people in New Castle County behind the Union cause, but the
two downstate counties of Kent and Sussex remained strongly
secessionist. Even Henry Belin was shocked when the Stars and
Stripes was fired on. As news of Sumter reached the Brandywine,
bells were rung, people ran out of their houses to listen to the report, and the men of the du Pont family, marshaled by that old
soldier, Henry, marched solemnly to the flagpole in the center of

the hamlet of Henry Clay, just outside the millyard gates, and hoisted the flag.

"I consider the Union gone forever," Charles wrote to his brother sadly. "Eight millions of people, whether agreed or not, will not quail for five times 75,000. . . . We have nothing to do in the quarrels of either section and if we had we could effect nothing."

Two days after Sumter was surrendered, Henry sent a letter on behalf of E.I. du Pont de Nemours and Company to its Richmond agent: "With regard to Colonel Dimmock's order, we would remark that since the inauguration of war at Charleston, the posture of national affairs is critical, and a new state of affairs has arisen. Presuming that Virginia will do her whole duty in this great emergency and will be loyal to the Union, we shall prepare the powder, but with the understanding that should general expectation be disappointed and Virginia, by any misfortune, assume an attitude hostile to the United States, we shall be absolved from any obligation to furnish the order."

An order also went out to all company agents, instructing them that du Pont would sell no powder to any of the seceding states directly or through agents. Nevertheless, a rumor spread that the company was doing business with the rebels.

"I do hope the du Ponts have done making powder for Bragg and Blackguard," wrote their minister, the Reverend Samuel Crawford Brincklé, first rector of Christ Church Christiana Hundred. "They have fallen very much in my estimation since I heard of it. Do they know it is treason to give aid and comfort to the enemy? I thought they were such strong Union men. I have it to be a fact that they have sold it to them!"

Off to Washington went Henry du Pont to pledge that the resources of his company would be at the disposal of the federal government. On the eve of the conflict, du Pont accounted for half of all American gunpowder production, and the head of the firm obviously wanted to make sure that it got its share, at the very least, of war orders.

When he returned, he heard drum and fife music from militia companies recruiting volunteers from among the strong Union men, men who wore on their breasts red, white and blue rosettes or miniature flags. The bustle and stir of the war provided new excitement to the people of the Brandywine. There was almost a holiday atmosphere about the place, for the horrors of the Civil War were still in the future and most of the people harbored a romantic picture of armed conflict. The women of the du Pont family, however, were pleased that Henry A. du Pont, just graduated from the United States Military Academy, was assigned for the present to a safe job at a military installation in New York Harbor.

Most of the hitherto undecided people in the Wilmington area had joined the Union side now that war had come. The Union spirit was so intense that the du Ponts thought their powder mills quite safe. Within a matter of days, however, they began to hear of Confederate plans to move against the powder works. Alarmed, Henry appealed to Secretary of War Simon Cameron for "200 or 300 stand of arms" with which to arm "over 300 good men, true and loyal," company employees and their relatives and friends, organized into four Brandywine homeguard units, two of them commanded by du Ponts, Charles and Lammot.

On the night of April 19, there was a bad scare: a report came that one hundred and fifty Maryland secessionists planned to seize or blow up the contents of the du Pont powder magazine at the ship-loading wharf at Edgemoor on the Delaware. Grabbing rifles, Henry and four other du Pont men, along with some workmen, leaped into seven wagons and dashed to the wharf, where they transferred the powder from the arsenal to the carts. They returned to the millyard with the powder at daybreak, red-eyed and exhausted, to find the du Pont women, their faces etched with anxiety, waiting for them with hot food and drink.

There were other scares. One night General Robert Patterson sent a dispatch from Philadelphia, warning that a "known desperado" had gone to the Brandywine to blow up the mills; the militia scoured the country, losing sleep and upsetting a good many peaceful citizens, but no desperado could be found.

On another occasion, it was reported that two men dressed in women's clothes had been spotted inside the powder company gates. No trace of transvestites, secessionist or otherwise, was turned up.

And then there was the day when workmen decided that a stranger in the Hagley Yard looked so evil that he must be a saboteur. "A spy! A spy!" the powdermen shouted, flailing him with clubs. But when Lammot and Eugene du Pont rescued the poor man and questioned him, they were convinced that he was nothing more than a harmless tramp.

As a Breckinridge Democrat, Charles I. du Pont might have been suspect in his loyalties, but his devotion to the Union was so well known that, on May 18, he was invited to address a Union meeting in Kent County. He declined because he regarded the rally as a political event out of place in a country at war. "I am for the country and the government," he replied to the invitation. "My first service is to throw politics to the dogs and let them devour its carcass; all party ties should be forgotten in the great effort to save our Union. Abolitionism, Native Americanism, Know-Nothingism, the proscribing of valued citizens for their religious opinions—all are passed away, and the task is now to save our nationality." The South, with no right to do so, had tried to deny Americans the birthright of a nation extending "from Maine to Florida and a clear line . . . from the Atlantic to the Pacific Ocean." Secession was morally and legally indefensible, and the rebellion had now reached a point requiring the use of force to suppress it. In such a conflict, Delaware must remain with the North whose interests were her own. "I am opposed to war," Charles said. "It is a relic of barbarism, but these Southern politicians are now the aggressors, and let the consequences be as they may—the loss of hundreds of thousands of men, and hundreds of millions of dollars—our government and Union we must support."

On May 11, Delaware's Governor William Burton appointed Henry du Pont commanding officer of the state militia with the rank of major-general. For a time a controversy of considerable proportions raged around du Pont who had confiscated the weapons of militia units which he suspected of secessionist sympathies.

It was just as well that Henry, who for the rest of his life was always referred to as "General" du Pont, did not know that the worst threat against his state, his Union, and his company came from a member of his own family. Charles du Pont Bird of Dover,

Delaware, a student at Loyola College at Baltimore, tried to organize a rebel move against the powder works.

On April 24, 1861, he sent a letter to the governor of Virginia, who thought it of sufficient interest to forward to General Robert E. Lee. The letter outlined a plan for sabotage and insurrection by secessionists within Delaware. "The powder mills on the Brandywine (owned by relations of mine) should be secured at all hazards," the young firebrand wrote. "With a not very large force, if we cannot hold them, they should be destroyed. Some of the du Ponts are friendly to the South. If it is possible to guard these works for a few weeks, the stock of powder for the Southern Confederacy would be largely increased."

Whether subsequent attempts by Confederate agents to destroy the powder works were inspired by Bird's letter has never been determined.

CHAPTER XXII

FATHER OF ANNAPOLIS

A T THE OUTBREAK of the Civil War, Captain Samuel Francis du Pont—"Frank" to his family—was in command of the Philadelphia Navy Yard. Fifty-seven years old, he was a very tall man, strongly built. His face was dignified but pleasant, with smile wrinkles at the corners of his eyes. A fringe of beard framed his face which was also embellished with a splendidly bushy mustache. He had "an irresistible voice and smile," his old friend Rear Admiral John A. Dahlgren noted, and he was "a good officer, an accomplished gentleman in and out of his profession." It appears that the old cliché was, for once, true: his men loved him. He practiced an old-fashioned, formal courtesy, charming to many people but somewhat bewildering and a trifle annoying to the few who regarded him as something of a "courtier." Obviously he was not the usual kind of naval officer. One of his close friends was Henry Wadsworth Longfellow, so Frank must have had considerable intellectual interests. Moreover, he was a genuinely religious man, unostentatious but deeply earnest in his devotion.

For forty-five years he had served in the Navy. Sea duty had taken him to every corner of the globe. In the Mexican War he had scored a number of victories over the enemy and his exploits won him the praise of the Secretary of the Navy. He had also learned a good deal about blockading a hostile coastline.

Afterwards he was appointed one of a six-man board charged with drawing up a program and plans for a United States Naval Academy; some have dubbed him "the Father of Annapolis." Then there was a period of service on a board that reorganized the lighthouse and life-saving services along the Atlantic Coast. A political hot potato was dropped into his hands in 1853 when the Navy Secretary, deciding that too many naval officers were unable to perform their functions properly because of incompetence and disability, named Frank du Pont to the Naval Efficiency Board that culled out the unfit. Many of the officers thus ousted had been political appointees; they had powerful friends in Congress, including Senator Sam Houston of Texas. The latter savagely attacked du Pont and the other members of the board.

Captain du Pont had been in command of the Philadelphia Navy Yard only three or four months when hostilities began. The emergency was brought home to him very quickly. Because communications between Washington and the rest of the North were cut off for a time in April, 1861, du Pont, on his own initiative, moved swiftly to establish and maintain a system of small, fast ships to carry messages between Philadelphia and Annapolis, Maryland. From Annapolis a rail line led directly to the capital, bypassing secessionist Baltimore.

As it became clear that the nation was in for a real war which might be long and hard-fought, the Administration appointed a board headed by Captain du Pont to draw up a major plan of strategy for naval operations against the Confederacy. The problems confronting them were difficult. On April 19 Lincoln had proclaimed a blockade of the rebel coast. A hasty and ill-considered act, it gave European powers an excuse to recognize the South's belligerent rights. If the President had merely announced that American ports below the Chesapeake were closed, he would have obtained the results he sought. Under international law, however, a blockade must be respected only if it is effective. So now the Union had to control 189 harbors and river mouths along 3,549 miles of shoreline from the Potomac to the Rio Grande. Every available ship was pressed into blockade duty.

The Board of Strategy selected three naval targets. The most important was Port Royal, South Carolina, twenty-five miles north of Savannah and some sixty miles south of Charleston—two ports that were favorites of the blockade-runners. As du Pont said, Port Royal boasted the finest harbor on the southeastern coast and could shelter "the navies of the world." Such a harbor could provide a headquarters for the blockading fleet right in the middle of the shoreline it was patrolling, a place to which ships could go for provisions, fuel and repairs.

The assignment of capturing Port Royal was given to Frank du Pont, now raised to flag officer, the highest rank in a navy which did not yet have admirals.

As he pondered his task, he must have thought a good deal about how this war was dividing families, for there were leading citizens of South Carolina who were du Ponts. This branch of the family had been in America longer than the Delaware du Ponts, for they were descended from Pierre Samuel du Pont's great uncle, Abraham du Pont, a Huguenot who fled to Carolina in 1695.

The greatest of the South Carolina du Ponts was Abraham's younger son, Gideon, born in 1712, who, as a planter on the Santee, had opened the way to the development of the state's rice crop. "South Carolina owes her successful rice culture to Gideon," a standard history says. "He first conceived and successfully carried out the idea of causing water to overflow and cover to a certain depth the [rice] fields, thereby killing the weeds which before his time had always stifled the rice plants." Gideon refused to take out a patent on his method of cultivation, so he and his family never profited by his innovation. Now his descendants were ardent secessionists, ready to fight any attempt to assert the federal authority in their state—even if the attempt were made by Cousin Frank.

Flag Officer du Pont's assignment was formidable. Port Royal was well defended. A large task force would be needed to overwhelm it. Du Pont's first task was to assemble a fleet.

Immediately upon his appointment as commander of the South Atlantic Blockading Squadron, Frank du Pont went to New York and checked into a second-floor suite at the old Astor House. He spent the latter part of the summer and the early autumn gathering his flotilla. Merchantmen were converted into men-of-war, a process "like altering a vest into a shirt," du Pont told Navy Secretary

Gideon Welles. In addition, Frank ordered the building of the famous "ninety-day gunboats." He bought vessels of every kind for conversion into craft suitable for naval warfare, even tugboats and ferryboats. And every last one of them had to be made seaworthy.

At last the fantastic fleet was ready. On October 16, signals flying, the unorthodox maritime array moved out to sea past Sandy Hook. In Hampton Roads, the deep, four-mile-wide channel off Virginia's Chesapeake shore, du Pont rendezvoused with the army transports of Brigadier General Thomas West Sherman—"the other Sherman," they called him. Sherman had a force of 13,000 green soldiers. And there the ships were forced to remain, as storms, unusual tides and rough water delayed their sailing from day to day.

All the soldiers and sailors speculated about their destination. Even the skippers didn't know; they were sailing under sealed orders, not to be opened until the fleet was at sea. To preserve secrecy vital to the enterprise, Welles had designated four possible targets: in Florida, Fernandina; in Georgia, Brunswick; in South Carolina, Bull's Bay and Port Royal. Du Pont and Sherman had been told to take Port Royal.

That a great undertaking was under way could not be concealed from the enemy, for nearly a hundred ships, the largest United States flotilla ever assembled up to then, were riding at anchor in Hampton Roads. At night the fleet looked like "a great city, so numerous are the lights," one naval officer recorded.

Such a vast assemblage must be aimed at Mobile, New Orleans, Savannah, Charleston, or Wilmington, North Carolina, the Northern newspapers speculated. The Southern press was just as uncertain. In Richmond, the *Enquirer* picked Charleston; but in Charleston itself, the *Courier* chose New Orleans. However, the editor of the *New Bern* (North Carolina) *Progress*, a nervous sort of chap, picked New Bern. LOOK OUT FOR OUR COAST! screamed a Georgia headline. Under it the editor proclaimed, "Let every man and every gun be ready."

Some people were not at all puzzled. As early as October 4, William H. Russell, correspondent of the pro-Southern *London Times*, knew of the Port Royal expedition; he asked permission to accompany it.

Worse still, on November 1, the Confederate Secretary of War, Judah P. Benjamin, telegraphed the governor of South Carolina and Brigadier General Thomas F. Drayton, commandant of Port Royal, to warn them, "The enemy's expedition is intended for Port Royal." At the time, Drayton did not know that one of the frigates in the fleet was commanded by his own brother, Captain Percival Drayton.

At length the weather appeared favorable. On October 29 the fleet weighed anchor. But it had scarcely rounded Hatteras when the sky darkened, the wind began to rise, and high seas tossed the ships about. As the wind reached gale velocity, du Pont, from his flagship, the steam-frigate *Wabash*, signaled that the order of sailing was no longer to be observed; every ship was on her own.

For the better part of twenty-four hours, the storm raged, reaching hurricane proportions before subsiding. Many of the vessels had not been designed for mountainous seas and wild winds, dangerous for even the most seaworthy craft, and it was generally feared that many would be lost in the storm. Du Pont's heart sank at daybreak the next day when only one ship could be seen from the bridge of the *Wabash*. But before the day was out, a number of other vessels appeared and fell into line behind her.

Eventually all but two of the ships arrived off Port Royal—ferryboats and all—and even the men on the two ships that sank were rescued before the vessels went to the bottom. The only human beings lost were seven Marines who, wild with fear, tried in vain to escape from their foundering craft to a rescue ship by swinging hand-over-hand along ropes made fast to both vessels.

For his assault against Port Royal, du Pont decided upon a remarkable plan. The harbor was guarded primarily by two strong points: Fort Walker on the western promontory, and Fort Beauregard on the eastern. Walker had been designed to ward off an attack from the sea, and du Pont decided that the citadel might be highly vulnerable to an assault from within the spacious harbor itself. On the other hand, Frank knew that the Confederates had three gunboats plus a converted river steamer, all commanded by one of his old messmates, Flag Officer Josiah Tattnall. To protect his fleet from a flank attack by Tattnall's ships, du Pont ordered a flanking squadron of five gunboats to sail into the harbor with the main attack force, there to remain on guard against any hostile move by Tattnall from the shore.

The principal fighting force was an array of nine of Frank du Pont's heaviest frigates and sloops ranged in line ahead. These ships would sail northward through the passage, midway between the two forts, into the harbor, then turn about to the south and come back again, still in single file, enfilading Walker. When each ship was broadside to the fort, it would come about again and head back into the harbor. In other words, the ships would describe an elliptical loop that would keep widening with each circuit. And both Walker and Beauregard would be blasted with cannon shot every time a ship was within range.

The Union cannonading was so fierce and steady that to an English correspondent aboard the *Wabash*, the columns of sand thrown up by the bomb bursts around the forts looked "as if we had suddenly raised from the dust a grove of poplars." A Northern naval officer said the shells fell into the forts "as fast as a horse's feet beat the ground in a gallop."

The du Pont strategy worked perfectly. His ships were raking the forts where they were least protected and the defenders had to fire on constantly moving targets. "No sooner did we obtain his range when it would be changed," a frustrated rebel gunnery officer later reported to his superiors, "and time after time rechanged, while the deep water [within the harbor] permitted him to choose his position and fire shot after shot . . . with the precision of target practice."

Inside the forts, there was no letup from the ordeal of screaming shells, bursting bombs, flying metal and bricks, showers of sand and dust, heaving earth, flames and smoke and the nose-irritating smell of powder, and over it all, the pitiful cries and shrieks of the wounded.

The action began at nine twenty-six in the morning. At one fifteen the attackers saw men streaming out of Fort Walker into the underbrush; the stronghold was being abandoned. At sunset a small scouting party found that Fort Beauregard, too, had been deserted sometime during the afternoon.

The victory destroyed forever the long-held belief that one gun on land was the equal of four or five guns aboard ship. Steam power, giving skippers more control of their ships when confronted with problems of wind and current, was a mighty new factor in naval warfare. And the first to adapt his tactics to the new conditions was Frank du Pont, although he had grown up in the old sailing Navy. His perception won him a great victory at little cost —six killed, twenty wounded, in his entire fleet.

Aghast at the fall of Port Royal, the Southern states withheld from the Confederacy troops vitally needed at the front; people back home insisted that the danger to them was too great now for their men to go off at Richmond's command. Sea-coast towns were deserted as the people fled inland. THE HOUR HAS ARRIVED, the *Sumter Watchman* headlined apprehensively.

In the North, the victory was received ecstatically. For months, the news had all been bad for the Union: Bull Run and Ball's Bluff were harsh lessons to a people who thought this would be a short and easy war. "On every brow sits sullen, scorching, black despair," Horace Greeley wrote to Lincoln not long before Port Royal. Afterwards his *New York Tribune*, hailing du Pont as a hero, headlined: ON TO CHARLESTON! On Wall Street the sale of government securities, hitherto sluggish, became brisk. Everywhere fireworks displays, parades, and other celebrations marked the first great Union triumph.

Nowhere was the jubilation as great as on the Brandywine. After a salute of the usual twenty-one guns, the Wilmington City Council was so carried away it decided that only another one hundred-gun salute could properly express the public delight. In the churches there were hymns and sermons of thanksgiving, and congratulatory telegrams poured into Louviers Upper House, causing Frank's Sophie, for many years an invalid, to weep with happiness. (Frank sent some war trophies to his cousins, asking them to hide the prizes until his return, lest Sophie see them and become alarmed.)

There were those in Delaware who predicted that du Pont would wind up in the White House. Meanwhile, as a token of appreciation from the public, a subscription was undertaken to buy a ceremonial gold and silver dress sword for the hero.

On Lincoln's recommendation, Congress tendered its thanks to du Pont for his "decisive and splendid victory" and he was promoted to the new rank of rear admiral.

In a report to Washington, Frank pointed out that his successful beachhead operation had the effect of "driving a wedge into the flanks of the rebels," enabling the Union to split the Confederacy in two if an army drove inland from Port Royal. No one in Washington took his hint. Such an offensive might have shortened the war: it was just what General Robert E. Lee, then in command of the South's coastal defenses, had expected and he had despaired of fighting off such an attack.

In the months that followed, Admiral du Pont captured the major blockade-runners' port of Fernandina, Florida, having first taken Brunswick, Georgia. St. Augustine and Jacksonville also fell to him, and then Fort Pulaski. Soon the entire coast from Hatteras to Key West was occupied or controlled by the Union's naval forces, except for Charleston.

Now Navy Secretary Welles, convinced by the historic battle between the *Monitor* and the *Merrimac* that monitors were invincible and omnipotent, ordered du Pont to take Charleston with a force composed of these strange little iron-clad ships. A sensible man, du Pont tested a monitor by sending it against a rebel earthworks at Fort McAllister. He found that the monitor was indeed relatively invulnerable to shot from the fort, but it had no fire power of its own to speak of, so it was unable to inflict any damage on the enemy. Repeatedly du Pont warned against reliance on the monitors as offensive vessels, but he failed to sway Welles.

The best plan, of course, would have been to send troops against Charleston from points up and down the Union-held coast, thus launching a simultaneous army-navy attack. But Welles specifically ordered du Pont to take Charleston without army support; the Navy Secretary wanted to get all the credit himself. He had set his mind on winning Charleston his way, and he would listen to nothing that challenged his decision.

Reluctantly, du Pont moved against Charleston on April 7, 1863. What he had expected occurred. The Union fleet had to pass through a rather narrow channel between Morris Island and Sullivan's Island, each of which had two artillery batteries that opened up on the invaders. A cable, stretching from Fort Sumter which was on an island to Sullivan's Island, forced the ships to halt as they came up to it, and there they lay, with enemy ships firing at them on both sides from fore and aft; they had been caught in a lethal circle of fire. Some ships proved unmanageable in the shallow water. "The fire of the forts was heavy and accurate and every ironclad was hit repeatedly," says Rear Admiral Bern Anderson in his naval history of the Civil War. The nearest monitor did not get within one thousand yards of Fort Sumter.

Du Pont, unaware that the Confederates had been trying in vain to detonate a mine on the bottom directly under his flagship, signaled his ships to retreat. Out of the channel they moved, a battered lot. The *Keokuk*, hit ninety times, sank the next morning, but the others somehow remained afloat despite the damage they had suffered: the *Nahant*, hit thirty-six times; the *Nantucket*, fifty-one; the *Weehawken*, fifty-three; the *Passaic*, thirty-five; the *Patapsco*, forty-seven. Du Pont's flagship, the *New Ironsides*, had been struck fifty-five times. The official records later disclosed that the Confederate batteries had poured 2,220 rounds at the Union ships while du Pont's men were only able to shoot 139.

"Welles and [Assistant Secretary Gustavus V.] Fox either did not or would not understand the limitations of the monitors, nor would they accept reports of the extent of the damage done them at Fort Sumter," Admiral Anderson says. "Keenly disappointed that the monitors had failed to take Charleston, they blamed the commander and determined to relieve him. . . . Welles . . . was blind to the true situation and du Pont was not at fault. Later events showed that he was shelved for being too realistic in reporting the limitations of the monitors."

Replaced by his old friend Dahlgren, Frank du Pont returned home to the Brandywine, hurt and angry that he had been made the scapegoat for the failure of an operation against which he had warned from the beginning. Dahlgren, too, failed to take Charleston, which was some slight comfort to du Pont who saw his own position vindicated. But he felt that a cloud remained on his name since the public was unaware that he had foreseen the disaster and tried to prevent it.

Living with his Sophie in Louviers Upper House, the admiral spent his time corresponding with friends, taking part in local civic activities, helping to direct the work of Christ Church, and discussing strategy with his relatives across the creek as military engagements were reported in the press. The war ended in April, 1865, two years after his retirement. That June he took Sophie with him on a trip to Philadelphia. There he met an old friend, Frederick Chatard, who had served with him in the Navy before the war and then had accepted a commission in the Confederate Navy. In answer to Chatard's plea, du Pont wrote letters to some of his influential friends in Washington, urging the restoration of his old comrade's civil rights.

During the night, Frank suddenly felt sick. Sophie called a doctor who did what he could but to no avail. Early the next morning, June 23, 1865, he died at the age of sixty-one. The cause of death is not recorded, but to this day the du Ponts insist that he died of a broken heart.

Rear Admiral Samuel Francis du Pont has not been completely forgotten: Du Pont Circle in the nation's capital is named for him.

CHAPTER XXIII

CONGRESSIONAL MEDAL
OF HONOR

ABOUT THE TIME that Admiral du Pont's career was coming to an unhappy end, Henry Algernon du Pont, his young first cousin once removed, was about to go under fire for the first time.

It was inevitable that young Henry A. would be a West Pointer. His father had attended the Military Academy and left the army only at the urgent request of the family. The elder du Pont never got over his disappointment; he was determined that his son should enjoy a way of life that had been denied to him.

At first Henry A. did not take to the Military Academy. Something of a snob, he found the Point not nearly as elegant or aristocratic as he would have liked. Its customs were particularly annoying. In time, however, he came to modify his views; two years after he entered the school he conceded that life there became "less irksome the longer you stay," and when he was graduated on May 6, 1861, just after the outbreak of war, he ranked first in his class.

Eight days later he was promoted to first lieutenant—the wartime need for officers was already making itself felt—and assigned to Fort Hamilton in Brooklyn, which commanded the eastern approach to

New York harbor. For two years the impatient young officer cooled his heels there, pleading in vain for combat duty.

At last, in 1863, Henry's regiment was moved out of New York and into the field. As the artillerymen boarded the trains that would carry them to Virginia, young du Pont was promoted to captain and given the command of Light Battery B, usually referred to thereafter as "du Pont's battery."

The battery and its commander saw a good deal of action, all of it in the Shenandoah Valley. In the spring of 1864, the Fifth United States Artillery was part of a Union army that invaded the Valley but got only as far as New Market, Virginia. Then it was thrown back in confusion by a hastily assembled rebel force commanded by John C. Breckinridge. Under relentless pressure from the cadet corps of the renowned Virginia Military Academy which spearheaded the Confederate assault, the blue line wavered and then broke, the Yankees fleeing in a complete rout toward the north. Once across the Shenandoah River the army would have a respite in which to rally against the Rebs. But it wasn't easy for the Northerners to cross the river; there was only a stone bridge which became a jammed bottleneck when the panic-stricken, disorganized horde reached it.

At the beginning of the battle, du Pont's battery had been in reserve. It was May 15, but the weather was already sultry, and Henry had seen to it that his horses were unharnessed and watered, so that they would be fresh for whatever the day might bring. Then his men harnessed the horses and hitched them to the gun carriages. When the infantry lines began to crumble, the battery was ordered to the front. As he moved forward with his men, Henry received contradictory orders from different superior officers too excited and inexperienced to know what ought to be done. Captain du Pont decided to take matters into his own hands.

There were six field pieces in his battery. Henry posted them in echelon, three pairs of guns in a narrow defile along the turnpike, in order to rake any forces moving up behind the fleeing Yankees. The guns were protected against flank attacks by the Shenandoah on one side and by Smith's Creek on the other.

As the men in gray, the rebel yell screeching from their lips, emerged wraith-like through the thick clouds of yellow dust, the muzzles of Battery B spat fire and iron at them with such terrible effectiveness that the Confederates faltered for the first time that afternoon. "The audacity of this battle," the cadet captain of VMI Company D later recalled, "caused us to think that it had a strong infantry support and we paused to form line before advancing further. This caused a delay of fifteen or twenty minutes and allowed the Thirty-fourth Massachusetts, the Twelfth West Virginia, the Fifty-fourth Pennsylvania, and perhaps some other troops time enough to slip through to freedom."

Soon the Confederate riflemen were shooting through the dust, seeking out the men at the cannons, and rebel artillery was brought up to blast open this last Union barrier. Du Pont ordered his first platoon to retire and take up a position behind the last pair of guns, there to resume firing down the road. This sort of leapfrogging operation backwards enabled Henry to carry out an orderly retreat. Because they were rapidly shifting position, the Yankee gunners were difficult targets for the enemy. But the pointblank fire of Light Battery B not only halted the South's infantry, but also a number of artillery units.

"For four hours du Pont's battery, singlehanded, held the pass, a Virginia Thermopylae," says military historian Fairfax Downey rather extravagantly. "At dusk it retreated over the Shenandoah span, destroyed it, and rejoined the army it had saved."

In the following spring, the North again tried to seize the Shenandoah Valley. In little more than a fortnight there were two battles in addition to a less serious engagement and three minor brushes.

During that period, a du Pont family legend was born. The story has it that Henry, ordered to shell the VMI buildings at Lexington, resolutely refused to obey the order because the institution was an historic site that must be preserved. As careful a scholar as Marquis James has described this as "one of . . . Henry Algernon's most gallant acts."

Unfortunately, it never happened.

In his own memoirs, Henry tells just what did happen on June 11 when the Northern army reached Lexington. It was greeted by desultory rifle fire from the stone cadet barracks of VMI. Major General David Hunter ordered his artillery to shell the barracks, and du Pont, now chief of artillery, executed the order. But after one round from six guns, the cadets retreated from the barracks and du Pont stopped firing. Then Hunter ordered the VMI buildings to be burned to the ground, asserting that he had found in them a Confederate proclamation "inciting . . . guerrilla warfare on my troops." When Hunter's troops moved out of Lexington, they left VMI a gutted ruin.

The legend of Henry's gallantry may have grown out of another occurrence a few days later. After the battle of Lynchburg had ended in a setback for the Union, Hunter retreated westward for a week until he reached White Sulphur Springs. There he was finally safe from pursuit. As the men in blue prepared to move out the next day, Hunter, who seems to have been something of an arsonist, gave orders to burn the famous old resort. This time Captain du Pont did speak up. He urged the general to reconsider, pointing out that the springs were part of the nation's heritage. Finally Hunter rescinded his order.

After Jubal Early used the Shenandoah Valley as a springboard for his raid against the outer fortifications of Washington in July, Phil Sheridan was given command of the Union forces in West Virginia with orders to take the Valley out of the war by a scorched-earth policy. Five days after Sheridan took over, the army had its first brush with the enemy. For two months there was fighting in the Shenandoah Valley and du Pont, now commanding the artillery brigade of Crook's Corps, saw action in every engagement. At the battle of Winchester on September 19, his favorite horse was shot from under him, but du Pont, "amidst the thickest of the fight, cheered the men onward and encouraged them by example to do their duty." So his chief, Brigadier General George Crook, reported in dispatches that named Henry as one of the officers who had given him "invaluable assistance." Du Pont received a commission of brevet major for his part in the battle. (A brevet commission promoted an officer to a higher rank without giving him more pay.)

Three days later Jubal Early tried to make a stand at Fisher's Hill but was routed. In the confusion of battle, however, Major du Pont was almost captured: a sudden charge by the Confederate troops brought men in gray around Henry, but he rallied his men and drove off the rebels.

At daybreak on October 19, as fog from Cedar Creek held back the day, three divisions of Early's Confederate troops, having passed through a supposedly "impassable" river gorge, fell upon the Union left flank, which happened to be Crook's Corps. The surprise attack panicked the half-awake soldiers who fled in complete disorder. Henry leaped to the back of his mount, a white horse that stood out in the dim light as an inviting target. Despite the warnings of his subordinates, he remained on the horse as bullets whined and snarled past him. When other soldiers ran, du Pont brought his gunners together, saw to it that they hitched the horses to the caissons and pulled out with his artillery pieces in orderly fashion. As soon as he found a place where the guns could be posted to sweep the advancing enemy, he put them into action, praising his men for their steady, cool work.

"This officer . . . by his brave bearing, most distinguished gallantry, and voluntary exposure to the enemy's fire at a critical moment when the Union line had been broken and defeated, encouraged his men to stand to their guns, checked the advance of the enemy, and brought off most of his pieces. In the later victorious advances of the Army, the same day, he also rendered valuable service. . . ."

The words are those of the citation which accompanied the Congressional Medal of Honor, the highest award offered by the United States to its fighting men.

On the same day that this medal was pinned to his tunic, du Pont also received a brevet commission as lieutenant colonel in the regular army. He was then barely twenty-six years old.

The battle of Cedar Creek decided the fate of the Shenandoah Valley. Laid waste by Sheridan, occupied firmly by Union troops, its charred fields and barns and gristmills could no longer feed Lee's army before Richmond. Its capture by the North helped to hasten the end of the war.

After peace came, du Pont served as commandant of various military posts and served on a board to co-ordinate tactics for the three arms of service. But a decade of the peacetime army was enough for him. On March 1, 1875, he retired to civilian life.

But the public had not heard the last of Colonel Henry A. du Pont.

CHAPTER XXIV

TIME OF ALARMS

Soon after the Civil War began, the nation faced the probability of a shortage of saltpeter, an essential ingredient of gunpowder. Lammot du Pont, summoned to Washington by Secretary of State William H. Seward, was told that he must undertake a mission of the greatest urgency.

Lammot was to go to England immediately with as much secrecy as possible, there to buy saltpeter, not in the name of the United States government but ostensibly for the private account of the du Pont company. Speed was vital, for saltpeter, a product of India, was controlled by Great Britain, and American relations with the British were growing increasingly strained. There was real danger that Britain might recognize the Confederacy. If this happened, the Union almost certainly would be barred from further purchases of Indian saltpeter.

So secret was Lammot's trip that even members of the family were not told about it. Only a half dozen of the older relatives knew where he had gone. His youngest brother, Antoine Bidermann du Pont, guessed that he must be visiting the firm's first plant away from the Brandywine, the mill at Wapwallopen near Berwick, Pennsylvania. His mother, who knew the truth, did not enlighten Antoine even when, as Christmas drew near, Lammot's continued absence puzzled and troubled other members of the family.

In London, within four days of his arrival, Lammot brought 23,000 bags of saltpeter and agreed to purchase another 10,500 bags still at sea en route from India. This made a total of more than 3,300,000 pounds, all the available saltpeter in the British Isles. Lammot felt pleased with himself.

And then, suddenly, the British put an embargo on all war shipments.

"The devil is to pay!" an exasperated Lammot wrote to his uncle, Henry du Pont.

Ironically, the embargo was caused by Admiral du Pont's successful blockade of the Confederate coast. One of the blockading ships, the *San Jacinto*, had intercepted a British mail packet, the *Trent*, on the high seas and seized two passengers, James M. Mason and John Slidell, Confederate envoys bound for London. The British were enraged by their abduction from an English ship, an act which London regarded as an affront to its rights as a neutral. The reaction of Whitehall had been the embargo.

For a week Lammot tried to get the British to release his saltpeter. Finally he gave up and sailed for home. At two o'clock Christmas morning he arrived on the Brandywine. For a few happy hours his family was able to enjoy his buoyant, energetic personality. Then, before sunset on Christmas Day, he set off again, this time for Washington.

On the twenty-sixth, the Cabinet was meeting to consider what is now known as the Trent Affair. During a recess in the Cabinet meeting, Seward received du Pont, who told him how the international incident had jeopardized his saltpeter stockpiles. When the Cabinet reconvened, this news—added to Lincoln's desire to keep England neutral—decided the issue. When the Cabinet meeting ended, Seward assured Lammot that Lincoln would acknowledge the fact that Britain's rights as a neutral had been violated. In turn, it was expected that the British embargo would be lifted.

On New Year's Day, 1862, Lammot sailed once again from New York. His fellow passengers included the Confederate commissioners, Mason and Slidell. About a week after du Pont reached London, the British authorized the shipment of his precious saltpeter. By mid-February he was back home, having crossed the Atlantic four times in three months during winter storms. A short time later he posed for a picture, leaning back in a chair, his hands clasped expansively behind his head, a cigar cocked at a jaunty angle from his mouth—the very picture of confidence.

On the home front, the Civil War at first brought on a business depression. Nobody wanted to enter into any major or long-term commitments when the future could not be foreseen. Credit dried up; markets evaporated; banks suspended payments in gold. During the last few months of 1860, unemployment became general throughout the North, and along the Brandywine woolen mills and cotton factories shut their doors. The few men still working took pay cuts.

The blight fell on the gunpowder business, too, but its impact was not so severe. For this, the du Ponts were grateful: "not only for our personal interest," said Sophie, Admiral du Pont's wife, "but for the large population [which the powder works] support. The other factories along the creek are all stopped except perhaps a paper mill. Some of them have been stopped since last fall and some of the people have not worked since then. There is a good deal of suffering already, and there must be much more if this unhappy division amongst our people is not settled soon."

Much earlier in the winter, Irénée had argued that the powder mills should be closed down until conditions improved even though such a move would cost the du Ponts' five hundred workmen their livelihood. His uncle, Henry the elder, head of the firm, wasn't too worried about the welfare of the working people, either, because he believed that the stories of their sufferings had been exaggerated. But Sophie, Henry's sister, disagreed and said so vehemently. She had received many appeals from workingmen's wives for sewing or any other kind of work that would earn bread for their families.

And conditions worsened with the outbreak of fighting. Many companies lost good markets when the South seceded and customers there defaulted on their debts. The du Pont company alone lost $150,000 in Southern inventories seized by the Confederacy and in bills that were never paid.

By fall, however, business started to pick up. Washington had come to realize that it was in for a tough fight which would require trained troops and first-rate equipment, including enormous quantities of gunpowder. In May, 1861, with not a single wartime order for powder on the books as yet, Henry du Pont expressed the belief that the war would cost the firm a good deal of money. As it turned out, the company did very well: its 1861 sales were $1,077,-444 compared with $752,000 in the last pre-war year. Other concerns in the area were awarded contracts for tents, ambulances, uniforms, and other war materiel. Before long a war boom developed.

The powder mills were now working around the clock—an especially hazardous state of affairs at a time when all lighting had to be done with highly combustible fuels. Looking out of her window in Eleutherian Mills at the powder yards full of kerosene lamps below, fifteen-year-old Sara du Pont thought the illumination "quite splendid."

Across the creek, Sophie, from the vantage point of age, took a grimmer view of things. She realized that the strain of working day and night was telling on the menfolk. Lammot was "killing himself," planning new inventions, supervising construction, watching every aspect of the powder-making, and developing dark pouches of fatigue under his eyes. Eugene was younger and stronger, better able to stand the pressure. "But just think of his mind, uninstructed and but half-educated," Sophie said, "and now entirely bound up in that refinery—no society whatever but Irishmen, and what little he can have of Lammot's time." As for Eugene's wife, she complained that he never talked at home any more.

At Henry's request, the government exempted du Pont workmen from the draft. But he had difficulty persuading Lammot and Irénée that they themselves should not enlist. The whole family kept telling them that they were contributing more to the country's welfare on the Brandywine than they could on a battlefield, but both were itching for a chance to get into active service.

There was, to be sure, more than enough action at home to satisfy any ordinary man. Indeed, the du Ponts and their workmen lived with danger as few soldiers did in the field. Between 1860 and 1865 there were eleven explosions in the powder yards, with a toll of forty-three lives and scores of men injured. More than thirty mills were wrecked or badly damaged. The du Pont houses on both sides of the creek at the top of the bluffs were hit by flying debris that knocked holes in walls and roofs, and the concussion of each blast shattered windows and sent china crashing to the floor; the same thing occurred in the powdermen's homes. Under the circumstances, employees might have been forgiven for leaving the powder works for less hazardous work but few of them did. After one particularly disastrous accident, Henry was able to report, "The men have behaved very well; none of the powdermen have quit and things are moving on smoothly." Each time that mills blew up, the du Ponts rebuilt them with a speed impossible before the war.

The cause of many of the wartime explosions could not be determined: by its very nature, a blast leaves very little evidence. However, it is probable that most, if not all, of the accidents occurred because of the stepped-up pace of production and the human and mechanical failures such a speed-up inevitably triggered.

On the other hand, the possibility of sabotage cannot be ruled out. The Brandywine was a breeding ground for rumors about rebel agents assigned to the job of blowing up the powder works. Mrs. Thomas O'Keefe's long absent husband and another man, both recent arrivals from the South, were arrested in her house in Rising Sun Village, a hamlet of du Pont workmen, after O'Keefe tried to bribe a powderman to give him a plan of the yards. The two men were hustled off to Fort Delaware where Mrs. O'Keefe frequently visited them—accompanied by a certain William Smith who had become her paramour while her husband was away. The tolerant O'Keefe and his companion finally were released after several months in prison without ever having been convicted of anything.

Whether the threat from saboteurs was real or imaginary, the powder mills were unquestionably menaced from another quarter. Thrice during the war, northward drives by Confederate armies put the Brandywine in peril of attack.

In September, 1862, Lee broke out of Virginia and began to move into Maryland, with Harrisburg, Pennsylvania, as his objective, hoping to isolate Washington and cut off Maryland and Delaware from the North. As the Confederate invasion got under way, Henry and Lammot du Pont were called to Washington. There they were informed that Union spies had bad news for them: 3,000 cavalrymen were being detached from Lee's force for a lightning raid to destroy the gunpowder works. For protection, the Northern government could only promise the du Ponts a body of 2,500 Pennsylvania militiamen. Fearing such a force would be inadequate to defend the mills, Henry said he would ship all the powder on hand and let the rebels destroy the works if they did show up. However, Secretary of War Stanton insisted that the powder mills were too valuable to the Union cause; they must be saved at all cost. Stanton then asked General Henry Halleck to send at least 4,000 men to the Brandywine. But in the end, only 2,500 arrived. They saw no action fortunately; some skeptics were certain they would run at the first sound of a gun. The battle of Antietam on September 17 quieted the fears of the du Ponts for the rest of that year.

In the following June, Lee again rolled his great army forward in an invasion that reached as far east as the Susquehanna River near York, Pennsylvania. Again the alarms were sounded in northern Delaware. Militiamen were called to their regiments and appeals were made for volunteers. Two hundred men left the powder yards to head west under the command of Lammot and Eugene du Pont. Charles I. du Pont, for his part, led his own home guard into the amateur army then assembling on the state's western border. The Brandywine was hushed that Saturday although it was Independence Day, usually the biggest holiday of the year.

In the evening, however, a wild celebration began when telegraph messages from Gettysburg told how Lee had been repulsed after three terrible days of battle. On the Brandywine, there were such fireworks as only powdermakers could provide and a fifty-gun salute to the Union troops. The next day the home guard arrived belatedly to join in the festivities.

The last scare came in July, 1864, when Jubal Early's gray cavalry dashed out of the Shenandoah, cutting across Maryland toward Washington, while another rebel force probed into Pennsylvania to ravage Chambersburg. It was five o'clock on a Sunday morning when a telegraph key in Wilmington began clicking out the alarming message that Union forces under General Lew Wallace were retreating toward Baltimore. Once again Delaware was in peril of invasion. That Sabbath, instead of church bells, the people heard the sound of fife and drums, calling every available man to service in defense of the state.

The next day it was reported—erroneously, of course—that Washington and Baltimore had fallen to the Confederates and rebel cavalry was not far from the du Pont powder mills. On the following day the Southern raiders did, in fact, capture two morning trains bound from Baltimore to Wilmington. Wednesday morning word spread that the Confederates were close to the outskirts of Wilmington—they would be in sight of the Brandywine at any moment. All citizens were asked to suspend their ordinary activities and join together in defense of their homes.

By night, happily, word was received that Early was falling back from Washington. The last threat to the du Pont powder works was over.

CHAPTER XXV

A MIND DESTROYED

Anxiously the du pont women awaited the end of the war. The more frequent explosions had rubbed raw their nerves. Their husbands' long hours of work had caused marital friction in many households. Even at its very outbreak, the war had brought the most serious family division the du Ponts had ever known, a feud between Margaretta, Alfred V. du Pont's widow, and the wife of her eldest son, Eleuthère Irénée II.

Charlotte Shepard Henderson, a beautiful and sensitive woman, was a Virginian who loved her home state and felt as close to her kinfolk as the du Ponts always have been to each other. In 1858, when she married Eleuthère Irénée II, there were no sharp conflicts in her heart. None of the du Ponts was a "black Abolitionist"; indeed the family often hurled this epithet against those whose politics displeased them. And Delaware was a slave state, a border state south of the Mason-Dixon Line which might—and nearly did—side with the South in a national schism over slavery.

When the war actually started, however, the clash of loyalties within Charlotte could no longer be denied. Her male relatives were in gray uniforms, fighting for the Confederacy, for the Old Dominion, and being killed with bullets and cannon shells for which her husband's family, her neighbors on the Brandywine, was making the powder. She felt isolated, almost a prisoner of war, in a community now united, as it had not been before the war, on the North-South issue.

Her mother-in-law was bossy and dogmatic. There is nothing quite so formidable as a *good* person untroubled by doubt: such a woman was Margaretta. She was devoted to her father, Daniel Lammot, who was fond of saying that the South was Satan and the Confederacy's struggle against the North proof positive of the secessionists' malignant design on religion. When the intolerant Margaretta attempted to force her unhappy daughter-in-law to acknowledge the righteousness of the Union cause, a breach became inevitable.

Thus began the worst estrangement the family had ever known. Irénée stood by his wife, refusing even to see or speak to his mother until she had made her peace with Charlotte. She never did. Even on his death bed in 1877, he told those about him not to let his mother into the room.

The cleavage—and the terrible years of war and bitterness—affected Charlotte's mind. She died in a mental hospital in Philadelphia twenty-nine days before her husband.

For most of the du Pont women, however, the Civil War was at first a time of excitement. They were thrilled when young Alexis I. du Pont II, a student at the University of Pennsylvania, taught the girls how to use pistols before he left home to enlist in the army. They felt quite brave.

The older women were less confident. Just before the battle of Gettysburg, when a Confederate move against the powder works was feared, Mrs. Alfred V. du Pont told her friends that if the rebels actually appeared, she intended to drop all her "bottles of wine into the pond" to prevent the marauders from getting drunk and thus increasing "their appetite for destruction."

The troops assigned to the task of protecting the powder mills brought color into the lives of the du Pont women. On the Fourth of July, 1861, a cavalry unit, the First Troop of the Delaware Light Dragoons, proud of their new uniforms and their handsome mounts, trotted to Eleutherian Mills to call on Major General Henry du Pont in his role as commander of all the state's armed forces. Henry invited them in and offered refreshments, while all the younger women of the family clustered about the guests. Afterwards everyone went up the hill to Sand Hole Woods where the general administered the oath to the horsemen. Then the company executed cavalry drill formations with more enthusiasm than skill. "It was a pretty sight to look at them galloping through the trees," Henry's wife wrote to their son, Henry A., adding drily, "Willie [her younger son, aged six] enjoyed it immensely, not discovering that they were beginners."

Sometimes the women would climb into carriages with their children and drive over to Camp du Pont on the Kennett Pike to watch the soldiers parade, and the troops occasionally reciprocated by having their band serenade the du Ponts in the evening. For a while, however, when an outfit composed of Delaware recruits was stationed at the camp, drunken soldiers became a common sight in the neighborhood and any young woman was the object of ribald shouts and lewd suggestions. Finally the young du Ponts were instructed by their elders to discontinue their afternoon walks and keep close to the house until a better-disciplined regiment took the place of the rowdies.

As the war wore on, more and more wounded and sick soldiers began to return to Delaware or to pass through on their way to places north. The church bells rang out whenever a casualty train was scheduled to pass through Wilmington and messengers would spread the news. There were fourteen hundred on one such train that stopped briefly at Wilmington early in September, 1862, carrying disabled soldiers to Philadelphia. The people were asked to send refreshments and "everyone turned out," according to Sophie du Pont. Whatever might comfort a sick man—fruit, bread and butter, milk, ice water, coffee—was brought in such quantities that enough was left over for the two thousand other casualties who arrived on a later train that day. What surprised the women most "was the cheerfulness of the men," Sophie said, "and they were so grateful for the tenderness shown them."

The months wore on, and season followed season, and the trains kept rolling north and south—south with huge numbers of raw young recruits being carried wide-eyed toward the armies in the field; north with smaller members of maimed and hurt and sickened veterans leaving the butchery behind them. New casualty lists appeared every day, and families grieved.

It was about ten o'clock on a Sunday night when news of Lee's surrender reached the Brandywine. The bells began ringing, first in Wilmington, then others picked up the jubilation until every bell along the length of the creek was crying out the happy news. Every house was lit up, people thronged the streets cheering, and the du Pont powdermen set off cannons, the blasts echoing back and forth with a crackling thunder against the walls of the valley. In the light of great bonfires, neighbors stood arm in arm and sang the songs of the war: the stirring "Battle Cry of Freedom," the sad "All Quiet Along the Potomac," the righteous "Battle Hymn of the Republic," the mournful "Just Before the Battle, Mother," the exultant "Marching Through Georgia," the optimistic "When Johnny Comes Marching Home"—the songs of a war now ended.

There were missing faces in the crowds around the fires. The war had claimed its dead. And the four years had taken their toll at home, too.

Early in the war, Victorine du Pont Bauduy died in her sixty-eighth year. She had been ill, but her condition was not considered critical. And then one night, her brother Henry suggested that he send for the minister, still the Reverend Samuel C. Brincklé, her beloved "Mr. B." But she said, "Oh, not tonight! I should like to see Mr. B. very much, but wait till morning." Just before the dawn, she opened her eyes and watched the doctor with his hand on her pulse. "How is it?" she asked. "Very low," he replied. "I can scarcely feel it." She nodded once, weakly. "I thought so," she said and died.

The old rector survived her by only two years. In the spring of 1863, he died of typhoid fever.

CHAPTER XXVI

THE POWDER TRUST

Lammot du Pont was a dashing, high-spirited young man with a mind of his own. The family had come to expect almost anything from him. But no one was prepared for the surprise he sprang on the du Ponts in the fall of 1865. He told them he was going to marry Mary Belin.

Everyone along the creek liked Mary, born and raised on the Brandywine. She had a cool, crisp wit, devoid of malice; a lively, friendly girl she was, with an original, keen mind. The Belins had been associated with the du Ponts for almost as long as the latter had been in America. Mary's grandfather, Augustus, one of the French planters who had fled Haiti in 1781, had settled in Wilmington where he later became the first Belin to work for the du Ponts. Mary's father, Henry Hedrick Belin, was the du Pont company bookkeeper as well as a trustee of Christ Church.

What shocked the family was the fact that Mary Belin was one-fourth Jewish.

In those days the du Ponts were probably no more bigoted—possibly a good deal less—than the majority of their neighbors, but most of the family, proud as they were of the du Pont blood, objected to bringing a girl of Jewish ancestry into the clan. Still, no one dared to try and dissuade the hot-tempered Lammot. So an alternative course was agreed upon: the young bride would simply be ignored by the family. They would act as though she did not exist.

On October 13, 1865, Mary and Lammot were married. For three months they held their tempers with some difficulty as the other du Ponts showed their disapproval of the match by avoiding Lammot's home.

On New Year's Day, however, a rig pulled up in front of his house and Henry, the head of the company and the real boss of the family, ostentatiously climbed down and walked inside with a present for Mary in accordance with the family New Year's custom. Other du Ponts, who had been watching Henry's performance from behind their curtains, put their heads together excitedly. They agreed that Henry's approval made it impossible for them to continue their boycott. So Mary was accepted as a du Pont in good standing.

In later years, Lammot's descendants sometimes would be the object of anti-Semitic remarks within the family circle, but the latent prejudice kept fading, especially after his sons, Pierre, Lammot, and Irénée, each in his turn became head of the company. It is Lammot's line which dominates the company today.

But at that time Henry had more important things on his mind than a quartering of Jewish blood in his nephew's wife. Chaos had fallen upon the powder industry. Government arsenals were overloaded with gunpowder for a war that was now over. The abrupt end of government purchases, not only of gunpowder but of uniforms, tents, blankets, wagons, horses, and provisions, had caused a nationwide depression. Now the government added to the blight by dumping surplus powder on the civilian market, selling it at auction for as little as five cents a pound compared with thirty-three and a half cents, the top wartime price. The public auctions continued for six years, and Civil War powder did not disappear from the market until 1890. The entire industry was disorganized by the flood of cheap powder.

To add to the problems faced by Henry, the western trade had been lost to du Pont during the war. Because of the difficulty of transporting powder in wartime when ships were threatened by Confederate raiders and trains by guerrillas, the flow of powder to the West had dwindled to a mere trickle. Miners, desperate for blasting powder, joined together and raised $100,000 to build their own powder mills. A western firm, called the California Powder Works, used cheap Chinese labor and obtained saltpeter at a lower cost than the du Ponts because of the shorter distance between America's west coast and the source of supply in India.

The answer to the industry's problems seemed obvious to Henry du Pont. Early in 1872, he sent letters to the five other largest gunpowder manufacturers, inviting them to a meeting with him and one of his principal agents, F.L. Kneeland, in du Pont's New York office at 70 Wall Street, "for the purpose of ensuring an equitable adjustment of prices and terms of sales of powder throughout the United States." All the companies sent representatives except for one small firm, and even it concurred by mail in the decisions reached at the conference.

Thus was the Powder Trust born.

The Gunpowder Trade Association, the official name of the Powder Trust, established rules governing prices and competition. When one company was accused by another of having violated the rules, the GTA held a trial of the issues and punished any company found to be at fault. In one two-year period, two hundred and thirty cases of price-cutting were investigated by the GTA, with many penalties being levied.

Other companies joined the GTA—some because they believed that its methods offered the best way to keep the powder trade healthy; others because they feared that they would be driven out of business if they stood aloof. By 1881, the GTA included eighty-five percent of the industry.

The Powder Trust carried on price wars against a number of non-member firms, including the California Powder Works, the Sycamore Manufacturing Company, the Lake Superior Powder Company, King's Great Western Powder Company, the Ohio Powder Company, and the Marcellus Powder Company. The GTA won every time.

On the west coast, for example, GTA firms in their effort to wreck the California Powder Works sold powder "at prices less than the actual cost of production and delivery," according to a study of the Powder Trust. As a result, stockholders of the California Powder Works sold forty-three and one third percent of their capital stock to du Pont. Moreover, in 1875 it signed an agreement with the GTA giving the association the right to set prices and terms of sale for powder disposed of in "the neutral ground" —Utah, Montana, Wyoming, Colorado, New Mexico. As the definitive history of the explosives industry points out, du Pont, through the California Powder Works, now had "a practical monopoly of the business of the west coast."

The same sort of maneuver brought Sycamore into line. This was a powder company in Tennessee, twenty-five miles from Nashville. The Powder Trust ordered a price war in Sycamore's territory, and soon powder was being sold below cost. Bankruptcy faced the company unless it came to terms with the association. Sycamore capitulated: it gave du Pont five hundred shares of Sycamore stock in return for capital and machinery. In 1876, du Pont bought the rest of the stock through a dummy. Once in control, du Pont compelled Sycamore to abide by the rules of the GTA. By 1879, more than sixty-one percent of all the powder consumed in the United States was made by du Pont or one of its innumerable subsidiaries.

Technological change, also, was affecting the industry during this period. Swedish inventor Alfred Nobel, best remembered today because of the prizes he endowed, including—ironically—a peace prize, having devised a system for detonating nitroglycerin with fulminate caps, now tamed that dangerously unstable compound by mixing with it the chalky earth called *kieselgühr*. At first Henry du Pont had sneered at nitroglycerin as impractically hazardous, an explosive that never could be used with safety, and his inflexible nature was unable to accept the idea that dynamite was an improved, safer form of nitro. In every one of their forms, Henry said, these high explosives "are all vastly more dangerous than gunpowder, and no man's life is safe who uses them."

But progress could not be denied and Henry permitted the California Powder Works and, later, other companies controlled by the du Ponts to manufacture dynamite largely as a result of Lammot's experiments with the blasting compound.

Henry still held out against the making of dynamite by the du Pont company itself, however, until 1880, when Lammot finally lost his temper and told his uncle he'd open his own plant to produce it if du Pont didn't. Lammot even went so far as to take an option on some land near Wilmington for a mill site before Henry announced, "We are going into the high-explosive business—that is, we are forming a company in which we are heavily interested to manufacture the same." The new organization became the Repauno Chemical Company, taking its name from a creek on the plant site in New Jersey across the Delaware River from Chester, Pennsylvania.

Those were the days of the settling of the West and, in the East, of the beginning of the transformation that would make an agricultural country into an urban nation. The railroads were spreading out over the western half of the United States, and they needed explosives. The Indians were being driven onto reservations—with gunpowder. Bessemer's process had provided a foundation for a whole new steel industry; dynamite was used to blast out the iron ore and the coal for it. The petroleum industry had just come into being; the new wells were being sunk with high explosives.

It should have been a boom time for the explosives industry, but it wasn't. For this was the era of the great speculators—Jay Cooke, Jim Fisk, Jay Gould, Commodore Vanderbilt—and the national economy was periodically shaken, in part because of their manipulations. After the panic of 1873, more than 23,000 business houses throughout the country collapsed and credit almost disappeared. In 1877, Henry du Pont said, "More than half the powder machinery in this country has been lying idle since the panic of 1873."

To survive such economic shocks, the du Ponts attempted to make their company as self-sufficient as possible. "We build our own machinery," Henry said in 1875, "draw our own plans; make our own patterns; and have never employed anyone to design or construct our mills or machinery, dams or races, roads or anything else; being our own engineers and superintendents of all work done at our mills, both here and in Pennsylvania."

This was the kind of operation Henry understood. The complete authoritarian, he wanted to have control of every part of the company. Change held no attraction for him. For years he scorned typewriters, forcing his tiny office staff to write letters in longhand and copy them with quill pen in a letterbook. Finally Frank Haley, the correspondence clerk, rented a typewriter for a month, took it home and learned to operate it, and then, without saying a word to Henry in advance, laid several typed letters on his desk. The old man signed the letters and told Haley the company would buy typewriters for the clerks. But he still refused to dictate letters to a stenographer; instead he laboriously scratched out twenty letters a day in longhand for the clerks to copy.

To his face the men called him "Mr. Henry" or "the General." Among themselves he was usually referred to as "the Red Fellow" because of the fringe of red beard that framed his face. He was supposed to be a disciplinarian and, in a way, he was; but he had a very human side, too: he liked to make his tour of the du Pont farmlands with several dogs, so that the noise of the dogs would awaken any dozing workmen before Henry could come upon them asleep.

The great du Pont estates today are the result of Henry's insatiable land hunger. Year after year he kept investing part of the firm's cash surplus in thousands of acres of land on both sides of the Brandywine, all the way up to the Pennsylvania border. Each new field or woods had a stone wall around it—Henry had a passion for stone walls. There was a family saying that he'd put a four thousand dollar fence around a two thousand dollar pasture.

Many members of the clan resented the spending of company money on the fences and even on land purchases. A more severe aggravation was the fact that the profits of the firm were divided unequally: Henry received as much money as all the other partners together.

Among the children Henry was a good deal more popular than he was with their elders. And "the Red Fellow" was just as fond of the boys and girls as they were of him. Whenever he appeared, he was surrounded by youngsters who could only be bought off with a piece of horehound candy and an affectionate pat on the head. In the cheerfully unscrupulous way of youth, however, the children were always ready to take advantage of the old gentleman. For example, in his office he had a collection of relics of the Revolutionary War's battle of the Brandywine. He was willing to pay ten cents to any lad who found a Revolutionary War bullet for him. So the boys cast their own bullets, buried them in the ground until they looked old enough, then exhumed them for sale to the unsuspecting patriarch.

One of the general's trade marks was the high silk hat he always loved to wear, especially in the evening, even if he were only going the few feet from his home to the office. This hat once helped to save one of the powder mills. It happened the night that Henry, in his office, heard a ringing or whistling sound from somewhere in the powder yard about nine o'clock. Only the glazing mills were in operation that night. In a powder works, any sound out of the ordinary is a danger signal, so Henry picked up a lantern and hurried to the nearby home of Thomas Kane, foreman of the Upper Yard. With Kane at his side, he made his way through the works, the whistling sound growing louder as they approached a glazing mill near the dam. A quick glance revealed the reason for the strange noise: the main shaft had become overheated at the point where it entered the mill; it was throwing off sparks. A fire and explosion might occur at any moment. As Kane stopped the mill gears, Henry rushed to the creek, filled his high silk hat with water, rushed back to the mill and doused the red hot shaft. Again and again he filled his hat and splashed water over the shaft until it had cooled and the threat of a blast was ended.

CHAPTER XXVII

THE LITTLE WORLD
ON THE BRANDYWINE

ONE MONDAY, in the last quarter of the nineteenth century, Alexis I. du Pont II made a passing comment to his brother, Francis Gurney du Pont, about the new vehicle he had seen him driving to church the day before.

"I didn't know you had a carriage like that," Alexis remarked casually.

That was all he said. But for the rest of the day Frank pondered his brother's words.

"I don't know why he said that," Frank told his wife that night. "It's none of his business what kind of a carriage I have." It was days before he got over his resentment.

Life was like that in the little world on the Brandywine. There were perhaps one hundred and twenty-five du Ponts living in the vicinity of the creek; so many, indeed, that the houses to accommodate them now stretched not only along the stream, but up and over the hills and across the rolling countryside in a broadening quadrant north and west of Wilmington, as well as in the city itself. The du Ponts had ceased to be French, but they remained, in Henry Seidel Canby's phrase, "a race apart from the Quaker-commercial town of Wilmington," although a few members of the family, mostly of Victor's line, had intermarried with some of the most distinguished families of Delaware.

The du Ponts were very rich now. As early as 1864, Henry du Pont's income was $119,453, the highest in the state, and when Eleuthère Irénée II died in 1877, he left an estate of a half million dollars, although he was not even one of the operating triumvirate. Nevertheless, the du Pont way of living remained simple and unostentatious.

One day a soot-smeared powderman in grimy work clothes walked into a Wilmington store and picked out a cheap rubber coat. He started to walk out with it, saying that he'd send the money over from the bank as soon as he could cash a check. The storekeeper refused to let him leave with the coat.

"But you should know me," the powderman said. "I'm Irénée du Pont."

"If you're a du Pont, I'm General Grant," the merchant snorted.

He should have known better, for the du Ponts were widely known as a hard-working family. As they had in the beginning, every du Pont still started at the bottom in the powder works, and this was not simply a token effort at learning the business from the ground up. The du Ponts had to work as hard as the next man, and they earned promotions slowly and by displaying those qualities that the business needed: perseverance, imagination, initiative, and, most of all, courage.

They worked close to their employees, and they lived close to them. The workmen's sturdy stone houses were clustered around many of the du Pont residences along Breck's Lane and elsewhere; the half-dozen or so of the powdermen's hamlets bore names like Henry Clay Village, Rising Sun, Hagley, Squirrel Run, Charles' Banks, Upper Banks, Free Park—inevitably called "Flea Park."

The children of the workmen and the du Ponts grew up together, at least until the du Pont youngsters went away to boarding school. The boys had their own groups, calling themselves the "Up-the-Creek Gang" and the "Down-the-Creek Gang" and so on, but each band included du Pont lads who played and fought and got into mischief alongside the powdermen's sons. Like the du Ponts, the powdermen were descendants of men who had worked in the mills before; jobs were handed down from one generation to the next.

In one way, the boys of the Brandywine were unlike other youths: they felt very much at home with explosives. Fourth of July celebrations on the Brandywine were the most spectacular to be seen anywhere because of the elaborate, homemade fireworks. On one occasion some of the boys prepared two dozen fireballs for insertion in Roman candles and laid them on a board to dry. One of the balls rolled off into the ashpit of a steam engine in a small shed behind a du Pont home. Flaring up, the first ball caused the others to fly into the hot coals. In such a predicament, Brandywine boys knew just what to do. Two dove out a window while the other two hurled themselves instantly out through the doorway. A moment later the keg of powder inside blew up. None of the boys was injured.

Most of the workmen were still Irish, and so too were the house servants. The fashion for French governesses had given way to a new taste for Germans. Whether this was a change for the better is debatable. When the wife of Eleuthère Irénée II returned from a long sojourn in Europe undertaken after one of her nervous breakdowns, she found that the Emma she'd left in charge of her five children had appropriated to her own use money given her for the household funds and that she had beaten the smaller children badly enough to raise welts on their backs.

Frank hired a *fräulein* for his children but he fired her in short order when he found it was her practice to show up in the kitchen—just about the time he was having breakfast—wearing nothing but a mackintosh and a pair of rubbers. She'd pour coffee into the mug in which she'd kept her false teeth during the night and then she'd proceed in stately manner up the stairs to her room. To Frank, it was a hell of a sight with which to start his day.

The du Ponts held family dances in Breck's Mill, once Victor's woolen mill, where Breck's Lane runs into the Creek Road. Between dances, the young cousins would hang out the windows to watch the moonlight dancing on the water as it roared over the dam, and some of the more venturesome or more romantically inclined would stroll arm-in-arm up along the stream, listening to the water splashing over the rocky bottom of the creek and talking with the desperate earnestness of youth.

Actually, it is not surprising that so many cousin marriages took place. Two of the children of Charles I. married cousins, and so did two of his grandchildren. That was the pattern. Soon the genealogical charts were crisscrossed by consanguineous matings.

Occasionally the du Ponts broke out of their microcosm. It was inevitable that an increasing number of boys going away to college, especially to the Massachusetts Institute of Technology, would expose the family to the pleasures of Boston and New York. Besides visits to the theaters, the opera and the concert halls of those cities, there were shopping expeditions to Philadelphia, particularly for the women of the clan.

To outsiders the du Ponts seemed aloof and cold, but this was merely a reflection of their relative isolation. Among themselves they were an exuberant, fun-loving people with a taste for flamboyance. Once, when a girl cousin was about to be married, Alfred I. du Pont borrowed a paddy wagon from the Wilmington police and carried the wedding guests in it to the home of the bride-to-be.

The most popular man in the family was Lammot, known to scores of juvenile du Ponts as "Uncle Big Man." After the organization of the Repauno company, he had moved to Philadelphia to be closer to those works, but he and his family still passed a great deal of time on the Brandywine. When the Philadelphia home office of Repauno was opened, George H. Kerr, Lammot's secretary, spent a thousand dollars renting space, buying furniture and equipment, and having the office elegantly decorated. Two weeks later his boss, returning from a business trip, asked Kerr if he had any money left. He didn't. Lammot looked around the office, unusually plush for du Pont taste, and said mildly, "Didn't think you had. You're certainly hell for pretty!"

Earlier, as paymaster for the Wapwallopen mill in Pennsylvania, Lammot stopped one night in a shabby coal-town hotel. In his traveling bag which he put under his bed was the month's payroll for the mill. During the middle of the night, the door was opened stealthily and a man entered the darkened room and knelt beside the bed to pull out the traveling bag. Lammot moved with lightning speed. Sweeping his bedclothes about the startled intruder, the six-footer picked him up bodily, carried him into the hall and tossed him down the stairs into the lobby. In the morning, Lammot learned that the hotel keeper had departed abruptly during the night.

Lammot was the chemist of his generation. It was he who discovered a method for using nitrate of soda instead of saltpeter for manufacturing powder. After that innovation in 1857, the cost of making powder dropped sharply, increasing demand and forcing the du Ponts to abandon their policy of building only mills that could be personally supervised by the partners.

It was one of Lammot's favorite sayings that anyone who went into an explosives plant when he didn't have to was a fool. In 1884, he did just that. It was a Saturday and ordinarily he would not have been at the dynamite plant that day. But A.S. Ackerson, a salesman for Laflin and Rand, another powder company, had asked Lammot if he'd show him around the plant. Reluctantly, Lammot agreed to do so.

For some time Lammot had been experimenting with methods for saving the acids that remained after nitroglycerin was manufactured. He wanted to recover the acids for two reasons: first, because it would be economically desirable; and second, because the waste acids, flushed into the Delaware, were killing the fish. In a specially designed NG—nitroglycerin—house at Repauno, the last charge of Friday had been drawn off into a lead-lined tank and left to stand overnight.

On Saturday morning, when Ackerson and Lammot were touring the plant, the superintendent, Walter N. Hill, was notified by a workman that the acid in the NG was fuming so much that it appeared to be boiling. Lammot and Hill went to the NG house and Lammot ordered everyone else out. Then, with Hill's help, he tried to stir the smoking, decomposing acid into a water tank beside it, hoping thus to quench the reaction. Finally Lammot realized that their efforts were useless.

He and Hill ran from the house and dropped behind an earthen bunker about ten feet from the building. The earthen wall had been thrown up on Lammot's orders when the NG house was built; he was certain that the bank would protect anyone behind it from the full force of an explosion. The place blew up with a deafening roar and Lammot and Hill were buried under tons of earth when the bunker was thrown on top of them. The three workmen who had been ordered out of the building earlier had stopped to watch from about thirty feet away; they, too, were killed. So was Ackerson, whose neck was broken by the shock.

That night, in her grief-silenced Philadelphia house, Lammot's widow began to pull down the shades in the living room when her eldest son, Pierre Samuel, then fourteen, stopped her.

"Let me do that, Mother," he said. "I am the man of the family now." To the day of his death, Pierre was called "Dad" by his younger brothers Irénée and Lammot.

On the Brandywine, as usual, explosions had been occurring with terrible regularity all along, but some freak of fortune had somehow saved the du Ponts themselves from injury and death. Their workmen were not so lucky, however. In 1866, one man was killed; in 1869, the death toll was two. And so it went: 1872, one; 1873, two; 1875, one; 1877, one; 1883, two.

The first American-born generation of du Ponts was also disappearing in these years. And now, on January 9, 1888, Sophie Madeleine du Pont died, having survived her husband, Admiral Samuel Francis du Pont, by nearly twenty-three years. Sophie, the adored aunt of du Pont children for so long, lived to the ripe age of seventy-seven, an invalid most of her life—proving the truth of the saying that the best way to insure a long life is to contract a chronic disease in youth and spend all your days taking care of it.

In business, too, the old order was passing. The du Ponts, through the Gunpowder Trade Association, held a virtual monopoly of the business throughout the entire country. "The only serious rival left in the industry was Laflin and Rand, a company that was in fact a comrade-in-arms," said du Pont executive William S. Dutton in his story of the company. From this position of strength, Henry wrote to a Texas du Pont agent who had warned that Southwesterners were growing hostile toward trusts:

We are a partnership—a firm composed of individuals. We are not an incorporated company, nor have we ever been a corporation. We have always been a firm and never had but the one firm name. We manage our own business in every particular, and allow no trusts or combinations to rule or dictate what we shall do or what we shall not do. We make our own powder, and we make our own prices at which it shall be sold, here, there, and everywhere in the world where it is for sale.

We are every day dictating to our agents as to prices, terms, and conditions to govern them; but we do not allow anybody to dictate to us as to what price, terms, and conditions we shall dictate. We do our own dictating.

If we choose, we can as quickly as wires can carry the orders change the prices at each and every point in the world where du Pont powder is for sale. And no trust, no combination, no set of people nor persons can interfere. We have not changed our mode of selling. Our mode today is the same as it has been since our firm was established very nearly a hundred years ago and we expect to continue a hundred years more in the same way.

All of this was strictly true. Nobody dictated to the du Pont company; the du Ponts laid down the law for the rest of the industry.

Henry wrote that letter in April, 1889. A "Fundamental Agreement," signed by members of the Powder Trust that same year, divided the country into seven sales districts and established the way business would be conducted by all GTA companies in each district. The GTA at that time controlled ninety-five percent of the rifle powder and ninety percent of the blasting powder produced in the United States. And du Pont had absolute control of the GTA.

The heritage of the du Ponts had been carried forward by Henry in a manner of which he was proud. But he was growing old; he had never liked change and he disliked it intensely now, and yet time was bringing about innovations that could not be avoided. 1889 appeared to be a year of major change. That was the year electric lights were installed in the powder yard, by virtual order of the Army and over Henry's protests; the year the old mule teams and their drivers vanished, supplanted by a railroad spur that ran from the powder yard to the main line of the Wilmington and Northern Railroad—Henry's son, Colonel Henry A. du Pont, had been president of this since 1879; the year that Alfred I., sent to Europe at the insistence of Army Ordnance Officers, negotiated royalty agreements under which du Pont would manufacture two new explosives: brown prismatic—or "cocoa"—powder for cannons, and smokeless powder for rifles.

One morning in June, Henry found himself so ill that he could not leave his bed to go to the office. For almost two months his condition deteriorated. On his seventy-seventh birthday—August 8, 1889—he died after fifty-five years of making powder, thirty-nine of them as head of the firm.

In the family burying ground in Sand Hole Woods, a verse from the Psalms was carved on his tombstone: "Mark the perfect man and behold the upright; for the end of that man is Peace."

A better epitaph might have been chosen from Proverbs: "Seest thou a man diligent in his business? He shall stand before kings."

CHAPTER XXVIII

REIGN OF EUGENE

AFTER MORE THAN a third of a century of authoritarian rule by Henry, the du Ponts were badly shaken by the loss of their leader. No one really wanted the responsibility of running the company—at least, nobody who had any chance of being entrusted with it. The eldest of the eligible du Ponts was Colonel Henry A., who had worked for the firm for four years after resigning his army commission. But during the last decade he had been a railroad president and he lacked practical knowledge of the powder business. His brother William was only thirty-four, too young for such a heavy burden. Thus the two sons of old Henry were eliminated.

The three sons of Alexis I. were possibilities. Of these, Francis Gurney du Pont probably would have been the best choice for the post, for he was a remarkably able man who had carried most of the administrative workload for the past few years—but he was also the youngest, only thirty-nine. Next came Alexis I. II, always called "Dr. Alexis" because he had earned a medical degree although he never practiced as a physician. After college he had worked for a time in a du Pont paper mill at Louisville, Kentucky, returning to the Brandywine only four years before Henry's death. He was forty-six. So, without enthusiasm, the partners chose the third brother, Eugene, who was ten years the senior of Alexis.

The mantle of Henry was too big for Eugene and he was in a

most uncomfortable position. Not only did he appreciate his own inadequacies, he also was painfully aware that the rest of the family recognized his shortcomings. Obviously, he reasoned, the business could not be run in the old way. So he made a valiant attempt to break away from the tradition of one-man rule. Now the country was divided into regions and Eugene appointed regional managers with considerable responsibility. He built a new office building, five times the size of the old stone structure used by Henry. When it was completed in 1891, he filled it with clerks, secretaries and stenographers. The force of carpenters and masons maintained as full-time employees by Henry was discharged and their work was turned over to an outside contractor.

Unfortunately, Eugene was only able to carry the modernization forward so far and no farther; then his own limitations brought progress to a halt. Accustomed to one-man rule by Henry, he could not delegate responsibility as broadly as the size of the company demanded. When all the changes had been made, the du Pont firm was still being operated as a benign dictatorship.

Some of the innovations were not popular. The carpenters and masons who had been thrown out of work were bitterly resentful, and a handful of them struck back with fire, the weapon most feared by powdermen. In 1889, a new barn close to the home of Francis Gurney was burned on the day after Christmas. Two weeks later, another du Pont barn went up in flames and some cattle perished with it. All through 1890 the barn-burnings continued, constantly menacing the powder works. Four men were arrested and convicted of arson, but to little avail. Incendiary fires kept bursting out until the end of 1893. It was an inauspicious beginning to Eugene's reign, but there was worse to come.

One of the greatest disasters in the history of the company occurred little more than a year after he had assumed command. On the seventh of October, 1890, two men were soldering boxes for prismatic powder in a magazine containing thirty-seven tons of powder. Although it might not seem so to an outsider, soldering is a perfectly safe task to carry out in a powder house if the proper precautions are taken. This time, however, the men were careless. Suddenly they realized that the soldering iron had ignited some loose powder on the floor. Plunging frantically through the door, they ran several yards from the building before it blew up, but they were killed by the blast.

That explosion set off a string of others. One after another, seven buildings, containing one hundred and fifty tons of powder, were blown to bits. Eleven men lost their lives, too, one of them being blasted into such small pieces that he literally could not be buried. The roofs were torn off du Pont houses and powdermen's homes, frame walls were ripped off buildings, the floors of stone houses caved in. A very old woman, the mother of a powderman, was killed outside her house, and a baby perished inside its parents' home when the ceiling fell on it. Horses and dogs and chickens were killed by the shock and flying debris, and in Wilmington hundreds of windows were shattered.

To a New Yorker who read about the accident in a newspaper and sent a check for the relief of the du Pont workmen, Eugene expressed his appreciation of the kindness. "Concerning the losses and needs of all our hands," he wrote, "we purpose [sic] to them and their families and to all who have suffered, to bring out of chaos an orderly state of affairs, to restore everything except life to all; to nourish, protect, and guide all and to do everything possible for man to do. Such being our purpose, it will not be necessary to use your check, which we therefore return with as many and as sincere thanks as it is possible for anyone to give."

After the ruined mills had been rebuilt and the younger du Ponts had time to consider the course of the company, they began to see that the changes initiated by Eugene were of form rather than substance, that the company was still basically under one-man rule. Two of the young men, Alfred I. and Charles I. III, had positions of substantial responsibility, yet were not partners. Growing restive, they now demanded a share of the business. They were cheered on by their contemporaries who felt that the older members of the family were holding back all the young men, leaving them with little hope for advancement.

In the end, William—"Willie"—for personal reasons, chose to resign his twenty percent partnership. It was divided equally between Alfred I. and Charles I. III. But in meetings of the partners thereafter, the older relatives ignored Alfred and Charles, carrying on the discussions as if the two were not there.

About the time that William retired from the presidency of the Repauno Chemical Company, two remarkable, thirty-one-year-old men, J. Amory Haskell and Hamilton M. Barksdale, took over the management of that du Pont enterprise with great success. Barksdale, who had been with the Repauno for several years, had already married into the du Pont family; his wife was Ethel, the sister of Charles I. III. Thus Barksdale was the first example of what became a du Pont pattern: the brilliant in-law. Over the years the family enriched itself by marrying its daughters to talented young men. Naturally, this gave rise to all sorts of cynical jokes about marrying the boss's daughter and in some instances the gibes were undoubtedly warranted. But usually the young grooms had already marked themselves as men on the rise before marrying into the family.

The elevation of Alfred to a partnership pleased the workmen, for he was the most widely liked member of a family which was still close to its employees. Many du Ponts were admired for their generosity: Francis G. ("Frank") built a public school with his own money at the Kennett Pike and Breck's Lane, and the du Pont women turned Eleutherian Mills, empty since Henry's death, into a clubhouse for the firm's workers, a project that eventually failed.

But Alfred's warm and impulsive deeds were in a class by themselves. For example, when a typhoid epidemic broke out among the children of du Pont powdermen, Alfred paid two physicians to care for the sick youngsters and told the doctors to do everything possible, regardless of cost. Ice cream and other delicacies from the du Pont larders went to the young patients, and the powder yard whistle was silenced so they could sleep more soundly.

The du Ponts joined with their workmen in many social activities. While Eleutherian Mills was being used as a clubhouse, three musical organizations—the Tankopanicum Musical Club, the du Pont Club Brass Band, and the Brandywine Fife and Drum Corps—had their headquarters there. The orchestra was led by Alfred and its members included two of his relatives, Felix and Pierre S. The latter had never studied music, but he had a natural talent for the piano that usually carried him through. However, one night during a concert at the Green Hill Presbyterian Church, he got badly tangled in a medley of Southern airs. Afterwards as they walked home, Alfred and Pierre were silent. Finally Alfred sighed and said, "You know, Pierre, tonight I wished I had had a baseball bat in my hand instead of this little stick." His cousin nodded sadly. "Alfred," he said in his mild way, "I can easily understand it."

Alfred was the first of the du Ponts to become car-crazy. He had the second automobile in Delaware. "They're going to bring in those new machines called automobiles and everyone will be killed," said Colonel Henry A. gloomily, with no pre-vision of the time when the du Ponts would put together General Motors, the greatest automobile manufacturing organization in the world.

The first car Alfred bought was a Locomobile which he soon sold to a Massachusetts man. A short time later, the buyer dropped du Pont a note: "I just want to report on the Locomobile I bought of you. It is loco, all right, but not so mobile."

As a partner in the firm, Alfred had more important matters than cars on his mind. There were three major contemporary problems: a threat of competition from Europe, the Spanish-American War, and a change in the nature of the company.

The European challenge resulted from an imprudent move by Aetna, one of the firms in du Pont's Powder Trust. Aetna made the mistake of shipping dynamite to South Africa. Until then, the European powdermakers had refrained from entering the American market. But Nobel considered South Africa part of its territory. In retaliation, the Nobel-Dynamite Trust Company, Limited, of London and the Vereinigte Köln-Rottweiler Pulverfabriken of Germany, two firms which had been co-operating as a cartel, decided in 1897 on an economic invasion of the United States. Both companies bought tracts of land in New Jersey, and Nobel actually began building a plant at Jamesburg in that state. The du Ponts were filled with consternation at this development. They hastened to send a delegation to Europe to meet with the British and the Germans.

Out of their conferences came the first cartel in which the Brandywine company participated—the Jamesburg Agreement of 1897. This barred the Europeans from the United States until at least 1907: it was later renewed and extended. In return, the Powder Trust pledged itself, as Eugene put it, to make "payments [to the Europeans] for preventing the competition." The scope of the cartel was global, dividing the entire world into spheres of influence, each party promising not to infringe on another's territory.

Toward the end of that year, Alfred, then visiting New York, told an acquaintance, "We're going to have war." His friend didn't think so—Americans were too sensible to fight with Spain. "Makes no difference," said Alfred. "They can't stop it. The newspapers will start this war."

And start it the newspapers did, with inflammatory headlines and slanted articles. The key issue needed by the irresponsible press was supplied on February 15, 1898, when the battleship *Maine* blew up in Havana harbor with a toll of two hundred and sixty lives. REMEMBER THE MAINE! the newspapers screamed, even though a naval commission was unable to fix the blame for the explosion. Hysteria swept the country. In April, Congress declared a state of war.

Arranging for a commission in the army, Alfred gave notice to his partners that he would soon be leaving. But the government insisted that he was needed on the Brandywine. Smokeless powder was still too new and the facilities for manufacturing it in huge quantities were just being built. Hudson Maxim, as brilliant an inventor as Sir Hiram Maxim, his more famous brother in England, had just sold his smokeless powder patents to du Pont and become a consultant to the firm.

The war would have to be fought with brown prismatic powder, and Alfred I. du Pont was the best brown-powderman in the country although he was now just thirty-three years old.

The government demanded 20,000 pounds of brown powder a day. At that time, the capacity of the Brandywine works was only 3,000 pounds, but Alfred promised that, within sixty days, the daily output would be pushed up to 20,000 pounds. He exceeded his goal. When the war ended with an armistice in August, his record was impressive: 2,200,000 pounds of brown powder delivered to the government in four months. The capacity of the du Pont plant had been increased nearly ninefold.

During that hectic summer, someone noticed Alfred's eight-year-old daughter, Bessie, playing with her dolls on the steps of a rolling mill in the Hagley Yard. He was asked if he didn't think it was an awfully dangerous place for a little girl to be. "Not *awfully* dangerous—no," Alfred said. "And besides, my men work there."

The company had been growing since Henry's death. Big as it had been then, it was still bigger now. "On the threshold of the twentieth century," said Willard F. Mueller in his scholarly study of the firm, "E.I. du Pont de Nemours and Company reigned over a vast explosives empire, the precise boundaries and composition of which were unknown to many of its own officials." To improve administration and control, Colonel Henry A. suggested that the company be incorporated. Some du Ponts—Frank, for one—opposed the idea vehemently. If the company were to be incorporated, he predicted, "in ten or twenty years others, no relation to the family, would largely own the business, and those who did own it would do their work as directors, perhaps living at a distance from this place." But he argued to no avail; the company decided to incorporate.

To clear the path for incorporation, the du Ponts applied political pressure and succeeded in having a state constitutional convention called in 1897. They wanted the new constitution to permit a change in the laws governing corporations. According to William C. Lawton, who made a study of the company, several members of the convention were "prominent in du Pont affairs." One du Pont man, Charles F. Richards, belonged to the convention's committee on corporations.

As a result of the constitutional changes and a legislative act passed in 1899, it is now cheaper and less troublesome to incorporate in Delaware than in most states. This law has made Delaware as important to corporations as Nevada is to the unhappily wed. Today thousands of the largest corporations call Delaware home—although their only connection with that state may be a mailing address there. Such firms include Ford, Coca-Cola, Commonwealth and Southern, Bethlehem Steel, American Airlines, Pullman, Allis-Chalmers, and Wrigley.

On October 23, 1899, E.I. du Pont de Nemours and Company, Incorporated, was chartered under the new Delaware law. The officers were Eugene, president; Francis G., Doctor Alexis, and Colonel Henry A., vice presidents; Charles I. III, secretary and treasurer. The first four were allotted twenty percent of the shares apiece; Charles was given ten percent, and so was Alfred I.

The younger du Ponts had hoped that the change to corporate form would also open up to them more avenues of advancement, but the announcement of officers and stock allotments showed that their expectations would not be realized. Disgusted, Pierre S. du Pont quit the company after nine years of work and went to Ohio.

The company was still under one-man rule, for this was the only way Eugene knew how to run the organization. Worse still, nobody was being trained in responsibility for the day when a successor for Eugene would have to be found. Except for Alfred, the only young man thus far able to reach a place near the top, none of those in control of the company had given any thought to this matter.

An enormous business enterprise depended on one man. When he died, the du Pont corporation would be close to death, too.

CHAPTER XXIX

SENSATIONS FOR THE PRESS

THE YEAR OF HENRY'S DEATH ushered in more than a period of trial for the company: it also marked the first appearance of the du Pont name in sensational newspaper stories. This was doubly offensive to the family because the du Ponts always had—and to some extent still have—the attitude that any interest in them was and is an outrageous invasion of their privacy.

So it was particularly painful for the family to learn about the marriage of Maurice du Pont in newspaper accounts. The marriage was described by the *Wilmington Evening Journal*, a Delaware newspaper not then owned by the du Ponts, as "the sensation of two continents." The paper wasn't exaggerating; the New York metropolitan dailies also gave it feature billing.

An alert correspondent for the *Chicago Daily News* broke the story on November 12, 1889. The headline read:

HE MARRIED A BARMAID
STORY OF MAURICE DU PONT'S ROMANTIC MATCH
—BEAUTY AND VIRTUE HER ONLY DOWRY

Maurice du Pont was the brother of Alfred I., but he had none of his brother's interest in the powder business. After briefly attending the Massachusetts Institute of Technology, he had gone to Johns Hopkins University, receiving an electrical engineering degree there. Then he set out to see the world. When his liner put in at Ireland, Maurice visited a Queenstown hotel—to get a drink in a hotel pub, according to the most believable story. There he saw a pretty, pink-cheeked lass who, with her ready laughter and gay, tart wit struck him as the most attractive girl he'd ever seen. The precise nature of Margery May Fitz-Gerald's duties at the hotel has been so obscured by legend that it can no longer be determined accurately. Some said she was a barmaid; others insisted she was a housekeeper or manager. Apparently she came from a fine old Irish family whose money had run out.

As a suitor, Maurice showed the characteristic du Pont stubbornness. He told Margery he wouldn't leave Queenstown until she agreed to marry him. Once they were engaged, however, he returned to America. But the betrothal was kept secret, possibly because he thought his family might object—he must have heard a good deal of critical comment about the Irish when he was growing up on the Brandywine. Then, after a few months, he went back to Ireland at the time appointed for the wedding. On October 12, 1889, the two young people were married in St. Peter and Paul's Church in Cork by the Reverend Canon Sheean.

The du Ponts, most of them, were furious at Maurice for not informing them in advance of his intentions, for letting them learn about the nuptials only in the press, and, possibly, for marrying an Irish girl. But *not* for marrying beneath his class. Throughout their history, the du Ponts often have taken penniless mates, so that snobbery on that score is unusual in the family although it appears occasionally. Offsetting the hostile majority reaction was a message from Maurice's older brother, Alfred I., congratulating him and urging the newlyweds to come to the Brandywine and stay at Alfred's residence, Swamp Hall.

They accepted the invitation and Alfred and his wife managed to soothe the ruffled feelings of some of the other du Ponts. The few who came to call on Maurice and Margery liked the bride. The calls were returned and soon the young couple were turning up regularly at family gatherings. Before long the excitement died down.

Although he was offered a job in the company—at the bottom where all the du Ponts began—Maurice decided against it. He had inherited about $105,000. By husbanding this carefully, he reckoned he could get along quite well without working for the powder company. Instead, he went into business as an electrical engineer in Asheville, North Carolina, where he made his home for many years although he and Margery spent a good deal of their time traveling to various parts of the world.

The second shock to the family came three years after Maurice's wedding, when the du Ponts had their first divorce.

Mary Lammot du Pont was the sister of Charles I. du Pont III and granddaughter of the first Charles I. Her father, Victor, had followed his own father into Democratic politics and even had inherited his seat in the state senate. Regarded in the family as a nonconformist, Victor was Delaware's leading lawyer and represented most of the largest companies which paid fat fees for his services. But he really most enjoyed defending the poor and the helpless, to whom he donated his services. A director of banks and insurance companies, he was also a political liberal at a time when the label still had real meaning.

In her father's law office, Mary made the acquaintance of Willard Saulsbury, an up-and-coming young attorney from a proud old Delaware family. She fell in love with the quick-thinking lawyer, but her family frowned on her attachment. The reason is not clear: it may have been a matter of age—Mary was almost seven years older than Saulsbury at a time when such considerations bulked larger than they do today.

So Mary was married off to her cousin William, the son of old Henry and brother of Colonel Henry A. William, incidentally, was a year younger than his bride. At the reception after her wedding in 1878, Mary plucked a spray of orange blossoms from her bouquet and handed it to Saulsbury. Those close to her saw her lower lip trembling.

As one might have expected, the marriage turned out badly. Everyone in the family soon knew that Mary and William were unhappy together, but even though other du Pont unions had smacked more of acrimony than of matrimony, the hostile husbands and wives had always somehow reached an accommodation. Mary and William remained married for fourteen years, so everyone as-

sumed they had long ago agreed upon some kind of mutually satisfactory arrangement.

In the spring of 1892, the family was shocked to learn that William had gone off to South Dakota, a state whose laws were unusually liberal for that time, and had divorced Mary there. It was
the first divorce in the clan and most of the members were appalled.

But worse was still to come. As soon as the divorce was granted,
William sailed to London and immediately married Mrs. Annie
Rogers Zinn, recently divorced herself from her first husband,
George Zinn of New Castle, Delaware. Within the du Pont family
circle, gossip had linked William and Annie for some time, but
nobody expected a double divorce and a marriage.

A year and a half later, Mary Lammot du Pont finally married
Willard Saulsbury; he had represented her in the divorce proceedings. She was thirty-nine now, he thirty-two. The difference in
ages seemed less important than it had a decade and a half earlier.

Outraged by the sensational publicity the change of marital
partners had given to the family name, the du Pont elders met and
agreed on a course of action. When William and Annie returned
from their European honeymoon, Eugene, the head of the company, told the groom that for the good of the family he must withdraw from the business. William bowed to the family edict: he
turned over his share in the firm to Alfred I. and Charles I. III, his
former brother-in-law. Then he resigned from the presidency of
Repauno and retired to Virginia.

Ostracized by almost all the du Ponts except Alfred I., William
bought President Madison's old estate, Montpelier, near Orange,
Virginia, and settled down to a comfortable life as a country
squire, breeding Jersey cattle and Hackney horses. But in 1913,
even though he and his brother, Colonel Henry A., were not on
speaking terms because of the scandal, William was called back to
E.I. du Pont de Nemours and Company, Incorporated, to serve on
the board of directors. Later he resigned that post in another family
schism and became president of the Delaware Trust Company. In
1925, he made the biggest income tax payment of any Delaware
citizen—a quarter of a million dollars in a time of very low tax
rates.

Besides Montpelier, William maintained several other residences: Bellevue, near Wilmington; a palatial estate with two private race tracks, just across the state line at Newtown Square, Pennsylvania; and a winter place, Hopeton Plantation, twelve miles from Brunswick, Georgia, where he died in 1928, a year after his wife Annie.

The family excommunication extended to Mary and her second husband, too. Most of the du Ponts, including Mary's sister Alice who had married T. Coleman du Pont, did not speak to the Saulsburys. And Willard Saulsbury, later elected United States Senator on the Democratic ticket, customarily referred to his wife's relatives as "that goddamned tribe."

Even the minister who married Mary du Pont and Willard Saulsbury was made to feel the family's wrath. He was the Reverend Ashton Henry, rector of Trinity Church in Wilmington. His bishop, the Right Reverend Leighton Coleman, a tyrannical patriarch who looked a good deal like the representations of Moses, apparently felt that he was the avenging instrument of the Lord. Bishop Coleman himself had married into the du Pont family, having taken to wife Frances Elizabeth du Pont, the daughter of Alexis I. Thus the prelate was a brother-in-law of Eugene, the head of the company, and of Francis Gurney, one of the principal partners. Bishop Coleman now charged Mr. Henry with violating the tenets of the Episcopal Church by performing the marriage and censured him so severely and relentlessly that the poor minister eventually found the pressure more than he could bear and fled to Switzerland. There the exiled clergyman received regular remittances from Willard Saulsbury.

The third family scandal occurred in November, 1892, just a few months after William's divorce and re-marriage. This time it involved a death.

The tragedy began with a wedding. A Virginia relative on their mother's side was getting married, so the offspring of Eleuthère Irénée II assembled at Swamp Hall before heading south. Louis du Pont, a student at Yale, brought with him Bessie Gardner, a cousin of the bride-to-be and therefore a very distant relative of Louis and his brothers and sisters.

Louis was quite smitten with Bessie's charms. So was his brother Alfred I. as he came to know her better on the trip from Wilmington to Alexandria. Virginia. Her father was Dorsey Gardner, a scholar then engaged on a new dictionary in collaboration with Noah Porter, president of Yale. She was twenty-one at the time, a good-looking blonde, gay and intelligent. She was far more cultured, informed and sophisticated than most of the Brandywine girls.

After the wedding when Bessie returned to New Haven, Alfred carried on an ardent correspondence with her. In the fall Louis went back to Yale, and his brother found excuses to visit him—and Bessie. There were other visits. Just before Christmas, Alfred told Louis that he and Bessie were engaged.

As though he couldn't accept what Alfred had said, Louis asked, "You're not going to marry Bessie Gardner?"

Alfred insisted that his plans were definite. In the days that followed, he was often troubled by the memory of the look on his brother's face. He had not understood the depth of Louis' feeling for Bessie.

On January 4, 1887, Bessie and Alfred were married in St. James' Church in Philadelphia where relatives of the bride lived.

That was the month Louis came of age. He received his legacy—and set out to win a reputation as "the only swell in the du Pont family," as one newspaper put it. Among other things, he began to drink heavily. His education suffered correspondingly. Originally in the class of 1889, he was dropped back into the class of 1890 and then of 1891; he spent three years as a senior at Yale and failed to graduate. Then he tried the Harvard Law School for a year before giving up any pretense of seriousness. Moving on to New York, he became a fixture of the big city's night life.

Toward the end of November, 1892, Louis arrived on the Brandywine to visit Alfred and Bessie at Swamp Hall, their residence. He attended an assembly at the fashionable Wilmington Club and appeared to enjoy the evening.

A few days later, on the afternoon of December 2, Louis strolled into the Wilmington Club. A friend stopped him to discuss a dance that was coming up, but Louis said he couldn't help with the arrangements because he was going "a long distance away." Half an hour later, a servant, hearing a shot, ran into the club's library and found Louis slumped in a chair in front of a writing table, a bullet in his head and a pistol on the floor beside him. He was dead.

The fourth scandal involved Louis' "Uncle Fred"—Alfred Victor du Pont II. A lifelong bachelor, Fred nevertheless served as guardian for two families of orphaned children—those of his older brothers, Eleuthère Irénée II and Lammot.

Fred had nothing to do with the powder company. In 1854, he and his brother, Antoine Bidermann du Pont, four years his junior, having decided that there simply wasn't enough room in the powder company for all the du Ponts now that the family had grown larger, went west to Kentucky. Near Louisville they bought a paper mill. They prospered and their business enterprises proliferated. At the time of his death, Fred was a vice president and director of the First National Bank of Louisville. He also was a major stockholder in the Central City Coal and Iron Company, in street railway systems in cities from Brooklyn to Chicago, and in a couple of steel companies. From his great wealth he gave freely, but without publicity, to private charities and philanthropic causes. When, for example, he decided that Louisville ought to have a high school for teaching young men technical skills, he built the school himself and gave it to the city, but he would not permit the city to put his name on the school. After his death, the Board of Education changed its name to the "A.V. du Pont High School."

No one, seeing Fred on the street, would have taken him for a multimillionaire. His tall, rangy body was always clad in a drab, black suit, and on his head he wore a somber black derby. "I declare," said one of the du Pont women, "he goes around looking as if he didn't have a five-cent piece in his pocket!" He also acted as though he didn't have a nickel. Although he provided an ample budget to insure that the horses drawing his street cars were sleek and well-fed unlike most horse-car teams of the time, he was reluctant to spend money on himself. Everyone in the family was surprised when he built a mansion in Louisville and laid out a private park for it at a cost of $400,000. He saw to it that "Central Park," as it was called, remained open to the public; and when the big house itself was completed, he couldn't bear to move there from his shabby hotel room. Instead, he turned the mansion over to his brother, Bidermann.

On Tuesday, May 16, 1893, word spread through Louisville that its richest and most public-spirited citizen, A.V. du Pont, had collapsed in front of his brother's house. Carried inside, he had died within minutes. As the *Louisville Commercial* put it the next day, "The quiet and simple character of his life [was] unbroken in the scenes of death."

To the du Ponts, not yet recovered from their recent public scandals, the newspaper accounts of Fred's life which extolled his virtues, his philanthropies, and his business acumen, were balm for their wounds. Louisville's officials and its leading citizens outdid each other in expressing sorrow in the passing of such an esteemed citizen.

Then the blow fell. The *Cincinnati Enquirer* came out on Thursday morning, May 18, with a front-page story about Fred's death. It seemed that he had not died quite as the official version had said.

Here is a summary of the *Enquirer's* description of his passing: About noon on Tuesday, a physician and an undertaker were summoned to Maggie Payne's bordello on West York Street. There they found a dead man. A death certificate was made out for a James G. Johnson, seventy-six years old, a widower, whose body was to be shipped to Bowling Green, Kentucky. However, the undertaker's hearse went, not to the railroad station, but to the du Pont mansion in Central Park. No trace of "Johnson" was ever found; and in the end, an official investigation, hushed up at first, established that the dead man was Fred du Pont.

The death certificate had listed "effusive apoplexy" as the cause of death, but it was known that there had been a shooting in the Payne bagnio that morning, and rumors intimated that Fred had actually been shot to death. According to one account, the shooting had been accidental; another version said that a blackmailer had slain the old man.

The *Enquirer's* account created a sensation in Louisville. Each incoming train carrying copies of the Ohio newspaper was met by men clamoring for it. Newsboys sold the paper for five dollars a copy and had no trouble getting the price.

The Louisville newspapers, however, stuck to the original story.

On Friday morning the *Courier-Journal* led off its front-page "News and Comment" feature with a denunciation of "sensational and incorrect reports published in newspapers in other cities." Choosing its words carefully, the paper said, "The *Courier-Journal* has made a thorough investigation of all the incidents in connection with the case, and unhestitatingly states its unqualified belief that there is no foundation whatever for the belief that Mr. A.V. du Pont came to a violent end." But the assertion that Fred had been stricken in Central Park was not reprinted, and the paper did not deny that he actually met his death in the bawdy house.

The attitude of the Louisville newspapers probably reflected their respect for the dead man. As a matter of fact, "Marse Henry" Watterson, the great editor who made the *Courier-Journal* one of the finest newspapers in the country, was in du Pont's debt and Fred had never pressed him for payment of the notes.

In the end, the *Enquirer* came to the conclusion that Fred simply died of a heart attack while visiting Maggie Payne who was sick.

The newspaper was wrong—if family tradition is correct. Within the clan, it was admitted that Fred had indeed been shot to death in the sporting house by a woman. The slaying supposedly climaxed a quarrel over financial arrangements for the child she had borne him.

But influential Louisville du Ponts, in their desire to avoid a public scandal and later to minimize it, induced city officials to describe the death as "natural." There was no arrest nor any attempt at prosecution, for a trial would only have attracted more attention to the unfortunate affair.

The tremendous public interest in the case, of course, arose from the fact that the death occurred in a disorderly house. Puritans could be smug about it, and men who were more conscious of their own human weaknesses could tell themselves that du Pont had been no better than he ought to be, either. All this was hypocrisy, for in those days every American city had its tenderloin and a great many solid citizens were to be found frequenting such resorts. Fred du Pont was simply a lonely old bachelor who tried to find companionship for a few brief hours now and then. Unlike the others, he met his death in a bordello, and because his name happened to be du Pont, it was news.

Regrettably, his lurid end tended to overshadow Fred's real character. He was widely known for helping penniless young men who showed ability. Most of the youths to whom he gave a boost were utter strangers, but some of the young du Ponts, frustrated by the barriers to promotion within the powder company, came west from the Brandywine to work in his enterprises. They knew Fred would not stand in their way if they showed real ability. Generous, sympathetic, warm-hearted, Alfred V. du Pont endeared himself to a great many people. As the *Cincinnati Enquirer* itself said, even after it broke the true story of his death: "He was unquestionably a fine old man."

CHAPTER XXX

I'LL BUY THE BUSINESS

FOR THIRTEEN YEARS the crisis created by the death of the benevolent autocrat, Henry du Pont, was held off—not resolved, simply postponed—by Eugene's valiant yet fumbling attempt to fill his shoes.

The day of reckoning came in 1902. Late in January, Eugene fell ill with pneumonia and, after lingering for a week, died on the twenty-eighth. With his death, the folly of the policy of holding back younger men became apparent.

Now the surviving officers and directors—the group from which the new president ordinarily would be chosen—were Eugene's brothers, Francis G., "Doctor Alexis," and Colonel Henry A.; Charles I. du Pont III; and Alfred I. For various reasons no consensus was possible on any of them. The colonel had little or no knowledge of the operations of the company and he wasn't much interested in it; at the moment, his major preoccupation was with politics. Frank and Alexis were both ill. Although Charles was only forty-three, he was in still worse shape.

By elimination, that left Alfred as the logical candidate to head the company, but in fact he was never seriously considered for the job. The kindest reason given was Frank's privately expressed opinion that he was "too young." In later years Alfred himself volunteered some of the real objections: "[I was] young, aggressive, and not popular. I suppose I was impulsive—and not always polite." By sheer force of talent and personality, he had forced the elders to admit him to a share in the partnership years before, but they had never forgiven him for challenging them. Then, too, when the elders ostracized William after his divorce, Alfred had championed his cause and visited him and his new wife. Alfred had rubbed the senior du Ponts wrong in a hundred ways, as a man of genius often irritates other minds.

The old men met privately day after day to mull over what seemed to be an impossible predicament. These were not official meetings of the directors, so Alfred was not invited to take part in the discussions. He knew that the conversations were taking place, but his first hint of the direction in which they were heading came when Frank was delegated to break the bad news to him. It had been agreed that the company must be sold, for there was no one available to carry on such a heavy responsibility. And since the du Ponts had a virtual monopoly of the entire powder industry, the only likely buyer was Laflin and Rand, the one company that had made any pretense of competing with them.

Usually tactless and outspoken, Alfred, for once, curbed his tongue and kept his own counsel. He contented himself with a terse statement that "a disposal of the assets of the company seemed advisable." Inwardly, however, he was seething with rage that this great organization, now in its centennial year, should be sold, that such a heritage should be thrown away to others after generations of du Ponts had given it their hopes, their labors, their health, even their lives. Five generations of hard work were to be tossed into the discard in exchange for mere money.

"I think the old company may need you sometime," Alfred's father had said on his deathbed. "I just have that feeling."

Now, Alfred felt, that time had certainly come. Quietly he made a trip to New York, where he arranged with bankers for a loan to re-finance the company if he should need cash to block a sale to Laflin and Rand.

For the moment he didn't want anyone in Wilmington to know what he had in mind, so he talked to his relatives a good deal about going into business on his own—manufacturing automobiles. But the others weren't talking much about the future; they were mainly concerned with justifying the sale of the company.

Somebody finally put to Alfred the question he couldn't answer truthfully any more: "*You* certainly couldn't run it, could you?"

"No," he replied, still determined to conceal his intentions. "Maybe I can push a wheelbarrow, but that's all the sense I have." The sarcasm was lost on his listener.

Nearly three weeks had passed now since Eugene's death, and the day of decision could no longer be put off. A meeting of the stockholders was called. Alfred came to it straight from the powder yard, wearing his work clothes and with his hands still black from the dust of the gunpowder. As secretary, Charles read the minutes of the last meeting at which the proposal to sell the company had been raised. Then followed some dispirited, rather shamefaced talk by the other directors about the inevitability of the sale. By general agreement, a minimum price of $12,000,000 was set for the property.

For the record, Colonel Henry A. offered a motion that the assets of E.I. du Pont de Nemours and Company, Incorporated, be offered for sale to Laflin and Rand, with Hamilton M. Barksdale as du Pont's agent in the negotiations.

All this time Alfred had been slumped in his chair, his eyes closed. Now he sat up and opened his eyes. He offered an amendment stating that the business must be sold to the highest responsible bidder.

Surprise greeted Alfred's action. Who could outbid Laflin and Rand? Nevertheless, it didn't seem worthwhile to dispute the quick-tempered Alfred at this point when everything had been agreed to. The colonel, therefore, accepted the amendment. After that, the question was carried unanimously.

There being no other business before the stockholders, the meeting was declared adjourned, to the satisfaction of the older du Ponts who had been worrying about what Alfred might do. A feeling of relief swept the room now as those present rose to their feet.

But Alfred was already standing, facing the stockholders, his eyes flashing. His back was to the door, blocking it.

"Gentlemen," he said, "*I'll* buy the business!"

There was a moment of stunned silence and then everybody began talking at once. In the hubbub, Frank told Alfred he couldn't have the company.

"Besides, the deal is for cash, you know," he said.

The blunt rejection stung Alfred into a rude retort. "If *you* can't run the company, sell it to someone who can," he snapped to the one man among his elders whom he had always respected. Francis G. du Pont was one of the ablest chemists the family had ever produced. Still addressing Frank as the most responsible person in the room, Alfred released a torrent of words, upbraiding the senior du Ponts for never giving the younger members of the family credit for having any brains.

On a later occasion Alfred testified to what he had said: "I pointed out to him the fact that the business was mine by all rights of heritage, that it was my birthright. I told him that I would pay as much for the business as anybody else; that furthermore I proposed to have it. I told him I would require one week in which to perfect the necessary arrangements looking toward the purchase of the business and asked for that length of time."

In at least one of his listeners, Alfred's words stirred a feeling of pride and sympathy. Colonel Henry A. understood tradition and fighting spirit if nothing else. The old soldier rose from his chair and put his hand on Alfred's shoulder. "All right," he said, "I'm with you."

Turning to the others, the colonel said, "Gentlemen, I think I understand Alfred's sentiment in desiring to purchase the business. I wish to say that it has my hearty approval. I shall insist that he be given the first opportunity to acquire the property."

At that point, Alfred left the room. He had important things to do.

Behind him he left confusion. Most of the others thought that his offer was no more than an off-the-cuff, harebrained fancy. Only the colonel regarded it as a serious proposition.

After the meeting, Alexis went home and, summoning Barksdale, he told him about the decision to sell the company. He asked the younger man to accept the presidency in order to handle the negotiations. Laflin and Rand was the best prospect as a buyer, of course. And then, as an afterthought, Alexis mentioned that Alfred "desires an opportunity to present a proposition" and that his wish "has, of course, been granted." In effect, Barksdale was being asked to take the presidency in order to surrender the company—a dubious honor at best although it was sweetened by the suggestion that he himself continue to run the concern if he couldn't arrange satisfactory terms of sale.

But Barksdale was too wise to put himself in such an uncomfortable position. "In my opinion," he said, "it would be a great misfortune for the company to place anyone at the head of the concern until you have exhausted all efforts to secure a man of your name to take the helm." For that reason, he said, he could not "at this time" accept the presidency.

That meant that the unhappy elders would have to deal with Alfred themselves. They didn't look forward to it.

Meanwhile, Alfred had been busy. He had never intended to swing the deal alone. From the time the notion of buying the company first occurred to him, he had hoped that he could bring T.— for Thomas—Coleman du Pont and Pierre S.—for Samuel—du Pont into the scheme with him. Both were his first cousins.

"Coly," the son of Antoine Bidermann du Pont, came of the Kentucky branch of the family. Born in Louisville, he had gone to Urbana University in Ohio but finished his education at the Massachusetts Institute of Technology. Six feet four, good-looking, a complete extrovert, he was a big man on campus at Urbana—stroke of the crew, captain of the football and baseball teams, track star, and a hit with the girls. He had gone to work in the family's Central City, Kentucky, coal mines, where he was vastly popular with the other miners; he even joined the union, the old Knights of Labor. Promotions gradually elevated him to the presidency of the coal company; one of his most striking achievements was to turn the place into a company town that stood as a model for others. Later he had been general manager of a steel concern in which the du Ponts had an interest and, after that, he became a promoter of street railway companies. Not all of his enterprises were successful: he built a button factory in Wilmington that never made a button, and a rifle factory was abandoned because the guns cost so much to produce that they couldn't be sold profitably. Like most promoters, Coly had the knack of using other people's money for his projects.

The other cousin, Pierre, had grown up on the Brandywine. In the beginning, he had worked for the du Pont corporation, helping to develop smokeless powder at the concern's Carney's Point works in New Jersey, just across the Delaware from Wilmington. Like other young du Ponts, he had been frustrated by the company's refusal to move him along as quickly as he felt he deserved. In time he had left and gone to Ohio to work in steel and traction companies controlled by Fred du Pont. Now he was president of the Johnson Company of Lorain, Ohio, which later was merged with other concerns into the United States Steel Corporation. Despite his shyness, the quiet, even-tempered Pierre was a consummate business man.

These two and Alfred himself would make a triumvirate if his vision could be realized: Coly, to head the company, using his promotional skills; Pierre, to run the front-office operations, keeping a watchful eye on the profit-and-loss statements; Alfred, to oversee the production end of the business, employing both his natural talent and the experience he had acquired working in the yards.

After leaving the stockholders' meeting, Alfred made a telephone call to Coly, who had moved his family to Wilmington when he launched the ill-fated button factory. Surprisingly, Coly was in town, so Alfred drove over to his house at 2023 Delaware Avenue and explained the proposition. It was breathtaking even for such an audacious promoter as Coleman du Pont. After discussing the idea with his wife, Coly asked time to think it over, but he warned Alfred, "I won't go in unless I get a free hand."

As soon as Alfred left, Coly telephoned to Pierre, then living in Lorain. Outlining Alfred's scheme, he said he would go along with it if Pierre would, too. Pierre already had received a wire from Alfred; he promised to come to Wilmington the following day to talk things over.

So, in the billiard room at Alfred's residence, Swamp Hall, the three cousins—plus John Jacob Raskob, Pierre's assistant from Ohio—discussed the matter from every conceivable point of view. For hours they considered all the angles. Then they decided to go ahead.

"There is going to be some tall hustling to get everything reorganized," Pierre wrote to his brothers, Irénée and William K. "We have not the slightest idea of what we are buying, but in that we are probably not at a disadvantage, as I think the old company has a very slim idea of the property they possess. . . . We are taking up a pretty big load; the prospects, however, are bright for making it a success."

Two or three days later, Coly, on behalf of himself and his cousins, made his presentation to the elders. Using the promoter's tactic of employing as little cash as possible, he proposed that the sellers accept payment in the form of four percent notes plus a bonus of stock in the new corporation. And to make the offer more attractive, he said the price would exceed the minimum of $12,-000,000. Exactly what it would be, he was not prepared to say until the cousins had had time to study the company's books more carefully.

The offer was accepted. Indeed, the old order changed faster than the three cousins had expected. A few days after Coly's meeting with the old board, Pierre dropped by the company's offices to talk with some of the senior du Ponts and, if possible, to study an inventory of the corporation's assets. Frank was just opening the morning mail as Pierre was ushered in. He handed the letters to Pierre and started to tick off for him some of the matters that needed immediate attention. Caught off balance, Pierre protested that he wasn't ready to take over yet; besides, the sale agreement hadn't been put into writing—in fact, the price hadn't even been agreed upon. Details, replied Frank with a wave of the hand—just details. Since the older generation had decided to sell, the younger might as well take over at once. And with that, Frank stood up, put on his hat and coat, wished Pierre good luck and walked out.

A week later, on March 1, 1902, the three cousins became the legal owners of the company. The price they paid was $15,360,000. But not one penny of it was in cash. The whole deal was on the cuff: $12,000,000 in four percent notes and $3,360,000 in stock—33,600 shares with a par value of $100 a share.

The total cash outlay of the three cousins was $2,100, the sum actually needed to incorporate the new company. More than fifty percent of the stock in the new company was held by Alfred, Pierre, and Coleman, the latter's share being larger than that of either of the other cousins as they had originally agreed. Alfred and Pierre had equal amounts.

What the three men obtained in the deal was far more than they expected. The old company proved worth more than $24,000,000— twice the price at which the elders would have sold out to Laflin and Rand. And now it was a company with the energy and outlook of youth. Coly and Alfred were thirty-eight and Pierre was just thirty-two.

One of the first acts of the new bosses was to move the home office of the company from the Brandywine to the Equitable Building in Wilmington. The corporation had long ago outgrown its simple office; now it was going to expand its executive operations as the largest powdermaking concern in America should.

Only sentiment still kept the Brandywine powder mills themselves in operation. The city of Wilmington had been moving out toward the du Ponts, and the explosive power of the gunpowder had been increasing—both facts that combined to make the century-old works somewhat less than practical. But as yet, Alfred and Pierre could not bear to put an end to the activity so long established and maintained on the Brandywine at such a great cost in labor and in lives.

Nevertheless, the moving of the main office to Wilmington meant an abrupt break with the old ways. Once all the du Ponts had worked in the same place with their powdermen, had known each man by name, had been ready to help with his problems, had shared a common danger. Now the only du Ponts still working in the Brandywine yard with the powdermen would be those whose production duties brought them there. The head of the corporation was being separated from its heart. This was unavoidable in the growth of the company, but it was hard to bear just the same.

On the Fourth of July in that centennial year of 1902, a great celebration was held on the Brandywine in honor of the coming of the du Ponts to the valley and the founding of their firm. Three thousand people attended—the du Pont families, the powdermen with their wives and children, and a few friends. Spectacular fireworks climaxed the dancing, games and merrymaking.

A few days later, a committee of workmen asked if they could meet with the officers and directors of both the old and the new companies. Self-conscious and nervous, the old powdermen on the committee shuffled their feet, coughed, lowered their eyes to their hands or focused them on the pictures covering the wall. Finally old Pierre Gentieu, their spokesman, read a formal statement:

> We, the employees of the E.I. du Pont de Nemours and Company at the home works on the Brandywine, in meeting assembled have hereby
>
> RESOLVED: That the record of one hundred years in the manufacture of gunpowder made by the du Pont company as a family is also shared with pride by many of the employees whose fathers and grandfathers have been identified with the history of the works.
>
> RESOLVED: That as one generation after another passes away, the record left by them has always been honesty, bravery, and kindness from the du Pont family and loyalty and love from their employees.
>
> RESOLVED: That we, the employees of the firm in nineteen hundred and two, wish to record the fact that we appreciate the kindness shown to us by the present officials and members of the du Pont family in thus inviting us all to mingle together in the celebration of this, to them, a Centennial Day; and as we have loved and been faithful to their fathers, we mean to do the same for the present generation.

Gentieu raised his eyes from the paper and gazed at Frank, Doctor Alexis, and Colonel Henry A.: "Gentlemen of the old firm, who have been our leaders and friends for so many years," he said sadly, "we are sorry that you are leaving us, for we will miss you."

Turning to Coleman du Pont, he added, "What the new company will do, of course, we do not know, but let us hope that after one hundred years more, as much good can be said of them as is said today of the du Ponts for the past century."

CHAPTER XXXI

STRUGGLE FOR THE SENATE

WHILE THE AFFAIRS of the du Pont company had been passing through a period of great change, Colonel Henry A. du Pont had become involved in a fantastic political war which was, in the end, partly responsible for the enactment of the Seventeenth Amendment to the Constitution of the United States. It was a struggle that was fought without letup for seventeen years, a clash of wills so fierce and ruthless that a respected journal of opinion, the *Outlook*, was led to observe, "This is not an ordinary political contest; it is a national scandal."

The year 1889 was only an hour or two old when four men stepped through the door of the barroom of the Hotel Richardson in Dover, Delaware, and pushed their way through the boisterous crowd to the bar. There, rubbing the chill from their reddened hands, they ordered hot toddies. Dover, like everything else in Delaware except the du Pont family and company, is small; even today the town's population is only 7,250. But it is the state capital and, on that festive occasion, the hotel's public rooms were crowded with politicians and newspaper reporters who had arrived for the opening of the Legislature the following day. None of them paid much attention to the four strangers, although one of the group was a man of impressive appearance, with a broad forehead, beetling brows, and a bristling mustache that swept both cheeks. He was expensively dressed and sported a huge pearl in his Ascot tie.

Suddenly his voice boomed over the crowd, demanding to be heard. The merrymakers turned to him with curiosity.

"My name," he announced expansively, "is Addicks—John Edward O'Sullivan Addicks. I have just returned from Europe and have learned that the Republicans have control of the Legislature. I understand that they may have some trouble in electing a United States senator. If they cannot agree on a man, they might elect me, and I will settle for it afterward."

Nobody in the hotel that night had ever seen Addicks before; in fact, it's doubtful if most of his listeners had even heard of him. And with good reason, since the newly proclaimed candidate for senator did not, at that time, own any property in the state. Actually, he did not even live there; he was a resident of Boston and a registered voter in Massachusetts.

Addicks was a robber baron whose manipulations of gas companies had earned him the sobriquet of "Gas" Addicks. A month earlier he had indeed returned from a European visit during which he had made a million dollars by a coup in Siberian railroad shares. In New York he had picked up a newspaper and read that the G.O.P., for the first time in years, had carried the Delaware Legislature.

In those days United States senators were chosen by the state legislatures. Now, according to the newspaper accounts Addicks read, a deadlock over the choice of a senator appeared likely in the state's legislature. It was then that the whim struck him: why shouldn't he cap his free-wheeling career by entering the Senate?

That whim brought Addicks into years of conflict with the du Ponts. During that time, he spent at least $3,000,000 trying to win election to the Senate—and trying to prevent the election of Colonel Henry A. du Pont. Because of the political warfare between the two groups, both Republican, Delaware had only one senator in the fifty-fourth and fifty-sixth Congresses and it was without any representation in the Senate during the fifty-seventh Congress. (Through the intervention of the G.O.P.'s national leadership, a compromise permitted the election of two other men as senators in the fifty-fifth Congress. Both were short terms.)

Born in Philadelphia in 1841, the son of a minor politician there,

Addicks quit school at fifteen to go to work in a wholesale dry goods house. At nineteen, he took a job with a Philadelphia flour merchant, one Levi Knowles, and within two years he was Knowles's partner. He made a permanent contribution to the flour business by introducing Minnesota spring wheat to the farmers of the East. Beyond any question, he was an extremely gifted man.

He was also inordinately greedy, ambitious, and unscrupulous. Inevitably, he moved into the promotion of illuminating-gas companies, with an occasional speculation in railroad securities—two industries being ruthlessly exploited by the financial pirates of the day. By watering stock and manipulating contracts, Addicks made huge profits.

While Philadelphia was the center of his operations, Addicks maintained a country home at Claymont in Delaware, just over the line from Pennsylvania; but he moved to Boston in 1885, and three years later Miraflores, the eight-acre Claymont estate, was sold to the widow of his old friend, Joseph Wilson.

When Addicks threw his hat in the senatorial ring, nobody took him seriously at first. One reporter, interviewing him at Mrs. Wilson's home, asked how he could possibly seek office in Delaware. "Oh, I live here," he said. "I've got a bureauful of clothes upstairs."

Despite Addicks' generous offer to sacrifice himself for the electorate, the Legislature voted instead to send to the Senate Anthony Higgins, a Republican lawyer of outstanding courage. Higgins had defied tradition by putting up a valiant—and successful—fight for the acquittal of a Negro accused of raping a white woman.

As soon as Higgins was chosen by the Legislature in 1889, Addicks prepared to challenge him in 1895 when his term was due to expire. As an unprincipled manipulator of public utilities in such centers of corrupt politics as Philadelphia, Jersey City, Brooklyn, and Boston, Addicks had acquired the conviction that anything could be obtained from politicians by the open-handed distribution of money. When the elections of 1892 came up, Addicks' fixers spent $100,000 and won almost complete control of the Republican organizations in Delaware's two downstate counties, leaving only New Castle County, the du Pont stronghold, out of their grasp. Two years later, while the Legislature was being elected,

Addicks expended $140,000 to good effect: the G.O.P. won nineteen of the thirty seats.

"Well, boys, we've won!" Addicks shouted in his coarse, arrogant way at a victory dinner he threw for fourteen leading Republicans from Kent and Sussex Counties. And then, referring to the Senate seat, he added, "I've bought it; I've paid for it; and I'm going to have it!"

But he wasn't going to have it—not if the responsible Republicans had their way.

When the Legislature convened to elect a new senator, only six of the nineteen Republicans were for Addicks; ten voted for Higgins. Neither man could muster the sixteen votes needed to elect.

Aggrieved at being, as he thought, cheated of the prize he had bought, Addicks declared that he was going to be senator regardless of the cost. He offered $10,000 to each member of the Legislature who would switch his vote to Addicks. But no one took the offer—to the bewilderment of the Addicks fixers.

"Damned queer," one of them was quoted as saying. "In Boston Mr. Addicks can get all the men he needs for $5,000 a throw."

Changing his strategy, Addicks hit upon the idea of deadlocking the Legislature until it would vote him into the Senate. "Me or nobody!" he proclaimed.

It was nobody.

After the battle had raged furiously for four months in Dover, Higgins tried to break the stalemate by withdrawing in favor of another candidate of blameless reputation and no partisan obligations. He knew a man who would just fit that description.

Higgins announced that Colonel Henry A. du Pont, holder of the Congressional Medal of Honor, champion of Civil War veterans, and a leading industrialist, had been persuaded to let his name be put before the Legislature.

For the colonel, fifty-five years old at the time, the decision had not been difficult. This was an opportunity to return to public service and, at the same time, to take part in a rousing fight. He was certainly not a typical political candidate: he looked every inch an aristocrat—rather on the German model. This "Junker" of Delaware wore silver-rimmed glasses; his hair, above his somewhat stern face, was rather thin and lay flat; his beard was cut in the

Van Dyke shape and there was a mustache to match. He favored dark suits, fawn waistcoats, high collars. On his lapel on any formal occasion, he wore the Medal of Honor. A greater contrast with the loud, boisterous, vulgar Addicks couldn't be imagined.

As soon as du Pont arrived in Dover, the anti-Addicks forces took heart. Two of Addicks' men deserted him for the colonel, which made the deadlock: du Pont—fifteen, Addicks—four, Democrats—eleven. If one man could be induced to leave either the Democrats or Addicks, Henry would win election.

At that point, the Governor died and William T. Watson, Speaker of the Senate, succeeded him as acting Governor. Watson was a Democrat, so his departure from the Senate cost the Democrats one vote. The lineup then stood: du Pont—fifteen, combined opposition—Addicks and Democrats—fourteen; thus giving the colonel the majority he needed for election. But before a vote could be held, Addicks persuaded Watson to return to the Senate and cast his vote with the Democrats, thus blocking du Pont's election. However, when the deadlocked Legislature adjourned, the du Pont men managed to have the Speaker of the House rule that Watson had been ineligible and that Colonel du Pont, therefore, was elected senator.

The fight was carried to Washington where Henry insisted upon his right to be seated. The Senate investigated the election and Addicks' agents contrived to bring the free-silver Republicans into an alliance with the Democrats in opposition to the McKinley Republicans. Since du Pont was a McKinley man, the opposing combination was fatal to his hopes. On May 15, 1896, by a single vote —thirty-one to thirty—the Senate denied the colonel's claim. And until 1899 that Senate seat remained vacant. Only one senator represented Delaware in the upper chamber.

While all this had been going on, Addicks had been plagued by domestic difficulties. Before he plunged into Delaware politics, his first wife had died and he had married her sister. Now his second wife sued him for divorce, charging adultery and naming Mrs. Wilson as corespondent. But Addicks defeated her suit. Later, when she changed her grounds to desertion and non-support, he allowed her to get the divorce, after which he married Mrs. Wilson.

In 1896, the same year that du Pont was rejected by the Senate, the state convention split and each faction sent delegations to the Republican National Convention at St. Louis. There the Committee on Credentials had to decide which delegation should be seated. The committee, dominated by McKinley men who still smarted from Addicks' appeal to the free-silver Republicans in Washington, voted to recognize the du Pont group, saying that Addicks and his crowd were merely "highwaymen on the road to political fortune, no matter what might be the result to the Republican Party."

After the convention, the Delaware G.O.P. split into two factions: the Regulars (du Pont) and the Union Republicans (Addicks). Money was scattered wildly through the state by the Unionists. Politicians who could not be bribed by direct payments of money or by big contributions to their campaign war chests were corrupted sexually. The Addicks organization provided women for their gratification and then, when necessary, used the prostitutes for blackmail.

As a result, Addicks was close to his goal in 1899. The membership of the two houses of the Legislature that year was fifty, so a candidate would need twenty-six votes for election to the Senate. The fifty legislators were twenty-nine Republicans and twenty-one Democrats. When the first ballot was taken, Addicks got fifteen, du Pont eleven, and an independent two; the Democrats gave all their votes to their own man. In the days that followed, three Republicans switched to Addicks and, a few days later, three Democrats did the same, to the outrage of the Democratic leadership which proclaimed all-out war on the turncoats. Now Addicks had twenty-one votes—five short of election. That was as far as Addicks got.

Again the Legislature was deadlocked. Delaware would continue to have only one man in the United States Senate.

By now the Addicks steamroller was in high gear. This time his faction, not du Pont's, was seated at the 1900 Republican National Convention held in Philadelphia. During the November elections, candidates put up by Addicks overwhelmed the Regular Republicans, leaving du Pont's faction only seven seats in the Legislature, all from New Castle County. Nevertheless, thanks to the Democrats, Addicks was still unable to win a majority and the Legislature again adjourned without breaking the deadlock.

This time, however, there had been two Senate vacancies to be filled. No one had been elected. And so Delaware, for the first time since the ratification of the Constitution, was without any representation whatever in the United States Senate. It was as though the state had ceased to exist as far as the upper chamber was concerned.

By now the fight in Delaware had become a national scandal, re-opening the national controversy over the method of electing senators. The Founding Fathers had ordained the indirect election of senators, but as early as 1826 this system had come under fire. Fraud, chicanery, and wholesale bribery marked many legislative sessions at which senators were chosen, but in no state had political morality deteriorated as badly as it had in Delaware.

From 1893 to 1902, as the Delaware test of strength went on, five resolutions to amend the Constitution of the United States passed the House of Representatives in Washington. All, however, died in the Senate whose members had been chosen by their state legislatures. But when Delaware was unable to send even one senator to Washington in 1902-1903, the leaders of the upper chamber at last had to acknowledge the need for direct, popular election of senators.

In Delaware, the prospect for the du Ponts was grim. The colonel could see the handwriting on the wall: in 1889, Addicks had been able to boast just one adherent in the Legislature; in 1895, six; in 1899, eighteen; in 1901, twenty-two. Could he be stopped?

At that point Colonel Henry A. du Pont called on his cousin, T. Coleman du Pont, to take time out from his duties as the new president of the powder company to serve as his campaign manager.

Delaware's Senate seats had been filled in 1903 as a result of a scheme dreamed up by McKinley's political strategist, Mark Hanna. Under this compromise, Addicks and du Pont both stepped aside to permit the election of substitutes to the fifty-fifth Congress— J. Frank Allee for Addicks and Dr. L. H. Ball for du Pont. But one of those seats fell vacant again in 1906, and then the fight was resumed.

Again Addicks' money was poured forth in a green flood over the state, but now he was up against an uninhibited, rough-playing opponent—Coleman du Pont, a graduate of the same school of dubious traction-company deals. And Coly was maneuvering from a position of strength. Addicks' outrageous vote-buying and the long deadlock had been exposed in a famous muckraking article, "Holding Up a State," by George Kennan in *Outlook*. And while the propaganda war was going against Addicks, Coly had been quietly undermining him with some of Addicks' own men. Addicks was shocked when Allee, whom he had put up for the Senate three years earlier, deserted him to throw his weight to Colonel du Pont.

It did Addicks no good to toss more and more money into the pot; Coly du Pont was ready to see him and raise the ante every day and, as a manipulator, Coly got better results with his vast expenditures than Addicks did with his. Every day more of Addicks' henchmen showed up at the du Pont campaign headquarters, to depart with fat cigars, swollen pockets, and complacent expressions.

After the Legislature was called to order on June 2, 1906, Colonel Henry A. du Pont was elected almost without opposition. Only one vote was cast for Addicks and the Democrats cast blank votes. President Theodore Roosevelt sent a telegram of congratulations to "the people of Delaware" on the results.

A more cynical view of the election was taken by the state chairman of the Democratic Party, who happened to be Willard Saulsbury. He said that Addicks was defeated because *he* didn't know how to buy votes like a gentleman.

Even in advance of the election, Addicks realized that he had lost. Eight hours before the Legislature balloted, he boarded a train at Dover for New York, vowing to return to the fight that fall. But his words were mere bravado.

Financial disaster followed political failure. Addicks lost a fortune when the bottom fell out of the copper market in which he had been plunging. Litigation arose out of his gas company deals and a federal court awarded a judgment against him of $4,000,000.

Before long he was in hiding from subpoenas, his known possessions had been attached, and he was reduced to poverty. Within two years of his last election attempt in Delaware, process servers found him living in a dreary Hoboken tenement under an assumed name, his gas and light turned off for non-payment by a utilities company he had once controlled.

For eleven years he was briefly in and then out of jails on various fraud charges, and his freedom was spent in the worst slums of New York. There he died on August 7, 1919, in obscurity.

By then, the possibility that another Addicks could hold up a state, blocking the election of a senator, had been eliminated by the Seventeenth Amendment which provided for direct, popular elections. Because of the scandal in Delaware, William Howard Taft, accepting the G.O.P. Presidential nomination in 1908, had announced his support of the proposed amendment. In 1912, a joint resolution of Congress authorized the amendment and a year later, on May 31, 1913, its ratification by the states was proclaimed.

Colonel Henry A. du Pont, serving his second term in the Senate, had the pleasure of voting for it.

CHAPTER XXXII

THE END
OF THE POWDER TRUST

COLEMAN DU PONT liked to call a department head into his office and ask him, "What time is it?"

The man would reach for his pocket watch, then fumble with a baffled look.

"Here it is," Coly would say, handing the man his watch. "You'd better keep a closer eye on your department than you do on your watch."

Coly had the joy of a small boy in simple magic tricks. Even loaded cigars amused him. He kept a box of such cigars in his desk, and when one blew up in the face of his victim, Coly would howl with laughter, holding his sides and gasping, "I never thought the powder business would be such fun!"

More than watches disappeared under Coleman du Pont's expert hand. Competing companies, too, had a way of vanishing soon after he went into action.

The first startling result of his leadership became apparent in October, 1902, when Coly and Pierre, without even consulting Alfred I., negotiated the purchase of Laflin and Rand, the very company to which their elders had proposed to sell the du Pont concern a half year earlier!

Asked what he had paid for du Pont's only significant rival, Coly roared happily, "Didn't pay anything! It's a matter of bonds to be worked out later."

That was almost literally true. The cash outlay by du Pont was only $4,000; and for that, du Pont got both Laflin and Rand and the Moosic Powder Company in which Laflin and Rand's major stockholders held a large interest. The total price, however, was $4,000,000 for Laflin and Rand and $2,000,000 for Moosic, both paid in bonds and stocks of du Pont subsidiaries.

The purchase tightened du Pont's grasp on the entire powder industry, and it also brought back into the du Pont fold J. Amory Haskell. A brilliant administrator, he had worked for Repauno until the opportunities there proved so limited that he took over the management of Laflin and Rand.

More than a hundred powder companies were now in the du Pont camp, some wholly owned, some only partially. This diffuse empire, built up by Henry du Pont during his reign, had begun to fall apart under Eugene. Now Coleman du Pont got a firm grip on the controls and carried the concentration of power to its logical conclusion, as Rockefeller had been doing with Standard Oil and Carnegie with Steel.

With breathtaking speed, companies were merged into the parent du Pont corporation. By 1906, sixty-four corporations had been dissolved. A year later, du Pont was producing from sixty-four to seventy-four percent of the total national output of each of five types of explosives, and one hundred percent of the privately produced smokeless military powder. Only the Standard Oil trust was as well organized.

The consolidation of the du Pont empire, while making for less duplication of effort and more efficiency, was not without opposition even within the family. One company affected by Coly's drive was the Peyton Chemical Company of California, whose president, William Charles Peyton, had married Anne Ridgely du Pont, a daughter of Eugene. The du Pont company owned three thousand of the Peyton company's sixty-five hundred shares and held Peyton bonds for $230,300. But when du Pont demanded that Peyton permit his company to be swallowed up in his in-laws' giant concern, he rebelled and the issue ended in the courts. "The ill feeling always a feature of family lawsuits is not wanting in this dispute," said a contemporary account. In the end, Coly won out. Over the years the rift in the family gradually closed.

Curiously, the muckrakers of the period who were lambasting the Oil Trust, the Meat Trust, the Steel Trust, and other combinations of that time paid very little attention to the du Ponts, probably because they were tucked away in Delaware, out of the main stream of journalism. Geography has saved the du Ponts from embarrassing publicity on many occasions.

But if the muckrakers were leaving the Powder Trust alone, Robert Stuart Waddell wasn't. Waddell had been general sales manager for du Pont until 1903, when he resigned to organize his own company. On behalf of du Pont, Coleman du Pont offered to put up some of the money for this enterprise, but Waddell refused. In later years the du Ponts charged that Waddell's real purpose in starting his own business was to force them to buy him out, which they declined to do. In any event, Waddell built his powder plant near Peoria in central Illinois. It was promptly destroyed by an explosion—a blast deliberately set off, according to Waddell.

He then began writing letters to congressmen and newspapers accusing the du Ponts of monopolizing the powder business. According to him, they had tried to prevent his going into powder-making as an independent, and when he had persisted in his plans, they had driven him out of the industry. Alleging that the du Ponts were overcharging the government by millions of dollars on powder contracts, Waddell hinted that only their political influence and their contributions to the Republican presidential campaign fund protected them from prosecution. "If a $70,000 campaign contribution is sufficient to obligate the executive and legislative departments of the government to take $12,000,000 from the taxpayers of the country and give it to the millionaires of this gigantic powder monopoly," he told reporters, "the independent powder companies and the voters of the country want to know it now."

Teddy Roosevelt was then at the height of his trust-busting crusade, so Waddell's bellow found a sympathetic audience. On July

30, 1907, the government filed an action against E.I. du Pont de Nemours and Company, Incorporated, for violation of the Sherman Anti-Trust Act, the first of many anti-trust suits against the company.

The case dragged on for five years. By the time a decision was handed down, the three du Pont cousins had been in charge of the corporation for nine years. In that time, the company and its subsidiaries earned a total net income, before deducting bond interest, of almost $45,000,000 on an original investment—in 1903—of $36,000,000.

The federal court ruled that du Pont was guilty. The decision found that for years—under the old Gunpowder Trade Association and, later, through direct means such as mergers—the du Ponts had been "suppressing competition and thereby building up a monopoly."

But the court was confronted by a knotty problem. More than sixty corporations had been dissolved into du Pont since the three cousins took over in 1902; those companies had been wiped out so completely that they could never be restored to their previous existence. Faced with a *fait accompli*, the court knew that it could not bring back the past. The question was: how could it break up this vast monopoly?

To solve this problem, the court asked the government and du Pont to get together and work out a plan for carving up the trust and reorganizing the company. Having been convicted, the company was going to be permitted now to figure out its own punishment. This aspect of the case led John K. Winkler to characterize that first du Pont anti-trust suit as "one of the outstanding farces of American judicial history."

As soon as the guilty verdict had been announced, the du Ponts went into action to obtain the best possible settlement. Taft was President now, and he had no heart for trust-busting. Senator Allee of Delaware was sent to arrange a meeting between Coleman du Pont and President Taft. This proved to be impossible because Taft considered Coly, who was also Republican national committeeman from Delaware, "slippery as an eel and crooked as a ram's horn." The Chief Executive would see Alfred I. du Pont, however.

At the White House, Alfred insisted that it would be to the

advantage of the government and of the nation as a whole for du Pont to retain its one hundred percent monopoly of smokeless military powder: the du Ponts were aware that war might break out soon in Europe. When it was pointed out that du Pont had been found guilty of violating the law, Alfred turned to Taft's Attorney General, George W. Wickersham, who was present, and reminded him that he had been du Pont's lawyer at the time the violations had taken place. If du Pont had broken the law, it was because the company had received bad legal counsel.

The conference was successful. When the court held a series of hearings on the reorganization of the company, an incredible parade of military and naval brass took place: the president of the Joint Army and Navy Board on Smokeless Powder, the Chief of Navy Ordnance, the chief of Army Ordnance, and a number of other generals and admirals—all testifying that it was vital to the national security for du Pont to retain its monopoly of smokeless military powder. Some of the witnesses became quite emotional. Said one of the admirals: "I am looking at it now, not from the point of view of the commercial interests of the government or the commercial interests of the manufacturer, but . . . from the point of view of the lives of the officers and men on board ships."

Unbelievably, the court accepted these arguments. To split up the military powder business among several competing companies would do damage to the close co-operation between du Pont and the government and thus jeopardize the security of the nation without any corresponding benefit to the public. Or so the court held in its final ruling in June, 1912. Thus du Pont was permitted to keep its one hundred percent monopoly of military powder.

With regard to the rest of the powder business, the empire was split into three parts: the largest to be kept by du Pont, with a substantial number of plants to be turned over to two new companies, the Atlas Powder Company and the Hercules Powder Company. In addition to the production facilities, both of the new companies were to be permitted to use du Pont's engineering, chemical and purchasing departments for five years until Atlas and Hercules were well established.

For the plants they took from du Pont, Atlas and Hercules paid in stocks and bonds of the new companies. The du Pont company did not keep these Atlas and Hercules securities but turned them over to du Pont stockholders. Since the bulk of du Pont stock was held by members of the du Pont family, the clan also ended up with the shares of the new companies. In short, the effect of the court order was to substitute "control [of the new companies] by the du Pont family for control by the du Pont company," as one economist put it. Another economist, William C. Lawton, pointed out that the du Ponts like to call Atlas and Hercules "healthy competitors" with "only one du Pont on the board of directors of either company."

On the other hand, a 1958 Twentieth Century Fund survey of anti-trust problems has pointed out that even if the court ruling did permit the du Pont family to retain control of Atlas and Hercules, "this control gradually faded as time passed and new shareholders replaced old ones."

The physical proximity of the Atlas and Hercules home offices—in a building just across the street from du Pont—raised eyebrows. (Recently Atlas moved to a Wilmington suburb.)

There was a sequel to the anti-trust suit against du Pont. Waddell himself filed a suit against du Pont for treble damages under the Sherman Act. Despite the earlier decision condemning du Pont, a jury now rejected Waddell's claim.

In 1942, du Pont and five other manufacturers, including Atlas and Hercules, were named co-defendants in a government anti-trust suit. The indictment asserted that the conspiracy had existed "at least as early as 1938." When the case came to trial, du Pont, Atlas and Hercules entered pleas of *nolo contendere*, signifying they did not wish to defend themselves against the charges, although they did not necessarily concede the truth of the accusations. Thus the defendants automatically were judged guilty. Since the case was a criminal cause, no injunction was in order. Thus the only deterrent effect was the penalty.

"It is quite clear that the government lost the case," said economist Edward W. Proctor. "No permanent or even temporary restraint was placed on any of the practices of which the government complained. In fact, the companies calmly continued doing business the same way they had been doing it before the government brought suit. The case solved nothing—it really did not punish the law offenders nor did it alleviate the restraints on competition."

This may not be as bad as it sounds. Proctor and other economists believe the wartime prosecution was politically motivated. Supporting this suspicion is the fact that the Department of Justice first tried to obtain an indictment in Norfolk, Virginia, but the grand jury there refused to return a true bill. Then the government took its evidence to Philadelphia, where another grand jury went along with Washington's demand for action.

CHAPTER XXXIII

THE OTHER WOMAN

ALFRED I. DU PONT saved the family enterprise, but he also caused the worst family scandal. It destroyed their legendary unity and, before it was over, resulted in a "war of the roses" among the cousins for control of the company.

Something of the sort was inevitable. Just as the business was evolving from a closed family partnership to a complex modern corporation, so the feudal clannishness of the family was bound to change in response to the transformations taking place in American society as a whole because of the Industrial Revolution. The du Ponts maintained the medieval concept of the closed family society later than most families, and even today they are more cohesive than one might expect. But the fragmentation of the family that is an unfortunate part of modern life could not be avoided even by them. Indeed, because the du Ponts were so very close-knit, the break when it came had a force as explosive as the product of the Brandywine mills.

Alfred's marriage had turned out badly. Perhaps it was doomed from the start, blighted by the shadow of the suicide of his brother Louis who had loved Bessie Gardner and lost her to him. Alfred's uncomfortable knowledge that he had taken Louis' girl seems to have given him a feeling of guilt after Louis shot himself, and that guilt must have soured his marital relationship. Yet even if the tragedy had not occurred, the marriage probably would not have gone well, for Bessie and Alfred were badly suited to each other. Her interests were those of her scholarly father, and her friends reflected her tastes: they were literary, artistic, or professional.

Alfred, on the other hand, was consumed by his work and even away from the plant he often immersed himself in technical engineering problems. His major outside interest was music: even after his marriage he remained leader of the Tankopanicum Musical Club, the odd name a derivation from an Indian word. But Bessie couldn't bring herself to pay much attention to her husband's musical activities.

There is no doubt that Alfred must have been a difficult man to live with. Sensitive, intelligent, proud, he carried the wounds of bitterness from his orphaned childhood. And for years he had labored in the company, galled by the realization that men of inferior abilities not only held positions in the firm superior to his but that they also were able to put a lid on his ambitions. As we have seen, even after he became a partner he was ignored by his elders at policy meetings. Frustrated, humiliated, Alfred would have been more than human if he had also been pleasant, agreeable, and understanding at home during those difficult days when Eugene was ruling the company and the crisis of leadership was growing closer.

Bessie's emotional equilibrium must have been unsettled, too, for she could not fail to sense the general disapproval of the family; she could not know that this attitude would change in the years to come. In those early years of her marriage, the du Ponts frowned on her because of her "airs." In the home that Bessie made for Alfred, the principal meal of the day was served in the evening and it was called "dinner." In all the other du Pont residences, to be sure, "dinner" was the main meal, but it was served at noon; the evening meal was light and it was called "supper."

Alfred's brothers and sisters considered Bessie's behavior toward them and her own husband rude. Once his sister Marguerite came from Washington to spend a week with them and then left, vowing never to return. Annie, too, swore she'd never go to Swamp Hall again. Even the easy-going Maurice lost his temper when he talked about how Bessie treated Alfred.

One of Alfred's Louisville cousins was Ellen LaMotte. After her father's business failed, Alfred invited her to come and stay at Swamp Hall. At first Ellen liked Bessie; then her feelings changed. She later told of the painful incidents between Bessie and Alfred that she had witnessed. "Frequently," so she said, Alfred had found it necessary to "leave his own table to save a scene and escape the direct humiliation." Ellen tried to persuade Bessie to behave differently; when she failed, she moved out of the house.

In the first year of their marriage, Bessie gave birth to a daughter, Madeleine, always called "Madie." Two years later, a second girl, Bessie, dubbed "Bep" to distinguish her from her mother, was born.

In the succeeding years, the friction between Alfred and his wife grew worse. In 1897, he summoned an engineer from New York to discuss plans for building a great house atop a hill in the gentle slopes east of the Brandywine. As they drove along the country roads, du Pont suddenly said to his companion in a sad voice, "I'm talking about this as if it would all come to pass and bring me what I want. It would cost a lot of money. I have the money—plenty of money. But will it buy happiness?"

The startled engineer sat silently, not knowing what to say, while the industrialist brooded. Finally du Pont roused himself and murmured, "I'm not a happy man. My home life is not happy." Before they returned to Wilmington, he had decided to postpone his plans for the house.

When the marriage was five or six years old, Alfred's hearing began to fail. This was a double blow: he had to learn to live with the embarrassment and loneliness of the hard-of-hearing, and he lost his greatest pleasure, music. Perhaps, in this private crisis, he was able to reach out, in his need, to his wife. At any rate there was, for a time, a new spirit of harmony in Swamp Hall. It was embodied, in 1900, by their third child, a son whom they named Alfred Victor.

Their happiness, unfortunately, was short-lived. Before long, in all the great houses of the du Ponts and in all the small cottages of the powdermen, the word spread that there was discord once again at Swamp Hall. And now Alfred and Bessie were like enemies rather than husband and wife.

But this time the gossips began to say that lonely "Mr. Alfred" was spending a good deal of time with a cousin, Mary Alicia Heyward Bradford. They were off for horseback rides alone out into the countryside, vanishing for hours on end. They picnicked alone in the woods. They laughed together and smiled into each other's eyes and had their own private jokes.

The family was not amused.

There have always been recognized heads of the du Pont family. At that time Colonel Henry A. was the acknowledged patriarch, but Elizabeth Bradford du Pont, wife of the ailing "Doctor Alexis," ruled the clan with a frosty eye and an iron fist. When the gossip about Alfred and Alicia—Mary Alicia was never called by her first name—reached her ears, Elizabeth summoned the colonel to her house for an earnest chat. Elizabeth had a special interest in the matter, for she was a twofold aunt of Alicia: Elizabeth's husband had been the brother of Alicia's mother, Eleuthera, and Elizabeth's half-brother, Judge Edward Green Bradford of the United States Circuit Court, was Alicia's father.

Judge Bradford was generally admired among the du Ponts because of his position, but he was thoroughly detested by his own daughter who regarded him as a domestic despot. Late in life Alicia told a friend, "As a child I was frightened all the time—terrified of everything. Suddenly it came to me that my father was the cause of this. He wanted me to be a boy. I saw it all and made up my mind to get even." In her mid-twenties, she had grown into a wilful, temperamental, imperious beauty, a girl of unusual intelligence but reckless and lacking in judgment.

After conferring with Colonel du Pont, Elizabeth had another discreet meeting with her brother, the judge. And he, in turn, called in his daughter to rail at her.

For a few weeks Alicia and Alfred were no longer seen in each other's company. But then George Amory Maddox suddenly appeared on the scene as Alicia's suitor. Now eyebrows rose again, this time with bewilderment as well as suspicion. For Maddox was Alfred's impecunious secretary, a handsome but not very attractive man chiefly known for his devotion to his boss.

Judge Bradford ordered Maddox to leave his daughter alone and he forbade her to see him. But she was twenty-six and legally free to do as she pleased. So she continued to see Maddox; and their clandestine meetings, the family soon discovered, were arranged by Alfred himself!

When Alicia announced her plans to marry Maddox, Judge Bradford was beside himself with rage. He virtually disowned his daughter and announced that he would boycott the wedding. He also forced his meek wife who had always been close to Alicia to remain away from the ceremony. Many of the powerful members of the du Pont family followed his example.

Nevertheless, Christ Church was crowded on April 30, 1902, when Alicia was married to Maddox, for Alfred had made all the arrangements and he was enormously popular with the younger members of the clan. After all, it was only two months since he had saved the company on which their hopes were centered.

The newlyweds settled down in Louviers Upper House, which was made available to them by Alfred. It had been the residence of Admiral du Pont. Later Captain Sidney E. Stuart, an Army inspector for government powder contracts, lived there. Three years before the Maddoxes moved into Louviers Upper House, Stuart had been killed in an explosion at the smokeless powder plant at Carney's Point. But du Ponts were too familiar with the terrible results of accidental explosions to be demoralized by them or to feel any superstitious dread of living in a house so recently blighted by tragedy.

In his bitterness Judge Bradford went to Coleman du Pont and appealed to him, as president of the company, to evict Alicia and her husband from their residence. Coly talked the matter over with Pierre and then sent the judge a letter saying that "radical" action of the kind Bradford had suggested would only aggravate an already painful situation. But even though Coly was obviously reluctant at this point to tangle with the cousin who had enabled him to become president of the company, he accepted Bradford's view of Alicia.

At first the du Ponts held their collective breath, hoping that Alicia's strange marriage might leave Alfred in a mood for reconciliation with Bessie. And for a while he did seem to spend more time at Swamp Hall. The family's hopes rose higher when it was learned that Bessie was pregnant again.

Disappointment, however, was in store for the clan. Alfred kept promoting Maddox to various "drag" jobs—as sinecures reserved for untalented members of the family were always termed—and each successive post kept Maddox away from home for longer and longer periods, until finally, as midwestern regional superintendent of du Pont black powder plants, he was scarcely ever in Delaware.

But Alicia was not lonely. Alfred saw to that. In Maddox's absence, he was a constant visitor to Louviers Upper House.

The gossip now reached the flood stage, and Judge Bradford snorted to members of the family, "I told you so."

In 1903, Bessie gave birth to her fourth child, a girl named Victorine.

About the same time, Alicia, too, was delivered of a daughter to whom she gave her own name, Alicia. The child not surprisingly had the unmistakable facial characteristics of her mother's family, the du Ponts.

Then, less than a year after Victorine's birth, Bessie gathered up all the children and went to Europe, settling in Brussels as though she were prepared to spend the rest of her life there.

In November of that same year, 1904, Alfred and some old cronies went on a hunting trip to Balls Neck, a peninsula in Northumberland County, Virginia, on Chesapeake Bay. Before breakfast one morning the hunters set out through the fields. Du Pont and Frank Mathewson, a powderman's son who had been a boyhood chum of Alfred and who was now inspector of black powder machinery, walked alongside a high, thick hedge. William Scott, a du Pont divisional superintendent in Pennsylvania, was walking parallel to them in the next field but on the other side of the hedge. Suddenly Scott, believing he saw game, whirled to his right and fired directly into the hedge.

Alfred's hat flew off his head; he dropped his gun, staggered a few feet and fell to the ground, his face streaming blood.

At first the men feared he had been mortally wounded. But in a few minutes he recovered consciousness and they were able to help him back to the plantation house where they were staying. To Scott, Alfred said, "Buck up, you couldn't help it."

A local doctor found that du Pont's left eye was badly damaged by the shotgun blast. After treating him on the spot, the physician rushed him to the University of Pennsylvania Hospital in Philadelphia, where those closest to him—his sister Marguerite, his cousin Ellen LaMotte, and a few friends—hurried to his side. So did Alicia.

The specialist told them that the eye might be saved, but only if Alfred had rest and quiet. Above all, the doctor said, his patient must not become emotionally upset.

At Alfred's request, one of his friends sent a letter to Bessie in Brussels giving her an optimistic report about himself. A few days later, the specialist received a cablegram from Bessie: "Wire me Alfred du Pont's condition."

Ten days after this, the wounded man was "frightfully distressed," as his nurse put it, to learn that his wife with their eldest daughter, Madie, had arrived in New York and was on her way to Philadelphia to see him.

At the hospital, Madie gave her father a warm and tearful greeting. Years later she described to Marquis James her mother's attitude when she was ushered into Alfred's hospital room: "She never once showed any pity, never once said, 'Alfred, I am sorry this has happened to you.' Not a kiss; nothing." It was a bitter memory for a young girl who adored her father. Madie could not know the years of heartbreak and anguish that no longer made it possible for her mother to speak with sympathy and love to the man she had married.

A short time later, when Bessie returned to Brussels with Madie, the situation was unchanged. She and Alfred, once lovers, could be nothing but strangers now. Worse still, by her visit to him she had done positive harm, for his emotional peace had been destroyed. Du Pont returned to Swamp Hall for Christmas, but he suffered a relapse two days later and had to be taken back to the hospital where the injured eye was removed. Later he was fitted with an artificial eye.

In January, Alfred went to Florida to recuperate. It was March when he returned, about the time that Bessie came back from Europe with the announced intention of living at Swamp Hall again. There wasn't a reconciliation, but there was a truce—for a few weeks. Then Alfred packed up and moved out for good, choosing for his new home a place east of the Brandywine called Rock Farms.

Nine months passed before Alfred and Bessie signed a legal agreement covering a financial settlement. It was not generous. Bessie surrendered her dower rights and pledged herself not to contest any will he might sign. In return, Alfred established a trust fund of $600,000 in du Pont four percent bonds, yielding $24,000 a year. That income was to go to Bessie as long as she was unmarried. With it she was expected to support herself and the four children and to provide for their education. For du Ponts, even in those days, $24,000 did not cover all that.

At the time of the settlement, Alfred's personal income was nearly $160,000 a year, and he owned more than $3,600,000 in du Pont stocks and bonds. Thus it might seem that he was downright niggardly in providing for his family. But, apparently he never intended the agreement to apply beyond his children's early years when he feared they might be spoiled by too much money. He fully intended to provide more liberally for his family in the future.

A small clue to the split that was developing in the du Pont clan appeared in the written agreement which included the names of two trustees, one named by each principal. Bessie's was Pierre S. du Pont.

CHAPTER XXXIV

I'LL SEE THE FAMILY
IN HELL!

In MAY, 1906, a month after Alicia was delivered of a son who was born dead, Alfred went to South Dakota, ostensibly to look at possible sites for a new plant, while she left for Europe. However, after spending six months in South Dakota to establish legal residence, Alfred obtained a divorce in Sioux Falls on a complaint charging Bessie with "barbarous and inhuman treatment." The only member of the family who had defended William at the time of his divorce now held the second du Pont divorce decree.

The divorce was not mentioned in the Wilmington newspapers. The private affairs of the du Ponts rarely were. If Wilmington people wanted to find out what the clan was doing, they bought the Philadelphia newspapers, a custom that continues to this day. The Philadelphia press reported Alfred's divorce fully, as well as the sensational events that followed it.

After returning to Rock Farms as a bachelor, Alfred filled his home in the evenings with young engineers from the company, with poker-playing cronies and with old friends. His cook, George, became famous in the area for the meals he served. Alfred saw a great deal of his children in those days, especially on weekends, for

Bessie was back at Swamp Hall now. She was growing closer to Pierre and his wife and many of Alfred's other cousins.

Madie and Bep looked forward eagerly to Philadelphia theater trips with their father, and once they went with him down to Florida. His son's big treat was to be taken for a ride in Alfred's automobile; this became a weekend routine. Occasionally, when Alfred and the children were out driving, they would stop by Louviers Upper House for a brief visit with Cousin Alicia. During one such visit, Alicia asked Alfred's son, "How would you like to have me for a mother?"

"Why, Cousin Alicia," the bewildered boy replied, "I wouldn't like it at all!" He never saw Alicia again.

During the summer and fall of 1907, Alicia was away from the Brandywine. It was generally assumed that she was off on another European trip, but her isolation from the family had been so complete that nobody really knew.

In her absence, a Philadelphia newspaper reported that Maddox had filed suit against Alfred I. du Pont but had withdrawn it before his attorney filed a bill of particulars. The gossips in Wilmington whispered what the newspapers could only intimate: that the suit would have charged alienation of affections. Maddox left the company and disappeared. It was rumored that Alfred had paid him a million dollars to go away quietly.

The gossips would have been puzzled if they had known that Alicia was not abroad, but actually was living in seclusion in Carlisle, Pennsylvania, a short distance southwest of Harrisburg and little more than a hundred miles from Wilmington.

On October 8, Alicia, appearing before Judge W. F. Sadler in a secret session in Carlisle, was granted a divorce from Maddox on a complaint charging abandonment. No word of the divorce leaked out. Only Alfred's brothers and sisters, Alicia's younger brother Edward, and a few very close friends were told about it. All of them kept the secret well. Apparently even Alicia's sister Eleuthera, widow of Pierre S. du Pont's brother, Henry B., did not know that her sister had presented the family with its second divorce in a year and only its third in the one hundred and seven years since the clan had arrived in America.

On the night of October 15, 1907, a messenger delivered to the editor of the *Wilmington News* an envelope from Alfred, who was in New York City at the time. This item appeared on the front page of the newspaper the next day:

Alfred I. du Pont de Nemours, vice-president of E. I. du Pont de Nemours and Company, and Mrs. Alicia Maddox, his cousin, were married at the Plaza Hotel in New York City yesterday. Only their immediate families were present. Immediately after the ceremony, Mr. and Mrs. du Pont left on an extended motor trip in Mr. du Pont's seventy-horsepower French car. On their return Mr. and Mrs. du Pont will make their home at Rock Farms near Wilmington, one of several estates owned by Mr. du Pont.

Mrs. du Pont is a daughter of Judge Bradford of the United States Circuit Court, and her mother was Mrs. Eleuthera du Pont. Upon leaving Wilmington over a year ago, Mrs. du Pont went to Paris, where she had a home on the Avenue du Bois de Boulogne. Last spring she instituted suit for divorce from her former husband on statutory grounds and was awarded the custody of their only child.

It was not only an announcement of a wedding; it was also a declaration of war.

Shortly after the wedding ceremony, Alfred received some bad news from his brother Maurice who had served as his best man. In Fontanet, Indiana, a du Pont powder works had been leveled by an explosion. Twenty-seven persons had been killed. Instead of embarking on the announced motor trip, Alfred and Alicia boarded the first available train to the Middle West. They were obeying the family tradition of visiting the injured and showing personal concern for their workers. But they were the only du Ponts who went to Indiana.

Angered by what he considered the family's failure to live up to the code that privilege imposes responsibilities, Alfred returned to Wilmington ready for a row on the subject. He never got a chance to bring it up, for as soon as he and Coleman met, the latter brought up the question of Alfred's marriage.

"Al, now you've done it," Coly said. "The family will never stand for this. Don't you think you'd better sell out to me and get away from here?"

"I'll see the family in hell first!" Alfred stormed.

He returned to Rock Farms to find Alicia's brother, Edward G. Bradford, Jr., waiting there for him. Bradford showed his brother-in-law a telegram just received from his uncle, Bishop Coleman, William du Pont's old foe. The bishop, wrathful as an Old Testament prophet, demanded to know whether Eddie had attended the wedding. He assumed that Eddie had not been there. And if this assumption was confirmed, the bishop and Judge Bradford were going to issue a public statement denouncing as false the newspaper reports that members of the "immediate families" had been present at Alicia's wedding. Eddie replied that he had indeed attended and "countenanced" Alicia's marriage to Alfred.

Now the du Ponts aligned themselves with the two opposing forces. Only about a fifth of the family paid courtesy visits to Rock Farms. The others ostracized Alfred and Alicia, sympathizing instead with Bessie. She was conducting herself with great dignity. Coleman, who was rumored to have been cold-shouldered by Alicia years before when he displayed an interest in her, took Bessie's side. So did Pierre and his brothers, Irénée and Lammot.

The men in the family continued to get together socially, but only on a stag basis; their wives were never involved. Obviously, despite the outward manifestations of friendliness among the male cousins, there were undercurrents that threatened trouble within the company, too.

Even Alfred's immediate family was sundered. His eldest daughter, Madie, quarreled with her mother and came to live with Alfred and Alicia at Rock Farms, but the three other children remained at Swamp Hall, where Alfred's name was never mentioned. In all the years of their childhood, Alfred never saw any of them again.

A couple of months after Alfred and Alicia were married, Madie eloped with John Bancroft, Jr., an undergraduate at Princeton, and went with him to live in Europe. A child was born to them there a year later. Three weeks after that, Bancroft filed suit for divorce, charging that Madie had committed adultery with a young student on their honeymoon trip to Germany.

It was then that Madie's stepmother, Alicia, made a threat that has become famous in the du Pont chronicles. She vowed to "rip the hinges from many Delaware closets, du Pont cabinets among them," unless somebody took care of the Bancroft matter. Everyone was frightened by the warning, and family representatives were rushed abroad to deal with Bancroft. In the end, he dropped the misconduct charge and obtained a divorce on the ground of desertion.

And still the tribal feud continued—comic, tragic, fantastic.

There was, for example, the fuss over the Wilmington Symphony. Alfred I. du Pont was the biggest contributor to the support of the orchestra, founded not long before his second marriage. But Mrs. Henry B. Thompson, the social arbiter of Delaware, excluded Alicia from the women's committee of the orchestra association, although every other Wilmington woman of any social standing was a member, including Mrs. Bessie Gardner du Pont.

Despite the snub, Alfred went on supporting the orchestra financially. Then one day it was decided that the organization would hold a special concert to raise money for a silver service to be placed on the battleship *Delaware*, then visiting Wilmington. Alfred contributed toward the cost of the concert and also wrote out a check for the silver service fund. But the stationery printed for the occasion omitted the name of Mrs. Alfred I. du Pont among the patronesses. After a friend of Alfred protested, new letterheads were printed with Alicia's name included among the others. But the letters which were actually sent out were written on the old letterheads. The stationery on which Alicia's name appeared was said to have been burned in the furnace of the Century Club, an exclusive retreat of Wilmington women.

That did it. Alfred cut off his support of the orchestra, and it was soon forced to disband for lack of funds.

Ugly tales were circulating, some of which reached Alfred's ears. He was not the man to put up with that sort of thing. On June 22, 1909, his attorney filed the preliminary papers for a lawsuit by Alfred and Alicia against Mrs. Mary H. J. Bush, the elderly widow of a manufacturer. Mrs. Bush was the mother-in-law of Alicia's younger sister, Joanna.

It was not necessary for the plaintiffs to specify the cause of action in the preliminary papers, and they did not. The preliminary papers, under Delaware law, simply served as a legal notice to the defendant that she was being sued. After a "reasonable time," Alfred and Alicia would have to file a bill of particulars.

A month later, another suit was filed. This time the defendant was Elizabeth Bradford du Pont, widow of "Doctor Alexis" and Alicia's twofold aunt, who had tried to break up the romance with Alfred long before.

Elizabeth Bradford du Pont retained as lawyer her son-in-law, Thomas F. Bayard, Jr. Years later, he was elected to the United States Senate on the Democratic ticket—with Alfred's help.

Mrs. Bush's attorney was, surprisingly, Willard Saulsbury, who had married Mary Lammot du Pont after her divorce from William. This was the Saulsbury who had long displayed hostility toward his wife's family.

Aware that the lawsuits undoubtedly would charge slander and that the resulting trials might air a great deal of dirty du Pont linen, the sorely divided tribe was desperately anxious to keep any mention of the litigation out of the press. The Wilmington newspapers, as usual, did not carry the story, but the Philadelphia newspapers were another matter altogether. Despite the alertness of those journals, however, it took them three months to ferret out the story. But then they—and the New York newspapers—had a field day.

The conservative *New York Sun* said flatly that the suits would charge slander. It added that other du Pont kin would be involved before it was over. The *Sun* stated that Alfred had discovered some of his kinswomen circulating "untrue and vulgar statements" about Alicia.

None of the newspapers specified the precise nature of the stories that were being circulated. To have done so would have been libelous, for the alleged slanders, according to the *New York World*, were "of such a nature that they cannot be published." The stories, the *World* claimed, had been spread for fifteen years, thus marking 1894 as the approximate beginning of the gossip. It is likely that the *World* was in error, for apparently Alfred's interest in Alicia began sometime after that date.

Labeling the du Ponts a family of "feuds and factions," the *World* added that "there are at least ten separate and distinct feuds" in the family. This factionalism, the newspaper said, was the reason why "a half dozen or so" du Pont girls had recently married men who worked for the company. "The cousins do not speak to one another," the *World* pointed out with more than a little exaggeration, "and if the du Pont genealogy is to be perpetuated, alliances with the outside world are absolutely necessary."

One Philadelphia newspaper carried a headline across the top of an entire page: THE WOMEN'S WAR THAT CONVULSES DELAWARE.

Eddie Bradford spoke out in defense of his sister Alicia: "The people who have circulated the scandalous stories about Mrs. du Pont do not even know her. She has not associated with them for years."

The emotional pressure in Delaware was building up unbearably. Everyone knew that if the suits came to trial, the private lives of all the du Ponts—and of many other people prominent in the state's affairs—would be thoroughly aired. No one really wanted that, not even Alfred or Alicia.

On April 8, 1910, Alfred and Alicia withdrew the suits. Their friends later said that Alicia had been opposed to the legal action all along and that she had finally prevailed upon her husband. Their enemies pointed out that the suits were withdrawn just four days after attorneys for the defendants had written to Alfred's lawyer, threatening that they would move to have the case thrown out of court if a bill of particulars were not filed within thirty days.

A short time later Bessie received a notice from Alfred to move out of Swamp Hall at once. Alfred blamed his ex-wife for the venomous gossip, although his own indiscretion had certainly provided fertile ground for malicious talk. When Bessie moved out of the old house on Breck's Lane, Alfred increased her income by $1,200 a year to cover the rental of a house in Wilmington. She moved with the two children who were still with her—Alfred Victor, then ten, and Victorine, seven—to a house in Red Oak Road. As soon as she left Swamp Hall, Alfred ordered the house in which he had grown up torn down until not one brick remained on top of another, until there was nothing at all to remind him of the past— or so he hoped.

A year earlier Alfred had begun work on a new home for himself and Alicia. That mansion, Nemours, was the first of the great du Pont chateaux. Nemours—which probably cost more than two million dollars—was set in the midst of a three-hundred-acre estate east of the Brandywine near Rock Farms, just above the du Pont Experimental Station. The main house was put up near five huge old poplars. Alfred remembered how as a boy he had walked there with his father, Eleuthère Irénée II. The elder du Pont had told him, "If I could do what I wanted, I'd build a house under those trees and sit down and read books and eat ice cream the rest of my life." But the simplicity of his father's tastes was not a part of Alfred's plans. Although he had been born and reared with the advantages of a du Pont background, he had soon become an orphan, and so he had done without many of the things his cousins' fathers gave them.

Now Alfred was rich and he gloried in his wealth. Nemours was the architectural expression of that attitude. There were seventy-seven rooms in the three-story limestone mansion when Alfred and Alicia moved in during December, 1910. Designed by the architectural firm of Carrère and Hastings of New York but strongly influenced by Alfred's personal tastes, the great house had something of the feeling of an antebellum plantation house in the South and a suggestion of a French chateau—a combination of dignity and grace and elegance and tranquility.

But it was many years before the master of Nemours was to know tranquility himself, and its mistress never found peace on this side of the grave. For years, work continued on the vast formal gardens and lesser buildings of Nemours, but it was work carried on in private. For Alfred had ordered the entire estate enclosed by a stone fence in which were set two grilled gateways of bronze, one from Wimbledon Manor in England and the other from the Russian palace of Catherine the Great. The fence was ten feet high and broken glass was imbedded on its top.

"That wall's to keep out intruders, mainly of the name of du Pont," Alfred said.

If that was his aim, he succeeded. Family legend has it that only two du Ponts—William and Francis I.—ever crossed the threshold. They brought their families, of course.

In January, 1912, little more than a year after she moved into the vast emptiness of Nemours, Alicia gave birth to a daughter who died almost immediately and was buried on the estate. It was the second such sorrow that she and Alfred had suffered; early in their marriage Alicia had lost a child through a miscarriage. The birth and death of the baby who lived only long enough to be christened

Eleuthera Paulina was a physical and mental blow from which Alicia never quite recovered.

Probably because of her emotional state after this misfortune, Alicia quarreled with Madie, the only child of Alfred's first marriage who had taken his side in the schism. Once again Madie went off to Germany—this time in a huff, her passage paid by Coleman's wife.

A year later, on February 3, 1913, occurred one of the most incomprehensible episodes in the entire du Pont warfare. A Delaware City member of the state House of Representatives, during routine action in that chamber on a number of ordinary, unimportant bills, introduced a measure bearing an innocuous title: "An Act to Change the Name of Alfred Victor du Pont to Dorsey Cazenove du Pont."

The name "du Pont," then as now, was quite enough to startle the drowsiest legislator into alertness. But Representative Swan, the Democrat whose name was on the bill, had already assured the other members that the boy's parents had come to an agreement on the change of name. He said that Thomas Bayard Heisel, a leading Democratic politician, had asked him to introduce the bill. The Democratic majority was satisfied with this explanation. The Republicans decided to follow their own leader who obviously favored the bill. He happened to be Alicia's brother, Eddie Bradford.

The measure was referred to the Miscellaneous Committee, approved by that body; it was passed by the House four hours later. The measure was then sent to the Senate.

In their editions the following morning, the Philadelphia and New York newspapers played up the story. While the legislators in Dover were still reading the speculative accounts in those papers, attorney Andrew C. Gray, representing Mrs. Bessie Gardner du Pont, arrived in town. He said that the bill had come as a complete surprise to the boy's mother. She wholly disapproved of it, he said.

When the House was called to order that day, the first member to seek recognition was Chairman Mooney of the Miscellaneous Committee, rising on a matter of personal privilege. He asserted that the lawmakers had been misled about House Bill Number 97. By unanimous vote with Swan abstaining, the measure was recalled from the Senate for reconsideration.

In a public statement Alfred said it had not been his intention to
mislead anyone into believing that Bessie agreed to the change of
name. He said he wanted the change "for reasons to me sufficient
and at the moment not of public concern." But since he had asked
a public body to take action, he could not get what he wanted unless he was willing to concede a legitimate "public concern" in the
matter.

Three weeks later, the Miscellaneous Committee held another
hearing on the bill. Although it was conducted behind closed doors,
the reporters, as usual, had no difficulty finding out what tran-
spired. Alfred testified that he had not seen his son in four years.
With obvious reluctance, he said that he wanted the change of
name because he feared Alfred Victor would "bring disgrace" on
his father, although he gave no justification for such an anxiety. He
said he had hit on the names "Dorsey Cazenove" because they had
been used in Bessie's family.

Lawyer Gray testified against the bill. He produced evidence
that the boy was earning good marks for scholarship at the Hallock
School and that his teachers rated his character as good. Then a
pathetic letter from the boy to his mother was read into the record.
In it young Alfred Victor asked why his father was trying to have
his name changed. It was a question that nobody could answer—
except the father, and he was unwilling to do so.

Although the legislators clearly viewed the whole matter with
distaste, Alfred was still determined to have his way. He sent a
lobbyist and four lawyers to Dover to go to work on the lawmakers. Just four days before Alfred's son celebrated his thirteenth
birthday, the committee voted the bill out for consideration by the
House. On the floor the measure was narrowly defeated, the vote
being seventeen to fifteen. Only one Republican voted for it—Edward Bradford.

The change-of-name incident even shocked and dismayed Alfred's most faithful supporters, whose numbers were rapidly dwindling. It was the sort of thing that was bound to bring down upon
him the reproaches of hitherto neutral people. Even a personal
tragedy the following year—when Alicia gave birth to a son who
lived just one day—did not balance the scales in the minds of most
people.

Why had Alfred, a brilliant, self-critical and essentially great-hearted man, made such an issue out of a petty, pointless and cruel proposal?

Probably the reason had nothing to do with the boy himself, but stemmed from Alfred I.'s frustration in his feud with the other du Ponts. The fight was going badly, very badly.

The feud had finally spread out from the family to embrace the company, and a no-holds-barred fight was getting under way for control of the business, on the very eve of a world war which would make it the greatest chemical empire in the richest country in the world.

CHAPTER XXXV

FIGHT FOR CONTROL
OF THE COMPANY

IN THE DECADE of the three cousins' company leadership, net earnings amounted to more than four times the price they had paid for du Pont in 1902. But more than profits were affected by the new management: the entire nature of the corporation had changed. In his quiet, efficient way, Pierre S. du Pont had drawn together all the loose strands of the far-flung organization, standardizing and co-ordinating management procedures. Many of the systems inaugurated in those years by the unassuming Pierre have since become standards for the best management practice.

One of Pierre's important changes was the formalization of the committee system which had evolved naturally during the preceding century because of the divided ownership of the business. Now a logical hierarchy of committees, which still exists, made policy decisions. The highest ranking, then as now, was the Executive Committee of which the president was chairman.

In January, 1911, Coleman was sick, and Pierre was acting president when the "Ex Comm," as it is called in Wilmington, held its regular meeting. With the advance approval of Coly, a plan for completely revamping the internal structure of the company was laid before the committee which followed the majority rule. Its most important effect was to remove Alfred I. du Pont, also a member of the Ex Comm, from his position as production manager for the corporation. Coly's brother-in-law, H. M. Barksdale, would become general manager and Pierre's brother, Lammot, would be chief of black-powder manufacture. As soon as the plan was put before the committee, a motion was made—and quickly carried—that it be adopted. It was put into effect March 1.

Without any prior discussion, Alfred—the company's second largest stockholder—had been fired.

His ousting was followed by a purge of the executives who had been closely identified with him. Nevertheless, the rank-and-file powdermen on the Brandywine insisted on holding a ceremony and presenting "Mr. Alfred" with a silver cup, even though they realized that their action might offend the new bosses. Pierre Gentieu, spokesman for the workers when Alfred and his cousins had taken over the corporation in 1902, helped to organize the ceremony. The actual presentation of the cup, however, was made by Frank Pyle who said, "We have hereby resolved that we feel keenly the loss of our leader and chief . . . [whom] we have always found a friend . . ."

With Alfred out, Pierre was now the sole survivor of the triumvirate that had come to power in 1902, for Coly had been ill and inactive in the company since 1908. His sickness had conveniently prevented him from testifying in the anti-trust suit, his critics pointed out skeptically. But now, in 1911, after all the testimony in that case had been heard, Coly emerged into public life again in his characteristically flamboyant way. He startled everyone by proclaiming, "I am going to build a monument one hundred miles high and lay it down on the ground."

What Coly actually proposed to do was to build a road—"the straightest, widest, and best in the world"—from one end of the state to the other. Forming the Coleman du Pont Road, Incorporated, he began work on a two-hundred-foot-wide right of way in Sussex County at the Maryland state line. Much of the land was given free, but wherever necessary Coly bought, until the project ran into two problems. Some shrewd downstaters demanded three or four times the value of their land, and local Democratic politicians asserted that the "General"—an honorary title given to Coly by the Governor—only intended to devote thirty feet of the right of way to the public. They said he would reserve the remaining one hundred seventy feet on both sides of the pike for commercial exploitation. The fight moved into the Legislature, and condemnation proceedings and suits brought the construction to a complete halt.

In 1917, the first section of the road, twenty miles in length, was finally presented to the state. By that time World War I had inflated costs, so Coly turned over the project to the newly created State Highway Department, agreeing, however, that he would pay up to $44,000 per mile for the rest of the road. Finally, in 1924, the highway was completed. By then Coly had contributed nearly $4,000,000 to it—money well spent, for the road was, indeed, a monument to him. Today the Du Pont Highway—U. S. 13 to Dover and U. S. 113 from there to Selbyville—is still a magnificent route, uniting the once isolated Delmarva Peninsula with Wilmington, as Coly had hoped.

But Delaware was already too small for "General" T. Coleman du Pont. He once said, "I like conceiving, planning, organizing, systematizing, and getting a project established successfully. Then I want to start something else." So Coly went to New York where there were always new schemes to mastermind. But he retained his legal residence in Delaware and remained boss of the Republican machine there.

In 1912, in partnership with Charles P. Taft, the President's brother, Coly built the McAlpin Hotel in New York, and on its twenty-first floor he established his Manhattan *pied-à-terre*. His parties there soon became famous for their gaiety and their pretty girls; Coly often had half the chorus of a Broadway show among the forty or more guests at an after-theater party. "The General is loyal to a myriad of pretty girls who are proud to claim him as a friend," a New York newspaper said in a needling story, "and no one, not even Mrs. T. Coleman du Pont, seems to raise an objection. In fact, some people imagine that Mrs. T. Coleman du Pont must be a myth. One never sees her, never hears of her."

A year after the McAlpin was erected, Coly hit upon another monumental idea: he would build the largest office building in the world. So he constructed the forty-story Equitable Building at 120

Broadway, a block above Wall Street, at a cost of $30,000,000. The structure long ago ceased to be the largest office building, but it remains one of the handsomest skyscrapers in Manhattan and contains the home offices of many leading Stock Exchange firms.

All of Coly's projects called for the investment of large sums of money, but the outbreak of World War I had knocked down security prices so drastically that the New York Stock Exchange had to be closed for a time to prevent a panic. The money market had suffered its usual shrinkage, and Coleman had trouble laying his hands on the millions he needed. Fortunately the war had also lifted the price of du Pont company shares: in late November, 1914, the common stock was quoted at $143 bid, $148 asked. As the largest stockholder, Coly had plenty of equity that could be converted into cash. He decided to sell some of his holdings.

Instead of throwing his shares on the market and thus exposing the corporation to the intrusion of outsiders, he offered to sell a block of twenty thousand shares at one hundred and sixty dollars to the concern, with the suggestion that the organization then resell the securities to "those in responsible positions in our company" so that they would have a personal stake in its welfare. The price he asked was above the current market quotation, but Coly explained, "I think it well worth one eighty-five today [December 7, 1914] and think it will go to one ninety or two hundred before the year nineteen fifteen is many months old."

Having been sharply used—or so he thought—by Coleman in some past dealings, Alfred was suspicious of the offer. He told Pierre he had no objection to the company's buying the stock, but he thought the price might be too high—in any event, the Finance Committee should discuss the matter before any action was taken.

However, before that committee met on December 23, Coleman was rushed from New York to the Mayo Clinic in Rochester, Minnesota, for treatment of complications resulting from an abdominal operation. The other members of the Finance Committee—Pierre, Alfred, and William—were present. Alfred objected to the price Coly had proposed, and William agreed with him; Pierre did not. A suitable price, Alfred suggested, might be $125. (This was ridiculously low; apparently Alfred intended his counter-proposal to be offensive to Coleman.)

Later Alfred and William would contend that the committee meeting had ended with a decision that Pierre should start at $125 in order to negotiate a satisfactory price; they claimed that the committee never rejected Coleman's offer outright. However, the minutes of the meeting concluded with the words: "We do not feel justified in paying more than one hundred and a quarter per share for this stock." The words "at the present time" should have been added, according to Alfred and William, but they had both signed the minutes book, thus conceding its accuracy.

On the other hand, a week later the board of directors received a report from the Finance Committee telling of the rejected offer but adding that the committee "asked Mr. P. S. du Pont to take the matter up with Mr. T. C. du Pont further." And Pierre approved that report.

In the meantime, the Hercules and Atlas companies had both accepted similar offers from Coleman for his stock holdings in those corporations.

Finally, in February, 1915, Alfred and William discovered that Pierre had understood their position to be a flat turndown of Coleman's offer. Appalled, Alfred immediately attempted to reopen the matter with Coly by writing him a letter. In it, Alfred again suggested a price of $125—although du Pont common stock was then being quoted at $198 bid, $203 asked, in the over-the-counter market: du Pont was not listed on the New York Stock Exchange until after World War I. Now Alfred was actually proposing that his cousin accept a loss of $1,511,100 on gunpowder securities in the midst of the greatest war in history!

Not surprisingly, Coleman's response was acid. Saying that he had read Alfred's letter several times, he went on, "I cannot, however, make out why you wrote it." Then, after analyzing just what Alfred's offer amounted to, he concluded bitingly, "To guide me, won't you please advise [me] how much of your common stock you are willing to let go at this time to the important employees at price suggested by you—one hundred and a quarter per share? Probably I can join with you in an offer. . . ."

Five days later the newspapers gave Alfred the first news of a startling development: Pierre "and others active in the company" had bought every share of du Pont stock held by Coleman.

What had happened was this: About mid-February, Lewis L. Dunham, Coleman's attorney and confidential secretary, had arrived in Wilmington to tell Pierre that Coly would sell, not merely twenty thousand, but up to forty thousand shares—not at the original offer of $160, but at Wall Street's current asking price of $200 a share. Pierre at once held a series of meetings with the men closest to him in the company: John J. Raskob, company treasurer; Pierre's brothers, Irénée and Lammot; his brother-in-law, R. R. M. ("Ruly") Carpenter; and Alexis Felix du Pont. At these meetings Raskob came up with two recommendations: first, that the group propose to Coleman that he sell all of his du Pont stock to them; second, that the group borrow from J. P. Morgan and Company the money to finance the $14,000,000 purchase. About the same time, Raskob told the Finance Committee that he felt "very substantial balances" should be maintained at the House of Morgan "as a matter of diplomacy." In those days one financial firm could combine the functions of commercial banking, investment banking and stock brokerage.

Raskob's plan was successful. As soon as the purchase had been consummated but before Alfred or William had any idea of what was going on, Pierre gave to each of three members of the board of directors—Harry F. Brown, Henry G. Haskell, and William Coyne—securities worth $125,000. Two other top du Pont executives, W. G. Ramsay and F. G. Tallman, received the same amount of stock.

Furious, Alfred accused Pierre of having used "the power and influence" vested in him "as an officer of the company" to swing the deal, and he urged him, for the sake of the family, to resell Coleman's stock to the company. William made the same demand. Pierre refused.

During the next few days, according to later testimony in court, there were several informal meetings of du Ponts sharing Alfred and William's attitude toward this sale of Coleman's shares that gave Pierre complete working control of the company. Then Francis I., one of the sons of Francis Gurney du Pont, asked the major stockholders who were not part of Pierre's new syndicate to meet in Alfred's office on the evening of March 4. The first to arrive, after Alfred and William, were Henry F., son of Colonel

Henry A.; Alexis I., secretary of the company and son of the Eugene who had once headed the firm; Francis I., brother to Alexis Felix who had been in Pierre's camp all along; and two brothers, Philip F. and Eugene E., whose mother, the widow of "Doctor Alexis," had been sued by Alfred. (Philip, the most unpredictable member of the group, known as "Fireman Phil" because of his joy in chasing fire trucks as a youth, was the poet of the family.)

At the stroke of eight, the door opened again, and this time Pierre and his brother Irénée walked in—to the astonishment of the others.

Always the soul of courtesy, Pierre asked if they might sit down, bade good evening to the open-mouthed group and launched into an easy, calm stream of family small talk. For an uncomfortable hour these du Pont kinsmen sat there, fidgeting, staring at the ceiling, fighting the deadly silences with banalities, and trying to out-wait each other. Although Pierre appeared less nervous than any of the others, in the end it was he who could no longer stand the suspense.

Clearing his throat, he said that all of them were aware of the stock transaction that had taken place. Cousin Willie (William) had charged him with "a breach of good faith." Now he wanted to know what Willie meant by that allegation.

Willie replied hotly that Pierre could not have made the purchase from his own funds. The loan arranged through Morgan obviously had been granted either on the company's credit or on Pierre's official position as president. If Pierre had been one of the du Ponts with little money and no control over the company, he could not have negotiated the loan or the purchase. Therefore he had used the company, and, for that reason, the company and not the members of the syndicate ought to reap the results of his dealings.

When Francis I. and Alfred expressed similar sentiments, Pierre replied that he had not used the company's credit in any way; the transaction was a purely personal matter and no charge of bad faith could be made against him.

The others again insisted that he should have bought Coleman's stock for the company, not for his own syndicate, and that he should now resell it to the corporation.

"Poppycock!" shouted Irénée. "The company had its chance and turned it down!"

Pierre reiterated his refusal to sell the stock to the company, and then he and Irénée left.

Thirty-six hours later, the board of directors met, but in the meantime Pierre had changed his mind. He sent a letter to his critics saying that he would "consider a proposition" to sell the stock to the company. He mailed the letter despite the opinion of John P. Laffey, du Pont's general counsel, that the corporation could not make such a purchase legally, for the funds would have to come from surplus and there wasn't enough money in the till.

Eighteen men attended the board meeting, and nine of them held stock in the Du Pont Securities Company which Pierre had set up to embody the syndicate: this later became the Christiana Securities Corporation. The attack was launched by William who said he didn't "think any officer connected with this company ought to use his position for his personal aggrandizement." Discussing the question of the financing, Francis I. then said, "I believe Morgan and Company loaned the money with a full expectation that, in case these notes were not paid, they could force the payment from the company's treasury by some financial scheme. Morgan could get control of the company if the notes are not paid."

Not so, insisted Irénée; the value of the securities themselves had been sufficient to persuade the bankers to underwrite the transaction. And Raskob added that the loan could have been obtained for four percent instead of the six percent that the syndicate had to pay "if we had used the company's credit."

The whole discussion, heated and angry as it was, had been disturbing to Pierre. He couldn't abide the hostility and suspicion directed against him. During a lull in the bickering he said, "I consider it intolerable to be in a position where an official has not the confidence of the board. If I do not, I do not care to remain with the company."

At this Coyne immediately moved a vote of confidence for Pierre and Raskob. Francis I., Alfred and another board member said no one had demonstrated a lack of confidence in either man, but Irénée demanded a formal vote on the motion. In the end this was done. The vote was unanimous, but Alfred and Francis I. abstained.

Laffey, du Pont's general counsel, then entered the room and repeated his opinion that Coleman's stock could only be purchased from the company's surplus which amounted to about $6,000,000, not nearly enough. So the board referred the matter to the Finance Committee of which Irénée was now also a member.

There the matter died.

Later, Alfred tried to make much of the fact that Pierre had given Laffey a $50,000 interest in the Du Pont Securities Company at the time. After learning the details of all the meetings, the Federal Court rejected his protest.

All these complicated maneuvers were publicized in a suit filed the following December by Philip F. du Pont in the Federal Court at Wilmington against Pierre and his syndicate. Alfred joined the suit as a plaintiff. The suit sharply divided the offspring of Francis Gurney du Pont. Alexis Felix, as a member of the syndicate, was a defendant, and his sister Sophie was the wife of Irénée, another defendant; against them were ranged as plaintiffs four of their brothers and a sister—Mrs. Eleanor du Pont Perot, Francis I., Ernest, E. Paul, and Archibald.

Earlier, however, Pierre had offered most of the plaintiffs and some of the other du Ponts and in-laws "an opportunity to become a stockholder of Du Pont Securities Company." Of his three leading foes, Pierre singled out Francis I. for this invitation, an invitation Francis I. declined. Pierre's letter was not sent to Alfred I. or to William. Most of the others who received the offer rejected it, but both Eugene and Henry F. accepted, as did Charles Copeland, William Winder Laird and Hugh Rodney Sharp, the husbands of Pierre's sisters. Since Eugene and Henry F. were already directors and Laffey also had been elected to the board, the syndicate now had thirteen votes in that body.

On January 10, 1916, the board, tightly controlled by Pierre, voted to remove Alfred from his posts as vice-president and member of the Finance Committee. And on March 13, when the new slate of directors was chosen, three of the insurgents—Alfred, William and Francis I.—were dropped from the company's governing body.

The suit came to trial in June, 1916. It was disclosed that fifteen banks and trust companies had been included in the group that put up the money—through Morgan—for the transaction, and all fifteen were depositories of the company's funds. Moreover, du Pont deposits in eleven of those institutions increased by three hundred percent the day after the loan was made. Pierre and Raskob said this was merely a coincidence. Then all the bankers took the stand and swore that they had made the loan to Pierre and his associates on their credit as individuals.

On April 12, 1917, Judge J. Whitaker Thompson delivered his decision, a victory for Pierre's enemies. The judge mercilessly assailed Pierre for trickery and double-dealing. "The only construction" which could be put on Pierre's actions was that he had "the intention of concealing from the Finance Committee the fact that he was negotiating with Coleman . . ." He had maneuvered the negotiations so that he might act "for his own benefit rather than that of the company." The transaction had been colored by "Pierre's breach of fidelity he owed to the company in misinforming and misleading Coleman as to the real action of the Finance Committee."

On the most important issue, however, Alfred's side lost. Instead of ordering the sale of Coleman's shares to the company, Judge Thompson said the stockholders must vote on whether to acquire those securities. The old Coleman shares would not count in the vote, of course. A majority—230,717—would decide the issue.

This plan gave Pierre a great advantage. He could count on 212,000 votes to begin with—the votes of himself and his fellow defendants, their close relatives, directors of the company, employees who owed their jobs to Pierre, and pensioners. His opponents could be sure of only 110,000 votes. Both sides campaigned vigorously for the decisive, uncommitted votes. In the proxy battle Pierre had an invincible edge: World War I had now inflated the company's profits astronomically and no stockholder would want to rock the boat.

So it proved in the voting. The shareholders decided, 312,587 to 140,842, that Pierre's syndicate could keep the stock.

The case was appealed by Alfred to the United States Court of Appeals. On March 6, 1919, the three judges of that court upheld the propriety of the stockholders' vote, and they approved the outcome of the balloting. But they went further: they disagreed entirely with the lower court in its condemnation of Pierre S. du Pont. The appellate judges found nothing in the evidence to sustain the charges of misconduct against du Pont's president. According to them, he had not been underhanded in his dealings either with Coleman or with Alfred's group, nor had he used the credit of the company to obtain the loan from Morgan. In short, "Pierre du Pont was most earnest in his efforts and sincere in his purpose to carry out Coleman's plan. . . . He had done his whole duty as an officer of the company."

The only recourse left to Alfred was the United States Supreme Court. He did attempt to carry the case there, but the nation's highest court, deciding there was insufficient basis to hear an appeal, put an end to the litigation once and for all.

The destiny of the company now lay with Pierre and his branch of the family.

CHAPTER XXXVI

A PRESIDENTIAL BOOM

OUTSIDE THE COURTROOM as well as within, the du Pont feud kept breaking forth in new areas.

In 1916, a boom was started for T. Coleman du Pont as a Republican presidential possibility. The "General," as he preferred to be called, modestly disclaimed any political ambitions but admitted, "I have received thousands of letters from small businessmen and farmers asking that I permit my name to be used." When a Business Men's Presidential League of undisclosed parentage opened its offices two weeks later—coincidentally, of course—Ormsby McHarg, the veteran political strategist in charge, said du Pont was vastly superior to any of the other possible candidates.

By this time Coly had formed a hotel chain in association with Lucius M. Boomer, building some hotels and buying others. The chain included, besides the McAlpin, the Waldorf Astoria, the Savoy-Plaza, the Sherry Netherland, and several smaller hotels in New York; the Willard in Washington, D.C.; and the Bellevue-Stratford in Philadelphia, plus, of course, the Du Pont Hotel in Wilmington. He also had acquired an interest in the Louis Sherry and Savarin restaurants in Manhattan. But he really established himself, in the words of one New York newspaper, as one of the "new giants of Wall Street" when he bought from J. P. Morgan control of the Equitable Life Assurance Society. The importance of this acquisition lay not in the actual earning power of the insurance company, but in the fact that Coly now controlled its assets, which at that time amounted to about $600,000,000. These funds had to be deposited in banks or invested in railroad and other stocks; the man who could decree how and where the funds would be used was a power to reckon with in Wall Street. Later Coleman mutualized Equitable and sold his shares back to the policyholders.

Although he spent most of his time in New York, engaging in high finance in Wall Street during the day and holding big parties in his suite at the McAlpin at night, Coleman liked to tell reporters, "I exist in New York, but I live in Delaware."

This sounded good to the people back home in Wilmington. Coly really meant, however, that his political base was in Delaware. If he wanted to get anywhere in politics, he had to keep that state as his legal home for voting purposes.

Despite the noises emanating from the Business Men's Presidential League, Delaware politicians believed that Coleman's ambitions were not directed toward the White House—at least, not yet—but toward the Senate. They assumed, however, that du Pont felt he needed the publicity of a presidential buildup in order to establish himself as a public figure before the voters of Delaware.

One man decided to thwart those ambitions. He was Frank Allee, former United States Senator and the politician who had helped to sink Addicks more than a dozen years earlier by switching his allegiance to Colonel Henry A. du Pont. He made that turnabout, it was generally understood, because Coleman had promised to support him for re-election after his Senate term expired. But when that time came, the du Pont-controlled Republican organization turned thumbs down on Allee because he had been "too close" to Addicks. Over the year that followed, Allee had been nursing his bitterness, waiting for a chance for revenge. Now he saw that opportunity. So he went to talk to Alfred I. du Pont.

Allee, like everyone else in Delaware, knew how Alfred felt about Coleman. Now the politician disclosed that he had been quietly working with discontented rank-and-file Republicans in rural New Castle County. When the State Republican Convention was held two weeks hence, that part of New Castle County outside Wilmington would be entitled to thirty-five delegates. Twenty of them were ready to follow Allee's lead. This offered a real chance to hit at Coleman and Colonel Henry A., for the state convention would choose the delegates to the upcoming Republican National Convention. Allee's scheme called for the rejection of the colonel as national delegate. The colonel's opponent, Allee argued, ought to be Alfred I. du Pont.

After considerable hesitation, Alfred agreed to join the insurgents. The next step came on April 10, 1916, when the rural New Castle County caucus at Dover voted for a delegate to the national convention. The results: Alfred I. du Pont, twenty votes; Colonel Henry A. du Pont, fifteen.

The outcome was a staggering blow to the colonel and it made Coleman uneasy. Henry had been so cocky that he hadn't even bothered to attend the state convention. True, Coleman was there, but he hadn't been able to accomplish a thing. When Coly's men threatened to take the delegate choice to the convention floor in a fight to overthrow the results, Allee threatened to extend the battle to other delegations with dissidents. If that happened, he said, he wouldn't remain on the defensive: he would attack and try to prevent the state convention from naming Coleman as its "favorite son" candidate—a political honor that Coly wanted most of all.

The threat succeeded. Alfred's election was not challenged. But in return, Coleman's men insisted that Allee support a resolution stating that the Delaware delegation to the national convention was "instructed" to vote for T. Coleman du Pont. For a moment it appeared that Coly had the advantage, but after the resolution had been passed by the state convention, it was found that Allee had changed the wording. The Delaware Republicans were no longer "instructed" to vote for Coly at Chicago; their state convention had merely affirmed that "we do hereby endorse" his candidacy.

The *Wilmington Morning News*, quietly purchased by Alfred in 1911, now became his political organ for the first time. It ridiculed Coleman's ambitions. So did six newspapers downstate which Alfred bought or subsidized. Only the *Wilmington Evening Journal*, acquired by Colonel Henry A. some years earlier, and three or four country newspapers that the colonel also owned supported Coleman's G.O.P. machine.

Matters were going so badly now that Coly's original strategy had to be changed. The Business Men's Presidential League furtively folded its tent and tried to slip away into oblivion, but Alfred's *News* found out that its offices at the Waldorf had been closed. The newspaper's headline over the dispatch read: BANG! T.C. DU PONT'S BOOM BLOWS UP!

The next clash came over the re-election of Colonel Henry A. to the Senate where he had served since defeating Addicks a decade before. (Delaware had had an all-du Pont Senate delegation when the Democrats had won an election and sent their man—Willard Saulsbury—to the Senate with the colonel. So bitter was the enmity between Saulsbury and the colonel, however, that Henry would not even observe the customary courtesy of escorting his state's new senator to the front of the chamber to take the oath. A Maryland senator escorted Saulsbury instead.)

On primary day, the insurgents were strong enough to drastically hold down the machine's victory. Eighty-four delegates to the state convention were machine men; they outnumbered the insurgents by only ten. And most newspapers outside the state reported that the election had been stolen by flagrant ballot-box stuffing and the voting of repeaters. Nevertheless, Colonel Henry A. was sure to be the party's choice for the Senate.

A few weeks before, Alfred had issued a statement concluding, "My deliberate judgment is that it would be a mistake . . . to renominate for this high office Henry A. du Pont. . . . There are many able men in Delaware who should be considered for this nomination, and in the desire for Republican success in the state and nation, I trust that someone who is not a du Pont may be nominated." Now that the colonel had been renominated, everyone wondered what Alfred would do.

His reaction was to enter a third party into the race. The Progressive Party headed its ticket with the Republican candidate, Charles Evans Hughes, for President. For senator it offered Dr. H. R. Burton of Lewes. It was felt that Burton would draw enough votes from Colonel Henry A. du Pont to elect the Democrat, Josiah O. Wolcott, a Dover lawyer. (Wolcott had won his party's nomination from Thomas F. Bayard, Jr., of Wilmington, a du Pont in-law by reason of his marriage to Elizabeth Bradford du Pont, a double first cousin of Alfred's wife.)

In the election, the colonel was defeated; in fact, he drew fewer votes than any other Republican state-wide candidate. Moreover, the results put Alfred into a position of considerable power and influence in the Republican Party, for every Republican who had been endorsed by Progressives was elected and every one who had been opposed was defeated.

Deeply hurt by this upset, Colonel du Pont returned to his handsome estate, Winterthur. Then seventy-eight years old, he had another decade of life ahead of him. Those years were spent in breeding cattle and writing family history and Civil War reminiscences. After he died in 1926, a woman in Washington, D.C., sued his estate for support of her son born in 1913. He had been sired, she claimed, by the proud old aristocrat. The case never went to trial.

Alfred did not enjoy his political supremacy very long. In the depression after the end of the war, he suffered financial reverses so severe that his liabilities in 1920 amounted to more than $10,000,000. Retrenchments were unavoidable. One of the casualties was his *Wilmington Morning News* which was sold by Alfred and quickly passed into the hands of Pierre S. du Pont. As soon as this happened, the *News* started thumping the tubs for T. Coleman du Pont.

For Coly still hadn't abandoned his dream of becoming a senator. Once, when it appeared that he could go to Washington any time he wanted—that is, before Alfred upset his apple cart—Coly had boasted that he wanted to organize that honored chamber into an effective body, adding with a laugh, "I'd leave it in the hands of salaried persons competent to run it right." Now he had a chance to show what he could do: with Alfred out of politics because of his money troubles, the G.O.P. Old Guard felt that it was safe to go along with Coleman's senatorial ambitions. But they didn't risk an election. Instead, the governor, a Republican of Coly's faction, appointed Senator Wolcott, the Democrat, to the highest judicial office in the state, the post of chancellor, and then named T. Coleman du Pont to complete Wolcott's unexpired term. Many newspapers—even Colonel Henry A. du Pont's *Wilmington Evening Journal*—castigated the scheme.

As a senator, Coleman du Pont was best known for his absenteeism. Nevertheless, when the elections rolled around again in 1922, he announced that he would run for *both* Senate seats, the regular six-year term and the remainder of Wolcott's term which still had a few months to go.

His Democratic opponent was Thomas F. Bayard, Jr., who had the support of Alfred. Although Alfred did not participate in the election as deeply as he had in the past, he was able to do some damage to his cousin's public image. An oddity of the campaign was the sight of Bayard and Willard Saulsbury, both du Pont in-laws, asking the voters at rallies, "Shall Delaware belong to the du Ponts? Are we a free people or shall we permit ourselves to be crushed under the weight of du Pont wealth?" Bayard beat Coleman by a hair's breadth—sixty votes for the short term and three hundred and twenty-five for the long.

Pleased at having helped to defeat his cousin, Alfred said, "No one really thought T. C. could be unhorsed for the reason that he apparently had all the cards. He had all the money; he had all the papers, both Republican and Democratic, because . . . [they are] owned by the du Pont company." Perhaps the "cancer" of du Pont political power in Delaware "has been removed for all time," Alfred suggested. In these comments, as in his actions, Alfred's motives remain an enigma. By temperament he was unquestionably an idealist. But was his political struggle against Coleman and the colonel inspired by his idealism or by his unrelenting thirst for vengeance? It seems likely that both factors moved him, but it is hard to avoid the suspicion that his primary interest was revenge.

In 1924, he abstained from any participation in the Senate election, and Coleman was finally victorious, swept along in the Coolidge landslide. Of course, Coolidge was not Coly's cup of tea; Harding had been more his sort. In fact, during the 1928 Senate investigation of the Teapot Dome scandal, a witness testified that $75,000 in bonds figuring in the case had been turned over to Coly in 1923. The bonds came from oilman Harry F. Sinclair, but Coleman, in taking the bonds, was supposed to have been acting for the Republican National Committee.

Coleman could not testify in his own behalf, for he was a very sick man. His throat had been bothering him for some time and in 1927 his doctors, finding cancer, removed his larynx. But the cancer had spread up and down his throat, and he continued to decline.

He talked with the help of an artificial larynx. "Can't talk, can't eat, hardly breathe—better dead," he told a visitor. By the winter of 1928, he knew he would never get well, so he retired from the Senate. Bearing his ordeal with courage that aroused the admiration of everyone, he would even perform his old feats of magic for visitors.

In his last months, Coleman received several friendly letters from Alfred, whose animosity had been modified by his cousin's fortitude in extreme pain. Coly, who above anything else always wanted to be liked by everyone, was pleased by Alfred's overtures. On October 28, 1930, he wrote a chatty letter to Alfred, concluding, "Your affectionate cousin." On Armistice Day, he died—the only du Pont to rank among those titans dubbed by Frederick Lewis Allen the "Lords of Creation."

CHAPTER XXXVII

PROFITS OF WAR

G AVRILO PRINCIP made the du Ponts one of the richest families
in the world.

During the first thirteen years of the twentieth century, E. I. du
Pont de Nemours and Company, Incorporated, enjoyed as much
business as any enterprise could want. The Panama Canal was being
dug across Central America with du Pont explosives. Under the
streets of New York, tunnels for the new subway system were being bored with du Pont dynamite. Everywhere America was building with the furious energy peculiar to its people, and the market
for du Pont products was growing constantly.

And then at Sarajevo the young Princip assassinated Archduke
Francis Ferdinand of the Austro-Hungarian Empire, and Europe
burst into flame. In the holocaust that followed, du Pont gunpowder poured across the Atlantic into Allied magazines in an ever-
greater flood. On the first of August, 1914, Russia went to war,
followed by France on the third and Great Britain on the fourth.
On October 8, du Pont received its first war contract: Russia ordered 960,000 pounds of TNT for high explosive shells. France was
next, four days later, with orders for 8,000,000 pounds of cannon powder and 1,250,000 pounds of guncotton. Before 1914 came
to an end, the Allies had contracted with du Pont for a total of
15,600,000 pounds of smokeless powder—most of it intended for

cannon—3,172,000 pounds of guncotton, and 2,160,000 pounds of TNT. But that was only the beginning. By mid-March, 1915, about ten weeks later, the orders had been increased three hundred and fifty percent!

Later Lord Moulton, director-general of British explosive supplies, said that the British and French armies couldn't have fought off the Germans in the savage trench warfare of 1915 without the help of du Pont, Bethlehem Steel, and J. P. Morgan and Company. The latter sold Allied war bonds in the United States.

Obviously, to meet the suddenly increased demand from Europe, du Pont would have to increase its productive capacity enormously. But such an expansion was clearly beyond the financial resources of any private enterprise. So the du Ponts were blunt with the Allied negotiators, insisting that, if they wanted explosives in such huge quantities quickly, they would have to assume the financial risks.

"Our demand was a cash payment of fifty percent to be made to us [at the time each contract was signed] without any conditions or restrictions attached—and the balance was to be paid as each lot was delivered," Colonel E. G. Buckner, du Pon't chief salesman, explained. "Our demand was finally agreed to. It was the wisest thing the Allies did. To it alone is due the credit of the huge job we did. It put our organization both in funds and in confidence. All limits were off. We were ready to accept any proposition involving any amount which contained the fifty percent cash payment clause. Contracts followed and were accepted so fast we were forced to start a new plant nearly every day. Sure, we made tremendous profits, but it wasn't extortion under the circumstances. If we had lost millions, we'd have been called idiots and fools."

Those were names no one could call the du Ponts. During the war years, the company's gross income totaled $1,000,000,000. The capital employed in the corporation jumped from $83,000,000 to $308,000,000. Net profits for the four war years reached the dazzling sum of $237,000,000, of which $140,983,000 was distributed to stockholders. Those dividends could be reckoned at four hundred and fifty-eight percent of the stock's par value.

Everything about the du Pont war work was on a vast scale. Forty percent of the shells fired by the Allies were hurled from the cannon by du Pont explosives. At the same time, the company met fully one-half of America's domestic requirements for dynamite and black blasting powder. At the peak of the war effort, more than 100,000 men and women were working for du Pont. Sixty-five thousand employees were housed in company-built hotels, boarding houses, dormitories, bunkhouses, and homes. The combined capacity of the pumping stations for all du Pont plants exceeded the daily water supply of Philadelphia and Boston together.

Sabotage was a constant danger, of course, and so were explosions, especially with so many inexperienced people working in the powder mills. During the war years, three hundred and forty-seven men lost their lives and property valued at $6,700,000 was blown to bits in accidents. One blast in the Brandywine works in 1915 claimed as an indirect casualty the Reverend William J. Scott, pastor of the Roman Catholic Church of St. Joseph's-on-the-Brandywine. As soon as he felt the force of the explosion, Father Scott ran down Barley Mill Lane carrying the Viaticum to administer the last rites to the dying. When he arrived at the powder-yard gates which were still locked, he collapsed with a heart attack. Although he lived for several years, he never regained his health.

In Alfred I. du Pont's family, both sides of World War I were represented. His eldest daughter, Madeleine, had taken as her second husband Max Hiebler, a German who served in the Kaiser's army throughout the war. Alfred's only son, Alfred Victor, had enlisted in the Marine Corps as a private when the United States entered the fight in 1917. And Alfred and Alicia adopted a French war orphan, christening her Adelaide Camille Denise du Pont.

For the child and Alicia, Alfred bought a two hundred and fifty-acre tract of land at Sands Point, Long Island, and began building a Georgian mansion, White Eagle, nearly as grand as Nemours. The grandiose architectural fancies of the du Ponts were now being realized with the help of the golden flood of wartime profits. In Kennett Square, Pennsylvania, just over the line from Delaware, Pierre was establishing Longwood, an immense palace of nearly two hundred rooms. Everything about the estate was on an incredible scale: the head gardener's house itself was a mansion, the gardens were horticultural masterpieces, and the largest privately owned organ in the world sent out its music over one thousand du Pont acres. Another great hall, Winterthur, was about to be enlarged by Henry F., the son of Colonel Henry A.; in the end it contained one hundred and fifty rooms, forty of them bedrooms, and represented an investment of $10,000,000.

As stockholders, even those du Ponts who had opposed Pierre's group made a great deal of money during the war. But some of the dissidents were also in business for themselves. Francis I. set up the Delaware Chemical Engineering Company and the Ball Grain Explosives Company which made fuses for the military. Ernest, Archibald, and E. Paul du Pont joined him in the latter concern. Later they were associated with the United States Flashless Powder Company.

For Pierre and his associates, one of the major problems presented by the war was how to put their immense profits to use. Remembering the anti-trust case against the Powder Trust, the leaders of the company decided to branch out into other fields. As Lammot later summed up their thinking: "The dissolution [of the trust] was notice to the du Pont company that it could not expand in the explosives field, having already been dissolved for being too large, and that was a very powerful influence for branching out into other lines." Some of the du Ponts have since observed privately that the breakup of the Powder Trust was a godsend to the company, for it laid the basis for du Pont's spectacular diversification.

Before the war the Germans had dominated the chemical industry, apart from explosives. Now the wartime shortage of important chemicals made this an inviting field for du Pont expansion. Actually, as early as 1908 the company had started to move in this direction. Wondering what to do with its excess nitrocellulose capacity, the Executive Committee assigned some men to study the problem, an assignment which eventually led to the establishment of the Development Department in which most of the top men in the company have served at one time or another. The result was the acquisition in 1910 of the Fabrikoid Company, manufacturing artificial leather and other plastics from nitrocellulose. Now the big war profits made additional expansion possible. In 1915, du Pont bought the Arlington Company, which turned out pyroxylin plastics, lacquers, and enamels. Then the Fairfield Rubber Company was acquired; and shortly one of the oldest paint manufacturers,

Harrison Brothers and Company, was brought into the du Pont fold. And so it went with company after company: Beckton Chemical; Cawley Clark; Bridgeport Wood Finishing; Flint Varnish and Color; New England Oil, Paint, and Varnish; Chicago Varnish.

The most important venture, however, was the purchase, on the advice of John Jacob Raskob, of a twenty-seven and six-tenths percent interest in the General Motors Corporation at a cost of $49,000,000. GM had been organized in 1908 by William C. Durant; it quickly swallowed up twenty-one automobile companies, including Buick, Cadillac, and Oldsmobile. More of a promoter than an administrator, Durant had run out of working capital within two years. To get the $15,000,000 he needed, he was compelled to let two New York banking firms—Lee, Higginson and Company and J. and W. Seligman and Company—select the board of directors for five years. "As a result," says economist C. Lowell Harriss, "he became so antagonistic to bankers that, to get a large sum of equity capital, he was willing to sell du Pont a large block of General Motors common stock at asset value when the auto company was earning about forty percent."

Before long, du Pont was once again competing with du Pont, for E. Paul, who had chosen the losing side in the company split, was now in the automobile business himself. He had been associated with motor car companies since 1914, and at the New York Automobile Show in 1919, he exhibited for the first time his de luxe vehicle, the Du Pont car. The automobiles were assembled at Moore, Pennsylvania, only sixteen miles from Wilmington; it was rumored that Pierre, conscious of his widely publicized interest in General Motors, had persuaded Paul to keep his plant out of Delaware, even though the home office of Paul's Delaware Motor Car Company was in Wilmington. The Du Pont never became a popular auto; it was jaunty and sleek as few cars were in those days, but it was too costly to achieve a mass market. A Du Pont was raced at Le Mans and Indianapolis. But the stock market crash and the depression of the 1930's put an end to production of this car. Today a knowledge of the Du Pont is the mark of a real antique car enthusiast; in the summer of 1963 a Toledo dealer offered a 1931 Du Pont sport phaeton, "overall winner many times," for sale at $12,-500. On the Brandywine, a 1928 model of that car has been seen in recent years on New Year's Day, when Paul's widow is driven in it to the traditional family gatherings.

Although the huge investment in GM was made about the time the war ended, du Pont did not cushion the shock of unemployment for its workers. In seven weeks the du Pont work force was cut from 85,600 to 18,000. Layoffs of such magnitude helped to precipitate the brief but painful postwar depression. In their defense, it may be said that the du Ponts were behaving no worse than any other industrialists of the time and considerably better than many. Moreover, they had to cut costs quickly, for they had no idea of how the peacetime market would function at first, and their wartime production facilities were far in excess of their probable peacetime needs.

In 1920, Durant, a persistent Wall Street speculator, was squeezed in a bear market. Trying to support a falling market in General Motors, he found himself, in the end, with obligations amounting to some $30,000,000. The du Ponts and Morgan bailed him out but the price was high: the man who had brought GM into being was forced to bow out of it entirely. Du Pont now had complete control of that great company.

"Well, it's moving day," sighed Durant as he packed up his things and left his office for the last time.

He left behind him a corporation in chaos, facing financial disaster. Pierre S. du Pont, though retaining his leadership of the family company, now became president and board chairman of GM as well. He brought Raskob along to help him. Two of the top executives at GM—Donaldson Brown and Alfred P. Sloan, Jr.—had the du Ponts' complete confidence; they worked as a team with Pierre and Raskob. By applying to the automobile company the same principles of management control that he had established throughout the du Pont empire, Pierre, in the words of the American Institute of Management, was "able in the eleventh hour to save GM from the jaws of ruin."

In 1921, GM suffered its first deficit, a whopping $38,000,000. Since then, it has never failed to show a profit, and by May, 1923, the company was in such a healthy state that Pierre turned over the presidency to Sloan.

CHAPTER XXXVIII

ALFRED MEETS HIS
CHILDREN

DURING THE 1920's AND 1930's the change in the du Pont world
from the prewar state of affairs was almost beyond belief.

In 1920, a deafening explosion shattered the Brandywine powder
works. A year later the company decided to close the powder yard
there forever in order to avoid the danger of another catastrophic
accident in an area now so close to Wilmington. The gates were
locked, grass grew high beside the mill race, the wooden roofs
of the ancient stone-walled mills fell in. No longer did the powdermen, black with the dust of their dangerous product, shout ribald
jokes at each other. Their women no longer sat in the lane, peeling
willow for the charcoal house. The laughter of children, once
loud and gay in the noisy creek, was heard only when du Pont
boys and girls ran down the hill to play by the water bubbling over
the rocks. The powdermen's hamlets—Squirrel Run, Free Park,
Henry Clay, and the rest—became ghost towns. St. Joseph's-on-the
Brandywine felt the change as its parishioners, the Irish Catholic
workmen, moved away. There were empty houses in Montchanin
and Rockland and Winterthur. Men whose fathers and grandfathers
and great-grandfathers had worked side by side in the powder

works with the du Ponts found it hard to understand why there was no longer a place for them on the Brandywine.

Some of them would never leave, their blood a part of what was now a quiet, peaceful glade, dappled with sunlight and shadow, harboring the abandoned ruins of mills that stood as crumbling relics of the past.

The end of powdermaking on the Brandywine coincided with a waning of the feud between the camps of Pierre and Alfred I. The latter was as hostile as ever toward his cousin, but the animosity less frequently burst forth in public incidents. Alfred and William had bought the Delaware Trust Company in order to have a bank of their own to compete with the big Wilmington Trust Company controlled by the du Pont company. They erected their bank at Ninth and Market Streets in Wilmington and made sure that it was fourteen stories high, so they could look down on the twelve-story Du Pont Building a block away.

Alicia died in January, 1920, and a year later Alfred married again. His third wife was Jessie Dew Ball, descended from an old Virginia family. Under her influence, he mellowed considerably. One indication of the change was his action in dividing $896,000 in du Pont securities among the four offspring of his first marriage, thus assuring each of them an annual income of $12,000.

Through an old powderman who had always been close to him, Alfred met and made friends with his second daughter, Bessie, who was shocked to learn that even now—in 1923—her father was unaware of her brother's war record.

Occasionally Alfred's estrangement from his son and daughters created *opéra bouffe* situations. There was the incident of the hotel dining room, for example. Many members of the clan liked to dine at the Du Pont Hotel when they were in Wilmington, and sometimes the management had to show a good deal of skill in order to keep warring elements of the family on different sides of the dining room. One evening Victorine was there with her mother, Mrs. Bessie Gardner du Pont. A tall man who had arisen from a distant table strode past her on his way to the lobby. Victorine looked up and recognized her father—he had been pointed out to her only once before in her life. The girl was so startled that she almost dropped her soup spoon.

It was not until the 1925 Wilmington Horse Show that Alfred, in turn, was shown his daughter. She was eighteen then; he had last seen her when she was four. Alfred would have been astonished to learn that she had twice walked beside him, unrecognized, on the sidewalks of Wilmington, and that she had once even sat across the aisle from him on a train from Philadelphia.

In 1927, when Victorine became engaged to the Philadelphia lawyer, Elbert Dent, she decided that she must be re-united with her father. She wrote to him telling of her betrothal and asked if she could call at Nemours with her fiancé. Alfred replied at once, and he also invited her brother, Alfred Victor, the son whose name he had tried to change, and his wife, Marcella, to come with the engaged couple.

"Isn't this just like a scene in a melodrama?" Victorine asked her brother as they held hands nervously and walked up the steps to the great door of Nemours. Down the long, stately hall the two couples walked in a cathedral hush, trying hard to maintain their composure.

In the formal drawing room they waited, wishing they could smoke cigarettes to relieve the tension, but not daring to because the rug was a seventeenth century masterpiece worth at least $100,000. Then Alfred and his wife Jessie appeared. At first the strain was almost unbearable, but after a while the conversation grew lively. It was the beginning of a new period for all of them. For the rest of Alfred's life, he was able to be a father to his children.

His son, Alfred Victor, who had been working for the du Pont company, quit to follow his real love, architecture. After studying in Paris, he formed a partnership with a young Frenchman, Gabriel Massena, and returned with him to Wilmington in 1930. Their first commission was the design for the sunken gardens of Nemours, one of the most beautiful features of that place of splendor.

But some of the old wounds never closed. Colonel Henry A., one of the directors of the family cemetery, did not speak to his brother William for twenty years. He was said to be determined to out-live Willie in order to prevent his being buried in Sand Hole Woods. Willie, however, survived his older brother by two years and the same sod covered them both.

Although Pierre and Alfred never buried the hatchet—Pierre was one of the very few du Ponts who did not attend Alfred's funeral in 1935—the company did not discriminate against young du Ponts of the opposition camp. In 1925, for example, Emile F. du Pont, son of Francis I., was hired by the company on Alfred's recommendation that he "should make a good boy in your work," being "strong and, so far as I have been able to determine, intelligent." Alfred's judgment was sound: Emile rose through the company to become a member of the board of directors and of the Finance Committee.

Emile's father, generally regarded as the best chemist the family ever produced—his discoveries in the field of smokeless powder and his development of the "sink or float" process of mineral separation were especially notable—made one of the most spectacular breaks with the past. At the age of fifty-eight, he became a member of the New York Stock Exchange—a strange place for a man who had once won fame as a "single-tax" radical. It was in 1931, in the depths of the depression, that Francis decided to launch this wholly new career. He began by handling his own investments and those of a few relatives who were especially close to him. Today, Francis I. du Pont and Company is the second largest brokerage house on Wall Street, outranked only by Merrill Lynch, Pierce, Fenner, and Smith, Incorporated.

Du Ponts who didn't want to patronize Francis's firm had another brokerage house in the family—located right in the Du Pont Building—to handle their accounts. This was—and is—Laird, Bissell, and Meeds. William Winder Laird was a son-in-law of Lammot du Pont, Pierre's brother. Alfred E. Bissell was married to Julia Andrews, granddaughter of the Eugene du Pont who had once headed the powder company. Hollyday S. Meeds, Jr., married Coleman du Pont's daughter Ellen, but was later divorced from her.

As might have been expected, Alfred, too, ventured into new areas of enterprise. In 1927, he bought control of the Florida National Bank of Jacksonville, the first in a chain of Florida banks that came under his influence. It was the beginning of a series of investments, which, under the active management of Alfred's brother-in-law, Edward Ball, was to make the name "du Pont" almost as potent in the economy and politics of northern Florida as it was in Delaware.

Still another path was taken by Henry Belin du Pont. Henry, who had owned the first private plane licensed by the Department of Commerce, opened the Du Pont Airport in 1927, when he organized a company now called the Atlantic Aviation Corporation, today said to be the largest business aircraft sales and service organization in the world. In 1958, Du Pont Field was closed and Atlantic moved to the New Castle County Airport. He also played a key role in the development of the company we know as Trans World Airlines.

Aviation became quite the rage among the du Ponts. Soon many of the younger men had their own planes and private landing strips on their estates. Richard C. du Pont was an expert on gliders, setting a world record. A. Felix du Pont, Jr., used to commute by private plane to his job in du Pont's Camden, New Jersey, plant, where he worked in the paint department inspecting aviation finishes.

Another fad of the younger du Ponts in the 1930's was motorcycling, probably because E. Paul du Pont had become president of the Indian Motorcycle Company. Squads of young du Ponts roared their motor bikes along the roads of the Brandywine country, startling their placid elders. Occasionally a couple of du Pont boys who didn't like the rector of Christ Church would halt their motorcycles outside the place of worship and gun their motors when the minister was preaching his Sunday sermon. But after one group of youngsters rode across the lawn at Granogue, Irénée's hilltop chateau, that territory was ruled off bounds to them.

Irénée's nickname was "Bus." One day he arrived at the estate to find that the Delaware Coach Company had painted a sign over an underpass used by buses in going to Granogue. There was a sharp turn just beyond the underpass, so the company sign warned: BUS—GO SLOW. It looked to Irénée as if somebody was pulling his leg. The next day the sign was changed to read: COACH—GO SLOW.

Yachting was one of the most popular du Pont sports. During the 1930's, a survey indicated that the clan owned more yachts than any other family in the world. One of the most enthusiastic amateur skippers was Ernest, who was commodore of one yacht club. One of the commodore's prerogatives was to fire the starting pistol for the club's races. An *éprouvette*—a small cannon used for testing the strength of powder—had been secured as a decoration

to the foredeck of his yacht. One day Ernest decided to fire a
blank from the little cannon to signal the start of a race, but when
his back was turned, someone slipped a shotgun cartridge into the
gun. In due time, the sailboats came up to the starting line, across
the bow of Ernest's boat. As the sloops reached the line, Ernest set
off the cannon—and was horrified to see a large hole, ripped by
shotgun pellets, open up in the mainsail of the nearest boat.

Public affairs also interested the du Ponts, and in this area of
activity, Alfred and Pierre still appeared determined to outdo each
other. When Alfred, as part of his political maneuvers, organized
the Non-Partisan League to improve conditions in the state, his
cousin countered by establishing the Service Citizens of Delaware.

During the period when Alfred was on top politically, he called
on the Legislature to change the tax structure, which, he said,
spared the rich at the expense of the poor. "The present system,"
he asserted, "taxes the poor man's horse at its actual value, and the
rich man's mansion at only its rental value." Such radical talk,
coming from the owner of the magnificent Nemours, led some of
his relatives to whisper that Alfred was, at best, a tool of the so-
cialists. But business men's organizations and taxpayers' groups rallied behind his campaign and, in the end, the Legislature was forced
to pass tax reforms.

In the same political manifesto, Alfred had also charged: "Education is at a low ebb, shamefully so, there being only twelve states
in the federal Union with a greater illiteracy than we have. Our
whole school system is archaic and lifeless from lack of funds. . . ."

This problem was tackled by Alfred's old foe, Pierre. He fi-
nanced a survey of Delaware's educational system which more
than substantiated Alfred's allegations. Experts engaged by Pierre
drew up a new school code, and while it was being fought through
the Legislature—with the support of Alfred's *Wilmington Morning
News*, by the way—he personally paid for the replacement of more
than a hundred dilapidated schools, spending a half million dollars
on Negro schools alone. Before he was finished Pierre had expended $4,000,000. In the next two decades, Delaware moved up
to tenth place in literacy and was able to boast of first-rate sec-
ondary schools.

His work with the school problem revealed to Pierre the weaknesses in the state's tax collections. For good schools, there must be taxes to pay teachers' salaries and maintenance costs, but the state wasn't getting the revenues to which it was entitled. So Governor R. P. Robinson appointed Pierre to the post of tax commissioner. Using his own funds, Pierre produced a list of every Delaware citizen who should be paying taxes. Then he began pursuing the delinquents. Those who refused to pay up found themselves in court. Soon the tax collection organization was operating with the same efficiency as the du Pont company or General Motors—both of which Pierre was running at the same time he was serving as boss of the state's schools and tax offices.

Before his involvement with the schools, Pierre had bought the Kennett Pike, a privately owned toll road, paved it, and turned it over to the state, thus anticipating his cousin Coleman's more grandiose gesture in that direction.

Not to be outshone by Pierre's civic achievements, Alfred took up the cause of the old and the poor. Even though he had moved his legal residence to Florida by 1929, he used his political influence, still substantial, to have an old-age pension bill introduced in the Delaware Legislature. At that time, before Social Security and private pension funds were common—the du Pont company, however, had set up a pension fund for its employees in 1904—almost forty percent of all persons over sixty-five years of age were dependent on others for their support. The aged, in Alfred's opinion, should enjoy independence and self-respect. "Most of them," he said, "have done their work in the world just as faithfully and just as well as you and I have done ours. That they have not saved enough money to see them through their declining years is nothing against them. We all owe these old people a debt, and we should meet it."

Only Montana at that time had a system of old-age pensions, and it was based on local option. Alfred wanted Delaware to be the first state to adopt a general old-age pension, but his bill, although it passed the lower house by a comfortable margin, was defeated in the state senate.

Something was needed to dramatize the pension fight. So Alfred offered personally to pay the elderly the pensions he thought they deserved until the Legislature enacted his bill. This gesture promised to be expensive, for the Legislature was not scheduled to meet for two years. A staff was hired, the state was canvassed, and lists of the aged were drawn up. Those who would have been eligible for a pension under the bill were selected to receive Alfred's personal monthly remittances. When the first checks went out on November 1, 1929, the maximum was $25 a month, the average $16. Although the payments were small by present-day standards, they were adequate in terms of the purchasing power of the 1929 dollar. About sixteen hundred men and women qualified for payments.

Governor C. Douglass Buck, who had married Coleman's daughter Alice, was impressed with Alfred's action. He appointed an Old Age Welfare Commission, with Alfred as chairman, to make recomendations for an official policy on pensions. This put the governor solidly behind Alfred's pension movement. Since Buck had inherited the political machine of his late father-in-law, this alone would have made Alfred a figure to be reckoned with in politics. But Alfred suddenly found himself riding the crest of a wave of personal popularity. The depression, unthought-of when he first began agitating for pensions, was now well under way, and the man whose name was connected with the pensions enjoyed tremendous influence with the voters of Delaware.

In 1931, the Legislature passed Alfred's pension plan and he mailed out his last checks. He had spent $350,000 to alleviate the plight of the elderly.

His big job done, Alfred relinquished the chairmanship of the Welfare Commission after urging that body to build a state home for the aged and do away with the county poorhouses. In October, 1933, the $500,000 State Welfare Home was dedicated at Smyrna, and Alfred attended, beaming with pride. Not only had his dream-child come into being, but it had been designed by the architectural firm of Massena and du Pont.

CHAPTER XXXIX

SPREADING OUT

JOHN JACOB RASKOB wrote to a du Pont vice-president in 1934: "You . . . are in a position to talk directly with a group [the du Pont family] that controls a larger share of industry through common stock holdings than any other group, including the Rockefellers, the Morgans, the Mellons, or anyone else that begins to control and be responsible for as much industrially as the du Pont company."

It was no idle boast. The wealth of the individual members of the family was so immense that it gave them a position of influence in many companies in which they had invested. An idea of the kind of fortunes they possessed can be obtained from the fact that T. Coleman du Pont, who had not possessed any du Pont company stock in fifteen years, left an estate of $17,000,000 when he died in 1930. In that year, the assets of Alfred I., who was on the outs with the company's management but still held a large block of stock, amounted to about $68,000,000. Even in the early days of the depression, the aggregate wealth of the family was probably close to one billion dollars.

Two holding companies represented the family's interest in the business. The first was Christiana Securities, Incorporated, which developed out of an earlier corporation formed to buy Coleman's shares. Now possibly the world's richest investment trust—shares cost about $20,000 each—it owns twenty-seven percent of the stock of E.I. du Pont de Nemours and Company, Incorporated. The second was the Delaware Realty and Investment Corporation, chartered in 1916 to hold the du Pont stock belonging to Pierre. Today Delaware R and I's interest in the du Pont company amounts to three percent. (Individual members of the du Pont family hold another seven and a half percent of the outstanding shares of their ancestral company.)

Through their own funds and the surplus of the company, du Ponts bought outright or gained control of an impressive number of other corporations during the 1920's and 1930's—so many other enterprises, in fact, that in the late 1920's, a Wall Street expert publicly predicted E.I. du Pont de Nemours and Company, Incorporated, was on the verge of becoming an investment holding company. In 1925, du Pont swallowed up the Viscoloid Company; in 1926, National Ammonia; in 1928, Grasselli Chemicals; in 1929, Krebs Pigment and Chemical, and Capes-Viscose; in 1930, Roessler and Hasslacher Chemical; in 1931, Commercial Pigments and Newport. Majority control of Remington Arms was purchased in 1933 and a du Pont executive was appointed president of Remington. At present du Pont owns 60.17 percent of Remington's common stock.

A du Pont family holding company, Rubber Securities Company, was established in 1927, and through this—and in their own name, too—the du Ponts acquired about seventeen percent of the outstanding stock of the United States Rubber Company, giving them practical control of that corporation. It is of passing interest that the du Pont purchase of the rubber shares was handled by Lewis L. Strauss, later chairman of the Atomic Energy Commission but then a partner in the investment banking house of Kuhn, Loeb and Company. Curiously, Strauss makes no mention of the du Ponts in his autobiography, although he was appointed to the board of United States Rubber, became chairman of its Finance Committee, and remained active in the corporation until 1945.

During this same general period, the du Ponts also began buying into other major industries, including North American Aviation, Bendix Aviation, and United States Steel. Their investment in Steel amounted to about $14,000,000 on the day that the Federal Trade

Commission announced that it was going to investigate the matter. A few months later, the du Ponts discreetly sold out their interest in Steel—at a profit of $2,000,000.

In products, too, the du Ponts were expanding at a rate probably unprecedented in American industry. In 1917, the wartime shortage of dyes and other organic chemicals encouraged the company to invest $50,000,000 in facilities for production in that field.

Rayon was the first new du Pont product under this program. In 1920 du Pont signed an agreement with the Comptoir de Textiles Artificiels which owned the patent on the new fiber that served as a cheap substitute for silk. Looking back now, it is difficult to recall the innovations in clothing, in fashions and in household furnishings brought about by rayon. "The greatest textile revolution since the invention of the cotton gin," someone called it—with good reason. For now women who couldn't afford expensive silk could still dress smartly.

The association with the Comptoir de Textiles Artificiels was fruitful again, three years later, when the French company licensed du Pont to produce cellophane, so closely akin to rayon that it might be called rayon in sheets. The name came from the first syllable of cellulose plus the Greek *phaneros*—"clear." It had been invented by Jacques Edwin Brandenberger, a Swiss chemist, trying to find a liquid viscose coating for cotton tablecloths. His first film was thick and brittle, but before long he succeeded in turning out continuous rolls that were thin, transparent and shiny. Cellophane was then used for wrapping gifts and other packages. In this country, the first cellophane was put on the market by du Pont in 1924. Though it quickly won wide acceptance, its popularity soon waned because it was not moisture-proof, as other far less expensive wrapping materials were. So du Pont chemists set to work devising a method for moisture-proofing cellophane, a goal achieved by one of them, William Hale Church, after two thousand experiments. The last obstacle removed, cellophane swept the field, wrapping candy, bread, cigarettes, and almost every other product.

And so it went: 1924, synthetic ammonia and photographic film; 1925, industrial alcohol; 1928, seed disinfectants.

Some of the new products were discovered by others. For example, tetraethyl lead, the "anti-knock" additive for gasoline, was discovered by Thomas Midgley, Jr., in collaboration with Charles Kettering when both were in the employ of General Motors; GM then joined with Standard Oil of New Jersey—which had been on the point of solving the same problem—to form the Ethyl Corporation. But the du Pont company got the contract to manufacture tetraethyl lead in plants built by the Ethyl Corporation. This was only just, for du Pont had developed the manufacturing process for converting the laboratory invention into a commercial product.

Midgley also was the discoverer of Freon, the refrigerating gas which was non-toxic and non-flammable. The rights to Freon were turned over to Kinetic Chemicals, Incorporated, by GM; and the motor company then gave du Pont fifty-one percent of the stock of Kinetic Chemicals, one of whose best customers was GM's Frigidaire division.

Other products most often identified with du Pont actually originated with others, including the plastic, Lucite, patented in the 1930's by Imperial Chemical Industries of Great Britain; polyethylene, whose manufacturing process was improved by the Max Planck Institute of Germany after ICI had discovered it; and the synthetic fiber, Dacron, which was discovered in 1941 by two chemists in the employ of the Calico Printers' Association of Britain, where it is known as "Terylene," a name given it by ICI.

Nevertheless, du Pont's own contributions to chemical technology have been impressive. Synthetic rubber was perfected by du Pont in 1931. At first marketed under the name "DuPrene," it later was re-designated as "neoprene," to give it a generic label. The du Pont chemists got their first clue in the search for a synthetic rubber from the Reverend Dr. Julius A. Nieuwland, professor of organic chemistry at the University of Notre Dame. When neoprene was perfected, du Pont paid royalties to Notre Dame for use of a catalyst that Father Nieuwland had patented. But the invention of neoprene was solely the achievement of du Pont.

The most important discovery ever made in du Pont's laboratories, of course, was the invention of nylon. The chemist responsible for this accomplishment was Dr. Wallace H. Carothers, a brilliant young man who was lured away from Harvard by du Pont after the company decided to support a program of fundamental research. In 1935, Carothers developed a polyamide that he called "66" polymer, a fiber that was strong, tough, elastic, water-resistant, and capable of withstanding high temperatures. In 1938, du Pont completed the pilot plant and a year later large-scale production of nylon got under way. Nylon has so nearly ruined the market for rayon that du Pont, once the only rayon manufacturer in the United States, has recently stopped making any of that fiber.

Carothers was not able to enjoy his triumph. In 1937, before the pilot plant was even completed, he committed suicide at the age of forty-one.

During du Pont's period of vast expansion between the two world wars, three brothers directed its operations: Pierre, Irénée and Lammot. Pierre was president from 1915 to 1919 when he became board chairman and Irénée succeeded him in his old post. In 1926, Irénée retired from the presidency, becoming vice-chairman of the board, and Lammot took his former place. He remained president until 1940 when he became board chairman. At the same time, Pierre and Irénée retired as chairman and vice-chairman, respectively.

But before that day arrived, the du Ponts had to run the gauntlet of the most adverse public opinion to which they had ever been exposed.

CHAPTER XL

THE LIBERTY LEAGUE

IN 1919, CAPTAIN WILLIAM H. STAYTON, an Annapolis graduate and lawyer, organized the Association Against the Prohibition Amendment. For years it appeared that his valiant crusade was hopeless. Most of the AAPA's budget came from Stayton's own pockets and it made little or no headway in fighting the evils of the Volstead Act.

Then, in 1926, the AAPA suddenly was "discovered" by a group of industrialists and financiers whose leaders were Pierre, Irénée and Lammot du Pont, John J. Raskob, and Charles H. Sabin, a New York banker. Pierre was appointed chairman of the AAPA executive committee of which Irénée also became a member; and Lammot was named head of the finance committee whose membership included Raskob. The three brothers and Raskob proved generous supporters: in 1929 they gave more than $130,000 to the AAPA, and two years later they contributed over $200,000. Together with the donations of other millionaires, these gifts by 1927 lifted AAPA's income to more than a half million dollars. Before Repeal ended the fight, over a million dollars was being spent by the AAPA annually.

Why were the du Ponts willing to pay such large sums to fight Prohibition?

That is a question that has never been answered satisfactorily, although the AAPA was investigated in 1930 by a Senate Judiciary subcommittee. Critics of the family have suggested that they were motivated by plans for entering the distilling industry, pointing out that du Pont had gone into production of industrial alcohol a year before Pierre and his brothers moved into the AAPA. More recently, an economist has asserted that "there is . . . some apparent du Pont connection with the National Distillers group through Francis B. Davis, Jr., chairman of the board of United States Rubber."

These explanations seem rather far-fetched. The fact is that the du Ponts did *not* go into distilling when the Twenty-first Amendment made the liquor business legal. (Although Pierre, after Repeal, did add to his other public duties the job of State Liquor Commissioner.) And the alleged connection between du Pont and National Distillers is so slight, if it exists at all, that it is likely to satisfy only those who see a plot behind all actions of big business.

Another reason advanced for the du Pont interest in Repeal was a desire to cut taxes. There is some basis for this hypothesis, since AAPA propaganda played heavily on the tax angle. If liquor were legalized and taxed, the AAPA argued, the huge revenues from the alcohol tax would obviate the need for many taxes. Irénée du Pont liked to say that "one of his companies would save $10,000,000 in corporation tax if we should have, say, the British tax on beer." And Pierre told large taxpayers that the British liquor tax "applied in the United States [if the Eighteenth Amendment were repealed] would permit of the total abolition of the income tax both personal and corporate."

Thus, the tax problem may have been a real consideration. On the other hand, the use of the tax issue in the AAPA materials gives every indication that it was raised only as a selling point to win over those who were unhappy about taxes. Nothing in the private correspondence or records uncovered by the Senate investigators supports the theory that the du Ponts opposed Prohibition because they seriously hoped their taxes would be lower if Repeal brought alcohol tax dollars into the federal treasury instead.

It is more probable that, like many Americans, they were simply fed up with the failure of the "Noble Experiment." Anyone with a sense of civic responsibility—and the du Ponts have never been accused of lacking that virtue, regardless of the way they displayed it—was bound to be troubled by contemplation of the lawlessness to which Prohibition had given rise, with gangsters operating openly.

Their AAPA activities carried the family into national politics in a role they had never filled before. Raskob was the key figure in this move. His friendship with Alfred E. Smith, who had risen from the tenements of Manhattan's Lower East Side to be Governor of New York state, was a decisive factor.

In 1926, during his last campaign for governor, the "Happy Warrior," as Smith liked to be called, was introduced to Raskob by Eddie Dowling, the actor. All three were ardent Roman Catholics, a fact which was to have some pertinence before long. Raskob was so impressed with Smith that he immediately wrote a $50,000 check for his campaign fund.

The next day James J. Riordan, head of the County Trust Company of New York and a close friend of Smith, told Dowling, "Eddie, your friend has $3,000,000 of General Motors and du Pont money on deposit in New York City. If I can get him to put it in the County Trust Company, my bank will jump from a $2,000,000 bank to a $5,000,000 bank."

Dowling later recalled, "I saw Raskob and he made the transfer. He also transferred the deposits of the General Motors Acceptance Corporation so that, instead of becoming a $5,000,000 bank, the County Trust jumped to nearer $10,000,000. Al then was made chairman of the board. That was the beginning of Al's desertion of the 'sidewalks of New York.' "

Al Smith won that election for governor, and it made him a leading contender for the Democratic presidential nomination in 1928, although it was recognized that Smith, as the first Catholic candidate for the White House, would have a formidable handicap to overcome. After he won the nomination, his forthright opposition to the "drys" made his already faltering campaign immeasurably more difficult.

The du Ponts and many of the other rich backers of the AAPA became generous contributors to Al Smith's presidential campaign fund because of his stand on the liquor issue, and their money helped him, of course. But when he got Raskob appointed chairman of the Democratic National Committee and thus his campaign manager, his foes raised the "Rum and Romanism" cry louder than before. On the other hand, Franklin D. Roosevelt told a friend that Raskob's appointment was a "bold stroke to try to end the ninety-nine percent of business—big and little—preference for the Republican Party."

In one of the dirtiest political campaigns in American history, Smith was defeated overwhelmingly by Herbert Hoover. The electoral vote was 444 to 87, with the Democrats even losing the Upper South, plus Florida and Texas. In Florida, Alfred I. du Pont organized the opposition to Smith, not because of the Catholic issue—Alfred was well known to be a warm admirer of the Roman Church—but simply because Pierre had come out for the "Happy Warrior" and because Smith supposedly had promised to make Pierre Secretary of State or ambassador to Great Britain. When Smith lost Florida by 44,000 votes, Alfred I. du Pont exulted to some friends, "I've just licked Pierre and Raskob and made Florida Republican and I am reeking with gore!"

The devastating national defeat nearly wrecked the Democratic Party, but Raskob, still national chairman, took his responsibilities seriously. He brought in Jouett Shouse, president of the AAPA, and made him executive chairman of the Democratic National Committee, that is, the operating chief. Most of the funds for running the national office came out of Raskob's own pocket. And with his genius for efficient organization, the party soon was in good form to take advantage of the political opportunity offered by the economic disaster that now was turning millions of voters away from the Republican Party.

The crash of 1929 was taking place, to be followed by the long, bleak years of the worst depression the country had ever known. People demanded action; they wanted a change. The Democrats made impressive gains in the 1930 congressional elections.

As the 1932 national convention approached, Alfred E. Smith and Franklin D. Roosevelt became estranged. FDR had won the New York gubernatorial election in 1928 while Smith was suffering a humiliating national defeat. Moreover, as governor, the young patroon from Hyde Park had shown clearly that he was his own man, not Smith's. There were many other factors at work driving the two men apart. By 1932, Smith and his group, including Raskob and Shouse, were so hostile to Roosevelt that they fought as hard as they could to prevent him from winning the presidential nomination.

Nevertheless, Pierre, Irénée, and Raskob voted Democratic in 1932, as they had in 1928, mainly because Roosevelt had pledged himself to repeal of Prohibition. Although FDR made good on that promise, the du Ponts always regarded their vote in this election as a great mistake.

The majority of Americans, however, thought otherwise. They came to regard Roosevelt as the man who had saved the American way of life from the chaos that threatened the very future of capitalism.

Today, looking back over three decades, it is well nigh impossible to convey to those who did not live through that terrible time just how frightening it was. Fifteen million men had lost their jobs by the time Hoover left the White House. One third of the nation's railroads had gone into bankruptcy. On April 1, 1933, United States Steel had not a single full-time worker. More than 5,000 banks had failed. On a single day in April, 1932, one-fourth of the entire state of Mississippi was lost in foreclosures. On New Year's Day in 1933, Calvin Coolidge, scarcely a radical, sighed, "In other periods of depression it has always been possible to see some things which were solid and upon which you could base hope, but as I look about, I now see nothing to give ground for hope—nothing of man." As historian William E. Leuchtenburg sums up that time: "In Hoover's last days in office, the old order tottered on the brink of disaster."

The du Ponts could have seen evidence of this all about them. For example, just off the Kennett Pike on the west, across from Breck's Lane and the Montchanin Road, was Westover Hills, a fashionable suburb which housed many du Pont executives among others. In those grim days, for obvious reasons, the section acquired the bitter tag, "Leftover Bills."

In his first hundred days in office, Roosevelt and his congressional forces pushed through legislation that gave confidence to the nation: the Emergency Banking Relief Act, the Economy Act, the Beer-Wine Revenue Act, the Civilian Conservation Corps law, the Federal Emergency Relief Act, the Agricultural Adjustment Act, the Tennessee Valley Authority law, the Federal Securities Act, and many others.

Although the nation as a whole took heart at having found a leader, many of the du Ponts, like most of their class, were genuinely alarmed at the radical nature of the New Deal's program. In March, 1934, R.R.M. Carpenter, whose wife Margaretta was a sister of Pierre, Irénée, and Lammot, asked Raskob if he had any idea what Roosevelt was really trying to achieve by his revolutionary schemes. Actually Carpenter, a vice-president of E.I. du Pont de Nemours and Company, Incorporated, was the company's political trouble-shooter.

Raskob replied that he, too, had been worrying about the direction the Administration was taking, but he explained that he had been out of politics since 1932. He considered that it was time "some organization" was established to get across to the voters "the value of encouraging people to work; encouraging people to get rich; showing the fallacy of communism. . . ." Jokingly Raskob added, "You haven't much to do, and I know of no one that could better take the lead in trying to induce the du Pont and General Motors groups . . . to definitely organize to protect society."

But in the end, Raskob himself took the initiative. He arranged a series of meetings in New York, attended by the three du Pont brothers; Alfred P. Sloan, Jr., of GM; Al Smith; and a number of other conservative industrialists and financiers. The result of these meetings was the American Liberty League, the founding of which was announced in Washington on August 22, 1934. Shouse, who held the press conference, told reporters that the League was "not inimical to the national administration," was "definitely not anti-Roosevelt," wasn't a movement "to stop Roosevelt in 1936," did "intend to try to help the Administration" and "would not actually participate in elections."

No one took these statements seriously. "The financial community," said the *New York Times*, "sees in the movement the nucleus of a new force for conservatism." *Newsweek* was more blunt: "The Tories have come out of ambush."

The Liberty League went to work in a big way. Its office staff occupied thirty-one rooms and employed more than fifty persons at a time when the G.O.P. national headquarters had only seventeen people in twelve rooms. The League's propaganda machine churned out material in quantity: pamphlets were issued at the rate of one a week and distributed to newspapers, libraries, schools, public officials, and anyone else who would accept them; a monthly bulletin was published; special "reports" were mailed to every part of the country; editorials and canned news stories were sent out to more than sixteen hundred newspapers; radio time was made available to the League; there were divisions for lawyers and college students.

Yet it was all in vain. The rich were talking to the wealthy; conservatives to tories. The du Ponts and their associates had lost all contact with ordinary Americans.

That was most vividly illustrated on January 25, 1936, when the American Liberty League decided to kick off an all-out drive to defeat Roosevelt in that election year by holding a dinner at the Mayflower Hotel in Washington, D.C. Two thousand guests gathered for the glittering affair, including a dozen du Ponts and a good many oddly assorted people—ranging from Dean Acheson, who would one day be Secretary of State under the liberal President Truman, to Elizabeth Dilling, whose activities on the crackpot fringe of the Right would cause her difficulties with the government in World War II. The audience "represented, either through principals or attorneys, a large portion of the capitalistic wealth of the country," according to the *New York Times*. Some wags had been calling it "dinner with the du Ponts," and the gathering lived up to its advance billing.

They played Al Smith's old campaign song, "The Sidewalks of New York," when he appeared on the dais, but it only served to emphasize the contrast between the "Happy Warrior" who had fought for the underprivileged and the embittered politician who had come out in 1934 against a measure to abolish child labor. "Jammed elbow to elbow, tailcoat to tailcoat, fluttery bouffant dress to sleek black velvet dress, the tables set so closely together in the main ballroom that the ushers in the Confederate gray mess coats and black pants scarcely could wiggle between the anti-New Dealers, Democrats and Republicans alike gathered to hear the magic, rasping voice of Alfred E. Smith belabor the present Administration," the *Times* said.

Belabor it he did. In white tie and tails, Smith tried his best to pin the Communist label on the New Deal. He charged that FDR was leading the country down the road to socialism, a familiar Liberty League refrain. If the President didn't mend his ways, Smith warned, he and his friends "probably" would "take a walk" at the forthcoming National Democratic Convention. As such speeches must be, his was wrapped in the flag at the end: "There can be only one capital, Washington or Moscow. There can be only the clear, pure, fresh air of free America, or the foul breath of communistic Russia. There can be only one flag, the Stars and Stripes, or the flag of the godless Union of the Soviets. There can be only one national anthem, 'The Star-Spangled Banner' or the 'Internationale.' "

Afterwards, Pierre S. du Pont told reporters, "It was perfect."

And so it was—for the Democrats. As Arthur Krock, the *Times*'s chief political writer, predicted, "Historians of this political year may unanimously conclude that [the Smith speech's] contribution was a rich one to the President."

The sight of Al Smith rubbing elbows with the kind of men he had long fought, the sound of Al Smith talking like a Hoover Republican, caused many Americans who might have been wavering to return to the New Deal with a new passion.

A week later, Eugene Talmadge, Governor of Georgia and bitter foe of the New Deal, held a "Grass Roots" convention in Macon, Georgia, to begin a Talmadge boom for the Democratic presidential nomination. Many organizations supporting Talmadge played heavily on the racist angle in their propaganda; a typical throwaway by the Southern Committee to Uphold the Constitution charged that "President Roosevelt has . . . permitted Negroes to come to the White House banquet table and sleep in the White House beds. . . ."

It was startling that many of the du Ponts, including Pierre, Irénée, Lammot, and Henry B., contributed substantially to this outfit, although they personally despised bigotry. There is every reason to believe that they were even unaware of the nature of the committee's appeals. "Yet in contributing without enough investigation to discover what sort of group they were supporting," said George Wolfskill in his recent study, *The Revolt of the Conservatives*, "they certainly failed in their responsibility to the nation and damaged their own cause almost beyond repair."

According to the *New York Post*, "the brood of anti-New Deal organizations spawned by the Liberty League are in turn spawning fascism." This was a low blow, for there never was any evidence that the du Ponts felt the slightest sympathy with fascism. Indeed, as the later cartel investigations brought out, even the most conservative members of the family were always unrelentingly hostile to fascist ideology.

To charges that he supported organizations dedicated to race hatred and anti-Semitism, Pierre retorted, "I have never entertained any prejudices that would mark me with disfavor to any race or people. I have one-eighth Jewish blood in my veins that I am not ashamed of." This was not the usual "some-of-my-best-friends-are-Jewish" line often taken by anti-Semites. Only a man who truly detested Jew-baiting would have drawn attention to his own Jewish ancestry. Unwise and gullible in his politics Pierre may have been; vicious he was not.

Franklin D. Roosevelt received the Democratic nomination as everyone had known he must, and the Republicans chose Alfred M. Landon, Governor of Kansas and a man of rather liberal views. The conservative du Ponts were so displeased that they talked about forming a third party, a "constitutional coalition," but the idea never got past the talking stage.

For lack of a better choice, the du Ponts threw their support to the G.O.P. A month before the election, it was disclosed that members of the family "and executives of companies bearing their name"—meaning in-laws mostly—had contributed $383,000 to the Republican war chest. By the time the campaign was over, their gifts to the cause probably amounted to a million dollars, directly and through other organizations such as the Liberty League. "Never before in political history," said a New York newspaper, "as far as observers could recall, has a campaign been so dominated by a single family or has any family donated a comparable sum in an effort to elect its man to the Presidency."

Most of the time it seemed as though the Democrats were cam-

paigning against the du Ponts—tagged by FDR as "economic royalists"—instead of Alf Landon. Jim Farley, linking the G.O.P. with
the American Liberty League, said the latter "ought to be called
the American Cellophane League" because "first, it's a du Pont
product, and, second, you can see right through it."

Liberty League propaganda was laughed off as "duPontifical."
Even writers bitterly hostile to the New Deal, like Frank Kent of
the *Baltimore Sun*, denounced the Liberty League for its "glaring
ineptitude" and warned that its support was the kiss of death. And
so it proved to be.

In the election, Roosevelt was re-elected by the most sweeping
margin of electoral votes since James Monroe. Only Maine and
Vermont held fast for the Republicans.

All that the Liberty League had managed to achieve was "the
conversion of America's favorite family—the du Ponts—into political enemy Number One," said Charles Michelson, witty publicity
director of the Democratic National Committee.

After the election, only the du Ponts continued to support the
League and their contributions were reduced. Before the 1940
presidential election campaign, the Liberty League, which had
been gradually dying for three years, breathed its last.

After World War II, some of the du Ponts were revealed as backers of a new version of the American Liberty League, this time
employing the name "American Action." Following a brief flurry
of publicity, the organization dropped out of the public eye.

The painful lesson of the 1930's had not yet been learned, it
appeared.

CHAPTER XLI

AUNT ZADIE ON THE
PICKET LINES

T HE PUBLIC FUROR over the American Liberty League gave birth to the general belief that all the du Ponts were conservative and Republicans. Of course, like most people of wealth, the majority of the family is tory. But the du Ponts have never been monolithic in their politics; since the Whigs vanished from the scene there have been du Ponts who were not Republican and not conservative.

The most striking example of the leftist tradition in the family was Miss Zara du Pont—"Aunt Zadie," as everyone called her—who used to lament the difficulty of finding a hat that would look well in the Unitarian church and also on a picket line. "She wasn't a Democrat," a du Pont who was very close to her said recently. "She was farther to the left. I guess she'd have described herself as a Socialist."

Beginning with woman suffrage, she became involved in many of the social struggles of her time, including municipal ownership of public utilities, birth control, civil liberties, abolition of discrimination and segregation, the labor movement, pacifism, and socialism. Because of her name, her participation often brought those causes more publicity than they would otherwise have enjoyed. "If I must bear the name," she once told a friend, "it might as well be of use helping good causes."

She didn't look or act like a radical. There was a rather delicate, patrician beauty to her features. Her voice was soft and as gentle as her manner. The toughest cop, seeing her on a picket line, instinctively lowered his voice, impressed by her dignity even though he might not be aware of her identity.

During one strike a curious policeman accosted her on the picket line.

"What's your name?" he demanded.

"Zara du Pont," she said.

He wrote it down in his notebook but said skeptically, "Another phony name. One of the Delaware du Ponts, I suppose?"

"Yes," she said, smiling sweetly at his sarcasm.

Zara was born in Louisville, Kentucky, on February 24, 1869, one of the eight children of Antoine Bidermann du Pont and his wife Ellen Coleman. Thus she was a sister of T. Coleman du Pont, not only president of the du Pont company, but a conservative and a Republican senator as well. Most of Zara's brothers and sisters were liberals, however.

She never married. "I never especially *wanted* to be married," she confided to an intimate late in life, "but I did long for children —and I've had them." She was referring to the fact that she raised ten du Pont children. Her political and social crusades were waged between periods of child-rearing.

Her sister Dora, who had married Henry Rodney Phillips, died when her daughter, Dora Coleman Phillips, was still a little girl. Aunt Zadie brought up her niece and saw her married to Egbert Moxham, son of du Pont vice-president Arthur J. Moxham, a friend of Zara's father many years before.

Then Mary Ethel Clark, the wife of Zara's brother, Antoine Bidermann du Pont, Jr., died in 1909, leaving three children: Aileen M., Ethel B., and Victorine. They lived in Cleveland, so Aunt Zadie moved there to live with her brother and care for his children.

In 1917, she went to Johnstown, Pennsylvania, where another brother, Evan Morgan du Pont, had lost his wife, the former Helen Augusta Quinn. Aunt Zadie raised Evan's six children: James Q.,

Bidermann T., Rosina, Ellen C., Dora P., and William B. "She drove us to the Catholic church more than our own mother would have done, simply because she wanted to bring us up as our mother would have," Jim du Pont recalls, "although she was not a Catholic."

Perhaps Zara's readiness to raise orphans was a reflection of her own childhood. Her mother had died when Zara was seven years old, and her maternal grandmother, a lovable woman, took the child under her wing. But later, an aunt who was "as difficult as Granny was nice," according to Aunt Zadie's own recollection, moved into the house and took over the chore of rearing the girl.

As a young woman, Zara refused to make her debut into society. Instead, she joined the board of the Children's Free Hospital of Louisville. That led her into other charitable activities, but she soon came to the conclusion that such work was "futile." She said, "It merely takes care of conditions, not causes." She was beginning to develop what one of her nieces, Ethel B. du Pont, calls her "insatiable desire for justice."

When, with the backing of all the women's organizations, she tried to get Louisville to establish playgrounds for children, she found that ladies were completely disregarded by politicians. This made her realize that "before women can bring about any social betterment they have got to become voters."

About that time she went to Cleveland to join her brother, A.B. du Pont, Jr., who was then helping Tom L. Johnson, the reform "Single Tax" mayor, in his battle for municipal ownership of public utilities. In Cleveland, she met Judge Florence Allen and Miss Elizabeth Hauser, then secretary of the Women's Suffrage Association in Ohio. Soon Zara was vice-chairman of the organization.

By a mighty effort of will, she was able to overcome her natural reserve and plunge into the give-and-take of suffragette agitation. In 1912, Florence H. Luscomb was sent to Ohio to work for passage of a state constitutional amendment giving the vote to women. There she first met Zara du Pont.

"We would assemble in the county seat," Miss Luscomb recalls, "and Aunt Zadie would lay out routes along the railroad lines for us and we would go forth, two and two, loaded with tons of leaflets in addition to our personal equipment, to spend a day in each of the small towns, canvassing the houses, stores, farmers in the fields, and at night holding an open-air, soap-box rally in front of the post office or general store. Up at five the next morning to move on to the next hamlet. At the end of the week or so, the troupe would re-assemble in the next county seat to repeat the process."

Years later, Zara moved to Cambridge, Massachusetts, where she settled down in a four-room apartment near Radcliffe College. Miss Luscomb lived close by and they became intimate friends.

"She was one of the most wonderful human beings I have ever known," Miss Luscomb says. "Seldom have I known anyone with such tenderness and sensitivity for human suffering and injustice, such willingness to give of herself in remedying them, such intellectual integrity and courage in taking unpopular stands."

Until well into her seventies, Zara was regularly seen on Boston picket lines. "One such instance was when five furniture-moving workers were locked out because they had tried to organize a union in their company whose labor conditions were atrocious," Miss Luscomb remembers. "The five men set up a picket line and for ten months, in summer heat and winter cold, at six o'clock in summer and seven in winter, Aunt Zadie, then in her sixties, picketed the firm's garage when the vans left in the morning." In the end the men won.

When the National Maritime Union was conducting an organizational strike in Everett, Massachusetts, the police broke up the picket line with tear gas. That night, the NMU strike leaders asked Aunt Zadie and Florence Luscomb to appear the next morning wearing gas masks. They did—and the police stopped using tear gas. The sight of a white-haired dowager in a gas mask on a picket line made good copy for the newspaper reporters and photographers who had been thoughtfully tipped off by the union. And the fact that the woman was a du Pont made the story even better. With that kind of publicity, the police didn't dare use gas again.

Often—as she did during the 1936 strike of the International Ladies' Garment Workers Union in Boston—she would step off the line to talk to a policeman pointed out to her as one who roughed up pickets. In her quiet, sincere way, she would talk with him, not as to an enemy but as to a friend. To him she would repeat what she always said to her nephews and nieces—that the most important thing of all was to *think*.

Throughout the 1930's, Zara made the headlines:

DU PONT RELATIVE GIVES $50 TO SOCIALIST PARTY AT BOSTON. . . . ZARA DU PONT BACKS SPANISH LOYALISTS. . . .

Another of Zara's favorite activities was the Women's International League for Peace and Freedom, a pacifist organization.

But the incident which aroused the greatest public interest came in April, 1941, when Zara attended a stockholders' meeting of the Bethlehem Steel Corporation—a meeting held, as it happened, in the Du Pont Building in Wilmington. There Zara launched a lady-like but vigorous attack on Bethlehem's management for its labor policies, which were, she charged, "sabotaging national defense." Speaking with her usual logic and clarity but without histrionics, she said, "Bethlehem's present policies are calculated utterly to destroy labor's faith in the devotion of America's industrial leaders to democracy, and so to destroy labor's will to co-operate with them."

Her assault so flustered Eugene P. Grace, Bethlehem's president, that he stumbled into an awkward, rambling apology for the company's stand. But Aunt Zadie's charges got most of the newspaper play.

That afternoon, when Grace stepped into an elevator that held Zara and one of her relatives, a du Pont with whom he was friendly introduced them, saying, "Do you know Aunt Zadie? We sometimes say that she's the crazy one in the family."

Zara, unruffled as usual, said mildly, "It takes brains to be 'crazy.'"

A month later Zara, as a stockholder, sued Bethlehem for wasting money fighting the unions. Soon afterward, she withdrew the suit, announcing happily that Bethlehem's management had promised to mend its ways.

Such activities led some of the younger conservatives in the family to refer to her irreverently as "Miss Kick," but none of them dared criticize Zara to her cousin, Pierre S. du Pont. When one of his relatives did venture to speak of her in unflattering terms one day, Pierre snapped, "I don't want to hear anything against her. She's a good woman."

At family get-togethers, Aunt Zadie was always treated with respect and affection by her conservative relatives. Although Pierre, Irénée and Lammot felt very strongly about politics, they recognized the right of others to disagree with them. And Zara, on her part, spoke of her cousins with warmth and kindness.

She once said, "I confidently expect to live till the time when a Jew, a Negro, a Catholic, and a woman will have been elected President of the United States." But in 1946 she died in Boston, at the age of seventy-seven, fourteen years before the first Catholic President took office.

Her heritage lived on in many of the nephews and nieces she had helped to raise. In the winter of 1945-1946, Ethel B. du Pont, as a stockholder, publicly supported the United Auto Workers' strike against General Motors, then controlled by the du Pont company. It was the sort of stand that Aunt Zadie herself would have taken.

CHAPTER XLII

THE DU PONT GIRL AND
THE PRESIDENT'S SON

THAT THE 1930's would be a decade of trouble for the du Ponts was foreshadowed in December, 1932, before the Roosevelt Administration took office. At that time, the Bureau of Internal Revenue notified Pierre S. du Pont and John J. Raskob that it could not allow an intricate, tax-saving securities swap between the two men. Both, however, insisted that their transaction was justified and proper under the tax laws. A long period of scrutiny and negotiation began.

Throughout 1933 and the early part of 1934, the New Deal ground out a series of laws radically changing the relationships between business on the one hand, and government, labor, and the consumer public on the other. And finally, on April 12, 1934—just about the time the du Ponts were starting to organize the American Liberty League—the Senate voted authorization for an inquiry into the manufacture and traffic in arms.

If their fear that the New Deal was paving the way for socialism led the du Ponts into supporting futile organizations like the Liberty League and shabby outfits like the Southern Committee to Uphold the Constitution, their folly was matched by that of millions of other Americans who, because of the depression, turned to the radicalism of the Communists, the Coughlinites, and other extremist groups which were ready to blame all the ills of the world on the rich.

In such an atmosphere, the du Ponts would have to fight to keep their name unsullied. But another development made matters even worse. Ever since the end of World War I, a spirit of disillusionment about that conflict had been spreading throughout all the world—except in Germany. And even there the people believed they had been betrayed. This was the time of anti-war poems by Siegfried Sassoon and Wilfred Owen. Books like Hemingway's *A Farewell to Arms* and Remarque's *All Quiet on the Western Front* were making clear the sordid, brutal truth about life under the gun. A new genre of pacifist plays was being ushered in, plays like *Peace on Earth*, produced in New York in 1933 and written by Albert Maltz who later—in 1947—was one of the "Hollywood Ten" convicted of contempt of Congress in connection with an investigation of Communism. But it would be misleading to suggest that the war-hating mood of the 1930's was created by the Reds. As usual, the Communists had to hurry to keep up with the people; they didn't lead the masses although they tried to.

After Gerald P. Nye, a North Dakota Republican, was named chairman of the Senate Munitions Investigating Committee, twenty-five thousand college youths took part in a one-hour stoppage of classes as part of the Student Anti-War Strike. They solemnly pledged themselves not to support their own government in any future war. This demonstration was indeed the work of the Communists; they took advantage of the cynical mood of American students to reap what benefits they could.

The du Ponts themselves did not make the mistake of blaming the Reds for every attack on munitions makers. In a statement Irénée said the drive to discredit them came from three wholly separate groups: idealists who wanted to prevent war and harbored the "mistaken notion that preparedness is a cause of war"; newspapers and magazines that were willing to hawk any sensational cause in order to increase their circulation; and Communists and fellow travelers who wanted to weaken the national security of capitalist countries.

No one paid much attention to the chief attorney placed on Nye's staff by Lee Pressman, then a New Deal lawyer and later counsel of the Congress of Industrial Organizations, the CIO. (Pressman was a Communist during that period and for years afterward, but this was not known then.) The new man's name was Alger Hiss and the munitions hearings marked the first appearance of his name in the newspapers. To many people, Hiss, during the Nye Committee hearings, seemed like a David out to slay Goliath. That was an image doomed to die years later after he was convicted of perjury for denying under oath that he had, as a trusted State Department official, given secret documents to Whittaker Chambers while the latter was a Soviet secret agent.

In his memoirs, Chambers later commented, "The penetration of the United States government by the Communist Party coincided with a mood in the nation which light-heartedly baited the men who manufactured the armaments indispensable to its defense as 'Merchants of Death.' It is not surprising that Alger Hiss should first have emerged to public view in the act of helping the Communist Party to abet that disastrous mood."

Late in 1934, the du Ponts were summoned to testify at public hearings. The three brothers all took the witness stand, and Pierre caused quite a stir when he disclosed that in November, 1917, Secretary of War Newton D. Baker had denounced the du Ponts as "a species of outlaws" because of the stiff terms they demanded from the government to build the Old Hickory powder plant, a government-owned mill near Nashville, Tennessee. The factory cost the government more than $85,000,000, of which less than $4,000,000 was salvaged after the war, but the enormous cost and waste were never clearly laid at the door of the du Ponts.

The star of the hearings was Irénée du Pont, who was neither shy like Pierre nor reticent like Lammot. A witness who talked in homely, down-to-earth terms, enjoyed a good argument, and rejoiced in a self-confidence that gave his words the strength of dogma, Irénée also presented the right appearance for a man who was in the fight of his life. His face had a plain, friendly quality that reminded one of Gary Cooper. His jaw was strong, and he had the usual prominent du Pont nose. Behind his gold spectacles were keen, blue eyes, and though the curved briar pipe in his mouth gave him a deceptive look of relaxation, he was actually as alert as a cat; he thought fast and tossed the ball back at his inquisitors as quickly as they threw it to him.

From the beginning, Irénée took the offensive. When the Senators and Hiss made vague general allegations, he demanded that they produce evidence or witnesses. He challenged them to find government officials or records to support an insinuation that du Pont had tried to interfere with the Geneva Protocol of 1924, an international code of procedure which attempted to prevent war by providing for arbitration of disputes. At the time of that conference, which had also tried to curb the traffic in arms, Irénée had publicly favored a limitation on arms but not disarmament. "To actually disarm," he said then, "is as absurdly Utopian as it would be to discontinue the police force of a city on the theory that everybody would be good. [On the other hand] to limit armament appeals to everybody's common sense."

And now Irénée told the Nye Committee, "If we had not shipped powder to France and England, the possibilities are that Germany would have won the war, and we would have been taken next and been a German colony."

Although the committee showed that a good many other companies had engaged in questionable acts, it proved nothing of the sort against the du Ponts. The worst that could be said about them was that their profits in World War I had been gigantic. To this undeniable assertion, they made these replies: until 1917 it was Europe's war, not ours, and the du Pont company could not be expected to risk money on plant expansion for the sake of other countries. Thus, when the United States entered the conflict, du Pont had the production facilities ready because it had been expanding during the previous three years. As for 1917-1918, when the American government was making purchases from du Pont, the company actually paid more money into the Treasury in taxes than it received in income from Washington's orders. The reason, of course, was that du Pont was still selling to Britain and France in those closing months and paying taxes on those foreign sales.

The evaluation of the investigation by *Fortune* magazine is significant, for "Arms and the Men," an article in the March, 1934, issue of that publication, had led the Senate to undertake the inquiry in the first place. "By and large," *Fortune* said after the hearings, "the du Ponts came away with a clean bill of health. Which is not hard to understand when you consider the facts: . . . peaceful activities account for ninety-nine percent of E. I. du Pont de Nemours' highly satisfactory current profits." Nevertheless, sensational headlines—DU PONTS ACCUSED OF SMOKE SCREEN FOR ARMS PROBE; ARMS MOGULS FOUGHT AGAINST CONTROL PACT—rather than sober, undramatic facts like these, stuck in the minds of most Americans.

The phrase "merchants of death" came into general use as a term of opprobrium for munitions makers. The propaganda against the du Ponts was kept up relentlessly as the pacifist campaign reached such heights that Congress was stampeded into passing three successive Neutrality Acts in as many years. Each law was passed on the assumption that wars were caused by the evil machinations of munitions makers.

This fantasy was given new life in two best-selling novels by Taylor Caldwell—*Dynasty of Death* and a sequel, *The Eagles Gather*—which pictured a family (most readers assumed that the du Ponts were the inspiration) that was forever plotting to bring about wars in order to sell more arms and ammunition and thereby fatten its profits. The novels were unbelievable in their portrayal of the wickedness of a muntions-manufacturing family, but reviewers, swept up in the mood of the time, were uncritical. "Rarely has a novel been more timely," reported the *New York Herald Tribune*. "It grips the attention in a powerful tale of the growth of a dynasty dedicated to the gods of war." Oddly, the du Ponts were upset, not by Miss Caldwell's books, but by a novel written some years later by Charles Wertenbaker. *The Barons* portrayed so clearly Alfred I. du Pont that it resembled biography more than it did fiction.

So long-lived was the "merchants of death" tag that it even popped up to cause an unpleasant incident for Irénée du Pont, Jr., after World War II. In New York to attend the theater with his wife, Irénée left her and some friends at their East Side hotel while he prepared to drive back to Wilmington during the night in his Volkswagen in order to report for work on time in the morning. Rain was falling, so Irénée offered a sailor and his girl a ride across

Manhattan. As the car pulled up at Pennsylvania Station, the sailor said, "I didn't catch your name."

"Du Pont," Irénée said. "Irénée du Pont, Jr."

Suddenly the sailor scowled. "One of those du Ponts from Delaware?" he demanded.

Irénée nodded.

The sailor was furious. "If I'd known that," he spat, "I'd never have accepted the ride." And with that he and his girl friend leaped out of the car and vanished into the railroad station.

Unfortunately, it was just after the Nye hearings that widespread publicity about the du Ponts and the American Liberty League appeared to lend substance to the wild charges against them. The public image of the family had never been at a lower point.

And then, early in January, 1936, the tax case against Pierre and Raskob came to a head—and a headline.

The transaction had taken place after the catastrophic market crash of 1929. Pierre and Raskob had sold each other large blocks of stock—Baltimore and Ohio Railroad, Warner Brothers, General Motors, Kennecott Copper, Anaconda Copper, and National Cash Register—well below the original price paid by each man. After the first of the year, each sold back to the other the stocks he had purchased from him a short time before. The brief exchange of securities, involving cross sales totaling nearly $30,000,000, left the two men only $46.86 apart. But the sales involved deductible losses under the income tax laws—or so the two men argued.

On January 10, 1936, the Commissioner of Internal Revenue issued his decision, disallowing the tax saving—which amounted to some $2,000,000. The timing of the decision, just two weeks before Al Smith's big speech to the Liberty League at the Mayflower, was more than coincidental. Although the decision was undoubtedly just, the timing was dirty politics. Headlines across the country labeled Pierre a "tax dodger."

That July, on the twenty-second anniversary of the beginning of World War I, George Bernard Shaw, celebrating his eightieth birthday, told reporters that there was no possibility of war in the foreseeable future because none of the powerful countries could afford it.

The *New York Daily Mirror* contacted Irénée du Pont and asked him if he agreed. He didn't.

"I have never seen a situation where there were a lot of dictators and nobody got hurt," Irénée said, adding with a touch of malice, "and Mr. Roosevelt is not excepted." Irénée continued, "Those boys [the dictators] will have somebody step on their faces, and to save themselves, they will have to do something. Hell will be the result."

To most readers, this sounded like war-mongering by one of those nasty munitions makers.

Throughout that election year, while President Roosevelt and the Liberty League were going after each other hammer and tongs, one of FDR's sons, Franklin D. Roosevelt, Jr., was paying an unusual number of visits to the homes of two of his schoolmates—H. Vaughan Morgan, Jr., and Drexel Paul, Jr.—who lived in the suburbs of Philadelphia. Soon the rumors began circulating that young Frank was coming down from Harvard primarily to slip over the state line into Delaware. He was spending most of his time at Owl's Nest, visiting a striking blue-eyed girl with golden brown hair. She was Ethel du Pont, daughter of Eugene, Jr., and granddaughter of the Eugene who had once headed the company.

Actually, young Roosevelt had been seen with Ethel du Pont from time to time over a couple of years. In April, 1934, he had smashed the camera of a newspaper photographer at a Philadelphia wrestling match, and it was later discovered that he was trying—successfully, as it turned out—to prevent the photographer from taking a picture of Ethel. In June of that year he was among the thousand young people at her Wilmington debut; in December she had been a holiday house guest at the White House; and the following May, Ethel had joined the Presidential party at Annapolis, Maryland, to watch yacht club races in which young Frank took part. When Ethel returned by ship from a European trip in September, FDR, Jr., chartered a plane to fly out and meet her liner. This had all the signs of a serious courtship despite the denials.

On November 14, 1936, with the election safely out of the way—and "That Man" in the White House again for four more years—their engagement was announced. During the next five months, each of them had to undergo emergency surgery: she, for appendicitis, he, for a sinus infection. But finally the big day—June 30, 1937—approached.

There were all sorts of problems in planning the wedding. It was to take place in Christ Church Christiana Hundred which only held three hundred persons, and there were probably twice that many du Ponts alone. Irénée and Lammot were coming; only Pierre, who was in Europe, would be missing. In the end, a few of the du Ponts who simply couldn't be left out were seated with Roosevelts on the groom's side of the aisle.

Thirteen hundred people had been invited to the reception and not even the two dozen big du Pont mansions could accommodate them all. A bevy of young things had to be put up at the Vicmead Hunt Club—*Vic* for Mrs. Victor du Pont, *mead* for Mrs. Hollyday S. Meeds, Jr., who had been Ellen C. du Pont. A buffet supper dance was held at the club one night in honor of the wedding party. Each of the bridesmaids wore star sapphire clips given by the bride. And Harvard's Fly Club, to which the President and all his sons belonged, held the traditional stag party for the groom.

The wedding gifts filled two large rooms and an upstairs hall at Owl's Nest. One room was devoted to silver and glassware, a second to the gifts in color: china, linen, pictures, spreads, pottery. Old prints and miscellaneous items like mahogany antiques and wrought-iron articles were in the corridor.

The press facilities resembled those for a mine disaster or a political convention. A press field tent was set up, with fifty telegraph operators to speed the correspondents' copy to the news services and newspapers all over the world. No reporters from newspapers were admitted to either the wedding or the reception and just one reporter from each of the then news services—Associated Press, United Press, and International News Service. Nevertheless, every tiny detail about the wedding was flashed to a world eagerly awaiting full reports.

The bride and her attendants presented a picture of misty, floating white except for touches of pale blue and orchid in their bouquets. The bridal gown was of shimmering white tulle. A tight bodice was shirred into a V neck caught with orange blossoms, and there were minute orange blossoms circling her slim waist. The tiny sleeves were puffed and very full. For five inches below a normal waistline, the skirt was shirred and then it flared into white billows to the floor. Set far back on the bride's simply waved hair was a little Juliet cap of miniature orange blossoms. The veil was also white tulle in three layers, floating twelve feet from her shoulders.

The time for the wedding was five o'clock, and only two minutes after the hour the strains of the traditional "Lohengrin" processional sounded through the small gray-stone church where so many generations of du Ponts had been married. As the bridal procession approached, the groom, attended by his younger brother, John, stepped from the vestry room into the chancel. The rector, the Reverend Frederick T. Ashton, and the Reverend Endicott Peabody, the venerable headmaster of Groton School who had married the groom's parents, were both waiting at the railing. Mr. Ashton opened the service and conducted it to the point where he asked, "Who giveth this woman to be married to this man?"

The bride's father stepped briefly from his pew as Dr. Peabody launched into the concluding part of the service. The word "obey" was omitted and so was the statement that the groom endowed the bride with all his worldly goods.

When the wedding party left the flower-filled church, with newsreel cameras grinding away, they found the roads to Owl's Nest on the Kennett Pike lined with the automobiles of the curious. Many were hoping for a glimpse of the President, of course. He had arrived by train from Washington that morning; his private railroad car was waiting at a siding at Montchanin station to take him to Hyde Park that night. State troopers, an army detachment from Fort du Pont, and Secret Service men cleared a way for the wedding party.

Forty persons sat down to the wedding dinner in the dining room. The rest ate a buffet under a broad, gaily striped tent on the grounds outside where an orchestra provided music for dancing. The new Mrs. Roosevelt threw her bouquet from the carved oak gallery in the two-story main hall.

But those who were superstitious had shaken their heads dolefully when a severe thunderstorm, with torrential rain and high wind, broke just as the wedding party left the church. It had been a beautiful, sunny day until only an hour or two before.

As a portent, the thunderstorm proved true. In 1949, after bearing FDR, Jr. two children, Ethel divorced him. A year and a half later she married Benjamin S. Warren, an attorney of Grosse Point, Michigan.

Young Roosevelt, who had been elected a congressman from Manhattan not long before the divorce, married Suzanne Perrin. He kept getting re-elected until 1954, when he chose instead to run for Attorney General of New York state. The only Democrat on the ticket to lose, he was defeated by a whopping 174,000 votes. Later he marred his political image further by representing, in this country, Rafael Trujillo, the Dominican Republic dictator who was later assassinated, and by serving as John F. Kennedy's hatchet man in the West Virginia primary in 1960. There young Roosevelt accused Kennedy's opponent, Senator Hubert Humphrey, of being a draft dodger in World War II, an accusation that FDR, Jr., retracted—after the election. Three years later, Kennedy, as President, repaid the political favor by appointing Roosevelt Under Secretary of Commerce.

Little more than three months after the wedding of FDR's son to the daughter of America's greatest munitions-making family, the international situation had deteriorated so far that President Roosevelt felt impelled to deliver his famous "Quarantine the Aggressors" speech, in which he said—in part:

> Without a declaration of war and without warning or justification of any kind, civilians, including vast numbers of women and children, are being ruthlessly murdered with bombs from the air. In times of so-called peace, ships are being attacked and sunk by submarines without cause or notice. Nations are fomenting and taking sides in civil warfare in nations that have never done them any harm. Nations claiming freedom for themselves deny it to others.
>
> If these things come to pass in other parts of the world, let no one imagine that America will escape, that America may expect mercy, that this Western Hemisphere will not be attacked and that it will continue tranquilly and peacefully to carry on the ethics and the arts of civilization. . . .

Irénée du Pont's prediction was coming true with frightening speed. Most Americans realized that the day was fast approaching when the country again would have to ask the du Ponts to roll up their sleeves and provide the nation with the materiels of war. The family, accustomed by now to being heroes in wartime and villains between wars, was about to become popular again. It was enough to make a powderman cynical.

CHAPTER XLIII

EYEWITNESS TO A NEW AGE

IN THE SPRING OF 1942, with World War II raging over a large part of the world, two major events happened—one public, the other secret. Senators, including Harry S. Truman, denounced many big American companies for "treason" because of their pre-war cartel agreements with the Germans and the Japanese. At almost the same time, the United States government asked E. I. du Pont de Nemours and Company, Incorporated, to take over the work of developing the atomic bomb.

That nasty word, "treason," was never applied specifically to du Pont, although it was one of the companies taking part in the cartels, and its role was widely publicized in Senate investigations. Inevitably, the epithets applied to other companies stuck to du Pont, too, regardless of the facts. So far as American industry generally was concerned, the charge was clear. In the words of Thurman W. Arnold, then Assistant Attorney General: "To our own cartels we owe the failure to expand American industry prior to Pearl Harbor. To the interests of these cartels in stabilizing prices and restricting production we owe our present scarcity in all basic materials."

A good deal of this accusation was unwarranted, of course. Not cartels but the worst depression in our history prevented the expansion of American industry before World War II. With few customers for its products, how could industry expand? And the wartime scarcity in strategic materials—although indeed partly caused by cartel policies—was to a considerable extent the result of a blind isolationism and pacifism on the part of all Americans who had refused to face up to the growing menace from abroad. During the 1930's, the government should have been stockpiling war materiel, but the country was so unprepared that it did not even have enough rifles to equip each soldier when the draft began before Pearl Harbor. American industry as a whole was blind to the economic aggression of the Nazis and the Japanese, but the vision of most other Americans was scarcely twenty-twenty.

Since the Jamesburg Agreement of 1897, the du Ponts had been engaged in cartels, principally with the I. G. Farben chemical trust of Germany, the Imperial Chemical Industries (Britain's famous ICI), and Japan's chemical combine, Mitsui. These cartels carved up the world into spheres of influence, fixed prices, and regulated production. Sir Alfred Mond, the head of ICI, summed up the philosophy behind cartels when he said, "The old ideas of the heads of great business meeting each other with scowls and shaking each other's fists in each other's faces and . . . trying to destroy each other's business may be very good on film, but it does not accord with any given facts."

However, in dealing with the representatives of German industry in the 1930's, the American businessmen did not realize that they were confronted with a new breed. The Germans hoped to obtain American trade secrets useful to the Nazi war machine, while restricting American production and withholding from its United States cartel associates patent information on new processes involving strategic war materials. In this aim the Germans were successful in dealing with most American companies, but not with du Pont.

"Du Pont," said economists Stocking and Watkins in a Twentieth Century Fund study, "had shown a singularly independent attitude in negotiations with I.G. . . . [This attitude] had stood in the way, as indeed it continued to stand in the way throughout the Thirties, of any comprehensive formal agreement, or entente cordiale, between these German and American chemical leaders."

And Joseph Borkin and Charles A. Welsh, in their book exposing cartels, *Germany's Master Plan*, published in 1943, conceded, "It must be stated, in fairness to du Pont, that in so far as its negotiations and transactions with I.G. are concerned, du Pont exhibited far greater respect for the national interests of the United States than many of its monopolistic brethren in other industries. To the extent that they were aware of I.G.'s desire to obtain veto powers over various branches of American industry, du Pont reacted in what could be called a patriotic manner."

Nevertheless, most liberals and many other Americans continued to confuse du Pont with other companies condemned for cartel policies hindering American preparedness. Probably the old Liberty League image of the du Ponts was responsible for this faulty identification.

In 1940, with Europe already engulfed in war and the United States threatened, Pierre, then seventy years old, retired as chairman and Irénée at sixty-four stepped down as vice-chairman. Lammot, almost sixty, moved from president to chairman of the board, his former post being taken by Walter S. Carpenter, Jr., fifty-two, a brother of R. R. M. Carpenter. The new leadership was confronted with the challenge of the atomic bomb.

Du Pont's first contact with the "Manhattan Engineer District"— the cover name for the atomic bomb project—was made in August, 1942, when Arthur T. Compton, Nobel Prize winner in physics and one of the leaders of the project, borrowed Charles M. Cooper, a chemical engineer, from du Pont. Compton sought advice from Cooper on construction and operation of a plutonium separation plant. Plutonium had been discovered only the preceding year. The scientists at the University of Chicago, the center of all A-bomb work at the time, were impressed with Cooper. They began to talk about drawing the du Pont company into the work.

A month later, General Leslie R. Groves was appointed head of the Manhattan District. Before he had been on the job two weeks, he approached du Pont to take over the design and development of the separations pilot plant to be constructed at Clinton, Tennessee. Groves naturally thought of du Pont, for he had worked with the company in the construction of military explosives plants. Not only was du Pont experienced and competent, but its own engineering department could build the plants the company would operate. Thus du Pont was an integrated organization, ideally suited to the needs of the atomic bomb work. On October 3, a letter of intent covering the design and procurement of equipment for the separation plant was signed. Du Pont got down to work immediately.

Within a week, Groves was meeting again with E. G. Ackart, du Pont's chief engineer, asking the company to take over design and procurement of equipment for the nuclear pile. Ackart told him that this sort of thing wasn't in du Pont's line; doing so would involve physics, and the du Ponts had always been chemists. Ackart suggested several other companies.

By now the scientists, as well as Groves, had come to realize the vast scope of the work lying ahead of them, the years of work that had to be done in little more than twenty-four months. Of all the organizations they could think of, public or private, only du Pont had the size, the breadth, the knowledge, the manpower, the experience, and the resources to carry through this project.

James B. Conant, president of Harvard University and one of the scientists directing the nuclear research, had been a consultant to du Pont and he was also a friend of Charles Stine, du Pont's research chief and member of the company's executive committee. So it was arranged for Stine and Willis F. Harrington, a du Pont vice-president, to go to Washington and discuss with Groves a matter vital to the war effort. However, because of the tight security curtain around the Manhattan District, they were not told the nature of the weapon under development—just that it was of the utmost importance and beyond the capacity of any other company.

Inevitably, some time later, a few top du Pont officials were informed of the true character of the work. Very reluctantly and at the government's insistence, the corporation agreed to take over the entire project which soon included the plutonium production plant at Hanford, Washington. A cost-plus-fixed-fee contract, a type frequently used by the government during the war, was drawn up.

"There were, however, extraordinary considerations which caused du Pont to introduce special provisions" in the contract, according to the official history of the Atomic Energy Commission. "The tremendous military potential of the atomic weapon posed a possible threat to the company's future public relations. The du Pont leadership had not forgotten the 'merchants of death' label slapped on the company during the Nye Committee investigations in the 1930's. Certainly it was clear that the company had not sought the [atomic] assignment; but to keep the record straight, du Pont refused to accept any profit. The fixed fee was limited to one dollar. Any profits accruing from allowances for administrative overhead would be returned to the government. Walter S. Carpenter, Jr., the du Pont president, disavowed not only profits but also any intention of staying in the atomic bomb business after the war. In his opinion, the production of such weapons should be controlled exclusively by the government. The contract provided that any patent rights arising from the project would lie solely with the United States."

Crawford H. Greenewalt of the du Pont Development (new products) Department went to Chicago to meet with the scientists at work there. Greenewalt, married to Irénée's daughter Margaretta, was a talented research man just elevated to the board of directors. On the morning of December 2, 1942, Greenewalt and Compton stood on the balcony of the racquets court under the Stagg Field stadium at the University of Chicago. They watched Nobel Prize Physicist Enrico Fermi and his assistants remove the cadmium control rods from the pile. At three-twenty in the afternoon, a sustained chain reaction began. In a few minutes, the rise in radioactivity in the room forced Fermi to shut down the pile. It had been done. Man had mastered the atom! For Greenewalt, this eyewitness role at the very dawn of a new age was probably the most exciting moment of his life.

Through the months that followed, du Pont not only built the works, but also put up housing and other facilities for a population that reached sixty thousand at Hanford. At the same time, the company's other plants were turning out an endless variety of war goods: nylon for parachutes, synthetic rubber, strontium nitrate for signal flares, methacrylate polymer for incendiary bombs, cellophane to protect rations, gas-proofing impregnants for fabrics, dyes to color water and attract attention to downed fliers, chlorinated hydrocarbons for smoke screens, Lucite for gun turrets on bombers and a thousand and one other things. As many as eighty-six chemical products from one du Pont plant alone went into the building of a bomber plane.

In contrast with World War I, when eighty-five percent of the company's war effort consisted of explosives, gunpowder accounted

established a full-scale International Department, and now it employs nearly sixteen thousand people in thirty-five foreign plants representing an investment of $320,000,000 in thirteen countries. Over fifteen percent of the company's current business comes from abroad.

Despite the foreign operations and eighty other plants scattered across the United States, the heart of the du Pont empire remains close to the Brandywine in the twin du Pont and Nemours Buildings in the heart of Wilmington, the home offices of the company. There are about twenty-five or thirty du Ponts on the payroll, not counting in-laws and other distant relatives. "I wish we had more," says Emile F. du Pont, a member of the board of directors and, until his recent retirement, the head of employee relations.

Usually a concentration of one family in a business means nepotism with all of its attendant evils, but this is not true in the du Pont company. Part of the reason is that so many members of the clan, in and out of management, own a substantial share of the business. Naturally they want their investment protected by the best executives obtainable. But the biggest bar against nepotism lies in an unpublicized practice in handling family members who are employees: if the du Pont in question isn't contributing to the company, he is encouraged to leave the corporation. Directors of the company vehemently deny that this is a policy, but several persons— not of the family—who have intimate knowledge of the internal organization insist that it is. When a du Pont has to be eased out of the company, the other members of the family try to set him up in a small business of his own.

This does not mean, of course, that du Ponts who work in other business organizations—or members of the family who prefer to live off the income from their capital—have failed to make the grade in the du Pont company. "Most of the men in the family don't want to work for the company," a du Pont executive says. "Some have the mistaken notion that they'll get lost in a huge company. Besides, they know that everyone is sure to assume that a du Pont is going to be pushed ahead, so they feel they must measure up more than most employees. The pressures can be severe."

Not long ago a du Pont recalled ruefully, "I saw Bus [Irénée] at a family cocktail party years ago and said to him, 'Honestly, Bus, what do you think my prospects are with the company?' He put his hand on my shoulder and he said to me, 'Why don't you take up boating?'"

On the other hand, Irénée du Pont, Jr., who joined the company as a plant engineer at Arlington, New Jersey, in 1946, has been rising steadily through the ranks. Now a member of the board of directors, he usually commutes to the office by bus, and his office is so plain and unadorned that it would be scorned by any self-respecting copywriter on Madison Avenue. A thoughtful, pleasant-faced man, he scoffs at those who say that the disadvantages of being a du Pont more or less balance the advantages. "I've risen much higher in the company than I would have if I hadn't been a du Pont," Irénée insists disarmingly. His self-appraisal is not shared by men outside the company who have dealt with him. They regard Irénée as an able, imaginative executive.

There are, however, some distinct problems in being a du Pont employed by the family company, in Irénée's opinion. "If you're a du Pont," he says, "you have to bend over backward to avoid throwing your weight around, because everyone is going to attach extra significance to anything you say. Have a minor, friendly disagreement over some decision with another man on the same level of authority, and the other guy is liable to be upset for days just because you're a du Pont.

"Personal relationships call for more formality, too," he goes on. "Where another man, say, might casually throw his arm around a stenographer and ask her how her family is, a du Pont can't because it might lead to all sorts of gossip. We've got to be somewhat reserved. Even at lunch, with other men in the company, it's best for a du Pont to stay out of some discussions—anything involving money, for example. Sometimes, when the other fellows are talking about the cost of sending their kids through school, we're tempted to join in, but we've found that it's better to keep a discreet silence. Nevertheless, a du Pont has an overwhelming advantage inevitably. The family relationship is an open sesame to a lot of things. If you're a du Pont, you can get the ear of your boss without any difficulty."

The company as such does not participate in politics, although it obviously has an official position on government policies that affect business. This attitude is of interest primarily because of the moderation it displays in contrast with du Pont pronouncements of the 1930's. A recent company statement said in part:

Political considerations aside, a number of American businessmen feel that the attitude of some government administrators is hostile to business and to the free market. This, of course, is not a one-way street: There are many in government who accuse certain businessmen of being blind "aginners" by nature, always opposed to any action the government takes in any area which might involve the expenditure of money. Undoubtedly there is truth on both sides. But where this hostility exists, it is harmful both to business and to the nation. The real difficulty, most thoughtful businessmen feel, lies not in the "hostile" attitude of government administrators. "They're *not* hostile," says one du Pont executive. "If anything, the government people I've met have been intelligent and well-intentioned." What is at fault is the jungle of law upon law and regulation upon regulation through which the businessman must pass to get approval for any action he might take. Thus, there is always the danger of attack because, as one du Pont lawyer puts it, "You never know where you're stepping next or what you've overlooked. . . ."

Businessmen are not opposed to government per se. They are not anarchists. They recognize a legitimate role for government in many fields—national defense, education, regulation of commerce, etc. They even accept a reasonable amount of government activity in the welfare field.

What they don't accept is the widely held belief that the government should play an active part in the production and distribution of goods, i.e., in the market place. They don't accept, nor do they feel it is proper, for government to act as a partner in their operations, or as a competitor.

The political impact of the company upon Delaware is difficult to assess. *The Government and Administration of Delaware* by political scientist Paul Dolan pointed out that "any material change in the employment policy" of the company would affect a great many people in the state, and Delawareans know it. "Employees are inclined to look at the company as the directing force of their lives rather than to the local communities and the social organizations such as the church, the club, or fraternal organization," a state of affairs furthered by the personnel practices of the company which even maintains a country club for its workers. This sort of thing also helps to keep out the AFL-CIO, which only represents about five percent of the company's ninety-three thousand employees.

"The influence of the company upon government in Delaware is not overt nor direct," Dolan wrote. "Members of the du Pont family have engaged directly in politics and in government, but the company does not intrude upon the operations of the state government nor force it to adopt any particular pattern which the policy makers of the company have pre-ordained.

"In fact, it might be truly said that du Pont is too big to bother with Delaware government."

CHAPTER XLV

THE FAMILY TODAY

Hexton stands on a promontory above the Sassafras River, an estuary of Chesapeake Bay, about thirty-five miles southwest of Wilmington on the Delmarva Peninsula. It is not a great house, not a Longwood or a Wintherthur or a Nemours or a Granogue. It is not even like the *fin de siècle* mansions that line the Kennett Pike and Rising Sun Lane and the other roads of the du Pont country. A comfortable house, this Hexton, a house that has dignity without formality, spaciousness without ostentation, ease without opulence.

This is a du Pont home today. It is not cast in a mold with all other du Pont homes, of course, but it is representative of the way that du Ponts now think. For they are not immune to the world about them; as society has become less formal, most of the younger du Ponts have become more casual in their way of life.

A mile or two of private road lies between the house on the promontory and the public highway outside. Driving along the lane, a visitor is likely to see a deer by the side of the road. The animal lifts its finely sculptured head on a graceful neck, gazes with frank curiosity at the stranger, and then moves with deliberation down the hillside into a wooded glade. There are forty deer in the wild herd that roams Hexton. They were captured and brought to Hexton from an army reservation where the herd was being killed off by concussion from shells on a firing range. Here they are safe and they know it; very little frightens them.

For humans, too, Hexton can be a kind of sanctuary, an asylum of tranquillity in a frenzied world. There is a timelessness to Hexton, a lack of urgency, an absence of stress.

This is the home of Samuel Francis du Pont. It was his father's country house, but times have changed and Sam regards Hexton as his real home. A handsome, powerfully built man in his middle thirties, Sam lives there with his wife, Joanne—"Jan"—and their children, Diane and Richard. Jan, an energetic, attractive woman, operated a well-known kennel of show poodles before their marriage and she breeds dogs at Hexton; another branch of the family, the S. Hallock du Ponts, maintains one of the leading dog breeding establishments in the country—the Squirrel Run Kennels, named for one of the now vanished villages of the Brandywine powdermen.

Sam himself has long admired the Quarter Horse, and a stable of that breed is being built up at Hexton. There are animals everywhere at Hexton, not only in the kennels and the stables, but also three house dogs and perhaps a dozen cats, all descended from one outstandingly virile tom, who appropriate the most comfortable chairs in the house and curl up companionably with guests in bed at night.

Animals are a feature of any du Pont home and landscape. Richard C.—"Kip"—du Pont, Jr., and his wife, Caroline, even tried keeping a black Angus calf as a house pet until it demonstrated effectively its determination not to be house-broken. The calf was moved outside, but it remains the baby of the family and wears a gold chain about its velvety, sable neck.

Kip's mother, Helena Allaire du Pont, a widow since the death of her husband, Richard Chichester du Pont, in World War II, shares the du Pont love for animals. Her Bohemia Stables on the Delmarva Peninsula not far from Hexton is most famous, of course, for the great Thoroughbred, Kelso, the first animal to be "Horse of the Year" three times in a row. Kelso likes people, enjoys wandering about sociably at picnics, and harbors a passion for chocolate sundaes. "If he were small enough, we'd keep him in the house," says Mrs. du Pont.

Sam is one of the sons of Ernest du Pont, who was usually called the handsomest of the du Pont men. Sam himself has the prominent nose and cleft chin—some du Ponts insist on calling it a "dimpled" chin—that have been family trademarks for seven generations. Ernest was a son of Francis Gurney du Pont, one of the company's most talented chemists. And Francis G. was a son of Alexis I. who was killed in an explosion. The father of Alexis was Eleuthère Irénée du Pont, the founder of the company, son of Pierre Samuel du Pont de Nemours.

An ardent yachtsman, Ernest passed on his interest in boats to his sons. For several years Sam raced boats, finally giving his fastest hydroplane, the *Nitrogen*, to the town of Madison, Indiana, where he has since been regarded as an honorary citizen. Madison maintains the boat as a civic project and races it against the best in the country at meets far from Indiana. At Hexton, Sam has a fifty-five-foot yacht, the *Gemini*, two runabouts, and a Star sailboat. The dock at Hexton is down a winding, ivy-covered lane from the house.

Across the creek is a landing strip. Most du Pont estates can be identified by their landing strips and wind-socks, for this is one of the most air-minded of all American families. Sam holds licenses to fly both single- and multi-engined craft; he's even piloted an airliner.

A large part of Sam's life still centers in Wilmington, although he doesn't live or work there. His father has been dead for twenty years, but his mother, now ailing, still lives in the big old mansion of Victorian Gothic at Montchanin Road and the Kennett Pike. In the 1920's, the newspapers made quite a fuss when it was learned that Ernest du Pont was engaged to marry Anne Thompson, a nurse at Johns Hopkins Hospital in Baltimore who had cared for him while he was recuperating there from a broken leg. But the family welcomed the Asheville, North Carolina, girl, and she soon became one of the adornments of the du Pont clan.

In-laws have a way of being swallowed up in the tribe, much as Kublai Khan's Mongols lost their identity among the thirteenth century Chinese. A leading du Pont explains it like this: "If the in-law works for the company, the fact that it's the *du Pont* company tends to make him an integral part of the family. As for the in-laws who are not associated with the company—well, usually they don't have much money before their marriage to a du Pont, and their new wealth has a way of removing them from many of their previous relationships, drawing them instead into the circle of du Pont family life."

During the schism in the family and the business a half century ago, Ernest was one of the du Ponts in the camp of Alfred I. With his brothers, Paul and Archibald, he organized the Ball Grain Explosives Company and later was president of the United States Flashless Powder Company. He was a member of the board of directors of the Atlas Powder Company and the Delaware Trust Company at the time of his death. It is indicative of the complete healing of the breach in the family that Sam's brother, Ernest, Jr., is an executive of the du Pont company and that Sam turns for advice on any major problem to Emile F. du Pont, who was regarded by Alfred as the most brilliant of the younger du Ponts thirty years ago. Emile has long been a member of the board of directors and of its finance committee.

Every part of the family now feels pride in the fact that the du Ponts have converted most of the palaces built in an earlier, baroque age into useful public institutions.

For example, Longwood Gardens is now the largest and most spectacular horticultural exhibit in America. Maintained on the income from a $33,000,000 endowment established by Pierre S. du Pont, its rare and beautiful trees, flowers, shrubs, conservatories, parks, lakes, waterfalls, chimes, and theaters cover a thousand acres near Kennett Square, Pennsylvania, about a mile from the junction of U.S. 1 and State Highway 52. More than six million visitors have wandered through the endless vistas of floral wonderland since Pierre first opened the gardens to the public in 1921; now five hundred thousand sightseers make their way to Longwood each year throughout the four seasons, for every month is the peak season of some kind of exquisite growth. Even in the depth of winter there are new blooms in the greenhouses—the largest in the world—which provide nearly three and a half acres of indoor gardens. The services of more than one hundred and twenty men are required to keep Longwood forever in blossom.

Winterthur's gardens, although natural and not formal like Longwood's, also attract professional and amateur horticulturists from far away, but the most famous feature of the Winterthur

Museum is its outstanding collection of Americana, including a hundred period rooms covering the domestic scene from 1640 to 1840. Unlike most museums, Winterthur permits visitors to go into the rooms and study the arrangements, furnishings, and decorations up close instead of roping them off. Even fireplaces and stairs have been brought to Winterthur from other places: a particularly graceful spiral staircase, for example, is from Montmorenci, a plantation house built in 1822 near Warrenton, North Carolina, by General William Williams. Winterthur's oldest section was built in 1839 by Jacques Antoine Bidermann, the first Irénée's son-in-law, born at Winterthur in Switzerland. Over the years the great house has been added to frequently, until it now boasts over one hundred rooms. The mansion itself is set in the midst of about a thousand acres of rolling land; the entire estate is believed to be worth more than $10,000,000. It was the home of Henry F. du Pont until 1951, when he and his wife, the former Ruth Wales of Hyde Park, New York, moved into a new house next door. Six miles northwest of Wilmington on the Kennett Pike (State Highway 52), Winterthur throws open its gardens from April 1 to June 30 and twenty-six of its rooms can be seen by the public without reservations for five weeks in April and May each year. At other times and to see the rest of the rooms, it is necessary to make arrangements in advance with museum officials.

In accordance with Alfred I. du Pont's will, his palatial estate Nemours has been turned into a center for the care of crippled but curable children. His second wife, Alicia, is buried there, and under the impressive bell tower lie the body of Alfred himself and, beside him, the remains of his beloved mongrel Yip, who followed him in death by a few days.

Even the original du Pont residence, Eleutherian Mills, the home of Eleuthère Irénée, is being opened to the public now as part of a one-hundred-and-sixty-eight-acre tract along the Brandywine which covers most of the old Hagley Yard. Just outside Wilmington, off Barley Mill Road, now State Highway 141, a short distance east of the Montchanin Road—ENTERING BRANDYWINE VALLEY, A CONSERVATION AREA, reads a state sign—a blacktop byway leads down into the gorge to the Hagley Museum which used to be the Henry Clay Factory. Exhibits there depict the industrial development of the area, and a jitney leaving the museum takes visitors on a leisurely ride through what is now a serene park, passing the ruins of powder mills, their roofs and doors long gone, that stare out on the rocky stream like empty skulls of the dead past. Near the upper end of the jitney route is a building in which the steps in the manufacture of black powder are shown. Halfway up the long slope is a gray stone building of contemporary design that nevertheless fits in with the architecture of the old du Pont structures. The family calls this the Hagley Library, although its official name is the Eleutherian Mills-Hagley Foundation. Endowed by the du Pont company in 1952 for $8,000,000 to collect and preserve historical records of the family, the company, and the area, it is used extensively by historians and economists.

The transformation of the du Pont palaces into public institutions reflects three things: the distaste of most du Ponts for the ostentation of the past; the difficulty of keeping servants and maintaining vast estates under modern tax laws; and, most of all, an acceptance by the family of the social responsibilities of the rich. For the sweeping gestures of generosity that characterized their predecessors—Pierre's gift of schools to the state, Coleman's construction of U.S. 13, Alfred's personal pension system for the aged—the du Ponts in the past two or three decades have substituted planned, long-range philanthropy which makes up in wisdom what it loses in spontaneity. The du Pont advisor on philanthropy is Dr. C. Lalor Burdick.

The major du Pont foundations are the Carpenter, Copeland d'Andelot, Crestlea, Chichester du Pont, Irénée du Pont, Jr., Eleutherian Mills-Hagley, Good Samaritan, Lalor, Longwood, Rencourt, Sharp, Theano, Unidel, Welfare, Winterthur, and Alfred I. du Pont Institute of Nemours. In addition, many of the du Ponts maintain smaller, personal foundations for charitable giving.

Grants of one or two million dollars are not unusual from the du Ponts. Although hospitals are a favorite beneficiary of many members of the family, education has been the principal recipient—a fact that would please Pierre Samuel du Pont de Nemours. The schools most closely linked with the family are the Massachusetts Institute of Technology, the University of Pennsylvania, the University of Virginia, and the University of Delaware. To these the bulk of the du Pont contributions have gone. Other institutions also have benefited, however. For example, Lincoln University in Pennsylvania, a Negro institution, has recently received large gifts from the clan. Even prep schools attended by du Ponts expect—and receive—financial support from them. In 1961, for example, Reynolds du Pont gave $360,000 to the Lawrenceville School. Two Wilmington private schools, Tower Hill and St. Andrew's, were founded by du Ponts.

To engage in philanthropy on such a scale obviously requires huge reserves of capital. Probably no one in or out of the family knows precisely how much money it possesses and controls. Estimates range from two to five billion dollars; three billion appears to be closest to the mark.

It is axiomatic that wealth makes a man conservative. But not all the du Ponts are rich, and not all favor the right in politics.

The range of political opinion still extends from conservative Republican to liberal Democratic, from Irénée du Pont, Jr., and Pierre—"Pete"—S. du Pont III on the right to Ethel B. du Pont on the left. But in between, almost every political shading can be found. Most of the du Ponts in the leadership of the company are conservative, as one might expect. "But not on the issue of race relations," Irénée, Jr., hastens to add. "I am in favor of doing away with segregation and discrimination; I'm very opposed to racial prejudice."

The minority leader of the Delaware Senate is Reynolds du Pont, a Republican. The state's G.O.P. national committeewoman and secretary of the Republican National Committee is Polly Buck, generally conceded to be one of the prettiest of the du Pont women; her husband, C. Douglass Buck, Jr., is a son of the former governor who was himself Coleman du Pont's son-in-law. Coleman's son, Francis V. du Pont, carried on his father's interest in good roads: after heading Delaware's Highway Department, he served as commissioner of the Federal Bureau of Public Roads during the Eisenhower Administration. There has always been a sprinkling of du Ponts in the state's Republican hierarchy.

On the Democratic side, the national committeeman from Delaware, William S. Potter, is a du Pont in-law; his wife, who was Alice Hounsfield Harvey, is a niece of Coleman du Pont's cousin-wife. A former lieutenant governor, Alexis I. du Pont Bayard, is a grandson of Elizabeth Bradford du Pont, one of those sued by Alfred I. du Pont during the family schism. J. H. Tyler McConnell, secretary of the Hercules Powder Company, ran for public office on the Democratic ticket a few years ago; his wife, Jean Ellen, is a daughter of William du Pont, Jr.

There are a good many other Democratic du Ponts in Delaware and elsewhere, including one of Irénée du Pont's sons-in-law, Colgate W. Darden, Jr., former president of the University of Virginia. Although Darden is a member of the board of directors of the du Pont company which manufactures pesticides, his wife, Constance, has been a Virginia leader in the fight against the indiscriminate use of those chemicals, a controversy started by Rachel Carson's book, *Silent Spring*. Mrs. Darden's participation in the conflict is accepted with resignation by her relatives in the company.

Regardless of politics, the du Ponts still cherish the traditions that bind them together. A family genealogy is kept carefully up to date. Years ago Pierre used to maintain the records of births and deaths; he carried cards in his pocket which he used to hand out to relatives, asking them to send him information to bring the records up to date. Later Miss Aileen du Pont handled the lists for him. When she became too ill to continue the task, Frank Battan of the Eleutherian Mills-Hagley Foundation took it over. He sends out requests for information periodically to all the du Ponts.

As they did in the beginning, the men of the family call on the women every New Year's Day. Du Ponts come from distant places for this annual reunion which helps to bind the clan together, because through this traditional visiting, many of the men and women of the family get to know each other. But unfortunately, since the men make the rounds in separate groups, there is no way for all of them to meet. Because of the size of the family, the women gather in a dozen different du Pont mansions and the men, assembled in small bands, must go from house to house. The arrangements are made by William Winder Laird, Jr., whose mother, Mary, was a sister of Pierre, Irénée, and Lammot.

One of the men, as a mark of special favor, likes to bestow on a few of his women relatives gift certificates for a special kind of cake baked by a Boston firm. Nobody, watching him at the January 1 visiting, has ever been able to figure out the basis on which he chooses who is to receive one of the gift certificates.

After New Year's Day, the family disperses again. Although the nucleus of the clan remains where Eleuthère Irénée and his Sophie settled over a century and a half ago, the du Ponts are now scattered throughout the world.

Just as the company now operates only one mill for manufacturing its original product, black powder, so change has swept over the family, too, and even against their own desire, the du Ponts are drifting gradually apart. Today they are held together, for the most part, only by a common financial interest, genealogical records, the New Year's Day reunions, and the common awareness of a colorful, danger-filled history.

The warning of Francis Gurney du Pont in 1899, when he was opposing incorporation of the company, has been coming true: "The business as it stands today is the one and only hope of keeping the family together on the Brandywine."

The company has changed and the family is no longer together on the Brandywine. These days, most of the du Ponts, if they return to that historic land at all, go back only to find peace in the burying ground in Sand Hole Woods.

BIBLIOGRAPHY

Amory, Cleveland. *The Last Resorts*. New York: Harper, 1952.

———. *Who Killed Society?* New York: Harper, 1960.

Anderson, Bern. *By Sea and by River: The Naval History of the Civil War*. New York: Knopf, 1962.

Betts, Raymond F. "Eleuthère Irénée du Pont and the Brandywine Sunday School." *Delaware History* (Wilmington), Vol. VIII, No. 4, September 1959, 343-353.

Bing, Arden Ellsworth. *Delaware Blue Book*. Milford, Delaware, 1958.

Borkin, Joseph, and Charles A. Welsh. *Germany's Master Plan*. New York: Duell, Sloan, and Pearce, 1943.

Bursler, Norman. "The du Pont Industrial Group." Monograph prepared for the Association of American Law Schools, 1951.

Caldwell, Taylor. *Dynasty of Death*. New York: Scribner's, 1938.

———. *The Eagles Gather*. New York: Scribner's, 1940.

Canby, Henry Seidel. *The Brandywine*. New York: Farrar and Rinehart, 1941.

Childs, F.S. *French Refugee Life in the United States, 1790-1800*. Baltimore: Johns Hopkins, 1940.

Chinard, Gilbert, editor. *Lettres de du Pont de Nemours écrites de la prison de la Force*. Paris: Librairie Historique, 1929.

———. *Thomas Jefferson: The Apostle of Americanism*. Boston: Little, Brown, 1939.

Clune, Henry W. *The Genesee*. New York: Holt, Rinehart, and Winston, 1963.

Cochran, Thomas C., and William Miller. *The Age of Enterprise*. New York: Harper, 1961.

"Coleman du Pont, 1863-1930." *Encyclopedia of American Biography*. New York: American Historical Society, 1935.

de Valinger, Leon, Jr., and Virginia E. Shaw, editors. *A Calendar of Ridgely Family Letters, 1742-1899.* Vol. III. Dover, Delaware: Public Archives Commission, 1961.

Dolan, Paul. *The Government and Administration of Delaware.* New York: Crowell, 1956.

Dorian, Max. *The du Ponts: From Gunpowder to Nylon.* Translated by Edward B. Garside. Boston: Little, Brown, 1962.

Downey, Fairfax Davis. *Sound of the Guns: The Story of American Artillery.* New York: McKay, 1956.

Drescher, Nuala McGann. "The Irish in Industrial Wilmington, 1800-1845." Unpublished master's thesis, University of Delaware, 1960.

du Pont, Bessie Gardner. *Du Pont de Nemours, 1739-1817.* 2 vols. Newark, Delaware: The Press of Kells, 1933.

———. *E.I. du Pont de Nemours and Company: A History, 1802-1902.* Boston and New York: Houghton Mifflin, 1920.

———, editor and translator. *Life of Eleuthère Irénée du Pont from Contemporary Correspondence.* 12 vols. Newark, Delaware: University of Delaware Press, 1923-1927.

———. *Lives of Victor and Josephine du Pont.* Newark, Delaware: The Press of Kells, 1930.

"Du Pont: Can It Stay on Top?" *Forbes* magazine, Vol. 90, No. 7, October 1, 1962.

The du Pont Company and Munitions. Wilmington, Delaware: E.I. du Pont de Nemours and Company, 1934.

The du Pont Company's Part in the National Security Program, 1940-1945. Wilmington, Delaware: E.I. du Pont de Nemours and Company, 1946.

du Pont, Henry A. *The Battle of Newmarket, Virginia.* Washington, D.C.: privately printed, 1923.

———. *The Campaign of 1864 in the Valley of Virginia.* New York: National Americana Society, 1925.

———. *A Genealogical-Biographical History of the du Pont Family.* New York: National Americana Society, 1923.

———. *Rear Admiral Samuel Francis du Pont, United States Navy: A Biography.* New York: National Americana Society, 1926.

du Pont, Pierre S. *Genealogy of the du Pont Family, 1739-1949.* Wilmington, Delaware: privately printed, 1949.

Dutton, William Sherman. *Du Pont: One Hundred and Forty Years.* New York: Scribner's, 1942.

Eberlein, Harold Donaldson, and Cartlandt V. D. Hubbard. *Historic*

Houses and Buildings of Delaware. Dover, Delaware: Public Archives Commission, 1963.

Errigo, Joseph A.L. *A History of St. Joseph's-on-the-Brandywine.* Wilmington, Delaware: Cann, 1941.

Folsom, Merrill. *Great American Mansions and Their Stories.* New York: Hastings House, 1963.

Foote, Shelby. *The Civil War, a Narrative: Fort Sumter to Perryville.* New York: Random House, 1958.

———. "Du Pont Storms Charleston." *American Heritage*, Vol. XIV, No. 4, June 1963.

Hancock, Harold Bell. *Delaware During the Civil War.* Wilmington, Delaware: Historical Society of Delaware, 1961.

Harriss, C. Lowell. *The American Economy.* Homewood, Illinois: Irwin, 1962.

Haynes, George H. *The Election of Senators.* New York: Henry Holt, 1906.

Henry, Allan Johnstone. *Francis Gurney du Pont: A Memoir.* 2 vols. Philadelphia: Fell, 1951.

———. *The Life of Alexis Irénée du Pont.* 2 vols. Philadelphia: Fell, 1945.

Hewlett, Richard G., and Oscar E. Anderson Jr. *The New World, 1939-1946.* University Park, Pennsylvania: Pennsylvania State University Press, 1962.

Holbrook, Stewart H. *The Age of the Moguls.* Garden City, New York: Doubleday, 1953.

James, James Alton. "French Opinion as a Factor in Preventing War Between France and the United States, 1795-1800." *American Historical Review*, Vol. 30, October 1924.

James, Marquis. *Alfred I. du Pont, the Family Rebel.* Indianapolis and New York: Bobbs-Merrill, 1941.

Jewkes, John, David Sawers, and Richard Stillerman. *The Sources of Invention.* New York: St. Martin's, 1960.

Kaplan, A.D.H., Joel B. Dirlam, and Robert F. Lanzillotti. *Pricing in Big Business.* Washington, D.C.: The Brookings Institution, 1958.

Kennan, George. "Holding Up a State." *The Outlook*, February 7, 14, and 21, 1903.

Lawton, William C. "The du Ponts: A Case Study of Kinship in the Business Organization." Unpublished doctoral dissertation, University of Chicago, 1956.

Lessing, Lawrence. "How du Pont Keeps Out in Front." *Fortune* magazine, December 1962.

Leuchtenburg, William E. *Franklin D. Roosevelt and the New Deal, 1932-1940.* New York: Harper and Row, 1963.

Lundberg, Ferdinand. *America's Sixty Families.* New York: Vanguard, 1938.

Malone, Dumas, editor. *Correspondence Between Thomas Jefferson and Pierre Samuel du Pont de Nemours, 1798-1817.* Translated by Linwood Lehman. Boston and New York: Houghton Mifflin, 1930.

———. *Jefferson and the Ordeal of Liberty.* Boston: Little, Brown, 1962.

McKie, Douglas. *Antoine Lavoisier.* New York: Collier, 1962.

Memorial of Charles Irénée du Pont. Wilmington, Delaware: privately printed, 1869.

Merrill, James M. *The Rebel Shore.* Boston: Little, Brown, 1957.

Mills, C. Wright. *The Power Elite.* New York: Oxford University Press, 1956.

Montgomery, Elizabeth. *Reminiscences of Wilmington.* Wilmington, Delaware: Johnston and Bogia, 1872.

Morison, Samuel Eliot. "Du Pont, Talleyrand, and the French Spoliations." *Proceedings,* Massachusetts Historical Society, Vol. 49, 1915.

Mueller, Willard F. "Du Pont: A Study in Firm Growth." Unpublished doctoral dissertation, Vanderbilt University, 1955.

Nettels, Curtis P. *The Emergence of a National Economy, 1775-1815.* New York: Holt, Rinehart, and Winston, 1962.

North, Douglass C. *The Economic Growth of the United States, 1790-1860.* Englewood Cliffs, New Jersey: Prentice-Hall, 1961.

Official Dispatches and Letters of Rear Admiral du Pont. Wilmington, Delaware: privately printed, 1883.

Packard, Vance. *The Pyramid Climbers.* New York: McGraw-Hill, 1962.

Proctor, Edward W. "Anti-Trust Policy and the Industrial Explosives Industry." Unpublished doctoral dissertation, Harvard University, 1951.

Pursell, Carroll W., Jr. "Peter Bauduy and His Shepherd's Dog, 1814: A Note." *Delaware History* (Wilmington), Vol. X, No. 2, October 1962, 181-184.

Quinn, T.K. *Giant Business: Threat to Democracy.* New York: Exposition Press, 1953.

———. *Giant Corporations: Challenge to Freedom.* New York: Exposition Press, 1956.

Saricks, Ambrose. "Pierre Samuel du Pont de Nemours and the French Revolution." Unpublished doctoral dissertation, University of Wisconsin, 1950.

Silliman, Charles A. *The Story of Christ Church Christiana Hundred and Its People.* Wilmington, Delaware: privately printed, 1960.

Smith, James Morton. *Freedom's Fetters.* Ithaca, New York: Cornell University Press, 1956.

Smith, Ophia D. "Daniel Lammot and His Role in the New Church in Delaware." *Delaware History* (Wilmington), Vol. VIII, No. 4, September 1959, 312-342.

Stelzer, Irwin M. *Selected Anti-Trust Cases.* Homewood, Illinois: Irwin, 1961.

Stevens, William H.S. "The Powder Trust, 1872-1912." *Quarterly Journal of Economics,* 1912.

Stocking, George W. *Workable Competition and Anti-Trust Policy.* Nashville, Tennessee: Vanderbilt University Press, 1961.

—— and Myron W. Watkins. *Cartels in Action.* New York: The Twentieth Century Fund, 1946.

—— and Myron W. Watkins. *Cartels or Competition?* New York: The Twentieth Century Fund, 1948.

Tebbel, John. *The Inheritors.* New York: Putnam, 1962.

Vaughan, Floyd L. *The United States Patent System.* Norman, Oklahoma: University of Oklahoma Press, 1956.

Wecter, Dixon. *The Saga of American Society.* New York: Scribner's, 1937.

Welsh, Peter C. "The Brandywine Mills: A Chronicle of an Industry, 1762-1816." *Delaware History* (Wilmington), Vol. VII, No. 1, March 1956, 17-36.

Wertenbaker, Charles. *The Barons.* New York: Random House, 1950.

——. "Du Pont." *Fortune* magazine, November and December, 1934, and January 1935.

Whitney, Simon N. *Anti-Trust Policies.* 2 vols. New York: The Twentieth Century Fund, 1958.

Wilkinson, Norman B. "The Brandywine Home Front During the Civil War; Part I: 1861." *Delaware History* (Wilmington), Vol. IX, No. 3, April 1961, 265-281.

——. "The Brandywine Home Front During the Civil War; Part II: 1862." *Delaware History* (Wilmington), Vol. X, No. 3, April 1963, 197-234.

Winkler, John K. *The du Pont Dynasty.* New York: Reynal and Hitchcock, 1935.

Wolfskill, George. *The Revolt of the Conservatives: A History of the American Liberty League, 1934-1940.* Boston: Houghton Mifflin, 1962.

INDEX

Ackart, E. G., 333
Ackerson, A. S., 200, 201
Adams, John, 41, 43, 45
Adams, Samuel, 136
Addicks, John Edward O'Sullivan, 231-239, 278
Aetna Powder Company, 208
A. F. and Company, 87
AFL-CIO, 342
Alcohol, industrial, 300, 304
Alexandria, Virginia, 43, 49, 77, 217
Alien and Sedition Laws, 44, 45
Allee, J. Frank, 237, 238, 243, 278, 279
Allen, Judge Florence, 315
Allen, Frederick Lewis, 283
America, 18, 33, 38, 40, 42, 43, 54, 115
American Eagle, 46, 47
American Fur Company, 87
American Institute of Management, 289
American Liberty League, 3, 303-312, 319, 324, 325, 332
Anderson, Bern, 171
Andrews, Julia, 293
Angelica, New York, 79, 80, 81
Annapolis, 164
Antietam, 183
Anti-Federalists, *see* Democratic-Republican Party
"Anti-knock" additive, *see* Ethyl
Anti-Semitism, 189, 190, 311
Anti-trust laws, 243-246, 338
Argentina, 338
Arlington Company, 287
Army, United States, 71, 104, 125, 126, 158, 173-177, 209, 244
Arnold, General H. H., 335
Arnold, Thurman W., 330
Asheville, North Carolina, 214, 345
Ashton, Rev. Frederick T., 327
Association Against the Prohibition Amendment, 303-306
Astor, John Jacob, 87
Atlantic Aviation Corporation, 294
Atlas Powder Company, 244, 245, 270, 346
Atomic bomb, 330-334
Atomic Energy Commission, 299, 333
Austria, 27, 33
Automobiles, 208, 223, 288, 289
Aviation, *see* Flying

Baden, 17
Baker, Newton D., 321
Ball, Edward, 293
Ball, Jessie Dew, 291, 292
Ball, Dr. L. H., 237
Ball Grain Explosives Company, 287, 346
Ball's Bluff (battle), 169
Balls Neck, 252
Baltimore, 118, 120, 164, 183, 184
Baltimore Sun, 312
Bancroft, John, Jr., 258, 259
Bank of the United States, 115, 117
Barbary States, 71, 72
Barksdale, Hamilton M., 207, 224, 225, 226, 267
Barksdale, Wisconsin, 4
Barnave, 25
Batten, Frank, 350
Bauduy, Alexandre, 55
Bauduy, Ferdinand, 84, 85, 86, 95, 96, 133
Bauduy, Pierre, 5, 55, 67, 68, 69, 73, 74, 80, 84, 85, 86, 89, 90, 94, 95, 96, 97, 98, 100, 102, 103, 106, 113
Baughman, Joseph, 87
Bayard, Alexis I. du Pont, 350
Bayard, James A., 56
Bayard, Thomas F., Jr., 260, 280, 282
Bayonne, New Jersey, 48
Beckton Chemical Company, 288
Belin, Augustus, 189
Belin, Henry, 157, 158, 189
Belin, Mary, 189, 190, 201
Bell, John, 157
Bellevue (estate), 2, 216
Bellevue-Stratford Hotel, 277
Belvedere, 91
Bendix Aviation, 299
Benjamin, Judah P., 167
Bergen Point, New Jersey, 48, 77, 79, 83, 84
Berwick, Pennsylvania, 178
Bethlehem Steel Corporation, 317
Betsy of Patterson, 56
Beugnot, Comte de, 36, 37
Biasutti, 3
Bidermann, Jacques, 43, 52, 53, 77, 96
Bidermann, Jacques Antoine, 96, 97, 101, 103, 107, 118, 126, 127, 347
Biltmore, 2
Bird, Charles du Pont, 161

Birth control, 313
Bissell, Alfred E., 293
Bladensburg, Maryland, 88
Boating, 294, 295, 345
Bohemia Stables, 344
Bois des Fossés (estate in Delaware), 2
Bois des Fossés (estate in France), 17, 18, 19, 25, 30, 32, 34, 35, 36, 37, 38, 46
Boissou, Mrs. Pierre, 148
Bonaparte, Jerome, 77-79
Bonaparte, Napoleon, 53, 57, 58, 59, 60, 62, 77, 78, 79, 98, 112
Book of Common Prayer, 150
Boomer, Lucius M., 277
Borkin, Joseph, 331
Boston, 199, 222, 233, 234, 316
Bowling Green, Kentucky, 219
Bradford, Alicia, 250-253, 255-263, 291, 347
Bradford, Judge Edward Green, 250-252, 257
Bradford, Edward G., Jr., 256, 258, 261, 263, 264
Bradford, Eleuthera du Pont, 250, 257
Bradford, Joanna, 259
Brandenberger, Jacques Edwin, 300
Brandywine Creek, 1, 2, 6, 55, 63, 67, 73, 82, 83, 84, 102, 103, 107, 114, 116, 133, 180, 188, 196, 229, 230, 249, 267, 290, 291, 347, 351
Brandywine Fife and Drum Corps, 207
Brandywine Hundred, 157
Brandywine Manufacturers' Sunday School, *see* Sunday School
Brandywine Powder, 87
Brandywine Rangers, 91
Brazil, 338
Breck, Charles, 134
Breck, William, 134
Breckinridge, John C., 157, 161, 174
Breck's Mill, 198
Bridgeport Wood Finishing Company, 288
Brincklé, Rev. Samuel Crawford, 134, 135, 136, 153, 159, 188
Brooklyn, 218, 233
Brooks, Captain, 46
Broom, Jacob, 55, 56, 67
Brown, Donaldson, 289
Brown, Harry F., 271
Brunswick, Georgia, 166, 170, 216
Buck, C. Douglass, 297
Buck, C. Douglass, Jr., 349
Buck, Polly, 349
Buckner, E. G., 285
Bull Run (battle), 169
Bull's Bay, South Carolina, 166
Burdick, Dr. C. Lalor, 348
Burton, Dr. H. R., 280
Burton, William, 161
Bush, Mrs. Mary H. J., 259, 260
Business Men's Presidential League, 277, 278, 280

Caldwell, Taylor, 323
Calico Printers' Association of Britain, 301
California Powder Works, 191, 192
Cambridge Modern History, 24
Camden, New Jersey, 294
Camden and Amboy Railroad, 143
Cameron, Simon, 160
Camp du Pont, 187
Canada, 59, 338
Canby, Henry Seidel, 130, 146, 196
Capes-Viscose, 299
Caracas, 105
Carlisle, Pennsylvania, 119, 256
Carnegie, Andrew, 241
Carney's Point, New Jersey, 251
Carothers, Dr. Wallace H., 301, 302
Carpenter Foundation, 348
Carpenter, R. R. M., 271, 308, 332, 337
Carpenter, Walter S., Jr., 332, 334, 337
Carrère and Hastings, 262
Carson, Rachel, 350
Cartagena, 105
Cartels, 208, 209, 330-332, 338
Catherine of Württemberg, 78
Catholicism, 8, 15, 24, 131, 132, 136, 137, 157, 213, 290, 305, 306, 315
Cats, 344
Cattle, 215, 344
Cawley Clark Company, 288
Cedar Creek, Virginia, 177
Cellophane, 4, 300
Central City, Kentucky, 226
Central City Coal and Iron Company, 218, 226
Century Club, 259
Chadds Ford, Pennsylvania, 55, 116
Chambers, Whittaker, 321
Chambersburg, Pennsylvania, 183
Charles' Banks, 197
Charleston Courier, 166
Charleston, South Carolina, 38, 43, 121, 165, 166, 170, 171
Chatard, Frederick, 172
Chemical industry, 287, 288, 300-302
Chénier, Joseph, 39
Chesapeake and Delaware Canal, 120
Chester, Pennsylvania, 64
Chevannes (estate), 2
Chevannes, France, 17, 20, 35, 39, 42
Chicago, 218
Chicago Daily News, 212
Chicago, University of, 332, 334
Chicago Varnish Company, 288
Chichester du Pont Foundation, 348
Chile, 121
Christ Church Christiana Hundred, 132, 135, 137, 154, 159, 172, 189, 251, 294, 326, 327
Christiana Hundred, 157
Christiana Securities, Incorporated, 273, 298, 299
Christina River, 55, 103, 111
Church, John Barker, 79

Church of the New Jerusalem, 135
Church, Philip, 79, 80
Church, William Hale, 300
Cincinnati Enquirer, 219, 220, 221
Civil liberties, 313
Civil War, 3, 6, 157-188, 190
Clannishness, 128-130, 196-199, 247, 260, 345, 346, 350, 351
Clark, Mary Ethel, 314
Clay, Henry, 120
Claymont, Delaware, 233
Clayton Act, 338
Cleveland, Ohio, 314, 315
Clifford, William H., 93-95, 100, 134
Clinton, Tennessee, 332
Club of '89, 24f
Codman, Richard, 44
Coleman Du Pont Road, *see* Du Pont Highway
Coleman, Ellen, 314
Coleman, (Rt. Rev.) Leighton, 216, 258
Colombia, 103
Columbus, Christopher, 2, 47
Commercial Pigments, 299
Communism, 310, 320, 321
Comptoir de Textiles Artificiels, 300
Compton, Arthur T., 332, 334
Conant, James B., 333
Confederacy, 157, 158, 159, 160, 161, 162, 164-172, 174-177, 178, 179, 180-184, 185-188
Congress, United States, 60, 71, 120, 121, 164, 169, 307, 308, 323, 338
Congressional Medal of Honor, 3, 177
Connecticut, 87
Constituent Assembly, 23, 109
Constitution, United States, 231, 237, 239, 304
Constitutional Union Party, 157
Cooke, Jay, 2, 193
Coolidge, Calvin, 282, 307
Cooper, Charles M., 332
Copeland, Charles, 6, 274
Copeland d'Andelot Foundation, 348
Copeland, Lammot du Pont, 337
Cormeilles, France, 29
Correa da Serra, José Francisco, 104
Cottons, 100, 101, 114, 133
Coughlinites, 320
Council of Ancients, 39, 109
County Trust Company of New York, 305
Cousin marriages, 2, 122, 127, 128, 130, 198, 199
Cowan, Christopher, 149
Coyne, William, 271, 273
Crestlea Foundation, 348
Crimean War, 142
Crook, George, 176, 177
Crowninshield, 3
Customs, 129, 130, 190, 350, 351
Cyane, 141

Dacron, *see* Synthetic Fibers
Dahlgren, John A., 163, 171

d'Alembert, 14
Dalmas, Charles Joseph, 46, 56, 95, 107, 111
Dalmas, Sophie Madeleine, *see* Du Pont de Nemours, Sophie Madeleine Dalmas
Darden, Colgate W., Jr., 350
d'Autremont, August, 81
Davis, Francis B., Jr., 304
Dearborn, General Henry, 71, 72
Decatur, Stephen, 50, 55
Declaration of the Rights of Man, 24
Deism, 132
Delaware, 2, 4, 5, 6, 56, 63, 116, 120, 136, 155, 157, 161, 182, 183, 185, 186, 210, 221-223, 231-239, 268, 278, 280, 282, 295-297, 341, 342
Delaware Chemical Engineering Company, 287
Delaware Coach Company, 294
Delaware law on incorporation, 210
Delaware Legislature, 106, 114, 137, 156, 214, 231-239, 263, 264, 268, 295-297
Delaware Memorial Bridge, 5
Delaware Motor Car Company, 288
Delaware Realty and Investment Corporation, 299
Delaware River, 55
Delaware State Journal, 123
Delaware Trust Company, 215, 291, 346
Delaware, University of, 348
Delessert, Étienne, 83
Democratic Party, 120, 157, 161, 214, 216, 235, 236, 238, 280, 281, 282, 305-312, 313, 319, 328, 349, 350
Democratic-Republican Party, 44, 120
Denizot, 113
Dent, Elbert, 292
Depressions, *see* Economic Conditions
Derna, 71
"Devil's Island," 39
Dickinson College, 119
Diderot, 14
Directory, the French, 39, 41, 44, 45
Dogs, 344
Dolan, Paul, 341, 342
Dominican Republic, 328
Don Pedro, 83, 84, 93
Doré, Madame, 12, 13
Dougherty, Michael, 147
Douglas, Stephen, 157
Dover, Delaware, 114, 155, 156, 161, 231, 279
Dowling, Eddie, 305
Downey, Fairfax, 175
Drayton, Percival, 167
Drayton, Thomas F., 167
Du Bourg, Dr., 12, 17
Dulux, 4
Dunham, Lewis L., 271
Duplanty, McCall and Company, 100, 101, 114, 133
Duplanty, Raphael, 81, 84, 85, 86, 100, 133
Du Pont, Abraham, 165

Du Pont, Adelaide Camille Denise, 286
Du Pont, A. Felix, 207, 271, 272, 274
Du Pont, A. Felix, Jr., 294, 335
Du Pont, Aileen M., 314, 350
Du Pont Airport, 294
Du Pont, Alexis Irénée, 5, 103, 126, 127, 132, 135, 136, 137, 149, 151, 152, 153, 154, 204, 216, 345
Du Pont, Alexis I., II ("Dr. Alexis"), 186, 196, 204, 210, 222, 225, 230, 250
Du Pont, Alexis I. (son of Eugene), 272
Du Pont, Alfred I., 5, 199, 202, 206-213, 215, 217, 222-230, 240, 243, 244, 247-276, 278-283, 286, 291-293, 295-298, 306, 323, 335, 346, 347
Du Pont, Alfred Victor, 46, 115, 118, 119, 125, 126, 127, 129, 131, 132, 134, 135, 138, 140, 143, 145, 150, 151
Du Pont, Alfred Victor, II, 218-221, 227
Du Pont, Alfred Victor (son of Alfred I.), 249, 256, 263-265, 286, 291, 292, 297
Du Pont, Alice, 216, 263
Du Pont, Amelia Elisabeth, 39, 80, 93-95, 134, 137
Du Pont, Ann Ridgely, 149, 150, 155, 156, 157
Du Pont, Anna, 248
Du Pont, Anne Ridgely (daughter of Eugene), 241
Du Pont, Antoine Bidermann, 178, 218, 219, 226, 314
Du Pont, Antoine Bidermann, Jr., 314, 315
Du Pont, Archibald, 274, 287, 346
Du Pont automobile, 288
Du Pont, Bauduy and Company, 69, 84, 93, 94, 95, 97, 100, 101, 114
Du Pont, Bessie (daughter of Alfred I.), 209, 210, 249, 256, 291
Du Pont, Bidermann T., 315
Du Pont Building, 291, 293, 317, 339
Du Pont burying ground, 6, 108, 109, 116, 123, 124, 154, 203, 292, 351
Du Pont, Caroline, 344
Du Pont, Charles Irénée, 39, 100, 114, 115, 127, 137, 142, 149, 150, 155, 156, 157, 158, 160, 161, 183, 199, 214
Du Pont, Charles I., Jr., 156
Du Pont, Charles I., III (grandson of Charles I.), 206, 207, 210, 211, 214, 215, 222, 224
Du Pont Circle, 172
Du Pont Club Brass Band, 207
Du Pont coat of arms, 19
Du Pont Company, 2-4, 6, 53-56, 60, 64, 66-75, 81, 86-92, 95-103, 107, 110-113, 118, 121, 122, 125-127, 129, 138-140, 145, 159-162, 178-184, 186, 189-195, 197, 200-202, 204-211, 213, 215, 221-230, 240-246, 248, 257, 266, 267, 269-276, 284-291, 296, 298-302, 305, 308, 314, 318-325, 330-342, 348, 351
Du Pont, Constance, 350
Du Pont Country Club, 5

Du Pont, Diane, 344
Du Pont, Dora (daughter of Antoine B.), 314
Du Pont, Dora P. (daughter of Evan M.), 315
Du Pont, Eleuthera, 72, 116, 122, 134, 135, 136
Du Pont, Eleuthera Bradford (sister of Alicia Bradford), 256
Du Pont, Eleuthère Irénée, II, 151, 180, 181, 185, 186, 197, 198, 216, 218, 262
Du Pont, Elizabeth Bradford, 250, 260, 350
Du Pont, Ellen (daughter of Henry), 158
Du Pont, Ellen (daughter of T. Coleman), 293, 326
Du Pont, Ellen C. (daughter of Evan M.), 315
Du Pont, Emile F., 293, 339, 346
Du Pont employees, 73-75, 101, 103, 112, 113, 115, 118, 136, 137, 145-150, 180, 181, 194, 197, 198, 205-207, 210, 229, 230, 252, 260, 267
Du Pont, E. Paul, 274, 287, 288, 294, 346
Du Pont, Ernest, 274, 287, 294, 295, 344, 345, 346
Du Pont, Ernest, Jr., 335, 346
Du Pont, Ethel (married FDR, Jr.), 325-328
Du Pont, Ethel (sister of Charles I., III), 207
Du Pont, Ethel B. (daughter of Antoine B., Jr.), 314, 315, 318, 349
Du Pont, Eugene (son of Alexis I.), 153, 161, 181, 183, 204-211, 215, 216, 222, 223, 241, 248, 293
Du Pont, Eugene, Jr. (grandson of Alexis I.), 325
Du Pont, Eugene E., 272, 274
Du Pont, Evan Morgan, 314
Du Pont, Evelina Gabrielle, 39, 103
Du Pont, Frances Elizabeth, 216
Du Pont, Francis Gurney, 196, 198, 204, 205, 207, 210, 216, 222, 225, 228, 230, 271, 274, 345, 351
Du Pont, Francis I., 262, 271, 272, 273, 274, 287, 293
Du Pont, Francis V., 5, 349
Du Pont, Grabrielle Josephine (daughter of Amelia), 94, 100, 134
Du Pont, Gideon, 165
Du Pont, Helena Allaire, 344
Du Pont, Henry, 99, 125-127, 129, 130, 132, 151, 157-161, 173, 179-183, 186, 188, 190-195, 197, 201-205, 207, 241
Du Pont, Henry A. (Colonel), 158, 160, 173-177, 187, 202, 204, 208, 210, 215, 222, 223, 225, 230, 231-239, 250, 272, 278, 279, 280, 281, 287, 292
Du Pont, Henry B., 256
Du Pont, Henry Belin, 294
Du Pont, Henry F., 271, 274, 287, 347
Du Pont Highway, 5, 267, 268
Du Pont Hotel, 5, 277, 291

Du Pont, Irénée (brother of Pierre S.), 190, 201, 227, 258, 271-274, 294, 302-304, 307, 310, 318, 320-322, 325, 326, 328, 332, 334, 336, 337, 339, 340, 350

Du Pont, Irénée, Jr., 323, 324, 337, 340, 349

Du Pont, James Q., 314, 315

Du Pont, Jean Ellen, 350

Du Pont, Joanne, 344

Du Pont, Julia Sophie Angelique, 79, 115

Du Pont, Lammot, 6, 142, 151, 160, 161, 178-180, 181, 182, 183, 189, 190, 192, 193, 199, 200, 201, 218

Du Pont, Lammot (brother of Pierre S.), 190, 201, 258, 267, 271, 287, 302, 303, 304, 308, 310, 318, 321, 326, 332, 336

Du Pont, Lammot, Jr., 335

Du Pont, Louis, 216, 217, 218, 247

Du Pont, Louisa d'Andelot, 6, 337

Du Pont, Madeleine ("Madie"), 249, 253, 256, 258, 263, 286, 335

Du Pont, Mrs. Marcella Miller, 292

Du Pont, Margaretta (daughter of Irénée), 334

Du Pont, Marguerite, 248, 253

Du Pont, Marie Le Dée, 13, 15ff, 19, 20

Du Pont, Mary (sister of Pierre S.), 350

Du Pont, Mary Lammot, 214, 215, 216

Du Pont, Mary Van Dyke, 142, 156

Du Pont, Maurice, 212-214, 248, 257

Du Pont motto, 19

Du Pont, Philip F., 272, 274

Du Pont, Pierre S., 190, 201, 207, 208, 211, 226-230, 240, 251, 253, 256, 258, 266, 267, 269-276, 281, 287, 289, 291, 293, 295, 296, 302-304, 307, 310, 311, 317-319, 321, 324, 326, 332, 336, 346, 350

Du Pont, Pierre S., III, 336, 349

Du Pont Powder, 87

Du Pont, Reynolds, 349

Du Pont, Richard (son of Samuel Francis), 344

Du Pont, Richard C., 294, 335, 344

Du Pont, Richard C., Jr., 344

Du Pont, Rosina, 315

Du Pont, Samuel, 8-13

Du Pont, Samuel Francis (Rear Admiral), 6, 99, 104, 122, 127, 134, 136, 141, 157, 158, 163-172, 179, 201, 251

Du Pont, Samuel Francis (son of Ernest), 343-346

Du Pont, Sara (daughter of Henry), 181

Du Pont Securities Company, 273, 274

Du Pont, S. Hallock, 344

Du Pont, Sophie (daughter of Francis G.), 274

Du Pont, Sophie Madeleine (daughter of Eleuthère Irénée, 99, 122, 127, 141, 151, 152, 169, 171, 172, 180, 181, 187, 201

Du Pont, T. Coleman, 216, 226-230, 237, 238, 240-243, 251, 257, 258, 263, 266-272, 275, 276, 277-283, 297, 298, 314, 349

Du Pont, Victor (son of Charles I.), 156, 214

Du Pont, Mrs. Victor, 326

Du Pont, Victorine (daughter of Alfred I.), 252, 291, 292

Du Pont, Victorine (daughter of Antoine B., Jr.), 314

Du Pont, Victorine Elizabeth, 30, 36, 84, 85, 86, 93, 95, 100, 132, 133, 134, 188

Du Pont, Washington, 4

Du Pont, William (son of Henry), 187, 204, 206, 207, 214, 215, 216, 222, 255, 258, 262, 269-274, 292

Du Pont, William, Jr. (grandson of Henry), 350

Du Pont, William B., 315

Du Pont, William K., 227

Du Pont, Zara ("Aunt Zadie"), 313-318

Du Pont de Nemours, Eleuthère Irénée, 6, 17, 19, 20, 22, 23, 25-32, 35, 37, 39, 42, 45, 46, 48, 50-57, 63, 64, 66-69, 72-76, 79-91, 94-103, 106-108, 110, 111, 113-116, 118-126, 128, 132, 133, 138, 345, 347

Du Pont de Nemours, Françoise, 38, 39, 48, 77, 98, 99, 103

Du Pont de Nemours, Gabrielle Josephine, 33, 34, 35, 36, 38, 79, 80, 81, 82, 94, 127, 137

Du Pont de Nemours Père, Fils & Cie., 43, 48, 49, 51, 52, 57, 76, 89, 114

Du Pont de Nemours, Pierre Samuel, 6, 7, 10-109, 113, 116, 124-127, 131, 165, 345

Du Pont de Nemours, Sophie Madeleine Dalmas, 25-27, 30-39, 45, 47, 54, 63, 72, 79, 82, 85, 86, 103, 106, 107, 111, 119, 133

Du Pont de Nemours, Victor Marie, 16, 19, 20, 22-24, 26, 27, 33, 34, 36, 38, 41, 43, 44, 46, 48, 49, 52-57, 68, 69, 76-82, 84, 88, 91, 93-95, 97, 100, 103, 104, 106, 107, 110, 113-115, 117, 118, 122-124, 127, 128, 131, 141

DuPrene, 301

Duquesnoy, 52, 53

Durant, William C., 288, 289

Dutton, William S., 201

Dwight School, 132

Dynamite, 192, 193, 200

Dynasty of Death, 323

Eagle Powder, 87

Eagles Gather, The, 323

Early, Jubal, 176, 177, 183, 184

Economic conditions, 81, 89, 96, 97, 101, 102, 106, 113, 114, 126, 138, 139, 180, 181, 190-193, 281, 289, 297, 298, 307, 308, 319, 320, 330, 331

Ecuador, 103

Eden Park, 5, 103

Edgemoor, Delaware, 4, 143, 160

Edict of Nantes, 8
Education, 16, 49, 132, 133, 136, 137, 157, 295, 296, 348, 349
E. I. du Pont de Nemours and Company, Incorporated, *see* Du Pont Company
Eighteenth Amendment, *see* United Sates Constitution
Elba, 98
Eleutherian Mills (powder yard), 68, 87, 90
Eleutherian Mills (residence), 73, 108, 109, 123, 158, 181, 186, 207, 347
Eleutherian Mills-Hagley Foundation, 5, 348, 350
Eleutherian Mills Historical Library, 348
Embargo Act, 81
Encyclopedists, the, 14ff
Ephemerides du Citoyen, Les, 16, 17
Episcopalian Church, 134, 216
Equinoctial states, 103, 105
Equitable Building (New York), 268, 269
Equitable Life Assurance Society, 277, 278
Essonnes, France, 23, 25, 50, 53, 73
Estates, 2, 194, 343, 346, 347
Ethyl, 300, 301
Ewell, Dr. Thomas, 88
Explosions, 74f, 88, 101, 102, 110, 111, 112, 135, 144, 145-150, 152, 153, 154, 181, 182, 195, 200, 201, 205, 206, 251, 257, 286, 290

Fabrikoid Company, 287
Fairfield Rubber Company, 287
Farley, Jim, 312
Farquhar, 3
Federalists, 41, 48, 59, 105, 120
Federal Trade Commission, 299
Fermi, Enrico, 334
Fernandina, Florida, 166, 170
Ferrières, 33, 35
Fingal, 99
Fires, 102, 107, 111, 112, 151, 205
First National Bank of Louisville, 218
Fisher's Hill, Virginia, 176
Fisher's Island, 336
Fisk, Jim, 193
Fitz-Gerald, Margery May, 213, 214
"Flea Park," *see* Free Park
Flint Varnish and Color Company, 288
Florida, 253, 293, 296, 306
Florida National Bank of Jacksonville, 293
Flying, 294, 335, 345
Fontanet, Indiana, 257
Forbes (magazine), 4
Fort Delaware, 182
Fort du Pont, 327
Fort McAllister, 170
Fort Sumter, 158, 159, 171
Fortune (magazine), 5, 322, 323
Foundations, 348
Fountain, Andrew, 87

Fox, Gustavus V., 171
France, 2, 7ff, 18, 19, 22, 39, 41, 44, 52, 58, 59, 60, 62, 66, 67, 72, 76, 77, 97, 98, 99, 105, 119, 122, 132
Francis I. du Pont and Company, 293, 338
Frankford, Pennsylvania, 50, 55
Franklin, Benjamin, 2, 10, 16, 17, 22f, 132
Free Park, 197, 290
French Guiana, 39
French Revolution, *see* Revolution, French
Freon, 301
Fulton, Robert, 42

Gardner, Bessie, 216, 217, 247-249, 251-254, 256, 258, 259, 261, 263, 264, 291
Gardner, Dorsey, 217
Garesché, J. P., 103
Gemini, 345
General Motors Corporation, 3, 4, 208, 288, 289, 301, 305, 308, 318, 337, 338
Genesee River, 79, 80, 81
Gentieu, Pierre, 230, 267
Georgetown, Maryland, 92
Germany, 17, 284-287, 320, 322, 330-332, 335
Germany's Master Plan, 331
Gettysburg, 183, 186
Gliders, *see* Flying
Good Samaritan Foundation, 348
Good Stay, 48, 51, 54, 56, 58, 77, 81, 83
Gould, Jay, 193
Government and Administration of Delaware, 341
Grace, Eugene P., 317
Granogue, 2, 294
Grasselli Chemicals, 299
Gray, Andrew C., 263, 264
Graziani, Josephina, 53
Great Britain, 2, 18, 19, 33, 44, 49, 50, 52, 58, 62, 88, 101, 105, 121, 178, 179
Greeley, Horace, 169
Greenewalt, Crawford H., 333, 337
Green Hill Presbyterian Church, 207
Greenville, Delaware, 6
Greiner, 3
Groton School, 327
Grouchy, Marquis Emmanuel de, 110, 112
Groves, General Leslie R., 332, 333
Guadeloupe, 49
Gudin, 32
Guncotton, 142, 143
Gunpowder, 22f, 50, 51, 52, 53, 54, 64, 66, 67, 70, 71, 72, 86, 87, 88, 119, 122, 127, 139, 142, 143, 159, 192, 198, 200, 229, 351; brown prismatic, 203, 209; smokeless, 203, 209, 244
Gunpowder Trade Association, *see* Powder Trust
Gustavus III of Sweden, 17, 18
Guyencourt (estate), 2

Hagley (hamlet), 197
Hagley Farm, 90
Hagley Library, *see* Eleutherian Mills Historical Library
Hagley Museum, 5, 347, 348
Hagley Yard, 90, 101, 114, 139, 151, 152, 209, 347
Haiti, 50, 55, 57, 62, 69, 72, 76, 77, 78, 189
Haley, Frank, 193
Halleck, Henry, 183
Hamburg, Germany, 46
Hamilton, Alexander, 2, 48, 56, 79
Hamilton, Paul, 88
Hamon, William, 56
Hanford, Washington, 333, 334
Hanna, Mark, 237
Harding, Warren G., 282
Harrington, Willis F., 333
Harrisburg, Pennsylvania, 182
Harrison Brothers and Company, 288
Harriss, C. Lowell, 288
Harvard University, 217, 301, 326, 333
Harvey, 55
Harvey, Alice Hounsfield, 349
Haskell, Henry G., 271
Haskell, J. Amory, 207, 241
Hauser, Elizabeth, 315
Hearst, William Randolph, 2
Heisel, Thomas Bayard, 263
Henderson, Charlotte Shepard, 185, 186, 198
Henry, Rev. Ashton, 216
Henry Clay (hamlet), 147, 159, 197, 290
Henry Clay Factory, 100, 347
Hercules Powder Company, 244, 245, 270, 350
Hexton, 343-345
Heywood, Charles, 141
Hiebler, Max, 286
Higgins, Anthony, 233, 234
Highwood, 2
Hill, Walter N., 200
Hiss, Alger, 321, 322
Historien, 39
Hoboken, New Jersey, 239
Holland, 33
Hoover, Herbert, 306, 307
Hopeton Plantation, 216
Horses, 215, 344
Houston, Sam, 164
Hughes, Archbishop, 136
Hughes, Charles Evans, 280
Huguenots, 8, 15, 115, 131, 165
Huidekoper, 3
Humphrey, Hubert, 328
Hunt, Wilson, 117
Hunter, Dr., 86, 87
Hunter, David, 175, 176
Hutton, James, 19

I. G. Farben, 331, 332
Imperial Chemical Industries, 301, 331, 334

Independence, United States, 2, 18, 19
India, 121, 178, 179, 191
Indian Motorcycle Company, 294
Indians, 80, 81
Inquiry into Nature and Causes of the Wealth of Nations, 14
International Ladies' Garment Workers Union, 316
"Investiture, the," 20
Ireland, 213
Irénée du Pont, Jr. Foundation, 348
Irish, the, 127, 136, 137, 157, 181, 198, 213, 290
Irving, 3

Jackson, Andrew, 120
Jacksonville, Florida, 170
Jacobins, 24, 39, 43
James, Marquis, 175, 253
Jamesburg Agreement, 208, 209, 331
Jamesburg, New Jersey, 208
Jandelle, 75
Japan, 330, 331
Jancourt, Chevalier de, 8, 14
Jay, John, 19
Jefferson, Martha, *see* Randolph, Mrs. Martha
Jefferson, Thomas, 2, 7, 15, 19, 44, 45, 48, 49, 52, 53, 54, 56, 58, 60, 61, 62, 67, 71, 82, 93, 94, 104, 105, 108, 132
Jersey City, New Jersey, 48, 233
Jesuits, 132
Jews, 189, 190, 311
Johns Hopkins University, 212, 345
Johnson Company, 227
"Johnson, James G.," 219
Johnson, Tom L., 315
Johnstown, Pennsylvania, 314
Journal de l'Agriculture, du Commerce, et des Finances, 15

Kane, Thomas, 195
Karlsruhe, 17
Kelso, 344
Kennan, George, 238
Kennedy, John F., 328
Kennett Square, Pennsylvania, 286, 346
Kent County, Delaware, 158, 161, 233, 234
Kent, Frank, 312
Kentucky, 43, 77, 121
Keokuk, 171
Kerr, George H., 199
Kettering, Charles, 301
Kinetic Chemicals, 301
King, James Gore, 2
King, Rufus, 45
King's Great Western Powder Company, 191
Kingston, New York, 83
Kirwan, 3
Kitchel, 3
Kneeland, F. L., 191
Knights of Labor, 226

Knowles, Levi, 233
Know-Nothings, 137, 157, 161
Krebs Pigment and Chemical, 299
Krock, Arthur, 310
Kuhn, Loeb and Company, 299

Labor unions, 226, 313, 314, 316-318, 342
Lafayette, Marquis de, 18, 46, 53, 108, 115, 116
Laffey, John P., 273, 274
Laflin and Rand, 200, 201, 223, 224, 225, 229, 240, 241
La Force prison, 36, 37, 39, 42, 52
Laird, William Winder, 274, 293
Laird, William Winder, Jr., 350
Laird, Bissell, and Meeds, 293, 338
Lake Superior Powder Company, 191
Lalande, Le Français de, 29
Lalor Foundation, 348
Lammot, Daniel, Jr., 135, 186
Lammot, Margaretta, 115, 134, 135, 185, 186
La Motte, Ellen, 249, 253
La Motte, 115
Lancaster, Pennsylvania, 110
Landon, Alfred M., 311, 312
Lane, William, 50, 55
Lavoisier, Antoine, 22, 25, 35, 38, 39, 50, 53, 64, 68
Lawrenceville School, 349
Lawton, William C., 210, 245
Lea, Thomas, 90
Lebrun, Charles François, 61
Le Dée, Marie, *see* Du Pont, Marie Le Dée
Lee, Robert E., 162, 170, 182, 183, 188
Lee, Higginson and Company, 288
Legion of Honor, 109
Legislative Assembly, 24, 28
Leuchtenburg, William E., 307
Lewes, Delaware, 90, 91
Lexington, Virginia, 175, 176
Liberty League, *see* American Liberty League
Lickle, 3
Lincoln, Abraham, 157, 158, 164, 169, 179
Lincoln University, 349
Livingston, Robert R., 58, 60, 61
London Times, 166
Longfellow, Henry Wadsworth, 163
Longwood, 2, 286; Foundation, 348; Gardens, 346
Lotteries, 117, 118
Louis XV, 9, 18
Louis XVI, 18, 19, 25, 27, 28, 32, 41
Louis Sherry restaurants, 277
Louisiana, 58, 59, 60, 61, 62
Louisiana Purchase, 2, 58-62, 71
Louisville, Kentucky, 204, 218-221, 226, 249, 314, 315
Louisville Commercial, 219
Louisville Courier-Journal, 220
Louviers (residence), 2, 110, 112, 113

Louviers (residence), Lower house, 82, 149, 150; Upper house, 169, 171, 251, 252, 256
Louviers, Colorado, 4
Louviers Woolen Mill, 101
Lower Works, 139
Lucite, *see* Plastics
Luscomb, Florence H., 315, 316
Luther, Martin, 136
Lycra, 4
Lynchburg, Virginia, 176

Maddox, Alicia, 252
Maddox, George Amory, 250, 252, 256
Madison, Indiana, 345
Madison, James, 60, 104, 215
Maine, 209
Malouet, 25
Manhattan Engineer District, *see* Atomic bomb
"Manifest Destiny," 140
Marcellus Powder Company, 191
Marcus Hook, Pennsylvania, 143
Margrave of Baden, 17
Marie Antoinette, 18, 25
Maryland, 6, 182, 183
Mason, James M., 179
Mason, Lewes A., 336
Masonic Order, 131
Massachusetts Institute of Technology, 199, 212, 226, 348
Massena, Gabriel, 292, 297
Mathewson, Frank, 252
Maxim, Sir Hiram, 209
Maxim, Hudson, 209
Max Planck Institute, 301
Mayo Clinic, 269
McAlpin Hotel, 268, 277, 278
McCall, Archibald, 55, 100
McConnell, J. H. Tyler, 350
McHarg, Ormsby, 277
McKinley, William, 235, 236, 237
Mease, Dr. James, 84
Meeds, Hollyday S., Jr., 293
Merino Wool Factory, 84
Merrill, Lynch, Pierce, Fenner, and Smith, 293
Merrimac, 170
"*Mes Adieux à l'Europe*," 54
Mexican War, 139-142, 163
Mexico, 59
Michelson, Charles, 312
Midgley, Thomas, Jr., 301
Mirabeau, Marquis de, 16, 18
Miraflores, 233
Mitsui, 331
Mobile, Alabama, 166
Mond, Sir Alfred, 331
Monitor, 170
Monitors, 170, 171
Monopoly, 121, 190-193, 201, 202, 208, 209, 210, 240-246, 338
Monroe, James, 60, 61, 107, 312
Montchanin (estate), 2, 290

Montchanin, Alexandre de, 8
Montchanin, Anne Alexandrine de, 8-12
Montchanin, Pierre de, 8
Montesquieu, 12
Monticello, 104
Montmorenci, 347
Montpelier, 215, 216
Moosic Powder Company, 241
Morgan, H. Vaughan, Jr., 325
Morgan, J. P., and Company, 271, 273, 275, 276, 277, 285, 289
Morgan, Stanley and Company, 338
Morison, Samuel Eliot, 44
Morrison, De Carrick and Company, 140
Mott, Lucretia, 155
Moxham, Arthur J., 314
Moxham, Egbert, 314
Mueller, Willard F., 210
Mullin, Mickey, 148
Municipal ownership, 313, 315
Munitions investigation, 319-325, 333
Munns, Charles, 87, 88

Nahant, 171
Nantucket, 171
Napoleon, *see* Bonaparte, Napoleon
National Ammonia, 299
National Assembly, 23, 24, 131
National Distillers, 304
National Education in the United States of America, 49
National Guard, 24, 28, 29, 35, 38
National Maritime Union, 316
National Powder Works, 22, 25
Naval Academy, 164
Navy, United States, 71, 87, 88, 104, 106, 107, 115, 163-172, 244
Nazis, *see* Germany
Necker, Jacques, 18
Necker, Louis, 52, 53
Nemours (Alfred I. du Pont estate), 2, 261, 262, 292, 347
Nemours, France, 12ff, 15, 17, 23, 42
Nemours Building (Wilmington), 339
Neoprene, 4, 301
Neoptism, 339, 340
New Bern Progress, 166
New Castle, Delaware, 56, 88, 115, 215
New Castle County, Delaware, 158, 233, 236, 278, 279
New England Oil, Paint, and Varnish Company, 288
New Granada, 105
New Haven, Connecticut, 132, 217
New Ironsides, 171
New Jersey, 81
New Market, Virginia, 174
New Orleans, 74, 166
Newport, Delaware, 4
Newport, Rhode Island, 47, 48, 157
Newport Journal, 48
Newspapers, 5, 212, 255, 260
Newtown Square, Pennsylvania, 216

New Year's Day visiting, 129, 130, 190, 288, 289, 350, 351
New York, 43, 48, 79, 81, 131, 165, 166, 173, 174, 191, 199, 217, 268, 277, 278, 305, 306, 323, 328
New York Consolidated Lottery, 117, 118
New York Courier and Enquirer, 120
New York Daily Mirror, 325
New York Herald Tribune, 323
New York Post, 311
New York Sun, 260
New York Times, 310
New York Tribune, 169
New York World, 260
Nieuwland, Rev. Dr. Julius A., 301
Niles, Hezekiah, 118
Niles' Weekly Register, 118
Nitrogen, 345
Nitroglycerin, 192, 200
Nobel, Alfred, 192
Nobel-Dynamite Trust Company, 208
Nobel Prize, 332, 334
Non-Partisan League, 295
Norfolk, Virginia, 246
North American Aviation, 299
Notre Dame, University of, 301
Nullification, Ordinance of, 120, 121
Nye Committee, *see* Munitions Investigation
Nye, Gerald P., 320
Nylon, *see* Synthetic Fibers

O'Banion, 3
Ogontz, 2
Ohio, 211, 227
Ohio Powder Company, 191
O'Keefe, Thomas, 182
Old age pensions, 296
Old Hickory powder plant, 321
Orange, Virginia, 215
Order of Vasa, 18, 109
Orléans, France, 42
Orlon, 4
Outlook, 231, 238
Owl's Nest, 325-327

Pacific Fur Company, 87
Pacifism, 313, 317, 320, 323, 325, 331
Palaces, American, 2
Pan, Mallet du, 25
Parent, Charles François, 73
Passaic, 171
Patapsco, 171
Patent of nobility, 19
Patterson, Elizabeth, 78
Patterson, Robert, 160
Paul, Drexel, Jr., 325
Payne, Maggie, 219, 220
Peabody, Rev. Endicott, 327
Peace of Amiens, 49
Peace of Ghent, 102
Pelleport, Gabrielle Josephine de la Fite de, *see* Du Pont de Nemours, Gabrielle Josephine

Pelleport, Reine Marguerite de la Fite de, 33, 34, 35, 38
Pennsylvania, 6, 55
Pennsylvania, University of, 186, 253, 348
Pensions, 296, 297
Peoria, Illinois, 242
Périgord, Abbé de, see Talleyrand
Perot, Mrs. Eleanor du Pont, 274
Perrin, Suzanne, 328
Peru, 121
Peyton Chemical Company, 241, 242
Peyton, William Charles, 241, 242
Philadelphia, 22, 26, 43, 64, 91, 114, 115, 117, 123, 158, 163, 164, 172, 199, 201, 217, 222, 233, 246, 277
Philadelphia Gazette, 48
Philanthropy, 5, 348, 349
Phillips, Henry Rodney, 314
Phillips, Dora Coleman, 314
Physiocracy, 14, 16
Physiocracy, or the Natural Constitution of that Form of Government Most Advantageous to the Human Race, 16
Pichon, Louis André, 76, 77, 78
Pickering, Secretary of State, 45
Pitray, Viel and Company, 121
Pittsburgh, 101
Planck, Max, Institute, see Max Planck Institute
Plastics, 4, 287, 301
Poivre, Françoise, see Du Pont de Nemours, Françoise
Poland, 17, 18
Politics, 91, 104, 105, 106, 107, 114, 115, 120, 121, 136, 137, 156, 157, 158, 161, 231-239, 277-283, 295-297, 303-312, 313-318, 319, 325, 328, 340-342, 349, 350
Polk, James K., 140
Polyethylene, see Plastics
Pompadour, Madame de, 15
"Pontiàna," 43, 51, 127
Porter, Noah, 217
Port Royal, South Carolina, 164-170
Portugal, 104
Potomac, 42, 43
Potter, William S., 349
Powdermaking, see Gunpowder
Powder Trust, 191, 192, 193, 201, 202, 208, 209, 210, 240-245, 287
Pressman, Lee, 321
Presidency, 169, 305-312
Press, freedom of, 16
Princip, Gavrilo, 284
Proctor, Edward W., 245, 246
Progressive Party, 280
Prohibition, 303-307
Protestantism, 8, 11, 20, 24, 128, 131, 136, 137
Providence, Rhode Island, 132
Prussia, 33
Pusy, Bureaux de, 38, 46, 48, 49, 77, 96
Pusy, Julie Ile de France, 38, 46, 77, 96, 98, 113, 116

Pusy, Maurice de, 46
Pyle, Frank, 267

Quesnay, François, 14ff
Quinn, Helen Augusta, 314

Race relations, 310, 311, 313, 349
Raichlen, 3
Ramsay, W. G., 271
Randolph, Mrs. Martha, 104
Raskob, John Jacob, 227, 271, 273, 275, 288, 289, 298, 303, 305-308, 319, 324
Rayon, see Synthetic Fibers
Reflections on the Wealth of the State, 14
Reign of Terror, 33, 35, 37, 41
Religion, 8, 16, 24, 115, 131-137, 157, 161
Remington Arms, 4, 299
Rencourt, see Du Pont, Marie Le Dée
Rencourt Foundation, 348
Repauno Chemical Company, 193, 199, 200, 207, 215, 241
Republican Party, 3, 120, 157, 158, 232-239, 242, 268, 277, 278, 279, 280, 281, 282, 306, 309-312, 313, 314, 320, 349
Revolt of the Conservatives, 311
Revolution, French, 2, 23-45, 81
Richards, Charles F., 210
Richmond Enquirer, 166
Richmond, Virginia, 87, 88
Ridgely, Ann, see Du Pont, Ann Ridgely
Ridgely, Henry M., 155
Ridgely, Nicholas, 156
Riordan, James J., 305
Rising Sun, 147, 182, 197
Roads, 5, 296, 349
Robespierre, 37, 38
Robinson, R. P., 296
Rochelle, France, 46
Rockefeller, John D., 241
Rock Farms, 253, 255, 257, 258, 261
Rockland, 290
Rodney, Caesar A., 115
Roessler and Hasslacher Chemical, 299
Roosevelt, Franklin D., 306-312, 319, 325-328
Roosevelt, Franklin D., Jr., 325-328
Roosevelt, John, 327
Roosevelt, Theodore, 238, 243
Rosendale, New York, 83
Rouen, France, 8
Rousseau, 12
Rubber Securities Company, 299
Rubber, synthetic, 301
Ruoff, Friedrich Hermann, 335
Russell, William H., 166

Sabin, Charles H., 303
Sadler, Judge W. F., 256
St. Amour (estate), 2
St. Andrew's School, 349
St. Augustine, Florida, 170
St. Bartholomew's Day Massacre, 8
St. John's Church (Wilmington), 134

St. Joseph's-on-the-Brandywine (church), 136, 137, 286, 290, 291
Saltpeter, 51, 121, 122, 178, 179, 191, 200
Sand Hole Woods, 6, 108, 116, 123, 154, 187, 203, 292, 351
Sandran, Alexandre Cardon de, 114
Sands Point, Long Island, 286
San Jacinto, 179
San Simeon, 2
Santo Domingo, *see* Haiti
Sassafras River, 92, 343
Saulsbury, Willard, 214, 215, 216, 238, 260, 280, 282
Savannah, Georgia, 165, 166
Savarin restaurants, 277
Savoy-Plaza Hotel, 277
Scandals, 212, 221, 247-265, 281
Schoenbein, Frederick, 142
Scott, William, 252
Scott, Rev. William J., 286
Seaford, Delaware, 4
Segur, Vicomtesse de, 33
Seligman, J. and W., and Company, 288
Senate, United States, 60, 62, 115, 216, 231-239, 260, 278, 280-283, 304, 319-325, 330
Service Citizens of Delaware, 295
Seventeenth Amendment, *see* United States Constitution
Seward, William H., 178, 179
Sharp Foundation, 348
Sharp, Hugh Rodney, 274
Shaw, George Bernard, 324
Sheep, 54, 63, 83
Shenandoah Valley, 174-177, 183
Sheridan, Philip, 176, 177
Sherman Anti-Trust Act, *see* Anti-trust laws
Sherman, Thomas West, 166
Sherry Netherland Hotel, 277
Shouse, Jouett, 306-308
Shubrick, Irvine, 115, 121, 122, 141
Shubrick, Thomas, 142
Shubrick, William B., 141
Siddal, John, 133
Silent Spring, 350
Sinclair, Harry F., 282
"Single Tax," 293, 315
Slavery, 16, 69, 81, 155, 157, 161, 185
Slidell, John, 179
Sloan, Alfred P., Jr., 289, 308
Smith, Adam, 7, 14
Smith, Alfred E., 305, 310, 324
Smith, Francis Gurney, 143
Smith, Dr. Thomas McKie, 122, 134, 135
Smith, William, 182
Socialism, 313, 317
Social Register, 5
Society for Promoting Manufactures, 120
South Africa, 208
South America, 103, 121
South Carolina, 82, 120, 121, 158, 165
South Dakota, 215, 255

Southern Committee to Uphold the Constitution, 310, 311, 319
Spain, 33, 49, 54, 58, 103, 209, 317
Spanish-American War, 209
Squirrel Run (hamlet), 197, 290
Squirrel Run Kennels, 344
Staël, Germaine de, 39, 53
Standard Oil, 241, 301
Stanton, Edwin, 183
Stayton, Captain William H., 303
Stewart, James, 151
Stine, Charles, 333
Stocking, George W., 331
Stockton, General John, 91
Strauss, Lewis L., 299
Stuart, Captain Sidney E., 251
Suffragettes, *see* Women's sufferage
Sumter Watchman, 169
Sunday School, 133, 134
Sussex County, Delaware, 158, 233, 234
Swamp Hall, 213, 216, 217, 227, 248, 249, 251, 253, 256, 258, 261
Sweden, 17
Swedenborgian church, *see* Church of the New Jerusalem
Swiss Guards, 28
Sycamore Manufacturing Company, 191, 192
Synthetic fibers, 4, 300-302

Taft, Charles P., 268
Taft, William Howard, 239, 243
Talleyrand, 18, 44, 46, 53, 60, 61, 76, 89, 98, 113, 114, 122
Tallman, F. G., 271
Talmadge, Eugene, 310
Tankopanicum Musical Club, 207, 248
Tannery, 100, 114
Tariffs, 101, 120, 121
Tattnall, Josiah, 167
Taxes, 16, 215, 295, 296, 304, 319, 324, 338
Teapot Dome, 282
Terylene, 301
Tetraethyl lead, *see* Ethyl
Theano Foundation, 348
Thompson, Anne, 345
Thompson, Mrs. Henry B., 259
Thompson, Judge J. Whitaker, 275
Tournai, France, 9
Tousard, Colonel Louis de, 50, 55
Tower Hill School, 349
Transportation, 126, 143, 144
Trans World Airlines, 294
Treaty of Amiens, 52
Treaty of Paris, 19
Treaty of San Ildefonso, 58
Trent, 179
Trinity Church (Wilmington), 134, 135, 216
Tripoli, 71
Trujillo, Rafael, 328
Truman, Harry S., 330
Tuileries, 25, 27, 28, 29

Turgot, 16, 17, 18
Twentieth Century Fund, 245, 331
Twenty-first Amendment, *see* United States Constitution

Unidel Foundation, 348
Union cause (in Civil War), 157, 158, 159, 160, 161, 164-172, 174-177, 178-184, 185-188
Unitarian church, 313
United Auto Workers, 318
United States government, 2, 22, 40, 41, 43, 50, 59, 66, 67, 71, 81, 102, 105, 138, 139, 246, 332
United States Flashless Powder Company, 287, 346
United States Rubber Company, 299, 304
United States Steel Corporation, 227, 241, 299, 300, 307
Upper Banks, 197
Upper Yard, 100, 101, 102, 111, 112, 113, 114, 149, 195
Urbana University, 226

Vanderbilt, Commodore Cornelius, 193
Vanderbilt, George, 2
Van Deusen, 3
Van Dyke, Dorcas Montgomery, 115
Van Dyke, Nicholas, 115
V. du Pont de Nemours et Cie, 68, 77
Venezuela, 103
Vereinigte Köln-Rottweiler Pulverfabriken, 208
Vergennes, 18
Vicmead Hunt Club, 326
"Villainy Detected," 88
Virginia Military Institute, 174, 175, 176
Virginia, University of, 49, 348, 350
Viscoloid Company, 299
Volstead Act, 303
Voltaire, 12, 15

Wabash, 167, 168
Waddell, Robert Stuart, 242, 245
Waldorf Astoria Hotel, 277
Wales, Ruth, 347
Wallace, Lew, 183
Wall Street, 169, 191, 223, 268, 269, 271, 277, 278, 288, 289, 293, 299, 338
Walsh, Rev. John S., 136
Wapwallopen, 178, 199
War, 3, 6, 67, 68, 88, 90-92, 101, 102, 114, 121, 139-142, 157-188, 190, 209, 268, 269, 275, 284-287, 319-325, 328-336
War of 1812, 88, 90-92, 101, 102, 114, 121
Warner, William, 102
Warren, Benjamin S., 328
Warrenton, North Carolina, 347
Washington, District of Columbia, 54, 55, 58, 106, 164, 172, 176, 178, 183, 184, 248, 277
Washington, George, 43, 48
Watchmaking, 8
Waterloo, 112
Watkins, Myron W., 331

Watson, William T., 235
Watterson, Henry, 220
Wealth, 2, 3, 197, 282, 298-300, 345, 346, 349
Wealth of Nations, the, see Inquiry into Nature and Causes of the Wealth of Nations
Weehawken, 171
Welfare Foundation, 348
Welles, Gideon, 165, 170, 171
Welsh, Charles A., 331
Wertenbaker, Charles, 4, 323
West Chester, Pennsylvania, 336
West Indies, 49, 77
Westover Hills, 307
West Point, 173
West Virginia, 121, 176
Whigs, 114, 120, 121, 157, 313
White, Dougal, 145
White Eagle, 286
White Sulphur Springs, Virginia, 176
Wickersham, George W., 244
Willard Hotel, 277
Williams, General William, 347
Wilmington, Delaware, 1, 4, 5, 50, 55, 56, 60, 63, 64, 71, 81, 84, 110, 111, 115, 123, 127, 128, 129, 131, 134, 142, 144, 147, 160, 169, 184, 187, 188, 196, 197, 199, 206, 216, 227, 229, 245, 261, 277, 291, 307, 343, 345-348
Wilmington and Northern Railroad, 202
Wilmington Club, 217, 218
Wilmington Evening Journal, 212, 279, 281
Wilmington Morning News, 257, 279, 280, 281, 295
Wilmington Symphony, 259
Wilmington Trust Company, 291
Wilmington, North Carolina, 166
Wilson, Joseph, 233
Wilson, Mrs. Joseph, 233, 235
Winchester, Virginia, 176
Winkler, John K., 243
Winterthur, 2, 281, 287, 290; Museum, 346, 347; Switzerland, 347
Wolcott, Josiah O., 280, 281, 282
Wolfskill, George, 311
Women, 112, 113, 115, 160, 181, 185-188, 198, 199, 207, 259-261
Women's International League for Peace and Freedom, 317
Women's suffrage, 155, 313, 315, 316, 318
Woolens, 83, 84, 100, 101, 110, 114, 198
World War I, 268, 269, 275, 284-287, 319-325, 334, 336
World War II, 323, 325, 328, 329, 330-335

XYZ Affair, 43

Yachting, *see* Boating
Yale University, 216, 217
York, Pennsylvania, 183

Zinn, Mrs. Annie Rogers, 215, 216
Zinn, George, 215